Therapeutic Misadventures

A Narrative Memoir

Martha Schaefer

ARCHWAY
PUBLISHING

Archway Publishing books may be ordered through booksellers or by contacting:

Archway Publishing
1663 Liberty Drive
Bloomington, IN 47403
www.archwaypublishing.com
1-(888)-242-5904

Because of the dynamic nature of the Internet, any web addresses or links contained in this book may have changed since publication and may no longer be valid. The views expressed in this work are solely those of the author and do not necessarily reflect the views of the publisher, and the publisher hereby disclaims any responsibility for them.

All photos are property of and in most cases were taken by, the author.

ISBN: 978-1-4808-0169-1 (sc)
ISBN: 978-1-4808-0168-4 (hc)
ISBN: 978-1-4808-0170-7 (e)

Library of Congress Control Number: 2013912795

Printed in the United States of America

Archway Publishing rev. date: 7/30/2013

CONTENTS

PREFACE

As I wrote the end of this memoir, I was surprised at how emotional I became. Here I was, in the same predicament thirty years later, starting life over.

I started this journey several years ago. It had always been in the back of my mind to write. There are references in the letters to and from my mom, as well as in my journal entries, to saving the letters and becoming a writer someday. The format originally was daunting, as I came to believe one novel could never cover forty years of journal entries and life.

When I finally sat down with the letters and journals, I realized that this would take more than one book and would speak to women (and maybe a few men) at different ages and stages of life. I concentrated on the first segment: my twenties and my perceptions of life as I literally moved through the world with my first husband. I wanted to capture the time for my daughters so they might know me better. I also wanted to acknowledge the universal struggles and joys in making peace with one's situation and knowing that change can be painful as well as magical.

The voices that flooded back to me through the entries were painful at times, but because hindsight is so forgiving, they ultimately brought peace in knowing they are not forever silenced. My mother is gone now.

We struggled to find the love and rekindle the amazing bond we shared before I left my marriage and came home to start over. I can now forgive us both for our egos and shortsightedness.

The letters and journal entries are all real. They have been edited for clarity (I hope) and cohesion. But the events are all true, and although they are portrayed as I saw them, I doubt much would change had anyone else given their perspective.

I never set out to hurt anyone or expose any secrets. The people in this book, living and deceased, are portrayed as best as I could.

Acknowledgements

Writing about myself in a past life brought back memories of people who helped shape that life. But it was those who are with me now or recently lost who provided the encouragement, and support to make this memoir actually happen.

My dearest doppelganger, Stephanie Sheridan sent me a copy of "EAT, PRAY LOVE" and said, "You should write your story."

My beautiful daughters, Lexie and Hannah, read early drafts and pushed me to continue, if only for myself.

In late 2012, my sister, Zanne, moved in with me for several months and flooded my life with love, encouragement and resources. She fed my fragile ego with her pride in my project.

Tom Krapf, brought me lunches, left at the door, on days I was so deeply immersed in the process, I could not be disturbed.

Lauren Garofalo Riccio listened to my incessant whining and self doubts. She and her mare, Blessing, provided the respite in trail rides that allowed me to go back to work on the days I felt most lost.

Steph Brann shyly told me she would love to edit for me and would only accept the loan of my horse trailer for payment.

Megan Rushford labored over my drafts and left me smiley faces and encouragement and never showed how frustrated she must have become with my poor punctuation skills.

Emmy Palange, young enough to be my daughter, not what I thought of as my target audience, but she read the very first draft and re-read it until it was dog-eared.

And finally, my mother. Without her love of letters and stories I would not have grown up loving the written word; nor would half of the letters in this novel exist.

December 13, 1978
Dear Marth,

I am saving my letters from you so when you are an old, well-traveled lady you can sit in your rocker in New Hampshire and re-read them.

INTRODUCTION

My story has been fifty-seven years in the making. The middle child between my older brother Duncan and my younger sister Susanne, I grew up in the tiny town of Byfield, Massachusetts. I received my first pony at ten years old, and my childhood was an idyllic mix of 4-H shows at county fairs and rural life. I took what is now known as a gap year between high school and college. My mom and I spent my college loan on a trip to Spain, and then my parents, and consequently we kids, began the long process of divorce.

College was two years in New London, New Hampshire, where I met Roger. His family was the poor country cousins of landed gentry. They owned and operated Twin Lake Villa, an old-fashioned resort on the shores of Little Lake Sunapee. The main hotel was cavernous and ancient, and the "cottages" were massive Victorian houses nestled in the pines. I fell in love with his quintessential Yankee good looks, his childish sense of wonder and adventure, and his amazing work ethic. Though five years my senior, Roger and I were best friends first and lovers by coincidence. We married in June 1977 with our reception at the Villa. The next day, we packed a U-Haul with a meager amount of furniture and our Datsun car with our shaggy dog, Mr. Mac.

The first year of our marriage was spent in the oil fields of southern Illinois. Roger sold chemicals to the oil rigs, and I sold insurance door-to-door to the farmers. We spent every weekend and every extra penny we had at auctions. As the farmers aged, their farms were sold to the oil companies and their belongings were auctioned off. I drove treasure troves of old-fashioned furniture, quilts, heavy pickle crocks, and all sorts of antique tin toys (Roger's personal passion) back to New England for storage and resale. We hoarded the earnings from these sales along with our meager salaries to buy stock in petroleum service companies that Roger felt were safe and growing.

My parents had divorced by this time. My dad was living in Houston, as was my older brother, Duncan. My mom was still in New England, and my sister, Susanne, was moving between the two places, searching for her own destiny as we all do in our twenties.

So here I am, an empty nester living in the woods of New Hampshire. My parents and brother have left this world, and I have raised two incredible women who live on the opposite coast. All my life, I have been driven to write my life down in letters and journals.

My story begins with Roger's and my move from the heartland of America, Olney, Illinois, to the Caribbean island of Trinidad. As an expatriate corporate wife, my main responsibility was to find happiness and be supportive of my husband's career. Not a bad assignment, and one that took me around the world as I pursued my own definition of purpose. Roger's career led us on adventures around the world but ultimately became the downfall of our relationship.

This is the story of marriages, divorces, dreams, and delusions—and all the lessons they bestow upon us.

The parallels and coincidences I am able to see as I reread my journals and letters are astonishing. So when I read of my frustration and depressions, my enthusiasm and blind hope, it reminds me that belief in myself has supported me in life.

If you were to ask me the key to eternal life and happiness, I would suggest a life well lived and well written.

My tropical paradise!

CHAPTER 1

This Will Take Some Getting Used To ...

11/30/78
San Fernando, Trinidad

Dear Mom,

You are the first on my long list of letters to write. Now, where to begin? I was so excited to finally get here Tuesday night after a disastrous flight that left me stranded in Puerto Rico for a day. Though I was totally sleep deprived my first night here, I just kept wandering around the house, amazed that I had made it to Trinidad at last.

The smells are so strange: spicy, burning garbage and rotting vegetation. My initial picture of what our house would be on a tropical island was far from reality. We live in a city on the side of a hill overlooking a neighborhood of similar houses. The highway is off to the left, and the downtown is below on the right. That first night, I arrived after dark, and the ride from the airport was hair-raising, to say the least. Cars and trucks know no speed limits here, and there are no lights on the highway, which winds through the sugar cane fields. It's a little scary here. We are definitely in the minority; I would say only about 2 percent of the population is white. Also, there is quite a bit of crime. We have all kinds of gates, locks, and bars on the windows. Roger keeps a monstrous machete under the bed, though I'm not convinced it's not just a little bit for affect. Chances are no one would really hurt anyone, but they would steal the gold from your teeth if they thought they could.

As of yet, I can't understand anyone here, though it's supposed to be English they are speaking. It is a musical bird-like sound all run together with a heavy British accent and lots of local slang. My favorite sign is the oh-so-common, spray-painted "NO LIMING" outside of shops and stores—the equivalent of "Don't Loiter." It is a strange sign in a society where liming is the national pastime of every male.

Some things are strange compared to home. We went grocery shopping in a filthy, dark cave of a shop. Milk and orange juice are scarce and come in paper and foil box-like packages. If you find some, you buy lots and hoard it, as you may not see it again for weeks. Butter comes in a round tin like a sardine can, and sugar (on an island covered with sugar cane) is prized like gold and difficult to find.

Rog is a manager and has to work a lot harder than in the States. He drives to the southern end of the island to visit the offshore oil rigs or spends long hours at the office in town. I hope to have a car soon so I am not so housebound, though driving is terrifying here. Not only do I have to get used to driving on the wrong side of the road from the passenger side of the car, but it also seems there are no rules of courtesy on these tiny, choked roads.

This will all take some getting used to ...

Love and miss you,
M.

12/9/78
San Fernando, Trinidad

Dear Mom,

Every day down here is better than the one before, and I learn something new each minute. Yesterday, Rog called all excited from the office to say we had lots of mail. We sat around for hours reading and rereading a letter from you, two from Susanne, one from Nana and Grampa, and one from Rog's parents, Marge and Rich. News from home is precious, and hearing about winter when the thermometer never dips below seventy degrees here is so strange.

I borrowed Roger's car and ventured alone downtown yesterday for the first time. It's a great confidence builder! People are a lot friendlier than I thought, and I found that I was the only one who even took notice of skin color. It's hard not to when I only see two white faces all day, but that is just my Yankee upbringing coming out.

It's not the right-hand drive that bothers me; it's the *way* people drive. The streets are incredibly narrow, and if someone decides to stop, they just get out and leave the car running in the middle of the road. No one seems to notice all the dogs, goats, and kids on the sides of the road. I guess they just figure they will get out of the way in time.

We drove south to Galeotta Point yesterday where Rog takes the boat to the offshore rigs. It is only forty-three miles, but the drive takes over two hours. The road winds through cane fields and villages and is bumpier than a New Hampshire road full of potholes in the spring. There isn't ten feet of straight road the whole way.

We arrived at the Amoco compound where Rog had a meeting. What a strange scene! I spent the afternoon with the wife of a coworker, and we went to a Christmas tea—thirty American and Canadian wives sitting around eating cucumber sandwiches and getting plastered on champagne punch while their maids were home taking care of the kids. Three quarters of them were pregnant, the other national pastime here. Talk focused on problems with domestic help, their last trip home, and what a hard life they all were living. I had a really tough time relating to the conversation, as I am still intrigued and fascinated by the culture and the place I find myself in.

Tonight we are off to the Baroid company Christmas Fete in Port of Spain. I can't get used to the fact that it is December and I am sitting around in a bathing suit—no snow, no smell of Christmas pine.

Can't wait for you to visit; I have so much to show you. Oh, by the way, be sure to get a yellow fever shot. All expat families are getting them next week. A dead monkey tested positive for the fever here two days ago.

Love and miss you so very much,
M.

12/12/78

Dear Marth,

Finally, three letters from you last night: November 30 and December 3 and 5. That Trinidad postal service is very strange. What do they do, save all the mail until someone says, "Hey, this is in the way," and send it all at once?

But what great letters! It all sounds so intriguing and foreign. Imagine coconuts and avocados right in your front yard … we are paying fifty cents for them now, and that's very cheap. And the sun and the humidity; bet your hair curls like a poodle!

Your house sounds positively huge. Hope your air shipment from the States arrives soon so you can make it feel more like home. Be sure to send some pictures for us all to pass around back here in Dullsville.

I am saving my letters from you so when you are an old, well-traveled lady you can sit in your rocker in New Hampshire and reread them.

Looking out on a gray and white world, all cloudy and barren, it is fun to think of you in a tropical green, hot scene. Miss you lots but are comforted by thoughts of your new world to explore and enjoy.

Mom

12/15/78

Dear Mom,

Well, happy birthday, Duncan. Do I really have a brother who is twenty-six??

I will try to place a call to Dad's later, hoping to catch him there. *Try* is the key word … I thought calling here from the States was bad ... it's easy next to this phone system. We actually have a scheme set up with some folks here who have a ham radio. If anyone of us has an emergency, we call the ham operator who will relay the info to someone in the States who will then call our families. How primitive is that in 1978?

Anyway, I got my yellow fever shot today. It takes ten days to take effect, so it should be just in time for Christmas ... Are you getting in the Christmas spirit yet? It is very hard to feel it here ... I keep having to remind myself that it really is December. Instead of Christmas music, we have parang (steel drums), which I really do love but find it hard to associate with the season. Since I have never heard it before, it just doesn't signify Christmas to me.

I am baking black cakes; they are a Trinidadian form of fruitcake. No one likes fruitcake at home, so why do I think it will be any different here? Doesn't matter. It's what us wives do at this time of the year ...

The fruit is soaked in cherry wine and then mixed with a pound of flour, twelve eggs, a pound of butter, and two pounds of brown sugar. (The government seems to time the arrival of brown sugar to the season, and the prices are sky high.) After the cakes are cooked, they are soaked in rum. Sounds yummy, but the mixing!!! I never appreciated electricity until I moved down here. I sure could use my mixer, can opener, toaster oven, etc. Lynette, my "maid," helped me with the mixing. I'm sure she thinks I am very spoiled considering my arms gave out partway through. I'll let you know if it is worth my tired arms.

Last night, a couple from Galeotta, who also work for Baroid, stayed overnight with their baby. I was so proud of my meal! I cooked leg of lamb (frozen from New Zealand), fresh pumpkin (think squash), baked bananas, and frozen peas. I am starting to get the hang of my kitchen, but it sure would be nice to get our shipment and have all my pots, pans, and linens. Still feels like camping out with someone else's stuff to me.

I am writing to you with one of my Christmas presents. Rog bought me a lovely German fountain pen today, but of course, "Kid Kidder" couldn't wait for Christmas and wanted me to try it out immediately. At this rate, I'll have nothing to open when the big day rolls around.

Lots of folks have invited us for Christmas Day, but we have decided to spend it together at the beach.

Tonight we are going to yet another Christmas Fete, our third since arriving. Olney, Illinois, was never this lively! These people really know how to party. Lots of drinking and dancing. Everybody dances; Rog and I have to loosen up and learn.

Can't wait for you to come and visit, Mom. So much to share and talk about. I miss you daily, hourly. Well, all the time.

Give my love to all,
M.

12/18/78

Dear Mom,

Finally got to talk to you tonight! I feel like I am in another world; it's so different here, so remote. We read about the States in the papers and think about home constantly. It's strange, to folks here the States is the ultimate ... the land of television, shopping malls, and the all-American buck $$$. It does look pretty good, I must admit.

I went shopping today with three Trinidadian women who are married to guys who work with Rog. They all have kids, which, as I've mentioned, seems to be the national pastime. I think it is something in the water and so will continue to boil mine! We went to the only mall on the island in the capital, Port of Spain. It is less than a third of the size of any strip mall at home. Unfortunately, between the high prices and the lack of imports, shopping is really frustrating. There is little creativity locally, though I did see some woodcarvings that looked interesting.

You wouldn't believe the prices in the grocery stores! American products, such as Shake and Bake (which I would never buy at home) are six dollars. Cans of cake decorating stuff and frosting are four and five dollars, and canned soda (called "sweet drink" here) is two dollars each. The women I shopped with were searching for toys for Christmas. The cheapest tricycle we saw was $120 and so poorly made it didn't look like it would make it out of the store, much less stand up under a four-year-old.

On the other hand, Roger is in heaven with his antique toy collection. Though they aren't technically antiques, he has found a wealth of imported Chinese tin toys (all would be outlawed for safety reasons in the United States) and is buying stuff up to add to his collection back in New Hampshire.

But the people and the surroundings fascinate me. So many different races, religions, colors, shapes, and sizes. I think the fact that Trinidad is not geared toward tourists is a plus as long as you have someone to show you around. The markets are bustling with shoppers and full of strange sights and smells. Fruits and vegetables in odd shapes and the smells range from sickly sweet to tangy spice.

The mountains never cease to amaze me. We drove back from the beach on the North coast yesterday on a different road than we had taken before. It was the narrowest I've ever seen, winding through the heart of the jungles. We stopped to sample a cocoa pod—sweet but not at all like chocolate. Some of the plants were so huge they seemed like green skyscrapers.

Great thick stands of bamboo, wild orange trees laden with fruit, bananas growing straight up in the air, and ferns so large you could easily sit beneath them and be sheltered in a storm. At one point, we even drove through a cloud! This beauty is balanced with a certain amount of danger and fear. We have been told by folks at the office that if you hit an animal or even a person to keep driving to the nearest large town and find the police and a phone. Don't stop under any circumstances, for as "wealthy" white people, we will be robbed or worse. If we break down, Roger's car has a radio that we can use to call the office for help.

The only thing I am really having a hard time adjusting to is my lack of patience … something you must have an abundance of here. Perhaps because of the number of people or just the "equatorial attitude of time," there are long lines everywhere—the banks, stores, the grocery checkout. Just to cash a check at the bank can sometimes take an hour standing in line. Perhaps it's because of the holidays too. I sure hope so.

Love and miss you,
M.

12/19/78

Dear Marthe,

I still can't believe I heard your voice last night! What a neat surprise. You sounded so little and far away, but it was really you, and that is what counts. You seem to be getting into the Trinidad scene more and more, and that is good to hear.

Just spoke with Rebecca Parsons at Baroid. She says she has sent three telexes about your air shipment, but apparently they have not arrived or been delivered. The problem is twofold: 1) The embargo left lots of freight backed up, and 2) the fire at the warehouse in Trinidad, which you are aware of. Your shipment is sitting in the Pan Air freight office in New York. She says they promised a January first departure date. She also tried to send it to Miami and then by sea from there, but the Miami freight people couldn't move it until January first either. Seems to be the magic date. So tell Marge and Rich to bring their own linens when they come to visit next month.

Called the travel agent this morning and asked her to make reservations for me to Trinidad on March 9. My boss will change his mind fifteen times between now and then, but with Carnival coming up, space is limited, and I am GOING! Job or no job!!

It doesn't seem like Christmas is less than a week away. I have no enthusiasm for a tree or cooking. My biorhythms must be way down ... as is my opinion of life right now. Having your favorite person in the whole world far away is ten times worse than losing a lover. They can be replaced, but you leave a huge hole.

Love to Rog and most of all to you,
Mom

12/22/78
Trinidad

Dear Mom,

Last night, Rog came home from Galeota all excited. He had bought a Ping-Pong table and a portable radio from some Americans who are leaving. They were rather expensive, but we are getting so sick of waiting for our shipment. At least we now have music—not rock and roll—calypso and Spanish sort of stuff, but it's music. We have also rented a black-and-white TV. It's not much, but only twenty-five dollars per month. I was hoping for news, but most of what is available is old American reruns of Mary Tyler Moore. On the plus side, it has a clock on the screen during the day when no shows are on. All the comforts of home!!

I took a taxi downtown yesterday to get some groceries. I have to call the office to get a cab. It's that or try to grab one on the street. The gypsy cabs on the street are never exclusive; they pick up as many people as they can cram into the car. Not something I am quite up to yet.

I got the same driver I had the last time I ventured out. He is wonderful—an elderly gent with a perky straw hat. He always has a crisp, white dress shirt and tie with a handkerchief around his collar so he won't soil it (I am assuming this is the reason.) In this heat, it is an unusual outfit. He drives a big, old Pontiac with no air-conditioning, late 1950s to early 1960s, I'm guessing (the car not him). The dashboard is adorned with an abundance of dusty, old artificial flowers. Here in the tropical land of beautiful flowers growing wild!! He is very polite and calls me "Mistress Kidder." Well, la-di-da!!

I looked for reading material. Magazines are fiendishly expensive, roughly ten dollars a copy and several months old. Can't wait until our subscriptions start up. I ended up buying three tins of butter (Australian), three bags of fresh rolls, a loaf of bread, and a dozen eggs. The total came to fifteen dollars!! There are often food shortages, especially around the holidays, so I stock up every time I find things like milk, OJ, butter, and eggs. When our shipment arrives, I will make bread once a week or so and freeze it. I hate to buy bread pans here when I have them coming in my shipment.

I have started doing water analysis for Baroid. It was a little dull at first, but now that I am beginning to understand what I am looking for, it makes more sense. Anything I can do at this point to give Rog more time off is helpful. He is so busy. I went over to the office to have lunch with him the other day, and there he was, out in the blazing sun, surrounded by large, intimidating Trinidadian workers, loading chemical drums on a truck right alongside them. I'm sure they thought it was very strange, this Yankee white man working along with them instead of shouting orders from his air-conditioned office like most bosses here. (That sounded strange when I just read it back. Guess you have to be here to understand.)

So I count the months and days until you arrive. It will be wonderful to wake up and know we can have breakfast together!

Love to all,
M.

12/24/78
Trinidad

Dear Mom,

'Tis the day before Christmas and all through the house, not a creature is stirring, not even a lizard. Well, that's not necessarily true. Rog is busy in the kitchen making brunch—banana pancakes. I've just been tidying up a bit. The day after Christmas is Boxing Day (whatever that means), so no Lynette to help me clean up until Wednesday. For some strange reason, with all this room in this big house, we manage to be pretty sloppy. Guess it's because we always seem to be running in to change our clothes and run back out somewhere else.

Friday, I ran water tests all day, and then we drove to Point Fortin to visit some New Zealanders. They are really neat people, middle-aged but very bouncy and interesting (please don't take that as an insult to middle age, just a description. I certainty wasn't inferring anything about age, but you must remember I am only twenty-three). She, Liz, said they have lived here four and a half years. She was kind enough to make us up a Christmas Care package of *real* cotton sheets and a tablecloth. Oh, *where* is my shipment??

We drove down with Wayne (the Baroid boss here) and his fiancée, Trish, who is Trinidadian of British descent. Because the traffic was so bad, Trish had brought her guitar and played the whole way. It made what normally would have been a tense, nerve-racking drive so much more enjoyable.

All the way down there were people gathered on porches and in the street singing, playing guitars, and dancing. Every house in every village was lit up and noisy. No matter how rundown and dirty, there were brightly painted coffee cans full of flowering plants in the yard. Washing decorated the shrubs and trees, spread on the branches to dry. It is easy to overlook the poverty and dirt when you really see the life.

I can't wait to get the darkroom set up when our shipment arrives. I am dying to do some photography of this place! Some of the houses are made out of mud and straw, packed and dried on frames of chicken wire. Others we have named the "Datsun houses" as they are constructed from the crates used to ship cars into the country that still say "Datsun" on the sides. You can always tell a Hindu's house by the colorful flags on tall bamboo poles out front. They also paint their houses the loveliest shades of faded pink, red, and blue. You must get out of the city neighborhoods, such as ours, to the country villages and see how the "other half" lives.

Saturday, we drove down to Galeota Point to visit our Canadian friends and pick up the Ping-Pong table Rog bought. I've told you how hairy that drive is, but combined with a holiday weekend, it was even more exciting. People really get into Christmas here like I have never seen before. They start the serious "Fete-ing" on Friday and never stop. All the villages along the way were teeming with people dressed in bright colors like so many parrots. The children were scrubbed and had colorful rags tied in their many kinky braids. The cars we met on the road all seemed to be completely out of control. One car was trying to drive a truck off the road that was loaded with kids and coconuts. The car finally sideswiped the truck, and they all stopped and got out to brawl. Needless to say, we didn't stick around to see the final outcome. The Indians are known for their tactics of "cut an arm off first, ask questions later."

Of course, the Ping-Pong table had to be put together right away upon returning home. I left Rog to work on that down in the garage while I made spaghetti for dinner. After dinner, we stopped over at a party in San Fernando for a little while. We just aren't used to this social whirl.

An important note I have made about the folks here is that they are all so spontaneous and happy. They make their own music when they have none and party and dance at the least provocation. Something these two Yankees need to learn.

12/26/78

Dear Marth and Roger,

First off, thank you so much for the terrific picture holder for Christmas. I look forward to choosing my best shots to go in it and having it handy to enjoy. One of my favorite pastimes is to climb into bed and go over pictures. That was a super idea!

Christmas was very low-key, and Susanne and I missed you both very much (and Dad and Duncan too). But everyone gave good gifts, and we had nice things to eat, so that was that.

The weather all weekend was warm and lovely until Christmas Eve when we got rain and wet snow. Susanne and I opened our presents on Christmas morning and took lots of pictures for you. She gave me a reproduction of an old sugar tin filled with lemon tea and a copy of the latest book by Erma Bombeck. I read it in part last night and just howled. She really brought back memories of carpooling with Celia Johnson to Miss Brown's nursery school and dear little Darrel Weaver. There is one in every nursery school apparently.

Just came back from a doctor's appointment. He specializes in diabetics. Found me fine but is a little puzzled with my fuzzy vision. Says it is definitely not related to diabetes. So he has made an appointment for me with an ophthalmologist. Little does he know it is really my brain that is fuzzy! Also says everyone over forty wears glasses to read. He is a nice, kindly, reassuring gentleman. I really can't complain about having to wear glasses; it's just that I never know where they are! A few weeks with you in the sun in San Fernando, Trinidad, will fix me just fine!

Hope to hear from you soon and all about your Christmas in the sun and warmth.

Love to you both,
Mom

12/27/78

Dear Mom,

December 13 seems a long time ago, but that is the date on the letter I received from you today. What a coincidence that you should ask what it is like to cook here.

Today was unfortunately a bit aggravating. Anywhere else in the world I would say it was a horrible day, but nothing is really horrible when the sun always shines and life is so interesting. I went shopping; we were down to one tin of tuna and a few ice cubes. The grocery store was out of a few things like bread, butter, fruit, veggies, milk, eggs, and OJ. I did find one frozen duck from New York (bet his wings were tired from flying all this way!) and a strange-looking frozen roast of something. All meat is frozen here. Somehow, I managed to spend one hundred Trinidad and Tobago dollars or TT, (about forty-five US dollars), but four rolls of toilet paper will do that down here. I also discovered that not only can I not buy anything to cook, I can't cook what I do manage to buy. I baked some potatoes (Irish as they are known here) with the roast of something … two hours at 375 degrees, and they were cold in the middle. You wanted to know about fruits, veggies, and meat? I can't even distinguish the bananas from the plantains from the cooking figs, potatoes, or potatoey-looking things. We have great lamb from New Zealand. I don't like to think about how long ago it was slaughtered, frozen, and then shipped here. I haven't gotten into the goat yet—too many roaming the streets, looking forlorn, for me to contemplate eating one. Blood pudding? I don't even want to know. The chickens are a real adventure. They look barely big enough to be hatched and are stuffed with the neck and usual giblets but also included are the feet, complete with toenails and, occasionally, if you are really lucky, the head! Cosmopolitan lifestyle, you say!?

My "maid" Lynette is black, but so is everyone else here. She lives with a local policeman who should make me feel safe, but with the corruption here, it leaves me feeling less than secure. We have an interesting relationship, mostly because we are fascinated by each other's lives. Most white Trinidadians treat the "help" like servants. I am just so happy to have someone to talk to and explore this culture with that I confuse poor Lynette with my enthusiasm.

As yet, none of our shipment has arrived, but I am just too busy every day figuring out how to do simple tasks that I haven't really been too bummed out about it.

You wrote, "When you get a chance ..." What, are you crazy? I'm writing my memoir here—time is all I have! You would like to know about the clothes folks wear. It's a strange mix, Mom. What you see on the racks in the stores looks like K-Mart rejects, but these women are so clothes conscious. There are two types of women: those who can't afford the garbage on the racks, so they take no personal notice and wear whatever is colorful and comfortable—garish mixes of prints in blousy tops and flowing skirts. Then there are the "corporate wives" who are forever tying to outdo each other for style setting.

For example, we went to a Boxing Day party yesterday. No, I still am not clear on what "Boxing Day" stands for. I have asked, and no one has given me a good answer, so I'm assuming it is a recovery day from Christmas, Caribbean-style. Anyway, this party was supposed to be casual. I grilled Roger (useless, as he lives in his khakis and button-down shirts) and was told shorts, jeans, or whatever.

So I wore my Spanish jeans and a silk blouse. But the other women were dressed to the hilt in cotton dresses, skirts, pantsuits, and "lounging pajamas." (*Yech!*) I felt a little odd until I found out how expensive jeans are here. Everyone got totally bombed on scotch, rum, and punch until four p.m when they brought out a huge buffet with champagne. Rog rode one of the kids' Christmas skateboards all afternoon. When I had my fill of discussing fingernails, jewelry, and toilet training, I found an interesting gentleman whose son works in the gold mines in Africa. He was a Trinidadian and told wonderful stories of growing up on the island.

The social life is taking some getting used to. If you don't have kids or have one on the way, you feel a bit left out. A far cry from the Midwest farm auctions and small-town life we left behind in Olney, Illinois. But, all in all, I can honestly say I am challenged and learning every day.

Love and can't wait to share this all with you.
M.

The beach at Maracas Bay

CHAPTER 2

Life as an Expat

Journal Entry,
2/10/79

My world is crushed. I can't believe all these months of waiting and anticipation for our shipment to arrive and now—total despair. There was a fire at the customs building in Port of Spain. It is unknown at this point what, if anything, of our shipment survived. Roger is going up today to see if he can sort it out. I am racking my brain to remember all those months ago what I packed: clothes, linens, books, photos, pots and pans, and the washer and dryer. There were two shipments; one was going back to New Hampshire, as we were told to not bring anything really valuable in case this happened.

Later same day ...

Seems there was a major screwup and parts of each of our two shipments went to the wrong address. We are sorting through soggy boxes of books and wedding photos that managed to survive the fire only to be drenched by the effort to put it out. All my good china came here instead of going to New Hampshire, along with our bicycles. Not real handy in this hilly city.

Amid all this, a friend of Roger's from New Hampshire has arrived for an undetermined amount of time. While I am thrilled to have a visitor and the prospect of playing tour guide, I don't know Harry, and he has a medical condition that makes me very nervous. He suffered colitis as a child and lives with a colostomy bag. Not that he isn't equipped to deal with this after all these years, but the medical community here is not top-notch, and I worry about infection.

2/13/79

Dear Marth,

Good to hear from you yesterday, but I am appalled at the news of your air shipment. Such gross inefficiency is hard to believe. Aren't you glad you heeded the advice not to take a lot of things you could do without? Think of all the good stuff safely stored in the barn in New London.

Susanne is trying to recall what was in the "disaster" boxes that she helped you pack prior to leaving Illinois. Do you want me to buy you linens, sheets, towels, etc? What about silver and your china? How about kitchen utensils and cookbooks? Did you have all your small appliances in that shipment like your blender and wok? Susanne and I will send our copies of the wedding pictures.

There is still a large void in my life with having you so far away and no handy phone connection. I am waiting for my phone bill to see how much our last call to Trinidad was and if it was not bad will call you before I leave to get any last minute things you need me to bring.

Love and miss you,
Mom

2/16/79

Dear Mom,

First, let me apologize for this week. I wrote you a letter on Sunday or Monday and just got it mailed today. (As if the Trinidadian mail system isn't bad enough.) The reason is our free postage from Baroid has been shut off. The nerve of these people!! Actually, I must admit, it probably was getting a little out of hand. I am quite prolific with my letters.

Anyway, back to why I'm apologizing. This week has been something else. Harry insists I am wasting my life away as a housewife down here, and I really don't need his advice and worldly views on the state of my life. He hasn't a clue. Meanwhile, as you heard in our wonderful phone call yesterday, our shipment was mostly intact. In fact, we found a few surprise extras, such as:

1. A neatly packed bag of garbage (not ours)

2. Three dozen felt tip pens in the original boxes—$.98 each

3. A cheap pair of women's sunglasses. They had a small mushroom growing on the lens, but Rog scraped it off and looks stunning in them.

So here I am all week, trying to organize my life (hooray for curtains, pictures, and pots and pans!) while this "mechanic" is working on my Volkswagen bug, Louise, every day. I feel like I'm living with the guy. Monday, I went with him to Port of Spain for parts. Wednesday, we spent the entire morning together. He was supposed to drop Louise off all fixed, but he "had a few things to do," so he picked me up, drove to his shop, and I sat around while he worked on the car. I then had to drive up to Port of Spain again to pick up the Carnival tickets. The traffic around here is horrendous and can really put you in a bad mood. Can't wait until you come so we can go exploring *away* from traffic.

But, to continue, I was supposed to bring the car back on Thursday for tires, taillights, and directional signals (yes, I was driving around without the benefit of these necessities) but took the day off to get groceries and clean the house. Lynette didn't show up all week. Constable Sheppard, her boyfriend, called to say her womb had slipped, and that she would be in tomorrow. (Hmm, that's an interesting excuse for missing work; I will file it away in case I ever have a job again.) I haven't heard from her since. I ran six loads of wash using our newly arrived machine and still have more to go. Lynette must have known what a killer week this would be.

Today, I realized by nine a.m. that she wasn't going to show up and that Roger's boss was arriving for dinner tonight. I ran to the P.O., supermarket (for things I couldn't get yesterday), and the market for fruits and veggies. At three p.m., I met the wife of the mechanic so she could take "Louise" for the weekend to finish up the repairs. Good thing Rog and his boss won't be home until seven p.m., as a long, hot bath is definitely in order.

I promise to get this in the mail tomorrow.

Saturday morning

Just thought I'd add a little before I go to the post office. It is very important that you get a yellow fever shot before you come. We've had an outbreak, and they are insisting that everyone get one. Forgot to tell you that when we talked on the phone the other day.

Went out to dinner last night with Rog's boss. Thank you, I did not have to cook! We went to Soons (best Chinese food I've ever eaten) with Ramish and his wife, Tara. Ramish is the other Baroid engineer here. He and Tara are native West Indians. I especially enjoy Tara; she is so lively and happy. She has promised to teach me some Indian cooking. Ramish is buying our electric stove for her. Right now, she only has a hot plate, and with three babies to cook for, I don't know how she does it. Actually, it is kind of embarrassing for me because here is Ramish, who is obviously a virtual genius and works as hard as Roger but because he is a national, his pay is a quarter of Roger's and they get no housing or car allowance. They live very frugally in a small village, and I am rather embarrassed by our big house with all of our luxuries. Welcome to the life of an expat in the Third World.

Love and miss you,
M.

A note on Harry.

Harry stayed with us for six weeks. He was tall, thin, and ghostly white when he arrived. I tried to warn him about the strong Caribbean sun, but he immediately burned so badly that he blistered. When I got sick of carting him around with me all day every day, he struck off on his own, grabbing route taxis and "exploring" parts of the island that no other white person in their right mind would venture to. Though he was never robbed or hurt, I lived in fear of getting a phone call that he was in trouble. When we finally told him his visit was over, he insisted on taking some of the great weed we had access to back to the States with him. The night before his flight, he bought a pound of marijuana, and we sat up until the early morning hours, grinding it down to powder. He emptied out several stick deodorant cases, and we packed the pot in those as well as his colostomy bag.

As he was landing at Logan Airport in Boston, the stewardess announced over the loudspeaker, "Would Harry please identify himself?" He was sure he had been caught with the pot, so he rushed to the bathroom and flushed it all. When he came through customs, it turned out his parents had him paged so they could let him know they were meeting him.

The Rape

I am sure I am not the first to say this, but rape is not about sex; it is about theft and assault. The theft of your awareness of self and the assault on your sense of security. I have never written about this incident in my life before. It doesn't appear in my journals, and certainly, I did not write about it to my mother, as I did not want to frighten or worry her. It had long-term ramifications on my life, but it was never recognized as having occurred. The pledge I made to myself to never allow anyone or anything in life make me feel so out of control unconsciously led me to my job at the racetrack and my work with our dog Winston and the police canine obedience classes.

Rape is about stealing that little piece of you that is the core of your knowledge of who you are; it is the most basic form of identity theft. Here is what little I will tell you about the rape.

We were well settled into our life in Trinidad. Good friends, Mo and Steve, had a small house on the other side of town. Mo was Trinidadian with relatives in Canada, which is where she met Steve. She worked as a secretary at the Baroid office, and Steve had moved to Trinidad to marry Mo and work for a construction company. Though he was an expatriate, they did not have the luxury of working for a foreign company to subsidize them. Their house was in a less desirable neighborhood than the rest of us. Nice by Trinidad standards, but not rich. Steve's sister, Donna, was visiting from Canada. I believe she was a psychologist in the government medical system there. Steve and Mo had to go off to work during the week, so I offered to entertain Donna during the day.

I drove to the house to take her sightseeing, and when I parked and walked up to the front door, I noticed a young Indian fellow, late teens or early twenties, standing just outside the front door. I said hello and walked into the house to find Donna in the kitchen, making a sandwich. When I asked her what was going on, she said the young man had come by looking for yard work and since she had none he had asked for something to eat. The hair on the back of my neck stood up as it dawned on me that this was not a good situation.

I turned toward the front door just as he slipped in and grabbed a knife from the counter. He told us he wouldn't hurt us but that we had to cooperate. He backed us into Mo and Steve's bedroom, locked the door, and proceeded to ransack the house. Donna and I were terrified … the stories of Indians and knives were legend. We couldn't escape the bedroom because of the bars on the windows, so we sat and contemplated our fate. I had a key ring with a canister of mace on it. Unfortunately, it was several years old, and neither of us had any faith in it or our ability to use it effectively. Then he came into the room. Holding the knife to my throat, he ordered Donna to tie my hands behind my back with a necktie. He then held the knife on Donna and tied her hands as well.

You know those dreams where you are terrified but your feet refuse to move? Where you know what your mind is saying but your body shuts down? That is the total terror I felt. Perhaps it was only minutes, but it seemed like hours. I know—two women should have been able to overcome one skinny Indian boy. But believe me when I say there was nothing but survival at any cost on my mind.

He left, and we managed to collect ourselves and yell out the window until an old black gentleman believed what we were saying and dared to enter the house and let us out of the bedroom. We called, and the police arrived. We were driven to the closest station. No physical, no rape kit, just our report. Roger and Mo came to get us.

I remember that night and many nights thereafter roaming through the house with a machete in my hands, feeling totally powerless and haunted by the memory of being so terrified.

Of course, the incident had to be reported to Baroid. They (the great faceless "they") offered to transfer us back to the States. I saw the look on Roger's face and knew he just wanted life to go back to "normal" and didn't want this to impact his dream of the career and life he had planned for us. I said I could stay. But Donna went back to Canada.

A few months later, there was another incident. This time, the perpetrator went into the Tesoro Oil employees compound and attacked a woman during the day. When he threatened her six-year-old daughter, she grabbed the machete we all kept under our beds and slashed at him. He ran but was caught on the compound and arrested.

The police showed up at my door one afternoon and asked me to come to the station to view a lineup and identify my attacker. I had a vision of the TV crime shows where the victim stands behind a one-way mirror and views the lineup. Not there. I was led into a close, hot room with eight men sitting on hard wooden chairs in handcuffs. I was then led by an officer as I walked down the line of men. I could smell their sweat and sour breath. The air was charged with fear once again, but this time, my fear was mixed with theirs. Immediately, I recognized my attacker. I signaled with a nod to the officer. He leaned into me and said, "Please place your hand on him to show positive ID."

I cringed. "I will NOT touch him again."

"You have to for positive ID" was the response. I closed my eyes and reached out. When I felt flesh, I opened my eyes and looked into the eyes of the man and saw terrible pain and sadness that caused bile to rise in my throat. It was not to be the last time I saw him.

The court date was set, but the government would not pay for Donna to come back from Canada to testify. Roger could not accompany me that day. I walked into the courtroom—the first I had ever been in. It was high-ceilinged and dark-paneled. The judge was a stately black man in a powdered white wig and flowing robes. A wooden cage held the defendants awaiting their trials. I was called and walked to the raised platform with a hard wooden chair to the right of the judge. My attacker was led from the cage. I didn't recognize him at first; his face and head were swollen and bruised like a ripe melon. The details of the case were read, and I was asked if this was the report Donna and I had filed. I answered in the affirmative. The judge told me I could step down. As I was leaving, I saw the courageous woman who had picked up the machete walk to the stand. I felt small next to her courage.

MAK (Martha Anne Kidder) at the track

CHAPTER 3

Life at the Racetrack

Over the next two years, Trinidad became home. I had visits from friends and family: my mom, my sister Susanne, and her beau-of-the-moment, Frank, to name a few. I adopted two dogs, one of which, Winston, became not only my constant companion but also a source of social interaction. I took him to obedience training with the local police force, and we progressed through the courses to the highest level of instruction offered.

I never did fit in with the other corporate wives and pursued my own interests, including the desire to ride horses, as I had done all my life. The only source of equine activity was the local racetrack. After many months of hanging around and inquiring, begging and pleading, I convinced one of the trainers to take me on as a groom and exercise lad. I often wonder what trainer Vince Cobb thought the day he agreed to let a skinny white woman ride at an all-male, black track.

2/2/80

Dear Mom,

I am actually doing it! I am exercising racehorses at the track in Trinidad! You are one of the few people who can really appreciate that statement.

I was so excited that I got up before the alarm went off at 4:30 a.m. Thursday morning. I dressed and made a cup of coffee, pacing and watching the clock. The stars were shining, and it seemed cold but tropical when I got to the barns. I waited in my car until two, three, four men wandered through the gate to the paddock area. Trying my damnedest to look nonchalant, I sauntered into the center of the paddock area and seated myself on a bench in front of Trainer Cobb's barn. A motley crew of grooms, exercise lads, and hangers-on came to life, meeting at the three central troughs in between the line of barns. Some bathed steaming, sleepy horses; others brushed their teeth and scrubbed themselves from the same troughs. A few asked where I was from and if I was a jockey. Trainer showed up at about 6:30 and assigned me a mare to ride. Until my legs get into shape, he wanted me to work at just a walk, trot, and canter out front in the parking lot. Believe me, that was just fine.

I borrowed a helmet, was boosted way up on my leather perch, and was led out through the gate. I bent to adjust my irons and noticed a small crowd following us to the parking lot. "Oh God, what if I fall off?" Trainer helped me lengthen my stirrup (to a frightening four inches above my ankle!). Walking was fine, trotting painful. I slipped off the irons, preferring the pain of posting without stirrups. Several other riders joined me, staring openly. "Canter her a few times around, and then come on in," quipped Trainer like I did this every day. My whole sense of balance was thrown off by the lack of leg contact. I tried to support myself with my knees on her neck, sort of hunched over, but it was no better. My muscles went into spasmodic cramps, yet I managed to hold on, dreading the thought of quitting in humiliation.

As I was led back into the paddock area, all I could think of was how I was going to get off this beast. I knew the proper finish would be to leap off; I also knew at this point that would be fatal. I waited until we stopped in front of the barn and then slipped to the ground. My knees buckled on contact, but I managed to steady myself against the mare's shoulder.

I spent the rest of my morning walking hot horses off the track, grooming, watching, and learning—soaking up everything. I have so much yet to learn.

Friday went equally well. I arrived later and much more confident. I rode the same mare and found my balance improving. I walked horses and groomed for about five hours. It makes for a long day, but a shower and a quick nap usually revitalize me.

Funny thing is, I practice perching on the tiny saddle by squatting in the water at the beach on the weekend. The waves help with my balance, and the saltwater heals the sores on my butt.

2/8/80

Dear Mom,

It's 4:30 a.m. I have realized this is a great time to get caught up on my writing; my head is clear and alert, and no one is around to interrupt me.

It was an easy day at the track yesterday—always is the day before a race. I am getting so I know names of horses and people now. The guys I work with are really good about looking after me and making sure none of the other grooms give me a hard time. I haven't ridden since I fell off Monday, but to be honest, I don't mind … it is just so good to be around horses again.

I am trying to get Rog to come out and see me ride, but the whole atmosphere of the track is just too intimidating for him. He was never a horse lover, but the addition of the rather rough crew of guys I work with is just not comfortable for him. He is happiest in his air-conditioned world of the office or mixing chemicals on the oil rigs.

The Christmas package finally arrived today! Thank you so much for all our wonderful treasures. Rog loves his leather Day-Timer, so rich and with his initials and all. We will stretch the cloth herb prints over the weekend, and I have spots all picked out for them on the dining room wall. The 1980 horoscope will sure come in handy when I get in one of my "what is wrong with me!??!??" moods.

Love and miss you,
M.

Ash Wednesday—How was Carnival?

Dear Marth,

What do you mean you haven't ridden since you fell off Monday? That's a good way to set a mother's heart throbbing!! How many stitches?

This mail system is driving me crazy. Went home last night and found your letter of February 2. It took two and a half weeks—talk about a slow boat …

Anyway, it was the one where you described your first day at the track, and I could share your keen excitement and smell the lovely leather and horses. I felt the muscles twitch when you described your eventual descent from the mare. It's a wonder you could get out of bed the next day. Shall I bring you some Absorbine? There is little doubt the Honky lady caused quite a stir ... and I am sure your performance was exemplary. Hope you are still grooming and riding when I get there; would love to go with you if they will let me into the paddock.

Please take care of yourself,
Mom

2/15/80

Dear Mom,

Would you believe I have been trying for the past two nights to put a call through to you? I wanted to ask you to be my valentine. Yesterday, we got your scented valentine cards. The whole dining room smells like you!

Life at the track goes on as usual. It gets easier every day (except the early hour), and I am learning so much. I rode yesterday; no mishaps this time. Jockey style is completely contradictory to everything I've ever learned. Legs are kept forward instead of back, feet placed all the way in the stirrups rather than just the ball of the foot, and you must lean back to maintain balance. It feels so strange perched way up there.

The horse I take care of is a five-year-old gelding named Master Bishop. His track record of late is unimpressive, but he is a lovely fellow with lots of heart and beautiful, flashy action.

The guys I work with are a strange bunch, though totally harmless and most amusing. I'm sure I amuse them as well. Chocko is about six feet tall and skinny as a zipper. His one outfit is a bumblebee-yellow jogging suit that was made for someone much shorter. He is arrogant and rascally, always jazzing up his horses so they dance around the paddock, appearing to be just on the brink of losing control.

Mallick is a Rastafarian, complete with the strange, tangled hair in dreadlocks. He is calm and quiet; his gray eyes depict an old soul full of wisdom. He handles his horses with the lightest of touch and can often be found in the afternoons snoozing in the tall grass outside the paddock with a giant black stud horse he cares for. It's a funny picture—man and horse stretched out side by side in the shade.

Skeggy is the middle ground. He is slight but muscle-bound and always keeping a watch on me around the paddock. No one gives me any grief, and I'm sure it is due to Skeggy and Trainer's command. He seems to be the one who is always coming to my aid whenever I have a confrontation with another worker or a problem with a dangerous horse. To watch him with the horses is to witness someone who is passionate about training with kindness and patience. Of the three, I think he is the most likely to go on to learn the craft and follow in Trainer's shoes.

Just a few of the cast of characters.

Meanwhile, Winston is doing so well in his obedience classes. Wednesday, he and I were the only ones to show up for class, so we had a private lesson with Sergeant Ramish. He heels without a leash and follows hand signals to sit, stand, stay, and lie down even as I walk away. The sergeant tried to tempt him with some food while I stood several yards away. He never took his eyes off me and passed the test with flying colors. There have been several break-ins lately, and the thieves poisoned the owner's dogs, so this lesson is very important. I sure wouldn't want to be the guy in the leather suit when we tell our dogs to attack during class. That is one scary job!

Carnival is coming up, and the bands are practicing all over town every night. We can hear the steel pan music from our house, and it is strange but lovely.

Love to you,
M.

2/19/80

Dear Mom,

Carnival in Trinidad! Wow! Rog and I went up to Port of Spain late on Sunday and met up with friends. We had dinner and watched movies until J'ouvert started at 4:30 a.m., the official start of Carnival. Customarily, on J'ouvert morning, bands of rabble-rousers get together to march through the streets, terrorizing the town. The marchers are called "jab-jabs" and traditionally dress as devils. We were in the only white band, and it was really strange to see so many white folks in one place. We wore our raggedy old clothes, and people smeared red, white, and blue grease paint all over themselves and everyone else. This strange-looking band marched through the dark streets of the capitol, drinking, smoking, dancing, and hauling the "pan wagons" full of steel pans and other crude instruments. Unfortunately, our musicians failed to show up in force, so when we reached Independence Square in the heart of the city, we disbanded and joined other bands, converging on the grassy oval from all directions. At some point along the way, sandwiched between hundreds of marchers, I caught the true spirit of Carnival—music beating on all sides, people jumping and gyrating in frenzied abandonment, the sun slowly lighting up the sky. It was a really fantastic experience, and such a feeling of total freedom.

Monday morning traffic started to clog the already congested streets, and the bands wound down, slowly dispersing. We made our way back to our car and stopped for a quick breakfast before heading to a friend's house for a nap. The festivities started up again at noon. Each year, the many bands have a central theme for costumes and decorations. The bands consist of about four hundred people split into groups of about fifty. Each section of fifty is costumed differently. For example, one band was Childhood Reflections and was split into sections of clowns, Raggedy Ann and Andys, etc. The costumes are all made by the bandleaders and designers and can cost anywhere from $150.00 to thousands of dollars.

We had not formally joined a band, so we watched the parade from the sidelines. At around 2:00, we had had enough sun and lack of sleep. We headed home to watch the remaining festivities on TV. Maybe we are just getting old, but J'ouvert was plenty of excitement for my tired feet and aching head. I don't know how these people live through three days of such madness.

Love and miss you,
M.

2/29/80 Leap Day!

Dear Mom,

Susanne arrived in good shape on Wednesday night. The airport was amazingly quiet for a change, and she whipped right through customs in no time at all. I can't believe she's finally here. We stayed up until four a.m. talking and then got up late yesterday morning. I didn't go out to the track, so we spent most of the day sitting in the sun, talking. This morning, though, I'm getting her up at 4:45 a.m. to go over to the track with me.

She brought your lovely long letter, which really caught me up on things. First of all, the schedule for our vacation sounds great. I'm really very excited to do some traveling with you.

Trisha has loaned me her car for a couple of days so Sue and I can get around. Still no decision on the fate of the burned-out "Louise." What a time to be without my car, just when I need it most.

3/2/80

Rog has just gone out to blend some chemicals, and no one else is awake yet, so I thought this would be a good time catch up on letters. Sorry I didn't get this finished before.

Sue and I had a good morning at the track, and she was definitely the center of attention. It really was a good experience for her and helped her relax here. All the guys I work with are really nice, and they treated her very well. Rode a little and feel I'm getting my confidence back.

Frank's flight was scheduled to arrive at 6:45 p.m. Somehow there was a lack of communication, and Rog didn't get home from work until 6:15. Sue and I grabbed the car and flew to the airport. We got tied up in traffic and didn't arrive until 7:45. I figured his BWIA flight would be late. The airport was a mob scene. Poor Frankie had arrived ten minutes early and had been hobknobbing with the natives. It was good to see old Frank with his devilish smile and ability to charm the skin off a snake. We got them settled at the house and had a quick dinner. Both Sue and Frank were exhausted, so we all turned in early. Suddenly, I heard screams and furniture crashing. Rog and I ran to the end of the house to Frank and Sue's bedroom and threw open the door. Sue was standing in the middle of the bed, and Frank was prostrate on the floor, half under the bed, swatting at a lizard with a broom. Too funny for words.

Saturday Morning

Dear Mom,

Not only do I not know what time it is, I don't remember the date either. Rog, Frank, Sue, and I are in Tobago. We rented a neat little house opposite Sandy Point on Thursday. Sue, Frank, and I came over Thursday night with tons of food and drink. We spent all day yesterday at the beach, swimming, eating, and relaxing in the sun. When we began to feel a bit burned, we headed back and were met by Rog at the house. The evening was spent walking over to Crown Point Hotel for drinks and the airport to reconfirm our flights on Sunday. We dined on pork chops, salad, potato salad, chili, and eggplant before turning in early. Since it is the height of the tourist season, we couldn't find a hotel or rental car, but this little house is perfect. It sleeps eight and is completely furnished for just forty $TT per day. I wanted Sue and Frank to see the rest of the island, but with no car, it doesn't seem likely. They seem content to just relax and get lots of sun.

We have several large bison tethered in our backyard, but once you get used to their mating calls and the airplanes coming and going, it is quite peaceful. Sue got a bit of a burn yesterday, so we'll have to keep her in the shade today. She is looking so healthy and brown I might just kidnap her for a few months!

Thinking of you always,
M.

3/3/80

Dear Marth,

Such a treat on Saturday to find two letters from you in the box. Was on my way to shop, and all the time I was out, I savored the idea of getting home and settling down to read your letters. Especially enjoyed the one in which you described Carnival—wild and hard to imagine. Is it really based on a religious observance or some long-ago tribal rite?

My horoscope (horrid scope) for February said I would be bored and impatient with the social life to which I say, AMEN! The list of eligible companions is nil. They are either unwell or too far away as to be useless.

Tomorrow is a big day in Massachusetts for Ted Kennedy. If he does not make a good showing on Primary Day here, he is dead. Listening to people discuss their political preferences is a very negative thing these days. Most everyone can tell you why they don't like Reagan, Bush, Kennedy, or Carter, but they don't have any alternatives. Leadership we don't have, just bodies.

Think of you so often and wish the phone calls were not so expensive/difficult.

Mom

6/2/80

Dear Mom,

June already? Half the year is gone. Imagine that?

Master Bishop came in second again this weekend at the races. I sure wish Rog liked horse races. I'd love to see that old Bishop run instead of just hearing about it later at the barn.

Just got back from work. It is a public holiday, Corpus Christi, but, of course, racetracks and oil fields know no holidays.

I am really enjoying riding these days. With my new boots, I've averted any new scrapes or bruises on my shins, and even the saddle sores on my butt seem to be healing. I exercise a mare named Vicar's Lass (aka Vicious Lass for her nasty habits of biting and kicking). We are out on the track every day now. Also, our two new two-year-olds are beginning work. They are always the last to be ridden and take the longest. They go out to the track when everyone else is finished to walk and trot twice around. These two mares are like Tweedledee and Tweedledum. They are distracted by everything, and whatever spooks one will instantly set off the other. I ride one, and an apprentice jockey named Badal rides the other. It seems to take forever to go just once around with all the stopping, turning, fidgeting, and bucking that goes on.

Of course, we are in the height of the rainy season, and the sand track is a quagmire. Any horse—or rider, for that matter—who works on it comes in looking like the creature from the lost lagoon, all sandy and gritty. I feel like I have been rolling around on the beach when I finally get home to my hot shower. But at least I have a home and a shower. For their measly $TT125 per week, the rest of the guys live in the barns in spare stalls and bathe in the horse troughs.

By the time you are reading this, I'll probably already have turned twenty-five years old. Right now, after a long day, I don't feel a day over fifty!

Love to you,
M.

Indonesia!

CHAPTER 4

Relocation—It's a Moving Experience!

6/18/80

Dear Marth,

Just got off the phone with you. What exciting news! You must be very proud of Roger with his promotion and the excitement of a transfer. Fascinating new places, people, cultures, and new adventures await you. Best of all, another warm climate, which suits you exactly.

I am still digesting the news and thinking of all the good friends who will miss you ... especially Trainer and the boys at the track.

Can't wait to hear your plans.

Love,
Mom

7/1/80

Dear Mom,

How did it get to be July already? Every day, The Day gets closer, and I get a little crazier. I'm so excited about coming home to the States and having time with you.

Meanwhile, one of the single guys who works with Roger, Dan, lived in Jakarta for two years. He has been very patient with my millions of questions and is teaching me some of the language to get started. I've made flash cards and try to learn a new word every day.

But then there is leaving. Leaving Trinidad will be very traumatic for me. Knowing that my time is running out seems to intensify friendships. Yes, the legend of the crazy white woman will probably live on for a while at Union Park Racetrack. Today, as I was headed home through the gates, a group of schoolgirls passed me. I heard one say, "She is a jockey. I've seen her ride." It gave me a funny, proud feeling. I know it seems small in the scheme of life, but what I accomplished here at this broken-down racetrack has changed my life forever.

This morning was Winston's graduation from obedience class. It started to rain at eight a.m. and never let up. Ten dogs and fifty spectators sweltering and wet was not a pretty picture. Winnie didn't win any prizes, but he, Rog, and I were the toast of the affair. The instructor gave a speech about all the hard work and dedication Winston and I had shown and said we would be missed. It made me feel wonderful until I remembered that Winnie would not be leaving the island with us. Just too emotional for words.

Rog just got a call from his boss. They want in him Singapore next week. He will be gone at least two weeks. Welcome to another "Relocation—It's a Moving Experience," courtesy of Baroid.

M.

Singapore on the Way to Jakarta
11/2/80

Dear Mom,

First day in Singapore. When I got in last night, we had dinner at the Jockey Club in the Shaw Center (where the Baroid office is). There is lots of shopping within walking distance of the hotel, and we covered a few places today. Also drove out to the Thieves Market near downtown. It was somewhat disappointing, mostly stereo equipment, luggage, calculators, and TVs. I expected more Chinese stuff in the way of clothing and furniture. So far, we've only bought a calculator for me, which does metric conversion—a very handy item!

Singapore is very clean and friendly, a lot like any American city with lots of traffic and shopping centers.

Rog bought a beautiful set of flatware from Bangkok. It's a brass-blend, gold bamboo pattern in a rich, wooden box.

We are supposed to go to Jakarta on Thursday, and I will start looking for a house, but due to our financial straits, I think it will take me awhile to decorate whatever we find. Relocation is an *expensive* experience! I think I am still suffering from a bit of jet lag—twenty-four hours to get here and then the time change. My mind is sort of fuzzy, and I float around not really seeing all the city and sights here.

More later,
M.

Dear Marth and Rog,

Tuesday, November 4, 1980—Election Day—and after all the months of campaigning by the Democrats and Republicans, the undecideds will choose our next president.

Hope you have caught up with each other and there is some semblance of order coming into your lives ... enough of this living out of a suitcase already, even a Halliburton case!

Can't wait for you first letters ... second, third, and all the rest.

We are into November and the true gray-style days. But not too cold and not yet dreary here in New England. The trick-or-treaters are behind us and Turkey Day is to come ... wonder what you will be doing?! Certainly not sitting down to a big bird with Pepperidge Farm stuffing.

Nana Doris has been on the phone daily since you left San Francisco, and by the time this arrives, I hope to have had something to report to her. She is sure you have been lost over the Pacific with Amelia Earhart, and I try to reassure her that Singapore Air wouldn't do that.

Weekend weather was excellent—thirties in the a.m. and forties during the day. I went to the cottage at the lake with my friend Roger. Lots of sun, and now with no leaves, the views from all windows are spectacular!

Got to rush to get this into the mail tonight. Love and miss you lots, Mom

11/7/80

Dear Madam B.,

Well, we've finally arrived in our new "home" ... not a very good beginning, I'm afraid. We went to Jalan Surabya, a market street, and somewhere between there and a taxi drive to the office, my camera disappeared. I may have left it in the taxi. Needless to say, I am devastated! Rog was most supportive, but I feel absolutely sick about it. Never even got to finish a roll of film.

One quickly realizes that you are in a very different culture here. Indonesians are far less attractive than Singaporeans. Not as many women are seen out and about. The market was filled with brassware, lamps, porcelain, and woodcarvings. The shopkeepers were really pushy and persistent.

The Baroid office park is very modern and most impressive. The Baroid people I've met so far are friendly—Americans, Australians, Brits, and a Scot who works for Rog. Still can't help remembering Pat and Mary who took over for us in Trinidad. Their first visit was so easy for them by comparison to this culture where we are trying to shoehorn ourselves into a busy city.

Journal Entry, 11/7/80

Arriving in Jakarta, I was immediately besieged with a bout of desolation and depression. Not that the city itself had anything to do with my feelings. On the contrary, Jakarta would normally fascinate me with its tropical heat, exotic vegetation, and polyglot of humans all racing around conversing in a bird-like, alien tongue. No, the depression came from deep within me, veiling my curiosity, as the dense smog veiled the surrounding mountains.

I spent the morning immersed in a book by the hotel pool. It's so easy to slip into another's world through the pages of a novel, losing contact with one's own sense of time and space.

Dining alone has always been an uncomfortable situation, but I crave a fresh fruit salad. The coffee shop offered a long buffet table laden with local delicacies but no fruit salad, so I ordered one from the menu. I figured my knowledge of tropical fruits garnered from two years of living in Trinidad would stand by me in this den of confusing culinary choices. The plate set before me resembled an artist's palette of bright and pastel shades and odd shapes. I recognized only the banana and orange slices. The thick, white stuff in the center proved to be Philadelphia cream cheese. The strange bright-yellow melon slice was the taste equivalent of watermelon, so why the strange color? Not, I hoped, due to the water it grew from! Some items were sweet, some tart and mouthwatering. I picked at it hurriedly and fled back to the comfortable solitude of my room and another novel to take me to fantasyland.

11/10/80
Hari Senin (Monday Morning)

Dear Mom,

Hardly seems like a week since I arrived in this part of the world; it must be longer!

We had a busy weekend starting right in on Friday afternoon. I went out to look at houses with a real estate agent. We saw five different places, mostly new ones in various stages of construction. Two had swimming pools, but we are not "allowed" a pool because no one else in Baroid here has one. The houses are more elegant than in Trinidad—mostly all one floor with little or no yard but lots of glassed-in, Japanese-style gardens. Didn't see anything that would fit our budget or was ready for occupancy.

Friday night, we went to dinner at a Baroid fellow's house. There were seven of us, and a good time was had. We are the youngest of the Baroid community, and the only ones without children. The women seem to be into playing golf, bridge, bowling, and the usual boring lifestyles of expat wives, but Jakarta certainly will offer lots more to do than San Fernando (except no racetrack).

Saturday morning, Rog had to work, so I went house-hunting again with a different agent. This lady showed me older houses in lots of different neighborhoods. I fell in love with one house. It's a two-story (quite rare here) with a master bedroom, bath, sitting room, and balcony on the second floor, complete with cathedral ceilings. The living room had lovely teak woodwork and a small garden and patio. Unfortunately, someone else had seen it first and has the first option on it, but we are keeping our fingers crossed. It's the first I have seen that is really "us."

When I got back to the hotel, Rog was there with Peter, the Scotsman, who works for him. Peter picked up his girlfriend, an Indonesian who works for Wang Labs and who speaks perfect English. We went to a park on the bay called Ancor. It was built in the 1960s by the Russians and is quite impressive, sort of a Disneyland. The main attraction was the swimming pools; one Olympic sized with waterfalls at one end; a "wave" pool, which, when the wave machine was turned on, almost made you think you were at the beach; and a huge, slippery slide that dumped you in a small pool. In addition, there was a river-like pool that encircled the area that actually flowed around with currents to carry you if you just lay back and float. The park also had pinball arcades (Kid Kidder was in heaven!), restaurants, and a sort of marketplace full of stalls selling batik, woodcarvings, brassware, and other local crafts. I am amazed by the amount of local crafts and artwork for sale everywhere. So unlike Trinidad.

Sunday, we went out to look at a few houses in the morning. One was really strange, sort of an open courtyard affair. It had two gardens inside with a raised terrazzo floor around them. The bedrooms were glassed-in cubicles around the corners of the central gardens with small, private, separate gardens in each. Rog really liked the house, but we questioned how practical it would be since there was no air-conditioning and you would have to mow the lawn in the living room. I had visions of snakes coming in on the lawn and cohabitating the house with us.

We spent the afternoon and evening with Brian and Linda Devinish, whose brother, Nyron, was the general manager in Trinidad. They drove us up to Puncak Pass in the mountains. Though it was rainy, we saw the tea plantations—acres of stunted little bushes covering the mountainsides and lower down the step-like rice paddies. I can see why after awhile of life in the city one would like to escape to the clear, cool air of the mountain resorts. It's not as tropical-rain-forest-like as Trinidad's mountains but so incredibly beautiful.

Brian and Linda (he is Trinidadian and she is Canadian) lived here for three years and then moved to London for eighteen months. They just moved back but know the area very well.

Today is Monday and more house-hunting for me, work for Rog. Can't wait to be settled!!

Love you lots and lots! Keep warm!
M.

Journal Entry,
11/10/80

Monday morning, and as the rest of the world goes off to work, I settle down to contemplate how I will fill my day. The weekend lifted my spirits, I was surrounded by people who spoke English and got out to see the city and surrounding area. Jakarta offers more to do than any place I have lived in the past. Roger and I ate out all three nights at various folks' homes he works with and one very elegant restaurant. I began my search for a house and toured roughly fifteen possibilities though only one struck me as being just what we want. Unfortunately, this one house may already be taken, so I am still in the market. Yesterday, we took a drive up to Puncak Pass. It is a beautiful area in the mountains to escape the heat and smog of the city. I realized it was somewhat lost on me, as I am not yet fed up with city life, but I still felt awed by the beauty of it.

My question at the moment is the type of women I have met and how I will function within this social framework. None seem stifled by their roles in life as wives and mothers. Perhaps the guilt that drives me to do something and seek a career is something I will never learn to overcome. It seems so hypocritical to take advantage of the abundance of domestic help and yet use one's free time for something so frivolous as golf or bridge. I am anxious to be settled enough to continue my writing courses yet so restless I can barely sit still long enough to write a letter. I crave companionship yet can't wait to be alone with my thoughts. Always, I feel out of my element and self-conscious, fearing people won't like me or worrying what they might think of me. In this feeling of total "lostness," I cling to Roger's warmth and familiarity and then am irritated with myself for my need for such security. Why am I always so impatient with myself?

Journal Entry, 11/13/80

My first reason for visiting the Central Museum was purely boredom. It seemed like a good place to escape the hotel. Sitting surrounded by ancient artifacts, I am awed by the inconsistencies of this culture. Their effigies are horribly grotesque—fearsome faces to rival any Hollywood horror movie. These creatures are found in their woodcarvings and painting as well as the many puppet characters and dolls.

Parts of Java trace back to the Early Stone Age while the area around Jakarta reveals artifacts from the late Stone Age. So where along the way did these cultures merge? In juxtaposition with the war-like, frightening creatures, I find intricate beauty: jewelry delicately woven with tiny shells and beads and baskets of thread-like grasses woven so painstakingly into geometric patterns and designs. The remnants of clothing all display a love for color and detail. Their musical instruments, jumbled into a small hallway, range from massive bronze gongs four feet in diameter to tiny bamboo flutes assembled by key in an ornately carved wooden stand.

I fell in love with a massive Chinese-looking bed. Low to the ground, it was king-sized with carved wooden posts and an ornately carved wooden canopy. Fitted with curtains and lots of pillows, it certainly looked inviting.

Perhaps, I think as I stroll back through the courtyard to the main entrance, I've begun to get a feel for Java. Seeing just what objects a society places in museums and how the importance of each object is displayed gives me a better insight into where in the world I am. I certainly don't feel as though I am far from my home—perhaps because I no longer require familiar sights to point out the differences between where I am and where I am from.

I must actively think in terms of geography to be aware of the miles that separate my country from here. I haven't felt the pangs of homesickness I first felt in Trinidad or the frustration of not being where I want to be. Originally, I felt this was a lack of curiosity to the place around me. I know now it is merely due to a surety about myself, who I am in relation to where I am. I mostly long for companionship, not through fear of loneliness, but rather through overexposure to my own thoughts.

Journal Entry, 11/14/80

The never-ending search for a home. I wander from house to house and try to imagine myself waking up in the bedroom, how I would decorate the living space, what I would buy for furnishings. I imagine Mom and I having breakfast together, perhaps at a rattan table in a garden with a small fountain and a pool full of giant goldfish. I look at each house with the eye for where I would sit and write; an office for both Rog and I perhaps? Our home in Trinidad was a place for people and parties; we had so many good times there.

Saw a lady today who raises German Shepherds. One husky, bold pup caught my eye. Do I really want that heartache again? I still dream of Winston—he is thin and unhappy in my dreams. If only I could send for him once we have a home.

Journal Entry,
11/16/80

Rog looked at a house with me yesterday afternoon. Now all that is left is for it to be approved by the big Baroid boss and then two weeks to finish the renovations. If only we could be staying at the staff house that is right across the street. I could learn lots of Indonesian from Anton, a kindly old gent who works there. Plus we would be close enough to watch things progressing with the house.

It's the little things like not eating in a restaurant full of people. I am so ready to be in a place of our own instead of this limbo on the eleventh floor. I doubt I would miss someone knocking on the door regularly to make up the room, check the bar, take away the laundry, change the towels, or turn down the bed at night. No more doors slammed by other occupants, voices in the hall, showers and johns gushing water all around. Solitude! I awoke with a horrible sinking feeling this morning. It was eight a.m., and my first thought was *Rog is late for work, and what will I do all alone today?* I searched my brain with terrifying anxiety and came up with nothing: nothing to do, no one to talk to, and no reason to be here. Then I was reassured. It's Sunday.

Journal Entry,
11/19/80

It is a rainy day in Jakarta. Last night, we had a fierce thunderstorm—so bad, in fact, that the Wisma Metropolitan was all but obscured from view from our hotel room window. I have managed to keep somewhat busy so far this week. Monday, I went out in the morning to buy Christmas cards and a large leather handbag. In the afternoon, I took a taxi over to Linda's house and managed to get totally lost in Simpruk. Linda and her husband live in an American compound outside the city where all the streets and houses resemble a mini suburb of Houston. Her husband works for an oil company, and we met them at the Petroleum Club (aka country club).

Yesterday was very productive. I called Virginia Wallette, whose husband is Roger's boss. She is an older woman with grown children—very "motherly." She picked me up with her driver at nine a.m. No one is allowed to drive here for two reasons: One is to employ folks, and the other is to avoid massive lawsuits if you ever got into an accident. We went to a grocery store, a drugstore, two furniture stores, and an Oriental rug store. I ordered rattan furniture for the dining room, living room, and a beautiful four-poster rattan bed. I'm absolutely amazed at how cheap it all is, though the delay of having it made is somewhat frustrating. The other furniture store specialized in antique reproductions and Chinese chests. I will order from them later when I am surer about the house.

Virginia is quite nice, though not someone I would ordinarily choose for a friend. We have little in common, but I appreciate her helpfulness. She had me back to her house for lunch, and I nearly fell off my chair when, as we finished our sandwiches, she rang a little silver bell on the table for the houseboy to come and clear away the plates!

Journal Entry, 11/21/80

I feel such total frustration and hate. It consumes me, reducing me to racking sobs of utter despair. Now we are told we are not even to have a house but rather an apartment with a month-to-month lease. I tried. I went out this morning and tried to find such a place. There is none anywhere in this city. Why? Why did we give up a life I had grown to love among friends in Trinidad to come to this awful hell on the other side of the world? There is no one for me to turn to. I've tried to call the office all day but cannot get through. I feel so alone.

Journal Entry,
11/24/80

My rage has subsided to a degree. I've looked for an apartment and found nothing above the level of low-income government housing standards. Roger questions whether we will be staying here or moving to Singapore. Either way is fine with me so long as we get settled *somewhere* soon.

The weekend passed quietly. We got word from Mom that she is out of a job. Though she doesn't sound worried, I know her too well to think it isn't bothering her. Wish I could call and console her, but it is impossible from here at the moment.

Saturday night, we saw an interesting sight. We had gone to a dinner/dance at Linda and Brian's club about twenty-minutes drive out of the city. The whole way back, the road was filled with youths, boys and girls of about twelve to twenty years old. They were marching into town from all over West Java. There must have been a thousand of them in all kinds of running suits, uniforms, and various outfits, some barefooted. Many were resting along the way, lying in the street with their feet propped up on the curb. It was one a.m., and they looked as if they had been marching all night. We wondered what or who had provoked the rally. What sort of reward could possibly persuade these kids to be marching all night? It was an amazing mass of humanity. They marched along, oblivious to the traffic as if totally invincible as cars and trucks weaved around them. How many would be hit and possibly killed before reaching Jakarta, and what would await those who made it? It was truly mind-boggling. Our company-supplied driver did not speak enough English to provide an answer.

Journal Entry,
12/1/80

A week has passed and with it Thanksgiving and our one-month mark in this hotel. We had a Thanksgiving dinner with Vickie and Mike Ratcliff, another Baroid couple. It was imported turkey and all the fixings.

I am still searching for housing as has become my routine. Still nothing definite, and my hopes of being settled by Christmas grow dimmer by the day.

One happy note is that we finally have our own driver and car. Masudi is wonderful, and I can't wait to work on my Indonesian with him. We spent Saturday morning driving out to Pamulang Riding Club and found it to be quite interesting. In fact, if I could get started doing some riding, I know my spirits would improve. Rog will be going to Balikpapan at seven a.m. tomorrow, and I hope to go out to the club again to investigate further.

CHAPTER 5

A Tale of Horse and Home

12/7/80

Dearest Madam B.,

All alone again for a few days. Rog went to Singapore at two p.m. this afternoon. I went riding after dropping him at the airport, but it was a thundery, rainy afternoon, so I didn't ride long. Keelendi and I are getting along quite well. He has a tendency to blow up every once in a while. Flashes of his racing days? Come to find out, he is ten years old, but the old devil sure has lots of life left in him.

No doubt we will be kicked out of this hotel soon. I'm sure they don't appreciate the fact that I "borrow" a few towels every day to give Keelendi his bath and rub down. They smell a bit odd when I bring them back, and I'm sure the laundry staff is thrilled with the abundance of brown horsehair all over them. No matter, we should be moving soon.

·   I have found a wonderful house in a neighborhood here in the city. It is on the end of a dirt road; yes, there are dirt roads right here in this city of millions. Well-to-do Indonesians and some foreign expats inhabit all the other houses on the road. A twelve-foot bamboo fence surrounds each house so you really can't see much from the road. Behind the houses and at the end of the road is kampong—villages of not well-to-do Indonesians who live without indoor plumbing, running water, or electricity (except what they help themselves to right off the telephone poles that bring power to the big houses). It is relatively safe and a wonderful warren of lives intermingling.

Our house is quite simple but lovely; it is all on one floor with a few steps down to a sunken living/sitting room, three bedrooms, three baths, HUGE living room, dining room, den/office, and kitchen. The front entry is a bridge over an enormous fishpond. Baroid is subletting the house (finally paid someone off enough to *get* a house) from Alcan. It is currently furnished, and we are buying some of the furniture. I can't wait to get the furniture I ordered earlier!

The house comes complete with servants, which brings me to my next point. Trinidad was one thing, with a maid who came in to do the laundry and help with the heavy lifting, but this is ridiculous! The hardest thing to get used to here is the fact that, although you may be alone, you are *never* by yourself. We must somehow learn to share our lives with a driver, a cook/maid, a gardener, a houseboy, and a *jagga* (night guard). Every house has servants' quarters in the back, and though they are quiet and unobtrusive, living in their own little world, they are there. As Rog pointed out last night, the discrepancies between rich and poor are so great it is frightening. I don't see any more poverty than in Trinidad, and for those who can secure a job and place to live with an expat, it is a giant jump up the socioeconomic ladder, but still I question how this sort of lifestyle can improve my self-awareness without leading me to become terribly spoiled and self-centered. It is so easy to say, "Enjoy it. It is handed to you once in a lifetime," but is all this going to make me a better person? Between you and me, I have an awful lot of self-doubts. So what is new, you ask??

About two weeks ago, things got really bad between Rog and me to the point where I made a decision. I set December 5 as my "D-Day" (departure day, that is) if our situation hadn't changed. I didn't stop looking for a house or trying to get settled mentally, but I refused to go on past the fifth if we couldn't work something out. I felt he was not making us a top priority. The job is much larger and more stressful than Trinidad or certainly Olney, Illinois. But all that aside, we are here together, and I just want my fair share of his time and attention. Last week, we went out to dinner and discussed my leaving very logically and carefully. Roger felt I could never be happy living in the shadow of his job with nothing meaningful of my own to do with my life. I need long-term goals and short-term accomplishments. He insists that if I go back to the States, he will support me financially, putting me through school if necessary until I can support myself at a job that is psychologically gratifying for me. Of course, the discussion ended with me in tears pleading that I don't really want to leave him. He says I am just scared and I'll get over it, but that I must make it on my own to be happy.

I am telling you about this now because the fifth has come and gone; I'm still here (obviously), and our situation is improving on all fronts. He is such a good, kind, and sensitive person. Why must I make life so tough for him? Why can't

I settle into my role in life here as just a wife like so many generations of women before me? What am I looking for???

I don't mean to sound like "Come on, you are the mother, you *must* have the answer." You are the only person I can share my thoughts with, good and bad, so unfortunately, you are the one I am turning to now. The last time I spoke with you on the phone was two days after Rog's and my monumental discussion. I knew I would break down and cry if I spoke to you for very long or didn't keep the conversation light. Emotions always get in my way. You would have been worried sick by my unhappiness, and that would be pointless. Perhaps someday I will leave; someday this marriage will be over. I know that no one, least of all Roger or I, will say we didn't really work at it. We enjoyed the good and struggled together with the hard times. And through it all, I have you to share my tears of joy as well as sorrow.

I am sorry this letter has begun to sound so sad. Fear not, lady! Today the sun is shining through last week's clouds!

You've no idea how much I love you,
M.

Journal Entry,
12/14/80

Lots has been happening, and I have been so busy that I have neglected my writing. I started riding and joined Pamulang. I tried out a couple of horses and decided on a ten-year-old Bay named Keelendi. He is an ex-racehorse and has good clean legs and a wonderful disposition. I leased him immediately and have been riding regularly. He needs lots of work over the jumps, as he tends to charge before and after. I also need work, so we will learn slowly together. We went out on a trail ride last Wednesday. It was a long ride out through the kampongs (villages) and rice paddies. Two other women from the club showed us the way. I was appreciative of their help, but they were really bossy about how I should be riding Keelendi. When I disagreed at one point, I was rudely rebuffed. Best that I ride alone from now on. I don't like their snooty attitudes and am happy in my role as a "barn rat" who is confident in my own abilities.

We moved into our new home on Thursday, December 11—just three days ago. It has been mass confusion ever since trying to get food, servants, and cleaning organized. The servants who were here had to be paid off and packed out. We have a maid named Lamina who is an absolute gem. She started yesterday and cleans like a mad woman.

I finally went out to the barn yesterday after a two-day absence, and when I got home, she had cooked a roasted chicken complete with stuffing, carrots, beans, rice, and a salad. I said she had done enough, and that she should go home and rest. She smiled her crooked smile, shook her head, and insisted on staying to serve dinner and clean up. This morning, she was back bright and early to clean out her quarters, move in, and make breakfast. An amazing lady; we must be careful to keep her happy, as she is such a help.

Tonight our new *jaga*/gardener starts work. His job is to garden, obviously, and guard the house at night. I'll get a houseboy to help Lamina with the heavy lifting, and we will be all set. I bought a bunch of baskets and hats at the market yesterday to cover the massive wall in the dining room. It is so nice to be in a house and have so much room to move around in!

12/20/80
New Seabury, Cape Cod

Dear Marth,

This morning, I had breakfast at the Passangrahan on Saint Martin! The whole thing—coffee on our beachfront cottage porch with rolling waves and Mr. Rooster strutting by, breakfast served by the grumpy native lady, small birds perched on the jam pots, and chickens chasing crumbs scattered by the middle-aged tourists next door from Ohio. And you and me—so proud of ourselves to be there together, savoring each morning and a new day. Isn't the mind marvelous?? Those days are ours, forever, indestructible.

My Roger (Hoy) dutifully made breakfast and has moved on to the post office and errands. It's a sunny, bright-blue-sky day, and, of course, no snow here on the Cape. The ocean is so dark—almost navy blue. The Cape is a brown, winter world, populated by scrub pines, squirrels, and some interesting small, sparrow-type birds. Brought your camera and will do some pictures for you.

We came down last night. Roger had not been here for a week. Stopped at an excellent little restaurant for dinner. I am always surprised at the real, honest-to-goodness American Indian population here. Some of the men wear their hair long in a black pigtail. And the women are so dark with lovely high cheekbones. You see them in shops, stores, restaurants, serving and being served. Somehow, I keep looking around for the cowboys and/or John Wayne!

I am reworking the interview I did with Truman Nelson. Hope to get it published locally. Getting into the art of doing nothing since the job ran out—has caused my mind to atrophy! I'll get my friend Brad to read the final draft. That's one person I can trust to be brutally honest about everything.

Been wondering about your horse, house, etc. No mail lately, but holiday mail is slow. You should know that from my last paycheck I put aside one thousand dollars—that is the Roger and Martha Fund. I'll be hard put to dig into that; it's for sharing your new world and adventures as soon as I can get there.

Thank you for all the marvelous memories you have made for me so far and for those we will have in the future. I love you, Marth

Madam B.

Journal Entry,
12/21/80

A week has slipped by, and I have come to the profound conclusion that there is no place in my life for complaint. Perhaps because my past week has been so emotion-packed, hectic, and educational that I haven't had time to appreciate my happiness. I am allowed the luxury of pursuing a lifelong interest in what before was mainly an expendable hobby—my riding. I think of all the people I have known because of horses and where their riding took them. I had an evil thought of what Suzie Horagan and the Colby–Sawyer College riding team would think to read about me in the alumni newsletter.

"Martha Walsh Kidder and husband Roger are living in Jakarta, Indonesia, where she is trying to get settled after the move and riding at the club daily. Martha's husband is the District Manager … blah, blah, blah …" It sure is a long way from what most people I used to know are doing.

Learning another language, no matter how simple, is an interesting experience. I have three levels of speech to consider. The many expats speak fluent English no matter where they are from, so one just rattles on in a normal manner to them. The second level is situations like Masudi, the driver. His English is far superior to my Indonesian by sheer vocabulary but is not particularly fluent. He thinks in Indonesian and converts it consciously to English with little or no grammatical structure. Then there is the bottom line, straight Indonesian. For this, I must rely heavily on facial expressions and gestures. My vocabulary feels grossly inadequate, though I work with my dictionary and flash cards and try to add a word every day. Lamina is a case of the third level—bottom line, straight Indonesian complicated by the fact that she is quite old, uneducated, and speaks a mix of Javanese and Bahasa Indonesian (the "national language"). I am surprised when I manage to convey my message; the trick is she often smiles and nods saying, "Okay, Mim," and I realize she doesn't have the faintest idea what I am saying. Then I realize I have been speaking in English! It happens most often in the morning when I first wake up and start speaking but with diminishing frequency. I am alone much of the time here, which is forcing me to really learn.

It's been a week of exploring and searching out stores. We (Masudi and I) do remarkably well in finding such necessities as gaskets for a leaky toilet and firecrackers for Mr. Roger aka Kid Kidder.

Masudi is sort of like a classic Hollywood butler. As our language liaison between so much of daily life, he has taken on the responsibility of "head servant." He interprets to and for the others, which gives him a definite advantage. When I get in the car, I sit behind him and to the left. If I want to talk, I make the friendly gesture of leaning forward to the passenger's seat in front, and he's always happy to work with me on vocabulary. On the other hand, if I am engrossed in thought or just not in the mood to talk, he never starts a conversation. If he needs to talk to me, he will start the sentence with "Excuse me, Mrs. Martha …," not wanting to intrude on my silence. He visibly walks proudly and takes care to dress neatly for his job.

I need only ask, "Masudi, where would I find _____?" or "How do I say _____?" and he takes command of the situation, sometimes going out on errands alone but more often taking me to the markets and teaching me to bargain for things.

Masudi is in a higher social class than the others. He has a small house, a wife, color TV, a motorcycle, and what is considered to be a very good job. He and Rog have grown quite close, and he is very protective of me.

Lamina is so great. She cooks well and cleans furiously from sunrise until the last spoon is in place at night. I have been trying to find a houseboy to help her since she is appalled if I try to help her in any way. Today, a friend, Sylvi, sent over a boy named Nyoto. Lamina was all smiles, and Masudi said she was very happy for the help. We have no modern conveniences whatsoever. The laundry is all done by hand—a tedious task, and the heavy work of washing floors will also be much easier with help. She is about forty years old and a grandmother. Originally, she was from Central Java but has lived in Jakarta for many years. She has a small house somewhere in the city with her kids and grandkids and has worked for foreigners for many years since her husband deserted her. She lives in the servant quarters in back and has Saturdays off. I really miss her when she is gone. She loves Roger and gets such a chuckle out of his antics. "Mister Roger" is next to impossible for her to say due to her thick accent with rolling Rs. It comes out as "Meesterrr Rrrogerrrr." She called him "tuan" at first until he discovered it literally means "lord, master, owner." He put a stop to that and asked her to call him Mr. Roger, but that is what she has said all her life, so it is a hard habit to break. I pay her thirty-five US dollars a month plus three dollars per week for food.

Yamin has become the world's hardest-working *jaga*/gardener. He is about eighteen years old. His family used to own all the land in this neighborhood. When they sold it, they were quite wealthy, but the elders spent it all going on hajjis, or pilgrimages to Mecca. He insists on working on the gardens that fill one side of each room in the house all day and then stays up all night to guard. My guarding gardener!

Our house is on a dirt street at the end of a row of lovely large homes. It has a bamboo fence all around, separating it from the kampong. Amazingly, skyscrapers are visible over the treetops as we are right in the city but just off the main thoroughfare.

Yamin and I have made a lovely garden together in the sunken den. It gives me endless joy to sit and look at its simple, peaceful serenity. At night, I light it with small spotlights and see a whole different effect. I grow to appreciate the beauty of this house daily. We tend to move around a lot when Rog is here, trying out different spaces and rooms. I have so many nooks to sit and write or read in or just gaze at the gardens around me. I think the sunken den is my new favorite as the garden is freshly planted with exotic greenery and plants. Yesterday, I sat on the back patio that runs the whole length of the house from dining room to living room to master bedroom. It was raining lightly and so cool and sheltered.

This was a weekend for meeting people. Rog and I went to two parties. The first on Saturday night was at the staff house. It was a fun, young crowd with good music, food, and dancing. Tom (American) and his wife Sylvi (Indonesian) went with us. They are fairly close friends now due in part to the proximity of our houses, their lack of a car, and our shared lack of children. Sunday afternoon, we went to Virginia and Don Wallette's house for the Baroid Christmas party. It was much more formal with an older crowd, including lots of Roger's customers. Not particularly my taste, but I have learned to play the good corporate wife scene. And their house is truly magnificent.

There is so much I want to get for our house to make it home, but these things take time. It is so big; I am at a loss as to where to start decorating. Should I concentrate on one room at a time or merely spread things out as we acquire them? So many bare walls and shelves to fill! A few trips to Jalan Surabaya will help.

In the meantime, I have Keelendi to fill any spare time. He is out of commission for the moment with some bad bruises from a fight with Valentino in the pasture. I wish I could get out to see him more often but know we will fall into a routine soon. I share Masudi and the car with Roger and obviously his work schedule comes first. I recently met another woman named Sonia who wants to start riding, so perhaps we can carpool. Also, Mrs. Gold, who told me about the club, will be back from New Zealand in two weeks. She goes out daily and has her own car and driver. I know I can hitch a ride with her every once in a while as well. I could never be lacking for things to do here, and not surprisingly, I find I won't be signing up for charity luncheons or bridge or golf lessons as I had feared!

7:30 a.m. Christmas Day

Dear Marth and Rog,

Ten below and blowing in Newburyport, but sunny. Here's the cast of characters:

Happy holidays from the arts and crafts center of New England! This town is beautiful at Christmas but entirely too cold. We must flee this place for warmer climates!

Love, Duncan

Hi, you guys! Thank baby Jesus that you aren't in New England right now. I'd forgotten what it felt like to be cold, but we are all having fun and staying inside a lot. Hit the Grog and the Steak & Stein for food and drinks yesterday. Same old song and dance there. The Christmas decorations downtown are so beautiful—fortunately, we got a good look at them before it got too cold.

Mom is in the kitchen, Dunc is watching TV (can you believe it? Sitting still??), and JT is puttering about with frozen car parts. Frank is debating about coming up from Connecticut, but by the time he decides, we will probably be on our way back to Texas. Mom's little Lydia just came in from the backyard, and she is so cold her tongue is chattering. Good thing she has no teeth left!

Love,
Susanne

I'm here soaking the battery to Duncan's "rent-a-wreck" car in the sink to try to warm it up enough so the car will start. My trusty Buick is hooked up to jumper cables. It is -10 degrees outside. Who in their right mind would be in New England for Christmas?? Look for all of us on the next boat.

Love,
JT

12/26/80
Hari Jumat

Dear Mom,

We were just sitting here (I'm sitting, Rog is playing Ping-Pong against the wall), talking about the changes we have been through since we lived at 225 East Cherry Street in Olney, Illinois. We had our third and best Christmas away from home. I guess I'm slowly adjusting to things like the holidays because of the love I feel from home. I thought a lot about Christmas in New England. We followed the time, commenting, "Well, it's Christmas Eve there now … Christmas morning …," keeping in mind the time difference.

We were very good and didn't open any presents until that morning. I got Rog a tennis racquet, balls, a pen set, and munchies. He bought me the most perfect gifts, things I'd admired but not felt we needed at this point. From Singapore, he brought an electronic lighter, underwear, and Chanel #19. From Jakarta, he'd gone back to the market and bought two heavy antique brass cookie molds. They are about six inches in diameter, round with seven molds in each like a Jell-O mold. Also, some colorful baskets. We opened our presents from you first. The ornaments are "Indah," that's Indonesian for beautiful. I regret not bringing my meager but precious collection of Christmas ornaments. They all represent a different year, so many from you. But these will begin a new collection and someday will join the first set. Rog sat right down and filled in all the pertinent info from last year's datebook into his new 1981 version. Susanne had also sent one, but he is carrying the one from you and using Sue's in his study.

My lovely leather address book is elegant and was put to immediate use, consolidating all the dribs and drabs and business cards I've collected. It seems at parties everyone wants to give you their card, it's "de rigueur," as Rog would say, to have both a business card and a family card with the home address and both wife and husband's names.

We are really getting into fixing up the house. We haven't gotten into the club scene yet, so we end up spending a lot of time here semi-alone. One does not feel particularly comfortable out walking the streets, though perhaps we will get to that point. It's not a fear-type thing because people are very friendly, but the roads are rather narrow and muddy with rainy season. Much like Trinidad, I'm just not up to dodging cars and other vehicles.

This house is a neat project that teaches me important lessons daily. This afternoon, Masudi and I went out to buy paint, brushes, and scrapers. Aside from learning a few new words, I had the mental exercise of trying to explain what I wanted exactly. I needed some WD-40, better known as CRE in Trinidad, that ubiquitous, graphite spray lubricant. I finally ended up with an oilcan and never did find paint stripper. The best part about doing things for the house is that everybody has to get into the act.

On the way to riding this morning, Masudi said he and Yamin (the *jaga*/gardener) talked about the fact that we have a fishpond and that perhaps Rog and I would like it dug up and reconstructed. From the garage to the front door is a very low footbridge over what appeared to be an overgrown garden. When I started digging out the weeds and rocks, sure enough, it is in fact a concrete-lined fishpond. Someone got lazy and threw some dirt, plants, and lots of rocks into it, but it wasn't beyond hope.

I was digging away merrily when Yamin showed up at one p.m. He took over the digging, and I was left with rock picking and weed pulling. Lamina came out and took over my rock pile, so when I finished the weeds, I got a basket and started hauling out the dirt. It amazes me how much pride and effort these people put into their work. And they all take such pride in the house as if it were their own.

Love and miss you. Can't wait for you to come here!!
M.

12/27/80

Dearest Madam B.,

Horror of horrors! They don't sell tampons here. Damn these Muslim countries. I accepted the lack of Santa Claus, but this is going too far!

Got your third Christmas card today and letter of 15 December. Can't wait to read your piece on Truman Nelson. Who knows, this may be the start of something big. I know with the right connections you could sell anything you wrote (Well, typed, that is. I can usually decipher your "unique" handwriting.) Then, when you run out of fresh material in Newburyport, bring your camera, and we will see the Orient together!

"Tidak, apa apa" on the bathing suit that finally came in at the Dancing Witch. I haven't had a suit on lately, and I ordered that two weeks before I left the country! Why so slow? Do they have a huge clientele in Newburyport seeking bikinis in December?

I am sitting in front of the window to my Japanese garden, watching the rain pour down. Don't know how long I'll last, but I can always finish this in the morning. We have solved the problem of mailing letters, though I will be interested to see how long it takes for them to get to you. Baroid has a strict policy of not mailing personal stuff even though their mail goes out of Singapore and would be much faster. I am now sending Masudi to the central post office with my mail. Lazy, yes, but it uncomplicates my life.

Finally got the fishpond cleaned up this afternoon. Yamin had worked yesterday afternoon, last night, and this morning until about ten. It is huge and will take all night to fill with water, even with the rain, as it is under the roof of the entry. It is a bit hard to describe, but I will send photos soon.

Must shut it down for the night. More "besook pagi."

Sunday Morning

Back again. Rog got up early for a tennis date. I slept in until 7:30—so lazy. Just checked the fishpond, and it has about four inches of water, so perhaps we can buy some fish for it today.

I imagine Susanne and Dunc have left for Houston by now. I trust all went well over the holidays. Did you get our telegram? We tried to call earlier in the week but couldn't get a line out. Just as well, as I have yet to see an overseas call cost less than fifteen US dollars.

We have to go to Singapore in January so Rog can get his Indonesian residence visa. I am looking forward to the trip to pick up necessary items like towels, sheets, and tampons! Rog figures he will be traveling a lot next month, so I will have Masudi and the car to myself most days. I usually ride four days a week but would like to work out a better schedule. Most of the ladies who ride out there live closer to the barn. If I could find someone here in town, perhaps we could carpool. I did meet a woman about my age from Columbia who is very interested in checking it out. Perhaps after the trip to Singapore I can get more organized.

We had two rather funny rip-offs yesterday. First, some background. The city is full of peddlers who come down the street all day, selling everything from Satè and soups to baskets, antiques, and birds in cages. One of my favorites is a fellow who pushes a fully loaded bicycle laden with every form of broom and brush known to man—I call him the Fuller Brush Man. For the most part, all are honest, and you can bargain them down on prices … in fact, bargaining is expected. So yesterday, two peddlers stopped at the gate, selling plants. Beautiful blooming orchids, marigold-type things, and such. They were each individually wrapped with a banana leaf around the soil and root ball. I paid too much for a huge bundle of them, and when Yamin and I started unwrapping them to plant them in the garden, we discovered they were all cut flowers. Boy, did I feel dumb! The second occurrence was when Rog, Masudi, and I were finishing up scrubbing out the fishpond. Two very polite men in army fatigues stopped at the gate and presented an official-looking document requesting twenty thousand rupiah (about thirty US dollars) for neighborhood protection. Masudi acted very uneasy and tried to explain to me not to pay them, but in the confusion, Rog paid them, and they left. It turns out they were not even vaguely related to the army or any type of protection agency—just common con artists. They were so polite, bowing and saying, "Hari Natal" (Merry Christmas). Rog now jokes "Hari Natal—twenty thousand rupiah." Best just to laugh and forget the whole affair.

Well, Madam B., I must go wash the rocks for the bottom of the fishpond.

Thinking of you hourly and love your letters.

Love to you,
M.

12/30/80

Dearest Madam B.,

Another morning at home. It's been four days since I rode. Yesterday, we had water problems, so I had to hang around for the repairmen. They showed up at six p.m. and are due back at ten this morning. Poor Keelendi will really think I've abandoned him, but I hope to go out this afternoon.

The work on the fishpond has come to a standstill. We tried to fill it Saturday night and Sunday only to discover it has a slow leak somewhere. We had bought sixteen lovely large goldfish and Sunday morning had to take them back out when the water level got too low. Then we had an electrical breakdown with the water pump (we are on a well), so there was no water for man or fish! Last night, six fish died in rapid succession. I put emergency measures into action and sent them all over to a friend who has a pond. At the moment, we have a lovely mess of rocks and cement but still no fishpond. I would give up and put the whole thing back as a rock garden, but Yamin, the gardener, is intent on patching it up and making a pond.

Sunday, Rog got up early to play tennis with a Phillips customer at the Petroleum Club. He called at ten to say he was sending the car for me to join them for brunch. The Club is quite posh with a lovely pool area, three squash courts, and tennis and nightly video movies. We had an excellent, *huge* brunch of omelets, bacon, hash browns, donuts, sausage, etc. The fellow Rog played tennis with is from Kansas and married to a girl from Denmark. I couldn't help wondering what she thinks when they go home to Kansas to visit his family. Must be quite the culture shock!

Well, here's hoping we have water soon.

Love,
M.

Journal Entry, 1/2/81

A new page of my journal for a new year. I get so much joy from just walking around this house. No one would believe that something so simple (though nothing here is simple, in truth) could bring such tremendous satisfaction. To begin with, I have numerous nooks and quiet places to sit and write letters. My first garden in the sunken living room is always a joy to contemplate. The garden in the yellow bedroom is completed and very secluded. It provides a private place to just sit and listen to the world going on outside the fence. The study affords a good view of the front entry and fishpond, which finally seems to be holding water. The main living room is comfortable for listening to music. I still have a few more corners to round out, such as the patio in our master bedroom, but considering we have been here just two weeks, I am amazed at the transition. (And so very glad to be out of the hotel!)

Masudi and I went back to the fish market and bought a second batch of fish and some really neat new plants. The plants look like very young floating cabbages with long, trailing roots. The fish are too numerous to count. Roughly nine huge angelfish, which are capable of quick bursts of speed and agility through the pond but also can remain perfectly still for minutes and almost invisible. I think there are four large black catfish, a mottled silver-and-black one, and dozens of tiny tetras and giant gold carp. At first, they were very shy, hiding under the bridge when you approached. This evening, they were all out, discovering their new home.

The new houseboy, Suparno, seems to be fitting in well with the rest of the staff. He is quieter than Yamin or Masudi and seemed quite terrified the first few days. I am guessing he is in his early twenties. I think he is fairly well educated, as he reads a lot and even speaks some English. I made some Indo-English flashcards so he and I can practice together. Like the others, he goes out of his way to please us and works like a maniac. It's strange, the relationships developing. Masudi and Lamina are our standbys. I am getting so I understand Lamina nine times out of ten, but she speaks a different Javanese dialect and some words are lost on me. Yamin is always smiling; he is a perennial clown and everyone's favorite. Suparno is more reserved and doesn't mix much with the others. I sometimes feel sorry for him for his lack of confidence, but perhaps that will come.

The fishpond was an interesting competition. Masudi, Suparno, and I started washing and arranging the rocks. When Yamin arrived, he went wild making giant arrows, stars, and hearts with the rocks. He pretty well covered the largest part of the pond, and everyone was egging him on. Suparno started on the narrow side and also made a heart, an arrow, and a star. By the time he finished, our small crowd had dissipated. I came back out and commented on Yamin's artwork. Sup looked crestfallen. I turned and saw what he had done. I congratulated him, and he positively beamed. Later, when I mentioned the episode to Sudi, he agreed there was some competition there. Sometimes I feel like they are just a bunch of kids, and I'm running a day care center.

1/7/81

Dearest Madam B.,

Just got home from Singapore—it feels so good to be back, and we got such a warm welcome from our crew. Masudi met us at the airport, and the other three were waiting at the gate where both the house and yard looked impeccable. Your letter of 12/20 was waiting at the office with a huge stack of mail.

Singapore was its usual hustle-bustle self. Great shopping; I have no idea how much I spent. When we were trying to cram it all into the suitcases last night, it sure seemed like a lot, but after unpacking, I can't believe how little we really bought. I picked up some veterinary supplies and brushes for Keelendi, lots of new towels, and several sets of satin sheets, eight Chinese silk paintings, three gorgeous framed (dead) butterflies, tons of magazines and books, a kitchen clock and coffeemaker, a bathroom scale, speakers for Masudi's stereo, lots of baby things per order of friends, cosmetics, a new terry cloth outfit (jacket, top, and pants) for me, a new pair of shoes, and a beautiful navy snakeskin evening bag. For Roger's birthday, he got a new Casio digital watch, a new tennis outfit, tennis glove, and a beautiful pair of Italian leather dress shoes. Sounds like a lot, huh? Well, I went absolutely crazy for two days straight collecting all that stuff. I bought the boys, Yamin and Suparno, each a t-shirt and Lamina an apron, which she went wild over.

Roger's partner, Peter, the Scottish guy, went with us. He's moving to Singapore in a month or so to handle the business up there. We all stayed at the Hyatt, which was pure luxury. Singapore's great for shopping and nightlife, but I found I much prefer Jakarta and our leisurely lifestyle here. We went out to a bar last night that had a great live band. The main attraction was the lead singer dressed in a black leotard, skin-tight, silver satin pants, and high silver boots with incredible glitter makeup. At first glance, the heavy blush, eye makeup, lipstick, manicured nails, and long, wild hair led one to think it was an overdone female. Wrong! He was quite the sideshow, teasing and taunting the old Chinese waiters and dancing on the tabletops. Only in Singapore. The music was quite good also.

Since we just got back, there is no food in the house, so we will have to eat out again tonight. There is a nice little restaurant down the street, Café Espresso, that we'll probably go to that is cheap, clean, and fast. Rog takes off again tomorrow for an overnight in Medan. Baroid sent him an airline credit card—bet they're going to regret that one!

I couldn't get my resident visa this time and will have to go back to Singapore next month. Too bad! My blisters from pounding the pavement should be just about healed by then, and the checkbook will have recuperated sufficiently.

Love you dearly,
M.

1/14/81

Dearest Madam B.,

No mail since we got back from Singapore. I feel very far away tonight.

I've ridden the last two days after not riding on Sunday. Yesterday, Keelendi was the best and worst he's ever been. At least, he was the best for me. We did about a half hour of dressage, and he is changing leads, cantering a figure-eight perfectly. We started with some low jumps and worked up to a small course of three. It was a first for him, and he was good about not charging at racetrack speeds between them.

My new friend, Sonia, had come out to ride with me. The school was closed, so we couldn't get a horse for her. When I finished with Keelendi, she got on to try him out. He was all charged up from jumping and immediately took off with her. Luckily, we were in the big indoor ring with no one around. I told her to just hang on and he would stop eventually. She was doing really well hanging in there until he took a sharp corner and lost her. She was okay, just shaken, and he was trembling. I dusted her off, calmed him down, and put her back up to walk back to the barn. Today, I rode alone, and he was almost as good as yesterday but refused twice on one jump. It's so satisfying to really see the improvement in him.

I don't know if I wrote to you about Sonia. She is from Columbia, twenty-eight years old and married to an American who is ten years her senior. He heads up the team of divers who work on the offshore rigs. They are a very rowdy bunch. Sonia has a daughter in Colombia who lives with her ex-husband. She doesn't say much, but I get the feeling it was not an amicable split. She is gorgeous, though a bit crazy; heavy on the makeup and fashions but totally fun and, like me, rebelling against the "corporate wife" image. She has some real problems with her current marriage to Ron, which is a bit of a drag since she needs someone to talk to and I end up having to do a lot of listening. Poor girl thinks in Spanish and must constantly translate to English or Indonesian. She and Ron have been here for two years, so she knows Jakarta and Bali fairly well.

When I got home from riding today, I worked out back in the garden off our bedroom. It is slowly shaping up, and all the rain we've been having makes everything grow so fast. I finally got some plants for inside the house the other day—a palm tree and some giant cacti. Still looks awfully bare in here.

Hoping for mail tomorrow!

Love you dearly, and you are always in my thoughts,
M.

Journal Entry,
1/22/81

Bandung. The ride was hair-raising, bouncing over the mountains on a narrow road crowded with buses, trucks, and lorries all creeping up the inclines and racing recklessly down the other side. The tops of the mountains were shrouded in thick clouds, and the cool air was saturated with rain.

Tea plantations rose up the steep roadside, giving way to stepped paddies of tender rice shoots in perfect plateaus. The towns along the way were choked with pony carts and becaks or marketplaces selling fruits and vegetables.

Bandung seemed more like a foreign country than Jakarta with less foreigners and a whole other language—Sundanese. The pace was slower and the people friendlier. The becaks were more abundant, smaller and artistically decorated. Architecture was not the modern, almost Western city atmosphere of Jakarta, but rather more gracious Old Dutch. It was pleasantly cool and dry—a perfect environment. I now understand why the Dutch fled Jakarta for this town when there was no air-conditioning.

I was surprised by the size of the city; it stretches out over the plains, rising to the mountains on all sides. Our hotel was supposedly one of the best places in town, however, it was drab, dreary had seen better days. The eerie Sundanese music wafting everywhere was enough to give me nightmares. Another fellow from the office, Juman, went with us. He said he was originally from a small village in Central Java. Strange person; he lived with his widowed sister in Jakarta. We ate at the same restaurant twice. It was good and very cheap. Glad to be home, even though, once again, we have no water.

Journal Entry,
1/24/81

Saturday afternoon, still no water. The pump is out of the hole, thirty meters down, and two young guys have been sweating over it all day. As I watched them painstakingly pull the pipe out a foot at a time, I couldn't help but marvel at their straining muscles bulging below the skin, sometimes so taut they shook from the sheer effort. Not once did they show anger or frustration at the task.

This morning, I arose at 4:45 a.m. Sudi was due at five to take Tom, Silvi, and I to Pasar Ikan (fish market). Unfortunately, he overslept and didn't arrive until six.

The market was alive with sights, smells, sounds, and activity. We were the only foreigners and quite obvious, towering above the mayhem. After making our purchases of oversized shrimp, undersized lobster, and a small shark, we toured the shops surrounding the market. All sorts of shells, sponges, sea-stuff, shops full of kitchenware, baskets, and several selling drums, violins, guitars, and odd, handmade musical instruments. I want to go back for another look soon.

Journal Entry,
1/26/81

Rog left Sunday morning for a week of travel to Singapore and Manila with a stop in Hong Kong. It would normally be a perfect trip for picking up some things for the house, but our financial situation is extremely shaky at the moment with the condo in New Hampshire unrented.

I have been spending the last three days here at the house trying to get our "pompa air" fixed. A week now without running water is no longer a laughing matter. I've become frustrated and beyond caring if we ever have water again. Yesterday morning, I planned to go riding as soon as the repairmen arrived and the work was underway. By eleven a.m., they still hadn't shown up, and it was raining incredibly hard. Our electricity went out, but I knew it was temporary, as the whole street was out. Sudi decided to go to the office to pick up my mail but realized the car battery was dead also. No water, lights, or car. I thought nothing else could go wrong. Just then, the tukan (peddler) showed up to finish the frames on my Chinese silk pictures. When the rain let up, he tried to leave, but his motorcycle had quit in the driveway. I looked out the living room windows and, to my horror, saw that the backyard was completely flooded and threatening to spill into the house! Nothing could possibly go this badly if Roger was here.

The day ended with all returning to normal with the exception of our water problems. Nick dropped by with an invitation to a hot bath and his condolences on my desperate plight. Lucy called to assure me the workmen would be here first thing in the morning, and Sonia called to check my state of mental health. If nothing else, my Indonesian vocabulary is improving!

Lamina made excellent satè ayam for dinner. From one skinny rooster, she made enough satè to feed the four of us (Yamin, Suparno, herself, and I) with two drumsticks left over. Amazing.

Journal Entry,
2/1/81

One month of the New Year gone. I'm restless and impatient for life to really settle down. I still feel like I've just arrived everyday. Talked to Mom yesterday morning. It was the first time since November. We are very worried at the moment about our financial state (albeit a far cry from the financial problems three years ago when we first moved to Illinois and the total balance of available cash seldom topped a thousand dollars). I just wish I could somehow be contributing or helping in a monetary way. (There's those nasty little "guilties" sneaking up on me again. I fear I won't be able to rent Keelendi again this month. Nothing to be done about it. I'll just go out when things improve.

2/8/81

Dear Marthe,

Your great letter of January 22 with pictures sits in front of me. Your peacock chair is marvelous! Can't wait to see your house. I'll bring a canteen of water.

Nana, Grampa, and I must find a map so we can follow your travels like the trip to Bandung. Grampa is digging through his old *National Geographic* magazines to look for articles about Indonesia.

Word from Houston this week: Dunc in love (small, blonde twenty-year-old named Barbara). He took her to New Orleans this weekend for her birthday. And he is pursuing his new career—a Houston cab driver! He's working as an independent and raking in the $$, two hundred dollars clear some days/nights. So he's happy doing his favorite sports—playing in the traffic and staying up all night.

Susanne is working full time at Texas Jeans and learning a lot of retailing. She is out of sorts with her beau, Cameron, and on the move again.

Good Lord, those two are enough to make a mother go gray!

Enjoying my three afternoons a week at the Phillips Real Estate office. But, oh, to find a full-time, paying job in this delightful town. The Coffin house on Jefferson Street just went on the market for $74,500! Choke, choke!!

Finally saw *Cousin, Cousine*, that marvelous French love story. They show foreign/old films at the YMCA twice weekly. Very primitive, chairs from the local undertaker, and small screen in a room off the gym. Movies are punctuated by bouncing basketballs. Where else but Newburyport?!?

Thinking I am bottoming out with my syndromes—empty nest/career, condo, life. I suggested my Roger stay home on the Cape today since my attitude was dull, but if he could survive his wife and six daughters, he seems to think he can handle me. You know how we Walsh ladies are about coming first with our men. I'm going through a semiannual fit of insecurity, and poor Roger pays the price. We are either very much alike or very much different. I can't figure it out. He seems so cool and quiet, but my therapist, Barbara Somers, says I come off cool and superconfident. How well, Marthe, you know that's not so. Who else knows me that well? Your love and understanding are my rock.

Love you and love to the Kid Kidder, my favorite CEO-in-the-making.
Madam B.

2/2/81

My Dearest Madam B.,

I was beside myself that Rog got a valentine first, but mine arrived yesterday. Of course, I'd forgotten all about Valentine's Day until it was too late to make cards.

Perhaps we are about at the same point in life at the moment. My letters have slacked off due to lack of major daily excitement, but I am not yet going stir-crazy from the lazy routine. Since George arrived, I've been rather housebound for lack of wheels and Masudi.

The job with Phillips Real Estate sounds perfect—interesting but not overly taxing on time or nerves.

I cherish the photo of Sue and Dunc and will see that it is suitably framed. Thought you might enjoy seeing some shots of the Chinese rattan bed I had ordered last November. It finally arrived last Friday. Since then, coincidental with the arrival of George (Roger's new employee), I have had to abandon certain habits and have retreated to the master suite much of the time. I moved the porch furniture onto the bedroom porch so I can sit outside in private more often and potted up eight large plants to screen the porch off from the rest of the backyard.

The bed is a king-size. You can note the Chinese silk prints from Singapore to the left of it. The other bed was quieter (rattan squeaks when you move, if you catch my drift) but no comparison for size and atmosphere.

Another new spot I've recently started inhabiting is out front by the fishpond. Yamin and Suparno hung a hammock that Sonia gave me from Columbia. It's a good spot to relax and "fish watch." Due to lack of a personable pet, I have begun taming the fish. They will eat from my hand and let me touch them, but that's about the extent of their intelligence. Sure miss Keelendi.

Our houseguest, George, has gone to Balikpapan for three days. It's not that I don't like him—oh, wait a minute, yes, that is the reason … He's a typical cold, pompous Limy, and I resent the amount of attention Roger pays him. All they ever talk about is work, and I am getting fed up with entertaining him. He makes little or no effort at conversation and must be pumped for even the simplest answers.

Oh well. I have to go back to Singapore in a week for my visa. That should break the monotony. Just wish I had lots of money to buy some pretty clothes.

Wish we could sit together with a cup of tea, but your letters really do help.

Love you muchly,
M.

2/15/81

Dear Marthe,

On the road again ... sitting in Norfolk, Virginia, terminal, waiting for a flight to Houston. We do see a lot of airports, don't we? My discount fare on Piedmont gives the opportunity to visit lots of places en route. Next stop is Charlotte, North Carolina. But at least I got to sit inside the plane. For the price, I expected to be strapped to the wing.

Hope a witch doctor has "unjinxed" your water/electricity/rain deluge whatever by now. Of course, you will have it all under control by the time Rog returns home. Manila and Hong Kong! No wonder the New London Kidders are green with envy. But wives were designed for holding the fort, and I never had any patience with those who called the office every time the refrigerator made a funny noise.

Love to you and the "Kid,"
Madam B.

2/25/81

Dear Madam B.,

Rog is off to Sumatra and Singapore to meet with his boss, Sonny Andrews, from Houston. I was really pissed off at him when he left at four a.m. yesterday. He "arranged" for me to go see an exhibition tennis match between Bjorn Borg and Vitas Garalaitis tomorrow night with two of his customers. Now, *tennis* is a dirty word to me, so I would never consider going alone anyway. But the customers are Linda and Brian Devinish, a couple of real wet blankets! Rog was dying to go so felt naturally I would feel the same. I tried to explain it's like me asking him to go to a horse show with two of the middle-aged, wet-blanket ladies from the barn. He woke me up at four a.m. again today to ask my shoe size so he could look for roller skates for me in Singapore. How can you be mad with such a person? If something tragic was to happen and I never saw him again, this would be my last memory.

It's coming on to four years since we've been married. I always set five years in my mind as the point, way off in the future, when I would do some serious evaluating of my life ... perhaps even consider children. Sounds like so long, but it is passing so quickly.

Since Rog left, I have not spoken face to face with anyone in English. I've spoken to Sonia on the phone, but all other thoughts and questions require translation to Indonesian. I rode yesterday morning, and Keelendi was his usual self—full of bounce and craziness. He was not sold at the auction (thank you, baby Jesus), as they had a poor turnout and he behaved particularly badly. Way to go K!! Saved himself for me!

This afternoon, I did some sightseeing with Masudi. We went to Monas. This is an obelisk structure, 132-meters high, that represents Indonesia's independence. It contains a small historical museum and a view of the city from 115 meters above. Sudi makes for a great guide because his national pride and enthusiasm flows evenly through his broken English-Indonesian conversation.

We later drove around the waterfront near the fish market, looking at the boats, and I thought of how much Dad would enjoy seeing this. Indonesia has the last remaining and largest merchant marine fleet that is totally sail-powered. Enormous wooden ships!

Tonight, Sudi and his wife took me to dinner. She speaks no English and is a typical Muslim wife, so it could have been a bit strained with my being the boss's wife. But they are such warm, friendly people that it was no strain at all. Sudi translated when I got stuck, and they came in for about forty-five minutes when we got home. It really was a very good experience.

2/26/81

Didn't get this in the mail, so I will continue. Sudi, Sonia, and I went to Bogor today. It's a mountain town about forty-five minutes from Jakarta with a museum and incredible botanical gardens. We wandered around for the better part of the morning and then had a lunch of local food at a roadside restaurant. I will never learn to divide people into their separate categories and treat "servants" as such. This baffles Sonia, who grew up with many servants in Colombia. It also baffles Sudi because he knows how to be a servant. I'm sure we appeared an odd threesome. We took dozens of photos of each other, which I will forward on to you. Sudi always seems to know just when to disappear so Sonia and I can talk privately.

Rog is returning tomorrow with Sonny Andrews in tow. I'll be glad to see him, but a weekend of Sonny sounds very dull.

Thinking of you always. Love you dearly,
M.

Journal Entry,
3/1/81

Some days are harder to get through than others. Time is my enemy, always being one step ahead or behind me, stealing away the months and years, dragging slowly through long days and countless weeks. My life is becoming increasingly stagnant as I try to keep a check on the monetary flow and spend more time within the confines of the house. We started a new outdoor project this week, building brick pathways and a small circular patio in the back garden. The physical labor, hauling all the materials around back, is satisfying, and the end result so far is well worth the effort. I still wake up with an empty feeling, though, as I face each day.

I'm beginning to believe through certain clues that Roger wants to have a baby. The thought of it terrifies me and makes me feel the walls are closing in. When I questioned him about it, his reply shocked me. If I "happen" to get pregnant, that would be okay, but he doesn't want to actively try to make a baby. I firmly believe the commitment must be made from the start, before conception. Mom and Dad planned long and carefully before family planning was popular (particularly among Catholics). They searched out a doctor who would "allow" them to have natural childbirth and actively shared the excitement and responsibility for each child. Granted, their marriage deteriorated beyond repair, but I always knew I was planned and very much wanted. Perhaps after four years of marriage with negative thoughts on the subject, Rog is afraid to show an active interest. Maybe he really wants a child but hesitates to say so because he thinks I don't. I look in the mirror. The eyes that gaze back at me are not those of someone who looks like a mother. Rather, I see the eyes of a child.

Oh, please, someone help me! Today I am my own worst enemy.

3/3/81

Dearest Madam B.,

At long last, I got a letter to beat all letters. It was from one of the guys I worked with at Union Park. The only problem is I really have no idea which one it is from!! It's signed C. Saroop, but I never really knew too many people's real names, so I'm clueless. He says "Mak [my nickname for Martha Anne Kidder], we miss you girl. I hope you don't mind I say girl, okay?" Talk about a flood of emotion and memories. I want to write back but must puzzle out who I'm writing to first. He said Vicar's Lass was going out to the farm for good after Christmas. I hope Trainer Cobb has some new stock to train.

Sonny Andrews, Roger's boss from Houston, finally left last night. It was really trying having him around as well as George. The man is a total and utter incompetent boob. Needless to say, we spent the entire weekend trying to occupy his feeble mind. We had him here for dinner Saturday night, and then he, Rog, and George went to Merek for the day Sunday. I went out motorcycle riding on Sunday. It was a beautiful day, sunny and warm. The *jaga*/gardener, Yamin, borrowed his brother's cycle, and we toured the area. On a motorcycle you can go all through the kampongs where there are no roads for cars. There are some beautiful villages out in the country away from Jakarta. Those right here in the city are pretty depressing because of the poverty and open-running sewers. Sunday night, we had dinner at Sonny's hotel.

I went back out cycling again yesterday afternoon with Masudi. We went quite a way outside the city to some really breathtaking places. Mountains rimmed with clouds surrounding florescent-green rice paddies. Rog and I have decided if we rent the condo and get on our feet financially, we might buy a cycle for me so I'd have a bit more independence. I would probably not learn to drive it myself but rather have Yamin drive me around on it. Great, if it's not raining!

Guess I forgot to tell you about our latest addition here. Sonia gave me a kitten. It's a fluffy gray female with a short tail. Indonesians believe that if you cut off a cat's tail, it will be better behaved and not kill chickens. When they are newborn, they tie the tail in a knot near the base and chop off the end. So Kucing has a little tuft where her tail used to be. Rog is not fond of cats, but since it was a present from Sonia, he's allowed it to stay. As all kittens, she is very cute and full of the devil. Lamina is in love with her and is no doubt the best-fed and cared for cat in all of Jakarta! I never realized how easy cats are to keep as pets. She made one mistake in the house so far, and that was because she couldn't get outside. She's very clean, and if she is tired out, she's quite loveable.

Thinking of you always,
Love,
M.

3/11/81

Dear Marthe,

Finally got an afternoon to myself with the office typewriter. Dot and Don Phillips have gone to Kennebunkport to ready a house they own there for a rental. Their real estate holdings are extensive—from Essex to Maine.

Before I forget, April 6 is Grampa Brim's birthday. He would enjoy an Indonesian birthday card if there are such things.

Lydia came to work with me today. We had been doing errands, and there wasn't time to take her home. It's in the forties and cloudy, so I didn't want to leave her in the car (read "spoiled Pekingese"). She is being so good and has only eaten one small customer.

Dunc and Sue called this morning. They were on their way to House of Pies for breakfast. Something they had to discuss and, not being able to handle talking and cooking at the same time, they had to go out. Are they really in our family tree? Sue had dinner with Dad and my Roger last night at a good Greek restaurant.

Dunc is still in the mood to buy his own cab and, as usual, has four ideas a minute about how to finance the car and medallion (license for cabs). No, I think I won't move to Houston, even if I go on Pekingese aid/welfare right here.

Had a marvelous interview with the vice president of operations for Gould yesterday. I would dearly love the job. But, of course, the money is a catch. I would be taking a five-thousand-dollar cut to start. If they offer me the job, I think I'll take it and just scale down my lifestyle. I could cut out things like clothes, food, and incidentals of that nature. From the looks of my typing, I could hardly qualify as a clerk, but this machine has no lovely automatic erasure button.

Your thoughts about the upcoming four-year anniversary are sensitive and arresting. It certainly doesn't seem like any such span by the calendar, and look at all the fascinating living you two have packed in. More than most families see in two generations, even if they are gypsies. Of course, as for having babies, I think you and Roger are so much fun and delightful you should be cloned. And we can always use a few more Yankees in this world, especially such classy ones as you two. I am at a loss to understand how I could have had such a good time growing up with my kids and yet only one of you three is interested in parenthood. And that one talks about doing it all alone … Sue told me something when I was in Houston, which really breaks my heart every time I think of it. Something was said about how good Dad is with little children. She said she has noticed that, but by the time she was aware of him as a father, she had passed the cute stage that he relates to and so she felt he never cared beyond that point. Tells me something about the built-in sensitivities of children. Choosing a father for one's children is a neglected area that sadly needs much more attention.

Dot Phillips's brother, Arnold Lessard, who is with Chase Manhattan, just returned from Jakarta. We got a card here at the office from the Jakarta Mandarin Hotel. Took him thirty hours from New York going out via Amsterdam, Karachi, Singapore. He conducts studies for new banking locations.

Enough of this rambling. Take care of the Kid/CEO. Lots of love to him but my best love always for you.

Madam B.

Journal Entry, 3/16/81

Jesus! I can't believe these people! Eiko and Jim Smith is a couple who just happen to be a very important customer. They just moved here from Tripoli; she's Japanese, he's American; two kids, a girl, four, and a boy, eighteen months. We took them to the Oasis restaurant Saturday evening and dropped three hundred US dollars—the works with a bottle of Dom Perignon. This is the second time we've seen them; they came for a disastrous lobster dinner first. Tonight, Jim called. Eiko got on the phone to invite us to dinner Wednesday night, and then Jim came back on to talk to Rog. I was in the shower when Rog called me, wanting me to talk with their servants. Mediating in two languages seems to be my new pastime. I wish they would learn Indonesian or hire servants who speak English!

I had spent the entire afternoon with Eiko shopping for tablecloths. I do enjoy her company, but they both get overly worked up about their servants. I refused to get out in the middle of my shower, but when I did emerge, they were still on the phone. First, Jim tried to talk to the *jaga* through and around me. Finally, he convinced the *jaga* to get on the phone. I got what information I could out of him and relayed it to Jim. That wasn't good enough. We played the same game three more times before Jim gave up rather rudely in disgust and asked to speak to Roger. This was after he ignored my correction of him on my name. Margaret??? As far as I know, he's still on the phone; must be an hour now.

Journal Entry, *3/18/81*

A very sad day in my life. My first inking of the problems ahead came when Yamin started a conversation casually by the front gate about Lamina going across the street to wash clothes in a neighbor's machine. Now, I didn't blame her for being ingenious enough to lighten the drudgery of washing clothes by hand, but as Yamin pointed out, the owner of the machine might not appreciate our using their washer. From there, it just sort of spilled over into a war. Sudi, Min, Suparno, and I went to investigate the price of materials for fixing the roof out back in their quarters. Along the way, I got the general drift of just how bad the situation is between them and Lamina. We dropped Min and Parno at the house, and Sudi and I continued on to the Mandarin Hotel. It was finally a perfect sunny day to use Sonia's pool passes. I needed to get away and think the problem through, but it was also nice to just get away and be "female," though that connotes "lazy." We lounged by the pool (I got totally burned) and then showered and went downstairs to the beauty salon. Sonia had a manicure while I went in for a trim on my "punk" short hair. I tried to avoid thinking in terms of anything but firing Lamina and solving the conflict once and for all. I didn't see her right away when we, Sonia and I, came home. We went to the kitchen for drinks, and I felt hollow. Confronted by Lamina, my mind was flooded with thoughts of all the good this woman has done for me.

I thought Sonia had saved the day for me with her idea of swapping maids. I breathed a huge sigh of relief and set about explaining the situation to Lamina. Yet, as I sat next to and looked at this small, dark, wizened lady, I saw the true injustice of life. I really had no good reason to fire her and many reasons to instead be giving her a raise. The fact that she had a sort of split personality when it came to her relations with her fellow employees could almost be explained away. Sonia's solution almost convinced me. Time will tell if I did the right thing by all. I never had to deal with four employees of my own, particularly such personal servants and the cultural and language differences. The line is so very indistinct between employee relations and human relations. How does one decide whether to react as an employer or a compassionate human being?

I haven't gotten a letter in so long I can't remember the last one from Mom. I tried once again last night to explain to Rog how lack of money and Keelendi has been affecting me lately. Tonight, he announced he has to buy Nick's golf clubs for $250 US. Is my life a losing battle here?

Journal Entry, 3/24/81

Eiko and I went to a newcomer's coffee at the American ambassador's residence sponsored by the American Women's Association. We both decided to pass on *that* little group—definitely not my style! I started getting really bad vibes upon filling out the initial questionnaire. The first question was "Husband's name, first and last. Please print." Under that was a line for "your name." The program went downhill rapidly from there. We listened to the ambassador's wife explain how she threw a successful "informal dinner" for seventy in honor of ex-President and Mrs. Ford. The crowning blow was each person had to stand up and tell a bit about herself. Each woman began (in a Texas drawl), "My name is Mrs. Joe Blow.

Mah husband is the president/vice president/head of (pick one), and mah children go to Hahvard/Yale/Columbia/Princeton ..." Wait a minute here. Who the hell are *you*??

For some reason I seem to be attracting problem cases this week. I went out last evening with Inga and Nonon. We went to Ancol, but the evening was rather a dead end with the news that Nonon is pregnant by her Australian boyfriend, Andy, from the staff house. He is not interested in marriage, so she is having an abortion. I am not sure how I managed to get involved in this, but it seems she will need somewhere to recuperate afterward away from the eyes of her family.

I swear Sonia has lost it completely. I caught her unconsciously grinding her teeth. She was furious with me for not spending the entire day with her at the Mandarin Pool. When I finally arrived at three p.m., she was sitting at a table with Kent (a diver friend of Ron's), ordering lunch, and was quite far gone from too many drinks. She spent the rest of the afternoon sitting fully clothed reading a book. Great company.

I headed back to the house where Nonon and Andy showed up following her abortion. She was in really rough shape, and I was worried. Shortly thereafter, a rather drunk and confused Sonia appeared at the door and made a beeline for the bedroom to pass out.

Journal Entry, 3/26/81

Weird one today. I started off well, thinking I'd spend the day, or the better part of it, cleaning the fishpond. Yamin, his friend, and I jumped right in, literally, as soon as Sudi and Rog went to the office. I was kneeling in two inches of muck, trying to catch the fish, when Dibby called. Let me go back a bit here.

When Nonon arrived the other day after her abortion, I was trying to distract her with conversation. She told me about a friend of hers who is making a film in Bali. They need a white woman for one of the parts who can speak Indonesian, and she told them about me. According to Nonon, acting experience is not a heavy requirement in the Indonesian film industry. She sent Dibby over today to take some photos to show this film-producer friend. Dibby called to say he'd be by at ten thirty the next morning.

Sonia showed up at exactly ten thirty the next morning just as the dog and monkey show was ending. I had opened the gates for the kids in the kampong and paid for the men who do the dog and monkey show. It was a great photo op and entertaining while I worked on the pond. A drum made of goat hide stretched over a bamboo log heralded the arrival of two men and their traveling show. Yamin negotiated a price of five hundred rupiah. The men put down two miniature stools, sat down, and set up while the crowd of kids and old folks gathered. A monkey in a pink dress performed first, jumping through a hoop, dancing, and pulling a wagon. It rode on a dog that later danced on its hind legs. An extra bonus came when one man took out a three-foot-long snake and wrapped it around his neck.

After they left, Sonia began applying makeup for me. By the time Dibby showed up, I no longer recognized (or felt particularly comfortable) with the face that stared back at me from my mirror. It took me about an hour to feel relaxed with the camera. God knows what the photos will look like. It was interesting, to say the least. The equipment they brought was fascinating—beautiful lenses, umbrellas, lights, the works. They totally transformed the living room into a full-scale photo studio. I was amazed the next time I looked at my watch. It was four. Sonia and I topped off the day with a Becek ride to the grocery store.

Journal Entry, 3/27/81

We arrived at the driving range to men surrounding the car, peering in the windows and gesturing wildly. We carried two clubs, paid the admission fee, and were led to a numbered stall. There was a rubber mat on the cement apron, and floodlights illuminated the range into which small white balls flew, disappearing amid signs designating distances. Rog set to work assaulting the balls as fast as Sudi could place them on the tee.

After about five balls, he turned to me. All day, I've had a strange pain in my side. I questioned whether the twisting action of swinging a golf club would help it any. When I declined, he turned to Sudi and gave him an impromptu lesson. As I watched them, I realized for the second time tonight how truly different we are. I feel my life is being centered on a series of small balls and ways to hit them. Tennis, gold, and Ping-Pong, though I must admit I do enjoy the latter.

My happiest moments are spent probing the mind—mine or preferably someone else's. The lack of a similar plane of thought is causing a drought in my mind, eroding my capacity to enjoy feeling life deeply. The problem is that I can't seem to communicate this problem of communication, and I think Rog believes doing what he likes best in life—hitting small white balls—will solve it. It's not that I don't enjoy sports per se. Like I said, Ping-Pong is good for concentration. I believe my past history of sports, though certainly not fanatical or professional, proves I'm no deadbeat in the realm of physical fitness. I get my share without making it scheduled into time slots. It pains me to admit I've let my riding slip so far away, but I seriously feel we cannot afford such a luxury at the moment. Things like the Indonesian Petroleum Club membership are more worthwhile since it helps with the social aspects or Rog's job, and we both can enjoy the facilities. But I'm going astray from the subject at hand. I feel walls slowly being built. They won't even be real stumbling blocks in the path for maybe many years. By the time we trip and notice them, it will be too late to halt the separation they will have caused.

Bali Man

CHAPTER 6

To Bali and Beyond

3/21/81

Dear Madam B.,

I am holding an all-out war with the Baroid office about picking up the mail. Today, I got three letters after two weeks of not hearing from you. The Box 2083 address is downtown at the main post office. It's a good half-hour drive each way in traffic, so needless to say, none of the drivers relish the responsibility. The staff car (secretary's) driver is supposed to go daily, but somehow the daily card game takes precedence. Sudi and I end up doing banking and PO runs for the entire office when I get fed up enough to go myself. It's becoming a bad habit.

Was fascinated to hear Dot Phillips's brother was in Jakarta. Baroid's bank here is the Jakarta Chase Manhattan. Please forward the word for him to get in touch with us next time he is in town. Maybe he'd like to hire me as a contact of some sort?!

We had a bit of an upheaval around here this week. Lamina, my cook/washing lady/maid, had to be fired. Never done that before! I traded her with Sonia for Sukari, Sonia's maid. Lamina has had trouble getting along with Suparno and had worked up to a royal battle with Yamin and Masudi as well. On Wednesday, it all came to a head, and the guys had a long talk with me about how bad the relations had become between them. I spoke with Lamina, and though I made it clear (as mud probably) that I had no complaints about her work, it was all quite sad. A problem of understanding not only another language but the sociological background behind the situation as well. Lamina took it extremely hard, and I was miserable about having to do it. I fear she may be a bit senile or something.

Sonia's maid, Sukarti, is probably in her late twenties and, like Lamina (and so many women here), was married and deserted by her husband.

I have a neat new friend named Inga. She's about twenty-four, daughter of a very wealthy Jakarta general. Inga's English is about as advanced as my Indonesian, so our conversation is always an odd mixture of both. She dates some of the guys from the staff house occasionally, which is where I first met her. Tomorrow, she is coming over to teach me to cook some Indonesian vegetable dishes. She fascinates me as, although she is quite Westernized, she comes from a very strict, old Jakarta family. When she turned twenty-one, her father gave her a house and garment factory in Bandung, but she works in her sister-in-law's jewelry shop in the Jakarta Hyatt. Inga has so much money that her joy in life is giving presents—a beautiful wicker framed mirror last week. There's no refusing her. She becomes indignant and rattles off all sorts of obscenities at you in Indonesian!

I feel so close with all your letters. Love you dearly, Madam B. If only we could cut the distance.

M.

3/30/81

Dear Marthe,

It certainly is exciting to listen to the news about the Indonesian airliner being hijacked in Bangkok and wonder if I know either of the two Americans on board. I pray one of them is not our CEO-to-be, Roger.

The workmen are here putting new green carpeting in the bathroom, and Lydia, the fifteen-pound monster, is objecting vociferously.

Had a lovely weekend with my Roger. Where would I be without his calm and supportive attitude? I would panic on the job front without him. We had Saturday here in Newburyport and a picnic at Nubble Light in Maine. Our spring temps are in the seventies, and everyone with wheels was on the road.

Had two interviews in Andover last week. A finalist, but not a winner. A sixty-mile daily commute, so I can rationalize it would have been a drag.

The Phillips' had a political coffee on Saturday morning where I made a couple of contacts that may be helpful. CETA is training women to be heavy equipment operators and electronic technicians. Perhaps I am poor and indigent enough to qualify by now!

Mr. Allen, your new tenant, called to say the heat pump was belching steam. However, a check with the contractor solved everything.

Two calls from Frank Carbone. He apparently called your dad in Houston (by mistake—he thought it was Susanne's number). Dad invited him to come to the Big H for a visit. That is a switch! Little does he know Frank has his eye on Susanne again!

If I could find a job starting in May, I'd hop the next plane to you and Rog.

Missing you and loving you,
Madam B.

4/1/81

Dearest Madam B.,

Got your two letters dated the twenty-third and twenty-fourth of March. Such good postal service lately—I'm likely to get spoiled. The second sounded so much more encouraging for the career situation.

I have a little something going myself. An Indonesian friend of mine told me about some friends of hers who are in the film industry here. They are making a film in Bali—a horror story—and they need a foreigner, "Orang Puteh," for one of the roles in the film. She said the main requirement was semi-fluency in Indonesian. I laughed the whole thing off, saying I had no talent or experience in acting. She claims this is not necessary—Hollywood this ain't! That if they accept me they would teach me what I need to know. She sent over a photographer with his crew last Thursday to do some shots for the producer. It would pay eight thousand US dollars, and I'd spend two months in

Bali (all expenses paid, of course) if I were accepted. Roger's first reaction was "What do you know about acting?" When he saw the photos, he said they were ugly. Does wonders for my fragile self-image. He has dismissed the whole idea as ridiculous and makes me feel foolish for even thinking about it. Just when I really need some positive moral support, he is too engrossed in his own problems to even discuss what this chance could mean to me. Not only the financial boost to my dwindling self-respect but also my self-image as a nonproductive entity. At twenty-six, I am feeling the door closing on my youth. The photos show the slight smile lines and crow's feet. I can't even be objective about my appearance any more.

You probably heard about the Garuda flight that was hijacked here. The two guys who attempted to escape are friends of Roger. The one who did get away lives down the street. They both worked for Baroid in the past but now work for Milchem, the competition. Today, Rog left for five days in Palembang, Sumatra, on a Garuda flight no less! Tell me not to be nervous about that!! I had wanted to go to the Borobudur Temple in Central Java while he is gone, but I have to wait to hear on this film thing.

We are now members of the Indonesian Petroleum Club. We were accepted and paid our dues on Saturday. I spent Sunday soaking up some sun and swimming in the pool while Rog played tennis. It's a really posh place—most impressive when you drive up to the huge marble building with impeccable grounds. They have only two tennis courts but three squash courts, three video rooms, an extensive library, badminton, Ping-Pong, billiards, a large swimming pool, sauna, gym, and a couple of very good restaurants. The clientele is predominantly British with lots of Scandinavian, Japanese, and Indians mixed in. Most Americans belong to the American Club. If the company doesn't pay for the membership here, most can't afford the $1250 US bond for membership. Thanks, Baroid!

I've been informed by my correspondence course that my time limit ran out, but I can extend it if I want to continue. As yet, I seem to keep sufficiently busy without it. I can't seem to get into it just now. I want to do something that pays!! I've been keeping the diary that Genevieve Fernald gave me when I left the States, and perhaps some day I'll get organized enough to make it into a book. For now, I just can't sit in one spot long enough to write anything longer than letters.

Hear Ronald Reagan had an attempt on his life. We won't get the full details until *TIME* magazine comes next week, so I really don't know what is going on. Would you believe we found out about the Garuda hijacking from England? Rog called George on Sunday (his new employee who had gone home to London to pack up his house and get his wife). George said it was all over the news there, but it didn't make the papers until Monday here. So much of our news is censored, we never know if what we hear is true or just the government's censored version of things.

Oh, to sit down and share a cup of Billy Goat Coffee and some real conversation with you!

You are so dear to my heart. Love you, Madam B.

M.-

4/6/81
New Port Richey, Florida

Dear Rog and Marth,

It's so nice to be warm in Nana and Grampa's backyard in Florida sunshine. After a teeth-chattering winter in New England, this is especially delightful!

What a joy to hear your voices Saturday night. It really seems like ages that you have been in Jakarta. Is it really only five short months?

Everything is fine in Golden Age Land here. The winter freeze left some badly browned palm trees, but all else is green and blooming—still a lingering fragrance of orange blossoms. I always feel renewed to see flowers in color and hear so many bird songs after a New England winter.

Spoke to Rog's mom, Marge, and she is arranging (with Baroid) for you to be home for Peter Bloch's wedding. I think Marge and my mother would be perfect cast as cruise directors for *The Love Boat*, don't you?

Grampa Brim has trundled off to have a new tire put on his bike this morning. Then we're off to see the new acres of tract housing in New Port Richey on bikes. I'll be nursing a sore crotch for weeks; he always borrows a boy's bike from a friend for me!

Susanne called this a.m. to wish Brim a happy birthday. I think she and Dunc and Dad and Houston have about played out. Dunc's girlfriend moved in with them this weekend. Susanne says her social life with rednecks is boring. She plans to learn as much as possible running Cleve's Texas Jeans in the next few months and then head east by fall. Frank beckons …

I'm thrilled to be on a labor force again, and looking forward to marketing and direct mail advertising beginning April 13. The offices are posh, and I'll be starting with the new president/CEO. He's only been there since March 15. Together we sink or swim. He has eighteen months to turn the business around. Cross your fingers, toes, and eyes for me!

Nana Doris tells me my bike is here, and the schedule says, "Bike riding *now*." Why wasn't I born to a Puerto Rican family of thirteen?

Miss you both muchly and love you dearly,
Madam B.

PS–My butterfly tattoo should make for interesting conversation—or perhaps profound silence—when my parents get a look!

4/12/81
Sunday afternoon

Dear Madam B.,

Just got in from our weekend on the IIAPCO Island. It was far from restful but interesting just the same. The island is a small dot of a sandbar among a cluster of other islands and coral reefs. It is owned by an oil company, IIAPCO, and contains three "cabins" for weekend use by company management and families. We went with two other couples and their four kids ages two, four, ten, and fourteen. The cabin was lovely and very large, completely screened, ceiling fans, two houseboys, and a boat and driver. We brought lots of food and drink, and with any other eight people, it would have been a fantastic party. Rog and I are considering a vasectomy for him first thing tomorrow morning!

The weekend was beautifully sunny although it poured for two days in Jakarta. We all got royally burned and well worn out from endless swimming and snorkeling. It was so similar to a Caribbean island—the clear, ice-blue water, and fantastic coral and shells. A nearby island has a hotel-type arrangement with cabins, so we want to look into the price of going again without our same companions.

Dad called Thursday morning and told me Nana Al seems to be nearing the end. I explained that if he wanted me to, I'd be happy to come home and spend some time with him and her. He seemed to be holding up okay, though, and said not to worry. He also stressed that I should not be disappointed with Duncan, as he's working very hard and now has two cabs and is making money. To quote Nana Doris, "Any Cuban refugee could aspire to that!"

Tuesday, I take off for Bali with Sonia. We first plan on going to Denpasar, the capital city, where she is trying to set up an export business with an Indonesian lady (to Colombia) and then on to Kuta Beach for about a week. Rog has a new employee here from the States and is going to Balikpapan next week, so I figured it was a good time for me to get out of Jakarta. I want to see how Sonia and her Indonesian partner are going to set up this business, and then maybe I'll try to make some contacts in the United States for a similar venture.

Wondering how you are and how the new job is going.

Love you dearly, and miss you by the minute.
M.

Balinese Temple

Journal Entry,
4/15/81
Kuta Beach, Bali

We arrived yesterday, Sonia, her Indonesian friend, CiCi, and I. First stop was a friend of CiCi's in Denpasar. The ride from the airport gave me pangs of homesickness for Tobago. The Balinese are predominantly Hindu, a gentle, gracious people dedicated to their shrines, temples, and awesome stonework. Each house along the way had a small shrine of some sort carved from stone and laden with flowers, food, and incense. The intricate brickwork and stone carvings show their gods among gardens not unlike the Christian version of Eden. CiCi's friend turned out to be a bustling, jolly mother of ten. She had two tables laden with lunch, one for us and one for her husband and his business associates. We borrowed a jeep and beat a fast retreat to Kuta Beach in search of a place to stay.

The first few "inns" were full, but we managed to find a fleabag hotel for five thousand rupiah with breakfast. We dumped our belongings and went off exploring in the jeep. Ci Ci hung around for dinner and then went back to her friend's house while Sonia and I cruised the streets, checking out the nightlife. It consisted of mainly very young, very fat Australian women—all so hungry looking for a date that I was embarrassed for them. Not for the first time, I am really proud to be different and am able to say I am American!

The sunset on the beach was truly spectacular and the highlight of the day. People appeared in droves to take pictures and worship the end of another day.

We awoke on our second day to the gentle patter of rain. The breakfast included in our room consisted of lukewarm tea and banana sandwiches. We decided that the hotel was no bargain with its leaky roof and abundance of wildlife, so Sonia and I set out in a light drizzle to shop around and find a new place to stay. The next place we found, another bungalow, was the same price but somewhat larger and much cleaner. It was the same style of Balinese brick and stone temple architecture, one room with two beds of questionable origins with lumpy mattresses covered with a rough sheet.

There was a small bath, Indonesian style, with the footprints on the floor for the toilet and the *mandy bath*—a large tank of water with a dipper for showering oneself. At least this place had tiles on the floor that were not slippery with slime.

In the afternoon, we drove over to the Hyatt in search of the Colombian ambassador so Sonia could get some adjustments made in her passport. We didn't find him right away, so we walked to the Bali Beach Hotel, a good mile down the beach. I arranged for my return ticket, and we bought lots of clothes from shops along the beach. For transport back to the Hyatt, we hired a Balinese fishing boat. Actually, there were hundreds of these beautifully painted boats pulled up on the shore for the tourists to dotter around the cove in. The main sails all advertised an airline, beer, or soap of some brand name. Two bamboo pontoons connected by brightly painted arches stabilized the center part of the vessel. We sat in a hollow hull about two and a half feet wide that turned up at the front in a smiling swordfish snout.

We eventually met up with the ambassador and arranged for a day of sightseeing for the next morning. I was yearning for a day on Kuta Beach at this point but figured I'd wait to voice my opinion.

Journal Entry,
4/24/81
Jakarta

This is the strangest week I've ever been through. The time in Bali is already a memory growing soft and fuzzy around the edges, and rock hard reality is so hard to face gracefully.

The day of sightseeing with a caravan of folks I didn't know, though not comfortable at the time, was well worth the time missed on the beach. I thought I could somehow escape going right up to the minute CiCi arrived. My period was at its heaviest, and I was not at all comfortable physically. My stomach was upset all night, and CiCi was late, so it looked like I could sneak off for the beach. Then CiCi arrived, and the group insisted I go. The ambassador was feeling cheap, so we all rode in the jeep CiCi had borrowed. Unfortunately, it was far from comfortable for six adults, and the windows had all been blocked out by the paint job. A perfect teenager's car to be seen in but not to sightsee in.

I was a bit turned off by the first place we stopped, which was crowded with tourist buses. There were masses of Japanese tourists— bespectacled with a tidy, exact way of dressing, toting the most modern, efficient-looking photography equipment. They are very polite people and well-behaved tourists. This theatre was offering a traditional Balinese performance called the Wayang Orang, a live performance of an ancient play. Despite the commercialized feeling I started with, I became totally enthralled by the performance. It was a mythological story similar to Paul Bunyan or Johnny Appleseed except much more profoundly religious. The characters represented good and evil and had amazing magical powers. The story was outlined in several languages and the characters were all self-apparent. The costumes were bizarre, and the high, squeaky, singsong Balinese language was eerie amid the gamelan gong music. I left entranced.

We wheeled into one of the many silver workshops lining the road and screeched to a dusty halt. As we climbed out, I could almost see the shopkeeper rubbing his palms and licking his chops in glee. The Colombians, Sonia included, bought altogether too much, though I must admit the prices were good. When we returned there on Saturday, I purchased a beautiful silver and boar's tooth necklace.

As we got further into the countryside, the roads became narrow tracks. We careened along, passing smog-billowing busloads of bored-looking people of every nationality.

The Bedulu Elephant Cave Temple (Goah Gadjah) was deserted when we arrived. CiCi got to the other side of the street first; the others were preoccupied at the basket market in the parking lot. She bought tickets for everyone before I saw the large, imposing sign next to the path down the mountain. It requested menstruating women to honor their custom by not entering the temple. That made sense to me from what little I knew of their customs, but when I pointed it out to Sonia, in the same state as myself at the time, she hooted with laughter. I refused to stand in front of the sign so she could have a photo taken. In the area between the temple's opening in the mountain and the dense drop to the tropical underbrush was a giant ledge, and the public baths and small outbuildings filled the space. The baths themselves were dug perhaps twenty feet down and were lined with stone with stone steps. Though I can only compare it to what I've seen in photographs, I would say it closely resembled the Greek baths with Hindu gargoyles spouting springwater from their bellies. Before the busloads arrived, I sat in the sun and pressed my imagination to see it as it must have been and marveled at how beautiful and unspoiled it was still. The rest of my tour group wandered into the temple and had returned to the path leading back up to the basket market. Clouds of dust drifted down in the sun as the buses caught up with us again.

On to Kinta Mani, so high up the in mountains a sweater would have been comfortable. Fog and drizzly rain obscured the view from above as we lunched at a Chinese-European restaurant. We then bounced down a dirt road to a volcanic lake surrounded by extinct volcano peaks.

A lot of confusion ensued, but we were finally loaded into a narrow, wooden motorboat and headed out across the lake. I was seated in the front of the boat next to Sonia and the ambassador's son with a local boatman fore and aft. Since all conversation around me was in Spanish and CiCi was in the back of the boat, I struck up a conversation with one of the boatmen. He explained that the people of this area are not poverty-stricken due to laziness. They are fanatically religious and believe the gods will provide for them as they see fit.

It was very cold and eerily silent as we slipped into the village to pay our fee for viewing the burial grounds. The boatman had instructed us not to give any money to anyone, but I was unprepared for the scene as we beached the boat. Old women and thin, starving children flocked to the boat with outstretched hands. The children threw off their thin t-shirts and sarongs and waded out into the cold water, shivering and whimpering. On the makeshift dock, a group of men sat playing cards and casting gazes toward our boatload of tourists.

The boatman returned, and we set out across the lake again. He pulled the boat up on a rocky shore and led the way through the undergrowth to a temple gateway in the dark forest. The ornately carved stone arch was strewn with human skulls, casting a pall over our silent expedition. A path led through the gateway to a jungle of massive, twisting black trees. There was no sound but our shuffling footsteps. We came upon a small clearing amid the roots of the trees and carefully picked our way amid piles of bones.

There were seven graves. The corpses were laid on straw mats with woven palm-leaf cages over them. All were quite decomposed with yellowish bones protruding from their sarongs. Though the most recent was only about a month old, there was no smell and very little left but bones. Small woven plates holding offerings of flowers, rice, and money lay at the foot of each grave. Everyone was silent on the boat trip back across the lake, absorbed in his or her own private thoughts and impressions.

The lure of the beach finally took hold on Friday. Sonia and I began our schedule of awakening with the first light, having a quick juice on the beachfront café and spreading our sarongs in the sun for the morning. I declined the urge to go topless though most of the women did. Since I had started my tan the previous weekend at Palau Putri, my breasts were very white, and I feared a painful burn. We played Frisbee, beach Ping-Pong, swam ourselves to exhaustion, and then retired to our sarongs for a massage.

The number of tourists was about equal to the number of Indonesian peddlers on the beach. They sold everything imaginable: clothes, t-shirts, bikinis, hats, sarongs, shells, jewelry, wood carvings, cold drinks, coconuts, and stuffed sea turtles. We employed the little ladies offering massages daily. For five hundred rupiah (about eighty cents US), these ladies unpacked their oils and creams and sat down to give you a good all-over massage. What a luxury! The peddlers were definitely a pain until you realized that if you ignored them most would wander off. Some of the hardier ones would sit down in the sand next to you and wait patiently by the hour until you decided you wanted a soda or whatever they were selling. At sunset, the beach filled up once again. It was a daily ritual—the tourists paying homage to their god, the sun, at the end of every day.

The nights were full of dancing and impromptu parties. On Saturday, we discovered the disco at the Hyatt Hotel. We picked up a Spanish friend, Dario, and met two Indonesian photographers from Jakarta (Udo and Anto) at the disco. CiCi took Dario, Sonia, and I out to dinner at the Hyatt first. The restaurant had a roving singing group. When they stopped at our table, Sonia and Dario requested a Spanish song, and soon the whole show was ours. They danced and sang their hearts out, and it seemed the entire place joined in. Udo and Anto were on an expense account from an assignment they were working and insisted on picking up the entire tab in the disco. We closed the show there then all discarded our clothes for a moonlit dip in the pool. I think the evening ended at about six a.m., though I never really knew what time it was all week.

From that night on, I started feeling whole and strong. There were no sexual ties or demands, yet I felt desirable and sensual being surrounded by males. We met up with two Italian guys on Monday. Luigi could speak some English, but his brother Benny only spoke Italian. Dario was staying with a French guy named Phillipe, who also joined our little band of fools.

CiCi left Monday, so we were one less female and the jeep. Dario and Phillipe had rented motorcycles Monday night. Anto and Udo already had bikes, so the eight of us rode the motorcycles to the Hyatt. Usually the ratio of females to males in Bali is about six women to one man. But we really lucked out with six guys escorting Sonia and me. The feelings of warmth and closeness were of a family sort—good friends for a short time with restrictions due to previous relationships, but no stress over that fact.

Wednesday, we had to leave. I went to Denpasar with Dario to pick up my ticket in the morning. Sonia awoke early to catch just a little more sun. I collected her from the beach; we took some photos, said our good-byes, and caught a taxi to the airport. We had just checked our bags, mailed our postcards, and sat down to wait the final hour before our flight. Our attention was suddenly drawn to a scuffle in the parking lot. Dario, Phillipe, Luigi, and Benny came roaring up on their motorcycles straight from the beach for a final farewell. We went out to a grassy plot in the parking lot and shot the rest of Sonia's film, making memories of the crazy days with wonderful people we would probably never see again.

Sonia's husband, Ron, met us at the airport in Jakarta, kissed us both in warm welcome, and took me to the office to find Rog. He was on the phone and very busy, having just returned from three days offshore. Though I know in my heart he was glad to see me, his cool, unemotional reception was like a slap in the face. Clouds of depression drifted in with the rain clouds of Jakarta. Back to reality, and life goes on. In desperation, I struck out at him verbally, and my tears of frustration were met by a wall of resigned understanding. And so we try again to learn to appreciate each other and this life we've chosen to build together.

Journal Entry,
5/7/81

I've let the weeks drift by, unaccounted. The adjustment to the anonymity of my life since returning from Bali has been tiring to my mind and soul, and to put to paper the petty passing of time seems too futile a task.

Dad called yesterday morning and introduced me (long distance) to his latest lady friend. She said she had read one of my letters and was so enthusiastic about the way I write. But what is writing but a mere outpouring of my soul that seems to be temporarily hibernating.

Six months ago today I began this book. It has followed my personal heights and chasms, documented my experiences, and served as a rubbish heap for spent emotions. But I am no closer, through these ramblings, to understanding who I am.

Mom called at 6:30 this morning. I had a strange feeling of floating somewhere near the ceiling, observing my life as I spoke with her. Suparno was clearing last night's debris from the coffee table and opening the doors. The whole scene seemed new and fresh to me as I viewed from above, imagining how different I now live from Mom. I pictured her sitting in her living room on High Street. It would be 7:30 the night before for her, and here I was ordering breakfast. In six months, it has all become so commonplace I rarely take time to view the total picture. Part of me believes I am a creative spirit waiting to be discovered. The other half is the ugly phantom of guilt that darkens my outlook and reduces my accomplishments to banal, time-passing activities. There just aren't enough tangible rewards to this lifestyle. My materialistic American mind insists upon money paid for time spent. Is there hope for life to begin at twenty-six?

4/15/81

Dearest Marthe,

Finally, a letter from you today—your April 1 with those way-out pictures from your photo shoot. Lady, you look fantastic. You exude class and cool … sorry you did not get the part, but how many kids from the Round School in Newbury, Massachusetts, ever even get a chance to try out for the screen in Bali?

From your phone conversation and now your letter, I sensed a crisis—identity and otherwise. Maybe you should try motherhood. I wouldn't trade mine for a minute of any career, before or since. It's a link with eternity and is so fulfilling for me. Hang tough, Yankee Lady. Something or someone will develop.

My career is most trying. The company is going to have to make a dramatic turnaround quickly. I'm learning the latest in word processing and am exhausted trying to cope with so much new technology. Enjoy yourself—don't insist on a career!

Dear God, it would be worth a lot to have a cup of Billy Goat Coffee and talk. Lydia is recovering from her dentistry—so funny before her tranquilizer wore off. Her palm tree tail was at half-mast.

Love you so much,
Madam B.

4/16/81

Dear Marthe,

A follow-on to my hand-written letter of last night. From now on, I'll try to use the machine and save your deciphering the scribble. Today, I mastered the monster (it really is a treasure)— IBM's latest electric memory typewriter. It will center, underline, remember, and type back all by itself. For the first two days, I could have cried, but looking at the three girls here who can use it, I knew any normal person could manage.

At lunchtime, I take my brown bag lunch and go over to Hardy's pond just around the corner. There is a huge selection of ducks, geese, swans, and wildlife. I think that is where the birds for the Upper Green and Barlett Mall are wintered. Anyway, they are such a tourist attraction; when you stop the car, they come waddling over and tap on the door for handouts.

And speaking of waddling and handouts, your little friend, Lydia, has developed two entirely separate sets of behavior: one for my Rog and one for me. When Rog is here, she stays in the dining room and waves the palm tree unless invited into the living room or, heaven forbid, the bedroom. Whenever he goes to the kitchen, she tags along all wiggles and terminally cute. Let him pull out of the driveway and she is back eating off my plate when I'm not looking and sleeping on my pillow! And he has never raised his voice to her ... just points a finger and speaks simple words. Why didn't we discover the formula ten years ago? She is much happier after her oral surgery and is as bouncy as a puppy. Lord, Lydia and Nana Al will outlive us all!

New England is trying to bud and be green, but it comes slowly this year. Lots of sunshine but still a cool wind from the north. Please tell my favorite CEO I have his new shares (split) of Petrolite and will put them in the safe deposit box. Such a bright boy to know what to buy ... and who has an elegant, personable wife, whom I miss severely and love dearly.

Madam B.

4/28/81

Dear Madam B.,

Here they are! The photos from fabulous Bali! I'm sure you will understand better after viewing these why I was hard-put to come back to Jakarta.

Your new job sounds so interesting! I never dreamed Agawam Associates was so large an organization. The press release about your boss Mr. Sheppard was very impressive. I was particularly taken with the fact that he speaks four languages. I have found that I am really enjoying languages. Hearing so much Spanish in Bali was frustrating because I could get the jist of a conversation but I couldn't reply.

I envy your job. To be mentally exhausted at the end of the day from so much new, stimulating information doesn't sound hard to take to me at all. You know how you were feeling after just four months of unemployment. Try four years!

In your recent short note, you said you sense a crisis, identity or otherwise, and suggest motherhood. It does not enter my mind. I can't seriously say I want to rule it out of my life forever. In fairness to Roger and a future person, I must rule it out of my life for right now, though. What hurts me most right now is that after having two of Roger's employees living with us for over a month, as well as people from the office commenting to me that Rog drives himself too hard, there never seems to be time for he and I anymore. Tennis seems to be his only release valve. I've tried, Mom. I have never hit so many various balls with various racquets in all my life as I have in the past four years. Tennis, Ping-Pong, now golf, squash, and bumper pool. It's okay. I can do it, though not with Rog's natural grace and ease. But I need to *talk*. I need eye contact, physical touch, and attention. I'm not about to give up on us, but a crisis is out there somewhere, you are right. The lack of actual time spent together is leading us to pursue different friends and interests. The identity crisis will always be with me so long as I am a Gemini, I'm afraid, and I don't see that changing anytime soon.

Loved the photos you sent. Your Rog struts across the bottom of my photo collage below my portrait of you and Sue. He is a remarkable gentleman and loves you, so he holds a special place in my heart.

My friend who I nursed through an abortion here recently became a lesbian, and I almost don't blame her for giving up on men. I could see it if they weren't so much fun to have around, even on a temporary basis.

Love to you, Lydia, and your Rog.
M.

5/9/81

Dearest Madam B.,

Just wrote a birthday card to Tara Chankersingh in Trinidad and thought I'd drop you a note to try to make up for my laxness lately.

Remember the two Italian guys I told you about that we met in Bali? Well, Thursday night, Luigi (the one who reminds me of a young Frank C.) called to say they had just arrived in Jakarta for a quick stopover on their way home. They were scheduled to leave Friday afternoon but wanted to extend their stay for a few days to see some of the sights in Jakarta. The problem was that they were short on cash, needed a place to stay, and didn't know anyone but Sonia and me. Sonia was with them and asked if it would be possible for them to stay with us for three days, as she lives in a tiny apartment and didn't have room. The only reasons Rog could give me for his terrible attitude toward the whole situation (and I guarantee you it was all very innocent) were: 1) "I don't know these people!" 2) "Who is going to entertain them and show them around Jakarta?" 3) "We already have a commitment to go out with some customers tomorrow night, and *they* can't go with us." I cannot name you one friend we've made in four years whom either I knew first and brought to the relationship or who was not in some capacity tied in with Roger's world of work. It makes me very sad to realize my individual preferences have been so repressed through the years.

The outcome was that the fellows left Friday afternoon as originally planned. Sonia, CiCi, and I saw them off at the airport, and I rushed home to shower and get cleaned up to go out with "our business" friends. When I arrived home, I was dumbstruck to find Rog had invited two single Baroid guys, one of whom I'd never met, and neither of whom knew the customers we were taking out.

Am I being unfair when I say I cannot see the justice of this? For two months plus we've had employees living with us when the company would have paid for hotel rooms. I do not feel I exaggerate when I state that 85 percent of all conversation during that time is related to business. I fear I've ceased to exist except as an ornament, politely sitting quietly or as a mirror image of Roger's personality and tastes. It all makes me so very sad, but I refuse to bring about a confrontation. All too often I am accused of starting fights and being the one who sees problems and is unhappy. I'm trying my damnedest not to appear changed in any way toward him physically or emotionally. Inside, I am waiting until I feel strong enough emotionally to start over again on my own. Hopefully, Roger is also aware of the situation after this discussion about my Italian friends, but after last night, I have to think nothing sank in and that he is unconscious of this aspect of our relationship.

We went to the disco at the Hilton with our assorted friends last night. I have never been able to get Rog to go there before; his distain for the very idea of a disco and dancing always made me feel very foolish in his eyes when I suggested it previously. It took a customer worth a million dollars of business to drag him there. Though I think he enjoyed himself, although not necessarily the dancing, when I suggested perhaps we could go there again sometime, I met resistance due to the old money excuse—too expensive to go on our own.

I do and forever will love Roger dearly as the closest person to me after you. I will always try not to hurt him, unless it means hurting myself irreparably. I enjoy so many aspects of our life here that I don't want to just throw it all away. I must start channeling all my excess time and efforts into realizing my own potential.

Thanks for listening, Mom. I love you dearly and hope you can get here soon.

M.

5/13/81

Dear Marthe,

The best birthday present of all—your letter and the pictures from Bali. What an exotic spot and interesting people! And you look terrific. The years are giving you an elegance and class that is indefinable but so striking. You touched on some subjects that had been bothering me, and I am confident you and Roger have much that is good in store for you. In four short years, you have both matured so much (yes, even the Kid who is my favorite candidate for CEO).

Spring is finally here, and the lilacs are out. But where is happiness? In the fragrance of the lilacs? Walking Lydia in the fog in Newburyport? A weekend at the lake with my Roger? None of the above. I know it's in me, and it still eludes me sometimes. Birthdays and holidays I bottom out without you and Sue. But she sends me funny cards and calls late at night, and we talk and talk, and it helps. I guess it's a good life. Are we ladies ever completely content? And would we like it if we were?

Opened up the cottage, and it was good to be back. Bruce is still in residence across the street and being wonderful to me. Have a pipe in the kitchen that needs replacing, and he immediately took measurements and offered to get a piece and fix it. The motor on the water pump burned out (oh joy, oh rapture) and, of course, Grampa Brim had a spare in his workshop. What a marvelous man! Davie Rochford is supposed to install it this week, but if he fails, Bruce also volunteered to do it ... all I have to do is keep feeding him. He even made brownies and spice cake for dinner on Sunday. Amazing person that redhead.

The black flies own the state of New Hampshire for the next few weeks. Marge and Rich will be back from Florida just in time to itch with the rest of us.

Did you know Bob Marley died of cancer this week? I am rushing out to pick up a tape of his.

My super smart typewriter just flashed a yellow light warning me, "End of the page, you turkey!" Amazing.

You are always in my thoughts.

Miss and love you,
Madam B.

6/2/81

Dear Mom,

Got your card and letter yesterday. All hell has broken loose around here, so I felt I'd better get up at six a.m. to have time to write back to you. Rog is off to Balikpapan again this week. It's beautifully cool this morning, and I really want to go riding while it is still chilly but guess I'll have to wait for the car to come back from dropping Rog at the airport.

When I said all hell had broken loose, I was referring to the arrival of Gary McFarland and family on Monday night. They are all very excited and enthusiastic about their new home here. Wife Sidney and two boys, Cameron, fourteen, and Wesley, ten, are all very anxious to get settled and start learning Indonesian. (I do remember those days, and it wasn't even that long ago!) I spent all day yesterday taking them shopping for furniture, food, and all sorts of necessities. Today will be more of the same.

I insisted on getting in my two hours of riding every morning, but after that, my time is all theirs. It is exhausting! I feel like a tour guide. Speaking of riding, a strange thing happened yesterday when I arrived after a three-day absence. Nikko, my coach, went on and on about "Oh, where have you been? It seems like so long since you last came out to ride?" We went out on a trail ride, and he started to profess his undying love for me!! Needless to say, I was flattered but somewhat taken aback. He is married with two dear little kids and has met Roger, so I never considered that he even noticed my presence beyond the role of teacher to student. As it got more intense, I put on the brakes and carefully explained that I like him very much also but as my coach, and that this was an impossible situation. He seemed to accept that, but the rest of the ride was a bit tense.

Also got a letter yesterday from Daniel in Trinidad. He claims he is returning to Jakarta soon to look for work. I would love to have him here. He taught me Indonesian in Trinidad before we left. He said Trinidad was brewing for a revolution since Dr. Williams died and socially was a real drag since Rog and I left. Also mentioned there had been lots of robberies in the old neighborhood. Even Pat and Mary's house (our old house) was broken into while Winnie and Churchill slept right through it!! That's not the Winnie I know and trained!!

Glad you finally got the birthday package. I'm so cross with the Houston gang. The day the McFarland's arrived, I also got a letter from Sue. She knew Gary had brought packages back to the States from us, and that he had offered to bring things back over here. Gary said he spoke with Dunc and/or Susanne but that they never came to pick up the packages, so he finally mailed your presents and gave Sue's to a friend to deliver. Sue and Dunc knew how much I need my riding clothes for the competition, and Gary would have been happy to carry them over for me. I can't buy what I need here. Singapore has a tack store, but it is wildly expensive, and I see no way I'll get them here this month.

On the subject of writing and photography, no, we haven't replaced the camera we lost as of yet. We looked into buying a medium-format box camera but decided that it was fantastic for studio work but you can't easily whip it out on the street for a quick shot. I guess we'll probably try to buy another 35mm sometime. In the meantime, I have two Indonesian friends, Yudo and Anto, who are professional photographers. Anto is working with me on an article/photo essay about transportation in Jakarta. We hope to try to sell it to GEO or *National Geographic* if we ever get it presentable enough to submit. I'll need your help/suggestions/critique when we get it finished. Both guys are really what I would consider excellent photographers, and I am very interested in setting up a show or in some way helping to market some of their prints in the States when I come home in August on vacation. The subjects are the people of Java, and you'll have to trust me when I say they are something anyone would be proud to hang on their walls.

Love you dearly, Madam B.
M.

6/4/81

Dear Marthe,

First, I must tell you that Mr. Allen, your tenant, has not come up with any rent yet for May. He had promised something by June 3, so I called him last night. He insists there is six thousand dollars tied up and he can get it in ten days. I told him I expected two months rent in full on June 13. He is very pleasant, but why wouldn't he be??

Saturday, I had to work so that blew the plans for going to the lake. Roger was off to Kennebunkport with four couples on Friday night. They all called me at the office on Saturday morning and said to please come up. After I had turned them down cold, I thought that was very decent of them. So that night, I packed up my little dog and headed north. The house was fantastic! A Victorian dream with porches, windows, turrets, jigs, and jogs. Six bedrooms and three baths right on the rocks and ocean. Near Vice President Bush's complex so that will give you an idea of the snotty neighborhood. It was crawling with secret service.

Anyway, they waited for me for dinner Saturday night; it was rainy and foggy. Lydia was the perfect guest, and, of course, turned on her "cute," including sitting on her haunches to beg. I had to hustle her off before everyone stuffed her like the Christmas goose. Roger and I walked along the oceanfront a lot. Sunday, we went out for drinks and then came back to Scandia in Newburyport for dinner. Quite the elegant weekend, and I was glad I went along. Now, since we have shared a bedroom in "public," Rog feels the jig is up and is mentioning marriage. I tell him he must have been drunk, and that the idea will go away. But he says it is Lydia, he, and I (doesn't she just worm her way in everywhere?) from here on out. Frankly, I like things just the way they are.

We are into hot, muggy June days. But so welcome. I avoid all air-conditioning.

Love you daily,
Madam B.

6/8/81

Dearest Madam B.,

Monday morning. Just got Rog off to work, I've balanced the checkbook, paid some bills, and since the Kucing is sound asleep on my lap, I'll sit here a bit longer and write to you. Kucing has really turned into quite a nice little cat. She is still not enormous like most of the street cats here, but she is a pretty charcoal gray and very affectionate.

Rog got home for Balikpapan on Friday afternoon. I was still out with Gary's wife and kids when he arrived. We started our day together at about six in the morning when their maid blew up their stove. Gary called in a frenzy, needless to say. I jumped in the car with Sudi and Sukarti, my maid, who also happens to be their maid's sister. We straightened everything out for them and took Sidney and the boys shopping and to the Petroleum Club for the day. I've really gotten to the point where I'm just about fed up with playing tour guide and feel it is time they started taking care of themselves. Rog took an instant dislike to Gary's wife, which doesn't help considering I've had to devote all my time to them while he was away.

Saturday, I snuck off early to go riding in the morning. When I got home, Anto, my photographer friend, showed up with more photos for my article. He is really pushing me to learn more Indonesian, and as much as I complain loudly, I know it is really helping to improve my vocabulary and grammar. When Rog got back from work, he, Anto, and I went to Jalan Surabya, our favorite antique market. I tried to explain to Rog that we really didn't need to buy anything, as we are going to Bali on Wednesday for four days. He bought some Chinese porcelain for his collection and a lovely present for you for Christmas. At least that's the excuse he gave. I doubt if he'll be able to wait until Christmas to give it to you.

Yesterday was Roger's day to take Gary en famil to the club while I went to watch the horse show. Nikko, my coach, was jumping, and I was very anxious to see how he would do. I was amazed that in this heat people compete in full dress regalia here—jacket, stock tie, gloves, the works. I only hope I can borrow enough stuff to get by for my competition in two weeks.

Haven't heard from Nana and Grampa in weeks. Hope they are okay.

I told Sue that if she wants to and can get her boss to give her cash in lieu of vacation, I will make up the difference for her to come over for a couple of weeks. I figured I'd borrow the money to make up the rest of the cost for her ticket from Rog and then later send and bring stuff back to the States to sell to pay him back. Don't know if she'd be interested in doing this, but she's welcome to think about it. The twenty-four-plus hours alone on a plane is not fun but is worth it when you get here.

We celebrated six months to the day—November 7 to June 7—in Jakarta last night, as well as our fourth anniversary (a few days early). I had a leather pouch/briefcase made for Rog. He gave me a three-and-a-half-foot-high, carved wooden garden god that he had shipped from Balikpapan. We are going to Bali for a few days, our first real honeymoon! No phones, no people with crises, no "friends" needing translations and favors ... just the two of us. Hooray!

Your card arrived yesterday. So nice to know someone is always thinking of me.

Love you dearly,
M.

Wednesday, 6/10/81
(One more day to your fourth anniversary!)

Dear Marthe,

Your neat little note from the plane returning from the Baroid weekend in Balikpapan arrived. Sounds fascinating but primitive. Never mind; Roger now has a blowgun with poison-tipped arrows. That will shake up New London society a bit.

Would really do almost anything for a few cups of Billy Goat Coffee at my kitchen table with you. If things don't get better fast around here, I may well be unemployed again. This company is totally supported by other corporations that are not doing well. However, my boss is scouting around for private money. I know he will offer to take my services wherever he goes, but there could be a lag in the transition.

Anyway, there are so many things we *need* to talk about … one twenty-eight-dollar phone call a month just doesn't cut it. I miss you and Sue more each month we are apart.

Had a fantastically busy weekend at the cottage. Rog and Bruce really worked their butts off mowing the lawn (Bruce repaired the mower in ten minutes flat that Grampa Brim had given up on), taking down dead trees, cutting brush, repairing water pipes, and priming the pump. The place really looks great and gets more sunlight now. Next weekend, Rog is getting plants from Jerry's wife for the hanging baskets and window boxes. As long as I keep the meals coming, those two keep working. They are extremely compatible. One hundred and twenty dollars worth of work for two pieces of French toast (that was breakfast). Bruce did talk a bit about his family and showed us some family albums on Saturday evening. He seems lonely, but I also think he is trying to create in his mind the family he never really had. He talks a lot about his father, whom I adored.

Nana and Grampa are toying with the idea of coming north in September, but only because they want to see you and Roger. Sue has volunteered to fly to Florida and share the driving with Grampa Brim, as Dunc's "straight through for thirty-three hours driving" trip would be too much for them. But he also wants to come to New England for the reunion. I would be in heaven with all of you here.

Lydia is so bright and perky these days. Dentistry was certainly the cure to her well-being. She has Rog wrapped around her funny, furry feet. Now he is the one who feeds her snacks, talks to her, and spoils her rotten.

Love to you both. Counting the days until you are on this side of the world.
Madam B.

Journal Entry,
6/10/81
Kuta Beach, Bali

Back in Bali! This place is so good for my soul. I can ignore the Australians, though they really do grate on my nerves. We met up with an interesting German gentleman in the airport, Hans something, who, of course, works for Baroid. He is an older man, single, who has taken American citizenship. He has lived in SE Asia for about twenty-five years and spun some amazing yarns about travel and living abroad.

Rog and I spent the afternoon playing Scrabble by the pool until sunset. This evening, we had dinner and drinks with Hans. Oh, it is so nice to be here with nothing more pressing to do tomorrow than sit in the sun and play.

Journal Entry,
6/12/81

I neglected to write yesterday due to our overindulgence on the magic mushrooms. We hired a van and driver in the morning and went to the silver factories to do some shopping. After lunch, we stopped by Juniors for a Blue Meany Special Omelet. We each had one and then headed to the beach. About the time I was finishing my massage, Rog was getting hammered. It really hit him, though I must confess, I got only a very mild case of the giggles. We were scheduled to go by Hans's hotel for cocktails at five p.m. but arrived a bit late and still in a rather silly state.

Today it was raining when we got up. We caught a Bemo ride to the Hyatt for breakfast. It's so strange to see a completely different side of Bali this time around. We haven't met anyone except Hans, who I could do without right about now. Even the beach looks and feels different.

We tried to nonchalantly hang out at the Hyatt pool, but while I was changing into my bathing suit, someone asked Rog for his room number so we had to move on. Came back to Kuta and walked down the beach to Legion to sun for the afternoon. Rog had a Frisbee date with Hans at five, and we took him to dinner after that. Enough already, Hans! This is *supposed* to be our delayed honeymoon.

Journal Entry,
6/14/81

Our Bali holiday has come to an end. We sit in the waiting room at the airport and contemplate our return to Jakarta.

We rented bicycles yesterday morning and set out on the road to Legion to do some shopping. I found a most cooperative shop owner and ended up spending fifty-six thousand rupiah on things we can hopefully bring back to the States and sell. After dropping our purchases off at the hotel, we set out in the other direction. The bikes were really in rough shape; both lacked brakes and had incredibly uncomfortable seats. We rode down quiet back roads much of the time, and I longed for a camera to capture the serenity. The brown cows grazing among the coconut palms reminded us of Tobago. Kids wheeled past on shiny new bikes all sporting crisp school uniforms, and everyone we passed offered a smile and a cheery hello. Rog took a nap when we got back to the room, and I went out to try to finish off our shopping.

This morning, we took a last walk around town. It was a different, quieter holiday this time but no less enjoyable.

Inge and I

CHAPTER 7

Wira Perkasa

6/16/81

Dearest Madam B.,

The birthday present from you arrived last week. After a day of torture from Kid Kidder about opening it, I hid it away until this morning and opened it at the breakfast table. Rog was immediately engrossed in the book as I sat weeping over your beautiful card. I stole a quick look at the book today after almost having to insist he couldn't take it to the office because it was, after all, my birthday present. Tonight I am again looking at the cover and the top of Rog's head. Guess I'll just have to wait for him to go to bed before I'll get a chance to read it!

We got a call from Sonny Andrews in Houston last night who said my riding things will be arriving in Singapore next week. Rog has to go up there anyway, so hopefully I'll be all set for the competition on the 27 and 28. Also, Suparno, the houseboy, said someone called from America this morning while I was out to wish me happy birthday. Damn, how could I miss a call like that? Got a package today from Nana and Grampa containing three natural sponges. They are so sweet to remember me.

Last night, my two friends, Inga and Anto, dropped off a huge (three foot by three foot) photo of me that Anto had taken one day when I was not paying attention. Next month, the three of us are opening an office here at the house. Inga's the financial backing and most of the business sense, Anto's the photographer and creative end, and I am ... well, I'm not sure exactly what I'll be able to contribute. There's a good demand for commercial and private photography here. Also, Inga has great connections in the entertainment business and is promoting lots of young artists. It's all very interesting and should keep me very busy. I'll have to let you know more about it as it progresses.

My "beastie," Revolino, came up lame yesterday. After four days of rest, I don't know why he is lame now with the competition looming, but hopefully by tomorrow we'll be back working on our dressage routine. In the meantime, I've been trying out different horses. As of yet, none can compare to my fat little friend Revolino. I've asked Anto to come to the competition and take some photos for me, so you will eventually get to see what we look like. Can't *wait* to have my own saddle and stuff here. Unfortunately, Rog is showing even less interest in riding since his first/last/only lesson. I get really irritated when I think of the hours I've spent sitting next to tennis courts, but perhaps if I do well in this competition, he'll show some enthusiasm.

Well, lady, Rog finally put down my birthday book, so perhaps if I'm quick, I can read a chapter before falling asleep. Thank you so much for your thoughtfulness.

You are always with me in my heart and thoughts.
M.

6/21/81
Sunday Morning

Dearest Madam B.,

I am in my usual position, seated beside the tennis courts at the club while Rog plays a quick game. He is taking off for Singapore afterward for about three days, so I figured he might as well mail a letter to you from there.

Hopefully, I can sneak a phone call to you while he is gone, but in case I can't manage it, here is what we need to talk about. Sue and Dunc called Thursday morning. In the course of the conversation, Dunc mentioned you were having some problems with our tenants at the condo. First, Madam B., please accept my apologies. From the beginning, that place has been nothing short of a royal pain in the arse, as Dad would say. I regret we ever got into it and even more that we got you involved. From what Dunc said, it sounds like we have to evict those fine folks and find some other tenants. As of yet, I have not discussed this with Rog because, well, basically because I have to live with him, and I know all too well what it would mean to have him worrying about it. Not only would his blood pressure suffer, but I don't want to have to listen to his unending rhetorical questions and pessimistic raging. Believe me, ignorance is bliss where things like this are concerned. Hopefully, you and I can work it out over the phone before he has to know about it.

So on to happier subjects. I have been meeting lots of new, interesting people lately and am quite hopeful at the prospect of working. Perhaps you remember my mentioning two friends of mine, Inga and Anto. Both are Indonesians who have been immensely helpful in teaching me to speak the language and immerse myself in the culture.

Anto is a photographer. He and I have been working on an article, which we would like to try to get published in *Geo* magazine or the like. It is about various modes of transport found in Jakarta.

Inga has been working for her sister-in-law's jewelry shop at the Hyatt. In July, she will quit that job and join Anto and myself in a joint business venture. We are going to do some commercial and private photography, special order photo printing, design work, and promotion of several local artists and musicians. I have a few ideas, such as a calendar using photos from around Java. The business connections and capital investment are coming from Inga. I am supplying the office in our house and a studio for Anto in the spare bedroom. This weekend, I met a movie director who is a longtime friend of Inga's. He has promised me a guided tour of the studio where he is presently filming two movies. Very interesting fellow.

Also, due to some candid photos that Ando took of Inga and me, two other photographers have asked me to model for them. One is Guntur Sukarno. His late father was the president of Indonesia before the current president, Soeharto. He has promised to help me improve my "Jakarta slang" much to the despair of Inga and Anto who want me to speak perfect and proper Indonesian. For sure, these photos of me will never be seen outside of Indonesian exhibitions, but it is interesting to meet some of the local celebrities. Now if I could just get Rog to broaden his social life beyond the boundaries of the oil field community.

Mas Tok, as we call Guntur, told me some fascinating stories of when his father was president. He visited the White House with his dad and attended a State dinner with President Kennedy. He said he was about eight years old and very much in awe of America and the Kennedy's, so he was totally devastated when at dinner his knife slipped and he sent a piece of steak flying across the table at President Kennedy. The president joked to his father that he was sending missiles at the United States.

Well, lady, the game is over (I don't even know who won!!), so I'll finish this off now.

Hope you are well and happy to have summer in New England.

Love,
M.

7/3/81

Dear Madam B.,

Tomorrow is the fourth, but today is the start of a month of fasting here. Ramadan is sort of like our Easter, and for a month, the majority of Muslims in Jakarta do not eat during the day (or smoke or drink anything). They can eat after the sun goes down and must get up at 4:00 a.m. to eat enough to last all day. It's really messed up my thoughts of the Independence Day tradition in the States. Tomorrow, the American Embassy is having a huge party, which should be interesting to say the least. Unfortunately, many families go back to the States for summer school vacation, but it will still be interesting to see how many Yankees live here.

Got two letters from you and a bank statement. Rog had perused all for some sign of payment from the tenants. I have offered no information about our phone call as yet, but I think financially we aren't in trouble … yet.

Your thoughts on the magazine article were well received. Unfortunately, we've had a bit of a setback. First, all of the photos we shot are prints, and we now realize that we have to use slides. Also, the new business has been taking all of Anto's and my time for the past two weeks, so we haven't done too much more about the article.

I am a bit concerned about *Geo* anyway. Rog has given away over three hundred US dollars worth of subscriptions to customers, and no one has seen a copy yet. Usually, with gifts like this, the subscription will start in a month or so. *National Geographic* is very prompt with overseas subscriptions. I wonder if *Geo* is going to make it against the competition.

Finally, I got my riding things Monday night. It was like meeting an old friend. I've worn my boots and britches every day since. Riding in jeans has left me scarred for life. The seams rubbed big holes in my knees, and because I was riding daily, they never had a chance to heal. Now I have a blister from the boots, but at least I know they will break in quickly. Nikko commented on how much better I ride with proper boots and claims I would have won the dressage no sweat if I'd entered … Thanks, now that it's over. He is still hot and heavy no matter how many rejections I throw at him. At least it's good for my ego every morning to think someone is excited that I showed up. A fellow from another stable rode Revellino in the jumping on Sunday and won … fat little brat looked really good. He's a flashy little horse.

Your description of your relationship with your Roger really hit home with me. We had a terrible scene about my riding stuff at a time when I was in desperate need of someone strong to be kind and consoling. Unfortunately, some people are incapable of giving these emotions. Damn all inhibited, cold, Yankees. I was met with rage at all the trouble I had caused everyone over the whole incident. It is unfair to criticize someone for character faults they are unable to change, but I find it very—no, increasingly—harder to live with.

Well, lady, I am rambling on, and August 28 is drawing near. We have an appointment for Saturday, August 29, 1981 with a cup of Billy Goat Coffee IN PERSON!!

Love you dearly ... always in my thoughts,
M.

Journal Entry,
7/5/81

Yikes, hardly remembered that yesterday was the Fourth of July—Independence Day!

The business, Wira Perkasa, has been keeping me really busy lately. We are slowly opening up new areas of promotion for local musicians and the possibilities of hotel promotion. Met up with Sayahrir Gobel, a fellow I met on the plane to Balikpapan. He is a definite possibility for future business in entertainment and photography. With Inga's connections and Anto's talent, I don't see how we could miss. I question my own contribution to the whole affair (outside of the physical space), and so often I feel somewhat left out and useless. I wish I at least had a camera so I could be practicing while Anto shoots. The article for *Geo* seems to have been put on a back burner for the moment, and I don't feel free to push Anto about photographing for it.

Life on the home front continues its fragile existence. Monday night, I finally received my riding equipment (a week after the competition that I gave up on), and I have been spurred on to try and achieve some sort of reputation in that field. No interest shown by my partner in crime here in regards to my riding, though, but I don't expect it anymore.

Communication is good on the surface, but my thoughts and emotions remain locked within. I feel stifled, and the pressure is building slowly inside. A letter from Madam B. concerning her relationship with her Roger got me thinking. This cold, stoic Yankee exterior is alien to me; closely controlled emotions are impossible for me to understand. But the time is not yet right for change.

7/16/81

Dear Roger,

How nice to hear from you ... still running the Baroid operation, I see. Did you make CEO yet? What are you waiting for?

Today, the environmentalists cried a lot. Shell started operations on George's Banks. One small spill and you will hear the uproar all the way to Bali.

July Fourth in Washington, New Hampshire, at the lake was uneventful. Rained for two days and lots of tourists packed up their kids and TVs and went home early. But us hardy ones were rewarded with a perfect day on Monday. And real fireworks in Hillsboro on Sunday night. Now there is a cosmopolitan group for you!

As to my job, Agawam is far from solvent but still in business. The creditors probably realize in the long run they stand to get more by waiting. Now it would be a race for the scraps. A government loan of five hundred thousand dollars is in the works; if that comes through, we will definitely make it. My boss is a good-natured workaholic and very capable of turning this mess around.

As you will see from the enclosed, the son and heir, Duncan, is still trying to take Houston by storm. Four cabs in his stable now. At least you should have no problem with transportation when you are there next. Even Chris Fitzgerald was driving for him temporarily ... she couldn't hack it, pardon the pun!

Our weather is gorgeous, hot and sunny days with cool nights. My Roger and I have worked out a perfect system for the cottage. He goes up midweek, I am allowed in on the weekends, and then he comes to Newburyport for a day during the week to check in at his office. I keep telling him all the other dads leave on Sunday night from the lake, and the moms get to stay on. He must be romancing a lot of those moms during my absence! The only one I know who still skinny-dips every morning at about 6:00 a.m. is well beyond my age, so I don't worry.

The Datsun is a blessing with its thirty-two mpg. Gas is now hovering around $1.50!

Been at this desk for nine hours now, and it's time to push off. Really looking forward to seeing you in September. Susanne is coming home from Houston on a Texas International flight mid-August for a week. Very cheap. She probably will be strapped to the wing.

Lots of Love,
B.

PS—Did you hug my kid today?

7/17/81

Dear Marthe,

I was sitting at the window this morning with Lydia poking me for some egg, coffee, whatever she could get, and I thought how soon it will be September and you will be here! Told Lyd, but her interests are so much more immediate. She perks up at the mention of "your mother is coming home," but immediately her gnawing hunger pangs blot out what I have said. I am so excited and counting the days.

A very good week for mail. Two letters from you and one from my favorite CEO-to-be, Roger. What a neat kid to take time to write to his mother-in-law. Can't wait to hear his amusing line of patter and candid comments on everyone and everything.

In his letter, Roger asked about my trip to visit with you guys. Any itinerary is fine with me. Give me my LL Bean duffle bag and a handful of traveler's checks and I'll go anywhere.

Always read your letters over and over at breakfast, lunch, and dinner. They are my constant companions. Thank you so much for being you!

Love to you always,
Madam B.

7/19/81

Dear Madam B.,

I finally broke down and bought a camera. It's a Nikon FM with a wide-angle lens. Anto also has a Nikon, so we can share his equipment. We all want to enter a photo contest sponsored by the department of tourism, and the closing date for entries is August 10, so I need to get shooting. I explained to Rog that since I would be using the camera the most, I expected only a loan from the savings account for it and would pay the account back as soon as I could.

I am still, as always, battling with the fact that after more than four years of marriage I own nothing outright myself in my own name and have never earned anything to compensate for the cost of my living expenses. I will never be able to reconcile myself to the fact of being a kept woman. Perhaps only you could understand my cravings for some form of spiritual, emotional, and material independence of identity.

The article I have written on transportation is finished and being edited at the moment by a friend who used to be the editor for *Gadis*, the largest magazine in Indonesia. He wants me to translate it and submit it to *Gadis*, but the translation part could take me awhile.

I've been so involved with Inge, Anto, and the business lately that I haven't had much time for other folks. The expats and their never-ending complaints only serve to piss me off these days. It is so easy to fall into their trap of idle bitching. With my new camera in hand, notebook, and Inge and Anto as guides, I plan to document as much of the island of Java as I possibly can cover. After the Muslim holidays, we are trying to plan a train trip to Central Java. If I could just summon up a little belief in my abilities (some optimism from Roger would help), I feel I might be able to make some money and grow my own personal identity.

Alas, no one could ever understand me the way you do … there is so much I don't understand about myself.

Love to you and the gang back home,
M.

Journal Entry,
7/20/81

Monday morning and a great start to the week. Inge, Anto, Sudi, and I set off for Puncak to spend the day shooting. The drive up the mountains did wonders for my state of mind. We left the smog of morning traffic for the shores of Lake Ciburbur. A deserted picnic area where we stopped to shoot the mountains from various angles bordered the lake. We headed back up the smooth new highway, which ended abruptly at the base of a mountain. Here we started our ascent on foot along narrow, winding streets. The first few villages were shrouded in rainy mist. I contemplated several shots and then decided it was too dark. Climbing around over the hills, we broke out into the tea plantations. I couldn't resist the first sight of the stunted leafy bushes, row upon row, winding up the ravines and plateaus and disappearing into the mountain's mist.

We stopped off at the first warung (shop) for my fellow travelers to grab some lunch. They settled down to steaming bowls of rice garnished with tempe, tellur (egg), and spicy sambal sauce. I wandered off across the street into a service road of the plantation. I came upon a little man squatting amid the manicured rows of bushes. He wore a large round, flat hat and was wielding a short blade, mowing the grass along the side of the trail. He smiled and greeted me and then went back about his work, providing a perfect subject for a few shots.

I wandered back to the warung to change lenses and found lunch just about over. We took a slight detour into a tea plantation: Cipoko Selatan— Gunung Mas. Masses of women were bending under their wide, flat hats, picking leaves and jamming them into satchels slung across their shoulders. Some shyly tipped their hats to hide their faces while others called out boldly for a few hundred rupiah. They laughed and chattered to each other as they went about their mechanical hand movements. I have no idea how much time elapsed, but I finished my roll of slide film and changed back to the print film I had started with.

Of course, the proof of the pudding will come when I see the slides and contact prints, but I'm really excited over this new camera. I itch to have a darkroom again and, at the very least, develop my own black-and-white shots. If I weren't so lazy, I'd be writing more to make use of the photos in some articles.

I'm starting to seriously consider the prospect of our trip back to the States in late August. I return to my native land a changed person. Never before have I felt so attached to a place as I do to Java. I doubt that I will choose to be away more than the minimum three weeks of vacation that Roger is taking.

Gunilla, me and Anto

CHAPTER 8

You Asked for It!

The weeks leading up to our departure for the States were fraught with stress as the work started coming in for Wira Perkasa and Roger was traveling constantly. He left for five days just a week before we were due to leave. I couldn't help but feel resentful that when he left he couldn't tell me where exactly he was going—Singapore or Balikpapan—when he would be back, and, worst of all, that he never called the whole time he was gone. I called the office daily, as he was checking in there. I struggled to finish up work, put the house in order, and pack. He took off for Singapore two days before our flight, so I met him there, dragging all our luggage.

I found I was strangely dreading this trip home. In my journal, I wrote, "I grow more and more apprehensive every day about this trip.

First of all, I feel so far removed from Roger, and I fear separation from my twin ego. I do really wish to see Mom, but other than that, I don't feel at all excited about being in the States, and I especially don't want to leave Jakarta. I can't imagine how this vacation is going to turn out. My resentment level with Roger is at an all-time high."

We flew from Singapore to Taipei and then on to Honolulu—fifteen hours on a crowded 747 with nothing to do but sleep. Rog is an absolute fidget when cooped up for so long and spent most of the flight walking the aisles. We found a hotel and spent a couple of days resting and trying to reconnect. Then on to Boston, where we rented a car, loaded it with our luggage, and headed north to Newburyport. We managed to find Mom's new place of employment and handed the receptionist a one hundred rupiah note to surprise her with. Needless to say, she was overwhelmed to see us.

Settling into Mom's tiny apartment, I felt so empty; there was a giant hole in my heart where I missed Jakarta. Rog and I are so far apart. We haven't even kissed since we met in Singapore. I feel we are like separate planets traveling in the same orbit.

I had planned on a quick, three-week vacation. Unfortunately, I suffered a miscarriage and ended up staying longer to recuperate at my mother's. I had to get a doctor's letter and fly with a wheelchair when I was finally able to leave. From there, I stopped over in Los Angeles to visit with a friend. Maura grew up with my sister and is the daughter of mother's partner, Roger Hoy. She was working in the television industry and thought there might be some interesting opportunities for me with a show called *You Asked for It*. The rest is history ...

Somewhere over the ocean, skies are blue ...

My Dearest Madam B.,

The hustle and bustle is over, and I am finally back on Singapore Air, headed home to Jakarta. I wanted to call from the airport in Los Angeles, but since I was "handicapped," they dumped me at the gate early and put a lock on my wheels. I considered requisitioning a final phone call—all prisoners have that right—but decided it would not do you any good to be woke up at 2:00 a.m. when I knew we would cry, and I couldn't bear to fly knowing you'd be upset for the rest of the night. This way, I sort of snuck away, and I'll sneak back even sooner!

I will be setting up a telex in Jakarta first thing on Wednesday, so please send me the telex number at Agawam as soon as possible.

Somehow I won myself a full-fledged Sugar Daddy Hollywood producer in Los Angeles—the producer of *You Asked for It*. Jerry Johnson seems to have fallen madly in love and wants me to come back to Los Angeles in January. Unfortunately, he is short, plump, and not at all my type, although he's very kind and generous. He took me to the airport Sunday night, and it's a very good thing I had someone there. Not only was my baggage *way* overweight, but I had more than the allotted number of pieces. We must have looked quite comical unpacking and repacking and strapping boxes together with my belongings spread all over the floor of LAX. He loaned me a three-hundred-dollar Sony cassette deck to listen to some new cassettes on the flight home and packed me on the plane. I was just settling in when the stewardess called me back up to the front of the plane. Though I had forgotten, Jerry remembered that I had just fifty cents in my pocket. He stuffed $150 in my hand, and off I went in total amazement. When I got to San Francisco, he had a message waiting for me to have a good trip and to call as soon as I hit Jakarta.

We are landing in Hong Kong, and the steward offered to mail this for me, so I'll sign off for now. More later.

Love and miss you terribly,
M.

10/7/81

Dearest Marthe,

It's easy to understand why you are loved around the world—from the Atlantic to the Java Sea! It's so much fun to be with you—an elegant lady always giving and growing. Being with you this year, I felt you have taken the step to womanhood. It's hard to define, but you have a sense of maturity and purpose that a young girl lacks.

Good to hear from you and Susanne today. Hope you enjoy your time in Houston with her. She's such a funny girl with her fast mouth and sophisticated style that only barely covers the warm, loving little girl inside.

The Cape was lovely today—clear and blue with white caps and lots of yellows and browns mixed with the prevalent scrub pine. This morning, I took a bird walk to the end of Daniel's Island. Emil Hanslin truly created an architectural triumph here, except for one log cabin (with spectacular oceanfront, no less). Saw lots of migratory small birds and squirrels and chippies scurrying around with full mouths—suppose they'll remember where they stashed the goodies come February?

Everywhere I look I see reminders of our good times and all the lovely presents, from the Bali bag (I brought it to the Cape) to the "Black Kid," my little kitten (aptly named Chocko after the devil at the Trinidad racetrack). I took him to the Cape as well and Lydia seems to find him companionable as long as she is number one when I am in view. Rog and I were watching them play on the breezeway. Chocko is so pleased to be near a warm, furry body, but he can't seem to understand why there's no milk supply.

All the good mornings over Billy Goat Coffee are etched in my memory. Although it's always so hard to have you go, I know we have a special relationship, and for that, I am eternally glad. Thank you, baby Jesus, as Meg would say.

A big hug for Rog, and congratulations to Wira Perkasa on the tourism contract. You have so many opportunities!

You are always in my thoughts.

Love,
Madam B.

PS—Are you taking your pills?

10/20/81

Dearest Marthe,

Yes, your letter from Los Angeles arrived while you were winging your way toward another sunrise. Interestingly enough, Sunday night (before you departed LA), I was going through my desk and found your sunrise letter of almost a year ago when you were first off to Jakarta.

So many sunrises from the Atlantic to Spain to the Pacific to Jakarta. What a rich life you have and how much we have deeply shared, visually and emotionally. You are so dearly loved for your joy and sensitivity. You know you could have stopped off forever at any of the stations during your trip home.

In the mail with your letter came one from Susanne. She, too, feels so attached (her word) to you and hated to have you leave. But her letter showed signs of maturity, which could only have come from long talks with her littler sister. I am so proud of my Yankee ladies and look forward to every successive year of sharing life with them wherever they go and whatever they choose to do.

Sent a letter to our CEO today with information on the condo. Will pay the lawyer's bill from the Arlington Trust account unless you tell me otherwise. But no rush, as I read it.

My cat, Mr. Chocko, is a model pet. Housebroken, warm, and friendly (even to kids), comes when called, and sleeps by himself at night without a word of complaint. Not like *some* pets we know (who will remain nameless) who will never be trained, hates little kids, comes only when they choose to, and throw themselves at the door if they aren't allowed in the bedroom. But delightful …

Everywhere I look, there are signs of your concern and love—the lovely bag, the marvelous yellow-and-white curtains at the lake, my rearranged kitchen, "our" oriental rug, my new wallet and change purse … the list is endless. But most of all, I hope you feel as surrounded by our mutual caring as I do. I refuse to dwell on distances; it hurts too much and isn't really important.

I believe it was W. Somerset Maugham who said, "It's a funny thing about life; if you refuse to accept anything but the best, you very often get it."

Go for it, lady. My love is with you all the way.

Madam B.

Hong Kong—Still En Route

This is crazy, Madam B. I just gave the steward one letter to mail to you, and since I won't bother to get off here, I'll just pick up where I left off.

This poor little guy who is the head steward is totally baffled. He came by during the flight when most of the other passengers were sleeping. I was working up some story leads for YAFI (*You Asked for It*), and he asked to look at my portfolio.

We had a nice discussion of cultures and politics. It seemed every time he walked by I was writing away. When I asked for some stationary, he looked totally exasperated and said, "Don't you ever get writer's cramp?" I explained that writing letters to my mom is recreational writing, sort of how I keep in shape.

Almost burst into tears when I opened the *Silver Kris* airline magazine. They have a photo essay on fall in New England. I swiped several copies and will forward one from Jakarta. The photos are magnificent though the text is somewhat dry.

It was kind of sad to finally leave Maura and her husband, Mark after my extended stay in Los Angeles. Their bungalow is really tiny, and we were just starting to get our routine worked out so the three of us weren't in each other's way sharing the bathroom.

Saturday, the three of us took a neat drive out through the canyons to Malibu. I always felt so comfortable with them, and Maura has turned into a smashingly beautiful lady. Mark is a gem. His wit and quick sense of humor is delightful. The Sugar Daddy producer, Jerry, has been totally captivated by the two of them, and I know he will look out after their interests. They remind me so much of Roger and me when we were first married … it was a refreshing pause that did much to restore my faith. Maura wants Susanne to come out to Los Angeles and find a job. It's a tough city, but it can be really fun, and they seem to have lots of friends both married and single.

But how are you, my Madam B? Here I am, dribbling on about myself. It certainly is not because you aren't in my thoughts. It's still a bit too painful to really concentrate my mind on where my feelings are. I picture you with Lydia and Chocko, all in the big bed, of course. I hope he brings you joy, Mom, and makes things bright while I'm away.

I almost, but not quite, of course, forgot about our purchase. It really is a beautiful carpet and looks so rich in our home.

There are about six rolls of film that I have not developed, so we will have many memories to share all over again soon.

Please stay warm and healthy until I return.

I love you, lady.
M.

10/24/81

Dearest Madam B.,

Got a letter from you already. As you can well imagine, it's been a bit crazy since I got back. I opened an account with a nearby hotel on Wednesday for telex, and they have been flying back and forth between here and Los Angeles daily. I've been researching story leads at the rate of about six per day. To get everyone organized, I wrote out a project proposal and weekly working schedule. Everyone is very excited about the project, but actually motivating them to settle down and work is another problem. Inge is in charge of finding us a new house, as the lease here is coming up and the house is falling apart. The possibilities are many, but I would like to stay as near to this location as possible. The boys (Anto and Yudo) will be in charge of getting permits and what is necessary to get the crews from Los Angeles in to film here.

I spoke with my producer friend in Los Angeles yesterday. He said the crew still has to go to Rangoon, Burma, and said there is a possibility I could go as well. Also, he is shooting in Hawaii in January. I've hired my Swedish friend, Gunilla (wife of another American with Phillips Petroleum), to help with the typing and my correspondence beyond the work on the YAFI project. I really need someone else fluent in English although I can only pay her fifty dollars per week out of my expense account.

Getting into Jakarta on the way home was a real problem. All my stuff came through fine, and I had "wheels" (wheelchair service) the whole way, but my exit permit expired the day I came in. Immigration kept my passport and let me go home, but Baroid had to pay over three thousand dollars to keep me here and get my passport back. Still, it sure is good to be home. The house is a wreck, full of workmen, and we have no air-conditioning in the master bedroom or water in the bathroom for some strange reason.

I keep thinking back on our conversations and the things we did together—the auction where we bought our carpet, going to lunch, brunch, and all our late-night talks. And the Billy Goat Coffee mornings! I revel in the wisdom I absorbed from you that will stand by me as I venture forward on a new career.

Enclosed is a copy of the telex I just received confirming my employment!!! God, that is so much fun to say. I keep repeating it to myself.

Actually, today is Sunday the 25th, but I am still in a fog. Last night, we went to a Gala Ball for Roger's company. Rog took along a copy of the telex and was showing it to everyone who would stand still long enough. I know he is very proud of me, but it is still all a bit embarrassing.

Having set up a telex, I now receive daily correspondence from Los Angeles. They call about every other day. It sounds like they will want about twenty stories from here and will be arriving on December 10 to begin shooting. Jerry Johnson called yesterday to congratulate me on the contract and to ask if I knew anything about Rangoon, Burma. I said no but that I could research it!

In the house-hunting department, we still do not have anything lined up, but to tell you the truth, I am not worrying too much about it. Roger will have an ulcer for both of us.

```
47243PACTOKM IA
GA
23673202+
WUI 10/24 0131
SANDYXRANK LSA

47243PACTOKM IA
```

TO:
SANDYFRANK LSA
MARTHA KIDDER, JARKARTA
FR: SANDY FRANK PRODUCTIONS, LOS ANGELES
TELEX 673202

DEAR MARTHA:

THIS WILL CONFIRM YOUR EMPLOYMENT WITH SANDY FRANK
PRODUCTIONS INC., AS FIELD RESEARCHER IN INDONESIA FOR THE SYNDICA
TED
TELEVISION SERIES, ''YOU ASKED FOR IT'', COMMENCING OCTOBER 12,

1981, AT THE RATE OF 500 DOLLARS PER WEEK.

PRIOR TO THE ARRIVAL OF OUR CREW, IF YOU ARE ENGAGED AS OUR PRODUC
TION
MANAGER FOR THE SHOOT, SALARY WILL BE 800 DOLLARS PER WEEK.

PLEASE CONFIRM YOUR AGREEMENT TO THIS CONTRACT AND GIVE INSTRUCTIO
NS
AS TO THE DESIRED METHOD OF PAYMENT.(WIRED, ETC).

SINCERELY,
J. JOHNSON
(EOT)
ABOVE VIA RCA FROM SANDYFRANK LSA
H
T

NEWS FLASH!!

This house is really in terrible shape. The electricity is so weak that you need a flashlight to read at night. We can only push two air conditioners at a time, and the unit in our bedroom has been out of service since we went on vacation. The plumbing seems to be backing up in our bathroom, so we have moved into one of the guest bedrooms until we can rent another house.

Everyone at Wira Perkasa is very excited about the project, but I am having a bit of a hard time convincing them of the urgency. Anto has completely taken apart the darkroom equipment and cleaned it all up. He is working twenty-four hours a day with me and has been such a help as far as researching locations and finding us contacts for each location.

Inge is not feeling well and is harder to motivate. I'm afraid there is perhaps a bit of jealousy regarding "Top Dog" on the project, but I haven't really had time to give it too much thought.

Hope you, Lydia, Chocko, your Rog, and everyone there is well, but most of all, missing you.

Love you all the time,
M.

10/26/81

Dearest Marthe,

Still the reports roll in from people who had a super time with you while you were in the States. JT called last week and said, without prompting, that you are his favorite of my children. You seem to talk so easily with him about the places you have been and what you are doing and take an interest in what he's doing. He so enjoyed his brief time with you in Houston ... and, of course, wants to come with me to see you and Roger.

Also a glowing letter from Maura telling how much they loved having you with them ... what good times she had reminiscing about Byfield and showing you around Los Angeles. She wrote most sensitively about my Roger and me.

And Susanne summed it up best of all. She loved having you with her and keeps enjoying your visit with all the great memories. She says your visit will last on and on.

Had a good chat with Dick also. I called to remind him and Dunc about Susanne's birthday. He had bought pearl studs for her, and Dunc had a jewelry box. Dick took her to lunch on Friday and was planning a brunch party on Sunday, as she was working all day on her real birthday. He seems very warm, friendly, and reasonable about your recuperation and subsequent visit in LA.

How's your Kucing? Lydia's new buddy is quite the star of our household. Whether one is brushing their teeth (fascinating as observed from the side of the sink), going to the john (he unrolls the TP for you), trying to read (he turns the pages), dusting (too bad we can't tie the duster to his tail), washing dishes (at the lake, he jumps up from the fruit bowl to my shoulder for a better view), he's everywhere—like Superman. He climbs like a Siamese, is twice as big as the day he pranced across the floor for my first introduction to him, and is *well behaved*. Rides well in the carrier and sleeps wherever he is bedded down without a peep. The wind chimes get quite a workout—it's a little like being in a bar when a good tip is recorded with a bell ring. Lyd plays with and chases him and lets him on the bed with her ... but not too close, please. He would enjoy snuggling up to her, but she is not that much of a good sport. And, Lyd's appetite has turned voracious since the cat arrived.

Next weekend is our last at the lake for this season. I find the trek too much now that the evenings are dark early and I do the two-way trip alone. But we have had six good months. And JT will be with us next weekend to help with the closing up.

Thoughts of you are all around me, and I still have that nasty ache every morning that says you are gone. But I'm looking for your first letter since getting "home" to Jakarta about things with our CEO, your housing, Wira Perkasa, the Kucing, and your career with Sandy Frank Productions.

Go, lady. You have all it takes.
Madam B.

10/29/81
Jakarta

Dearest Madam B.,

I'm becoming quite the little typist these days with sending out telexes daily and the letters. I'm trying to get enough work set up so that if/when I take off for a couple of months with YAFI to do the reporting, Wira Perkasa will keep busy and start working on projects from the States.

Guess I have to tell you about my latest proposal from Los Angeles. Jerry called the other day to say he wanted a screen test on me as soon as possible. IF, and that's still a really big IF, I pass the test they want me to go from shooting here to Rangoon, Burma, and two sites in India. I would be gone for about a month and a half, but when I told Roger that I would be making two thousand dollars per week, of course the old Yankee was packing my bags and asking to see the contract!! Hopefully, we will start shooting the screen test by tomorrow if the script arrives by telex.

In the meantime, today is a national holiday, the first day of the Muslim New Year, so most offices are closed, and it makes it tough to get anything done. Anto and Yudo were here working earlier as was my new research assistant, Gunilla. Inge is becoming a real problem. Not only is she not well, female problems and a pregnancy I suspect, but she has been keeping the books for Wira Perkasa, and now I find many discrepancies in where the money has all gone. I have taken over the bookkeeping on top of everything else, and she cannot be depended on to do anything definite for the YAFI project. Luckily, Gunilla is very available and willing to help, so I will be able to rely on her to cover the office while Anto, Yudo, and I go on location in December with the filming crew.

We still have not found a house, but I refuse to let that get in the way of my work for YAFI. I will never have a chance like this again, and I don't intend to let *anything* blow it for me. Rog is quite upset about the house situation, but I know it will work itself out. Also, Rog found out yesterday that he didn't get the water-flood business from IIAPCO. That was the big proposal he had worked on for months. The only reason they could give was that he had most of their business already. Crummy excuse. To top it all off, the American family he has working for him are causing many problems. The wife has had to go to Singapore for various unknown reasons just about every month, and she calls the office to bitch someone out every day. Now they are talking about going back to the States. "It's just too hard on us here." Sheesh! I babysat them for months in the beginning. Poor Rog is really having his fill of troubles.

I spent yesterday afternoon at the Hilton beauty shop getting myself in order for the screen test. Sonia, my Colombian friend, met me there, as I had not seen her since getting back. Had my hair henna-ed and trimmed per order of the producer, Jerry, and also splurged to have my nails done. I could almost get into this "movie star" scene if I had the time. Sonia was, of course, shocked by my news of employment and wanted to know if they might want to go to Colombia.

Can't wait for you to come over. By then I'll be an expert on Java and Bali as well as a bit richer, so we can really splurge on travel!

Thinking of you a million times a day and picture you in every setting. The time we spent together is all recorded in my diary, and I read it over and over. You are my inspiration. Can't think of distances or I'll cry.

Take good care so you can come soon.
M.

11/1/81

Dear Madam B.,

Still using this crummy manual typewriter. It seems all the companies who rent machines are out of electrics at the moment. Hope you'll bear with me; it's better than my handwriting at least.

Lazy Sunday afternoon, and I just finished up my research and telex for the day. Rog has gone to play tennis at the club. I offered several times to go with him, but he doesn't seem to enjoy my company these days. I just don't know how to deal with him anymore. He is never happy and so negative about his job, the office, and life in general. To add to his troubles, Marj called first thing this morning to tell him that Rich has cancer. They are going to have to remove his colon and rectum. I thought surely Rog would want to go to New Hampshire, but he says no. I offered to go for him just so he would know for sure what is going on there, but he says no to that also. He is in a slump, but everything I offer for suggestions to try to cheer him up brings on more negativism.

Meanwhile, I got my script yesterday and will begin filming of the screen test tomorrow. The script is from a show they shot in Rio and does not make much sense to me, but I have decided that I want this job desperately. The screen test *has* to be harder than the actual shooting of the show, so I will just go ahead the best I can. Keep your eyes, nose, fingers, and toes crossed for me for luck!

11/3/81

Sorry, lady. I got waylaid for a day or so. Yesterday was devoted entirely to making the screen test. It took three hours to film ten minutes worth of action … remind me never to want to go into the technical end of this!! I had to play reporter for seven takes, each with a change of clothes, with the director of the Indonesian film crew YAFI will use when they come to shoot the programs. They were really good, I think; they were moonlighting from the TV station here in Jakarta. The script was really dumb, but we managed to shoot one take in the back garden and six in the house. Rog came home in time to catch the first two takes. His only comment was "Don't you think you sounded a bit stiff?" Thank you, Mr. Optimism, for your vote of confidence!!! I know I can't be hard on him, as he has enough problems as it is, but really, a little emotional support would go a long way to helping the state of affairs around here.

I just got a call from Los Angeles from a lady whose husband is number four worldwide in the USAID, whatever that is. She is setting up some help from a diplomatic point of view here for me. Well, la-di-da! Now we are into the diplomat scene. Whoever said, "*I* Asked for It?"

I am very encouraged with the way the screen test turned out. Though I will never see the film itself, I felt relaxed and good about it while I was doing it, and Jerry assures me they are not entertaining any thoughts of sending a reporter over for this shoot. Of course, this could all change in a minute's notice the way these people operate, but I am very hopeful.

Love you dearly,
M.

11/6/82

Hey, lady!

It must be nice—an early retirement from the business world and reentry at over twenty thousand dollars per year?! Has Roger given his notice at Baroid yet? Susanne is quitting Monday, and I'll work my two weeks. Then we're all coming to live with *you*!! (Just kidding.)

Got your copy of the telex yesterday, and we are all bursting with pride for you.

Love to our CEO and most of all to our favorite field researcher for TV.

Madam B.

11/9/81

Dearest Madam B.,

I'm really feeling guilty about how little I've been writing to you since getting home. Dad called today, and I realized I haven't written to him at all since I got home. He said it was most important that when I do write that I write to you, and you would keep everyone else informed. He also said Sue had quit her job. Another Walsh once again joins the ranks of the unemployed.

We are just about finished up on the research end of the project and ready to move on to the advanced production stage. Remember I always wanted a title in life? Well, now I've finally got one, and they want to change it every week! From field researcher, I will now become advanced production manager and later, hopefully, field reporter. I should find out if they got the screen test later tonight when I call. Mondays are always a bit unproductive; we lose communications for two days over the weekend, and they don't start back to work until midnight my time, which is Monday morning their time. My biggest hassle at the moment is the bookkeeping. I don't know anything about it, and neither does anyone else here.

Guess I forgot to mention that Inge has left the company, and now that we are moving and have to change the address, we figured we might as well change the name too. A fresh start, so to speak.

Inge's attitude was a problem from the start, and with all the employee relations problems while I was away, I think she had known all along that her time was limited. Yudo and Anto insisted I take over the books and the general management of projects on the threat that they would leave if Inge were in charge. One week after we started the project with YAFI, she disappeared for ten days of unexplained absence. She showed up last Friday in the height of a really busy afternoon. I had a filmmaker waiting to talk to me, and the phone was ringing with a call from Los Angeles. I couldn't give her much of a greeting, and she seemed to expect much more than she got. After about an hour, she called a taxi and as she was going out the door, she asked what I wanted her to work on. I explained I was really tied up and that if she could hold on for about five more minutes, I'd finish up and talk to her about the project. "Just write it all down for me, and I'll call you tonight," she said as she left.

Sure, Inge. Don't strain yourself! It turns out she had been in Singapore for some secret operation … abortion maybe. In the meantime, Anto, Yudo, and I were frantic for help and had hired Gunilla full-time to help out until we knew what Inge was doing. Gunilla had not only enthusiastically pursued the research we gave her, but she went out and brought in some great story ideas of her own that YAFI accepted.

Since we were so far into the project, there was no way we could slow our pace for Inge to catch up. We decided she would do better to keep up our contacts here in Jakarta and help us out with the typing, etc. But that did not appeal to Madam President at *all*. She came back on Saturday morning and started packing up the typewriter. Now, true, it was hers (and not a good one at that), but it was the only one we had available, and I had four telexes to type that day plus lots of notes to type up from the research. She said she needed it for an article she was writing and would bring it back in the evening. I asked if the article was written yet. NO. Did the article have to do with the YAFI project? NO. I tried to diplomatically point out that the YAFI project was earning us a tidy sum and that I thought it was important we have the tools available that we needed to do the job. She said again, "It's my typewriter, and I need it." Okay. So don't do me any favors.

The next time I looked up from my work, she had disconnected the phone and was heading out the door with it. I called out, but she ignored me. When she came back in, I said, "Okay, Inge, let's talk about this." Nothing to talk about; she claimed it was her telephone and she needed it. After several threats, begging, and finally just plain losing my temper, she left with my tossing her belongings out the door after her. It raised quite a crowd out by the front gate, but at least I felt a bit better after letting off steam. I went by her house later to take her the rest of her things and try to talk it out. She was just like a little kid and stubborn as some other Scorpios we know. Just as well. It's all out in the open, and she's gone. Employee enthusiasm has picked up one hundred percent since then. But I can't help remembering that if it had not been for Inge's contacts and guidance, I would not be where I am today just one year after coming to Indonesia. I feel badly it had to end the way it did, and I have lost someone I had thought was my friend. Now I will be forced to buy a new typewriter, as this borrowed one is no better than hers.

Hopefully, this extended diatribe of a letter will make up for some of my recent neglect. We are moving on Friday, November 13. The new phone number is 790082. It's a nice little Spanish-style house that Rog picked out; two-story with a small garden and porches around the second floor. Good neighborhood and closer to work for Rog. I will miss my kampong neighbors.

We are still in the final voting stages, but I think the new name of Wira Perkasa will be Media Budaya, International. *Budaya* means "arts and culture" in Indonesian.

My Kucing is well and gaining weight since I came home. He has a lady friend, and they sit and howl at each other day and night. I told him we have to move before he gets hit with a paternity suit. The turtle has just laid two eggs, which has all of us mystified since Ernie/Ernestine has lived all by him/herself in our pond for the last six months!

I miss you painfully, and wish you could be here now to help me understand all this bookkeeping.

Love you dearly,
M.

Journal Entry,
11/10/81
2:30 a.m.

I can't believe what is happening to me. Walls are crashing and I sit in total late-night, black silence.

I just called YAFI to make my daily report and check into a few things. Kathy called back. We went over the basic dailies, and she was very enthusiastic. "No holds barred. Go with it!" about Gunilla's idea for a segment on Nina Thompsen, the snake lady.

She then switched me to Marlene, and I can only quote her. "Just relax for a week. Other foreign researchers are off salary at the moment. Don't go to Bali just yet ... reevaluating ... foreign production is on hold for the moment." "Decisions were made on Friday night. There's a cash-flow problem. I'll get back to you in a week—sooner if you are off payroll. Oh, we'll pay you what we owe to date. Just relax for a week."

A WEEK!!?? Holy shit! I had her switch me over to Bob Schaefer, the moneyman. Bob sounded sad, hopelessly so. "Supposed to try to wire the money today sometime." The more I pushed, the less I got. I hated to let go the lifeline of hope, but I couldn't ask him to switch me to the top—to Jerry.

Not about to go to bed in this state, so I put a call through to Jerry directly. The message, of course, was that he was "in a meeting" and would call me back. It's been forty-five minutes since, and to say I'm nervous is to miss the whole point of my writing this down.

11/10/81

Dear Ms. Executive,

What happened with the screen test? Isn't this all just too much to believe? Nothing, but nothing, is serious/important enough to interfere with such an opportunity.

Glad you have Gunilla. Inge is perhaps too young to handle the responsibility of an office such as yours is becoming. And maybe not mature enough to work well alongside you just now. Thank heaven for Anto and Yudo. Hope they are up to the challenges of the coming months.

The November issue of *Travel & Leisure* has a feature story on the Borobudur temple. Your part of the world is certainly coming into its own for lots of play right now and you are *on the spot*!!! I'm having Nana, Grampa, and everyone who knows you writing to YAFI to request stories from Indonesia. Operative word is *YOU* asked for it, right? Can't hurt.

Roger must be dreadfully disappointed with the turn down of his proposal for the Indonesian government. Do you think someone else got ahead with a big/bigger payoff? Or would it really have been embarrassing to give him such a major contract? Is it Gary's wife who is fussing to go home?

We are into November weather now … down in the forties and thirties. You would chatter your teeth! Been keeping the apartment in the mid-sixties during the day (better for plants and my little zoo) and only turning the thermostat up for a couple of hours in the evening. Hopefully, if we all cut back, Jackie won't have to raise the rents. Les, my boss, just had his first delivery of oil at his new house—$651!! The price is $1.23 per gallon. Enjoying your warm climate? It's a lot cheaper too.

We are hanging on here at Agawam Direct Marketing. The federal loan is definitely out. Reaganomics. But I think I agree it is time to stop all the giveaway programs—just unfortunate that I'm on the payroll for one that needs it. A local bank has made a small personal loan to Les, and our creditors are holding back. It's that or get only a few cents on the dollar for what we owe. So we're all working like mad to get a major client. Les is in Washington today to see AMTRAK (there's a loser too) and Time Life. Cross your eyes, nose, fingers, and toes for us.

Our telex training session is scheduled for 1:30, so I must dash this over to the post office and get back in time for it. Some evening soon when I'm here after 7:00 p.m., I'll try to raise you on the machine. We're 951223 AGAWAMROWL. What's your answerback?

You are always with me in my head and heart. Love to our CEO. Madam B.

Journal Entry, *11/20/81*

New House! New Office! New Company!

Not only did money finally come in from Los Angeles yesterday, but also this morning a telex from Mom verified the deposit of an additional five hundred dollars from YAFI for production costs.

We've been on a two-day spending spree around here. First, we were able to pay everyone's IOUs and salaries up to date, and second, we paid Rog one thousand dollars toward expenses. With that expense money, Rog and I started whittling down our list of "things we can't live without."

Today was company shopping day. I'm glued to the new portable, electric mesin tulis, and we invested in the darkroom curtains.

Slowly, things are falling back into a routine and sorting themselves out. Yudo left for Bali last night to scout locations, and the bookkeeping system is coming together. From all this vast amounts of money, I have not set aside a single rupiah for the office co-coordinator extraordinaire— myself. I weep if I stop too long to think about it.

Nine hours until YAFI's telephone call. I'd better have some more pertinent information to report than a new typewriter and darkroom curtains ...

Journal Entry,
11/24/81

Well, it certainly looks like we are back in business. I sent out three telexes today and received two. I'm sure Kemang Hotel was glad to hear from me again for our telex business. Anto went out after the Debus story today. That may be our best yet. Yudo got back from Bali, and although he wasn't as thorough as I would have been, I feel we have some good locations and stories.

I spent the morning at the Reuters news agency. Just being that close to such a world-famous news organization gave me goose bumps. I had a meeting with an Australian cameraman, Walter Burgess. He was a bit of an ass (aren't all Australian men here?), but I think he could be helpful to our cause. Though I couldn't bear to work with him, he's not a bad person, and influence-wise, he will be good to know. It sounds like his stock footage might make for good documentary stuff, but *where* does the funding come from??

I should go to the bank tomorrow a.m., but I really want to set up the "Nina Thompsen, Snake Lady" story and the zoo filming. I'm ending up doing all the administrative bullshit and none of the actual production. I want to take some shots too. It's so hard to have all this newfound equipment and knowledge and never have a chance to use it. I've got to get out of this office tomorrow and work in the field, so to speak. It is *my* project after all. So far, no money and little field experience but a *hell* of a change in my life.

11/25/81

Dear Marthe,

Got your "moving" letter last night. That's got to be the least pleasant experience in life—moving is worse than a toothache! But the new house sounds interesting, and with your fine touch, you'll make it a lovely home as was Olney, Illinois, San

Fernando, Trinidad, or Timbuktu. Roger is so lucky to have a built-in decorator. How does Kucing like the new home? Are the servants happy with their new arrangement?

It's such fun having a telex to respond to Roger's messages from the Baroid office. Hope mine are arriving. The bank was most cooperative about taking your YAFI checks, and Bill Kidder (el presidente) was actually friendly and curious about what you are doing. How much? From where?? By check or wire? I told him you were running a house of ill repute in Singapore and this was laundered money through Los Angeles. That should keep the town talking!

All business in the States seems to be slow and suffering. With the auto and construction industries in such a slump, the ripple effect is finally getting to everyone. Americans just have to realize that for a while their standards of living are not what they were two years ago. President Reagan is turning out to be much stronger than many people thought he would be, and probably it's high time someone said whoa to all the spending, arms race, and giveaways.

I'm looking into the tickets and dreaming of sitting over coffee in the morning with you in your exotic home.

Love and miss you terribly,
Madam B.

Journal Entry, 11/26/81 Thanksgiving

It all depends on where you are from. Gunilla and I did some grocery shopping yesterday at about noon, and I spent the afternoon putting together the feast. We were five at dinner: Gunilla, her husband Lou,

Rog, Anto, and me. The turkey (ayam raksasa!!—BIG chicken) was good with lots of traditional condiments from the American commissary at Phillips Petroleum's expat village. The servants, Parno and Sukarti, were fascinated by all the strange food—the cranberry sauce (jellied, unfortunately), olives, and stuffing with smoked baby clams. Sukarti made a pumpkin pie, and Lou brought canned whipped cream. Just to make it all very American, we even had ketchup on the table, with which Anto proceeded to douse his turkey. Gunilla wasn't too familiar with the whole procedure.

Back home in the USA, people will be dressing in coats and boots and thinking about upcoming Christmas parties ... a whole world away.

December 1, 1981 ... winding down 1981 and probably just as well ...

Dearest Marthe,

Talk about being on a high and then plummeting to the bottom. I know what you mean. The summer/fall were great, but the last two weeks have been so low I could walk upright under Lydia. Must be a sign of the times—holidays, time of year, cold weather (no heat above sixty-eight degrees no matter where one goes), and low finances all around. How many times a day I yearn for a talk with you over hot Billy Goat Coffee in the sunshine of the dining room.

Susanne starts her trek north and east today from Houston. She and your hairy dog, Mac, are planning to be on the road before sunup. She was trying to talk a friend into going along. Pulling a U-Haul with her roll-top desk, bed, and packing boxes alone could be a chore. First stop is New Port Richey to visit Nana Doris and Grampa. Strong Yankee lady, but still I won't be *un*-anxious until she lands in Connecticut at Frank's house. By then, Frank will have been in/out of the family business a few more times and hopefully will have found a place for them to live.

Doris called last night and said the last electric bill for the lake was two hundred dollars. The joys of electric heat and no insulation. That rips the possibility of my paying the whole tax bill for now. I had wanted to take the financial burden off of Nana and Grampa, as they no longer get to use the cottage. That and four hundred dollars to fix the Datsun this fall. But these are tough times for everyone's budget, so no complaints. It was a good summer/fall in Washington, and the Datsun's running great. And what's the Public Service Company going to do? Shut off the lights? They are already off for the winter!

Things with my Rog have been less than good of late for me. No one will ever know what goes on behind the bushy eyebrows; articulate he is not. I was feeling neglected and resentful (sound familiar?) about cooling my heels alone most of last weekend, Thanksgiving. Finally, he came to Newburyport Saturday evening. We had a good dinner and a walk. Guess I was fed up with being a homebody. Sunday, he refused to go to Boston with me to meet my friend Prim and her daughter Chris (and I also wanted to kill the winter blues with a visit to the Gardner Museum). He didn't feel well, so we canceled. Quiet day. Like I needed another of those?

Monday morning, I was very teary and took my turkey sandwich and went off to work. I got there so early everyone thought I must have been there all weekend sleeping under my desk. At noon, I went to the landing to watch the ducks as I ate and wept in true female fashion. Rog showed up. He had no more idea what was wrong than Chocko would have had!

God! Do you believe men sometimes? So the upshot of the whole discussion (mine, not his, of course) was that he is just reserved and quiet and "that's the way it is." Now, that sounded a bell somewhere in my head. Only the last time I heard it, it went something like "If you don't like the berries, get away from the cart." He came back and stayed with me last night, but there is this debate in my head. Does he wish I would go away? Should I go away anyway? Why does it all make me feel old and bored and like the best of life is all over?

Pay no attention. By the time this arrives in Jakarta, things will be better. It must be the time of year. More people lately have said they are in a bad mood, depressed. Even Les is being nasty. And with good reason—our financial house of cards is shakier than ever, in spite of new clients. And, of course, he bought a house he could ill afford and has a whole drawer full of unpaid household bills. And still no bank loan/assistance. Whew. I really don't have a thing to complain about.

Next time I'll be more upbeat.

Love and miss you ever so much,
Madam B.

12/2/81

Dearest Madam B.,

Monday, we got our first Christmas card. I opened it thinking, *Now what fool is rushing the season with cards this early?* Then I happened to look around at the calendar and realized I'm the one who is late. Usually I have the cards all written by Thanksgiving, if not mailed. Guess things have really snuck up on me this year with all the excitement of YAFI.

Rog has taken off for the week to Kalimantan, Borneo, and points north. I can't complain, as it is the first trip he has made since getting back from vacation. Also, it takes some of the pressure off me so I can finish up all my production work before the cameraman arrives on Saturday.

Anto and I took ourselves out for boiled shrimp at the Seafood 99 last night. It's a bit rough for Roger's taste but it's cheap, and with my cast-iron stomach, I have never had a problem. Imagine eating in the rough at some place like Woodman's Clam Shack only Indonesian-style with boiled baby shrimp and lots of hot sauce. They had a big bucket of crabs sitting out waiting to be cook, and all through our meal, one crab kept hopping out and scurrying across the floor in search of the door. A waiter would grab him and toss him back in the bucket. Quite the floor show.

Good news for YAFI yesterday. Now they think they will try a few stories with me doing the narration. If Burt, the cameraman, thinks it is going okay, he will make the decision to go ahead with the rest of the stories. Keep your eyes, toes, and everything else crossed for me!

March or April sounds great for you to come over, though I wish it could be before that. Is Susanne planning on coming too? Perhaps by now she has outgrown her traveling blues and will be a good companion for you on the long flight over. No word from Houston in weeks, but Sue had written that Dad was starting a new "career," so I guess everyone is busy. Where exactly is Sue planning on living when she comes north? Moving right in with Frank and his mother? Coming to Newburyport first to visit with you? I need to know where to send her Christmas card, if I ever get around to sending any.

Love and miss you more than you know,
M.

12/4/81

Dearest Marthe,

A wonderful surprise last night—two letters from you and the pictures you took around Newburyport. Such lovely colors and reflections.

Interesting reaction to the screen test. Now you know the foibles of using untried film crews. Find comfort in your own strength in dealing with a bilingual situation and the stress of the camera work. No wonder Jerry is impressed! How could he not be with all the retakes and having a reporter/director all in one? Such a bargain he is getting.

Dunc called last night to tell me he is getting out of the cab business ... too many hassles, twenty-four-hour duty, and the "pits" for colleagues. What else is new? Next, are you ready for this? He wants to bail out by selling the cabs at auction, hopes to clear fifteen thousand dollars. He thinks it is a great profit, and it is if one doesn't consider their time worth zip! And ... sit down. He wants to go into the business of manufacturing hot tubs! Didn't you always want one in your backyard? In this economy of higher than 8 percent unemployment?

He wants to buy a going (down?) business and pick up the limited equipment—a tired truck or two and the molds to make TV antennae discs—plus two Mexican laborers. He plans to mortgage his soul to the current owner for three years plus all his capital. Dad thinks it is a ridiculous idea from start to finish. Dunc would be the manufacturer and would wholesale the products. This has to be an even worse time to go into business than when he tried it two years ago and now with a totally useless product. I begged him to search the market for a product or service that people need, not just perhaps want and can't afford. Something related to the oil-service industry, insurance, banking, food, or computers—something with a future. But he sounded very down in the mouth with me for not being all excited. Surely, I was delighted he's getting out of the cab rat race. But he has sales ability and has learned something of running a small business. Why throw it all away—again?

Hope your Rog is finding the adjustment to your business life easier. It's different, no doubt of that.

Feeling better about myself since the two previous letters. Sorry about bottoming out and letting you know all about it. It must have been something in our biorhythms; even heard a girl on the radio say she felt like she was on another planet these last few weeks. But Les keeps plugging along with this business and is pleasant to work with again, Roger is trying to be more attentive, and Susanne is back east. The worst part is we are still so far apart. It never gets better after you leave. It is always there, thinking of you and wishing we could have a good talk. Take good care of yourself.

Love you ever so much ... you who are closest to me in the whole world.
Madam B.

12/6/81

Dear Madam B.,

I am enclosing a clipping from yesterday's front page of the paper. The small person crouching in the upper left-had corner is yours truly. This was the charity event I telexed about that we covered in hopes of selling an article/story. Perhaps if I write it up anyway and submit it in time to various papers, there will be someone interested for next year's event.

We took a lot of shots, and Gunilla went back the next day and sold copies to all the embassy stalls and individuals we had photographed, so it wasn't a total loss.

We are awaiting the arrival of Bert Van Munster, the cameraman who is doing some work for the United Nations. He will shoot for ten days for the UN and then begin shooting for us. We will probably only do five or six stories, but they have promised me I can try a couple as the reporter with Bert's direction. If they turn out okay, we will shoot all with me as the reporter! Hopefully when YAFI starts shooting for the 1982–1983 season in February, they will come here first because we are all set up with dozens of more stories. I will not make the millions of dollars I had planned on this time, but as you say, the experience is well worth the money I don't make.

I don't exactly know when Rog will be back. He called the other day, but I was out. He told the servants he would call back again, but as yet, not a word. I think he is in Irian Jaya, and they don't have very many telephones there.

Trish Dean from Trinidad wrote that she has Winnie and loves him dearly. She says he is so affectionate now that he is over the trauma of separation from Churchill. He is becoming like his old self again and is very protective of her. I would give anything to have him back, but since that is impossible, I am glad he has such a good home.

Anto just came in to the office and asked if I had started on my autobiography. Guess this is a long one. In truth, you are the only one to whom I can write exactly what is on my mind, and once I get started, I just can't stop. The words flow faster than my fingers can type.

Well, all is well from here except that I deeply miss being able to talk to you. Hope you are keeping warm and getting your vitamin B shots regularly.

I love you dearly and can't wait for you to come and share my world here.

M.

12/8/81

Dear Miss Marthe,

Slipping and sliding after our first blizzard of the season … nothing small to start this year! Saturday afternoon, it started and went right on for twenty-four hours. A very pretty, sticky, wet foot-and-a-half, all over everything. But what a picture-perfect scene with the holiday lights and wreaths and white frosting.

Rog arrived ahead of the storm. He had been down in New York with his daughter Kelly. We were snowbound until Monday morning. He's still here—dentist today and the office tomorrow. Four days with Lyd and Chocko and the poor, nonanimal lover is going stir crazy. But he made a terrific pot roast dinner last night. The strain of being so well behaved must be awful for Lyd. She is such a little lady when Rog is here. And Choko is always himself—running straight out or asleep. I took him out in the snowstorm in my arms. He was having none of that stuff!

Susanne rounded out her weekend with the grandparents in Florida, and they all seemed to have enjoyed it thoroughly. Sunday night, Frank flew in to Tampa and spent the night with them. You know what a charmer he can be, and he still was! Monday, he and Sue were off to Busch Gardens and left that night for "the road." They called me from Tampa. Frank wanted to hook a right to Key West, and Sue wanted to come back to New England. Little does it matter to Frank; another diner-table coup at his parents' house and he will be out of the family business anyway. Someone loaned him five thousand dollars until his insurance money comes in, and you know Frank, not a care in the world and a twenty-two-year-old on his arm.

We're doing great at Agawam. The *Boston Sunday Globe* carried the auction notice for the land and buildings. And still we keep rolling up new clients, but that does not mean money for the cash flow for at least six weeks. Clients seem reluctant to pay before we produce. Les is a lot more subdued but is still most pleasant when one thinks of the total strain. He has a house he cannot afford, even when we are making money. He took a second mortgage to help the business. He has a wife and three daughters who can't think of enough ways to spend the money, and they have no idea how things are at the office! Still, it's a great job, for all that.

What will you do Christmas Day? Someday, we'll have a huge family Christmas again with all the in-laws and outlaws.

Love you ever so much,
Madam B.

12/11/81

Dear Madam B.,

Friday afternoon and all is quiet in the office. Gunilla and Yudo have gone home for the day, Mr. Roger has gone to Singapore to buy Christmas presents for his customers, and I figured it was a good time to get my thoughts together by writing to you.

I should be pumping out articles but have reached the saturation point with reading my own stories so that will have to rest a while. Gunilla is really good about finding markets for articles and pushing me to write. If anything, she pushes too hard! I explained that I am not a word-processing machine and that even those machines have to have some input! But she is seriously good for me in that she is so enthusiastic about selling articles and hunting through the *Writer's Market* for magazines to approach. She has some very good ideas for stories on the various animals we researched for the YAFI project and selling them to children's magazines, such as *National Geographic Kids*. Also, she has a friend here who belongs to a country-western musical group. They have three American members, three Indonesians, and one Australian. She thought it would be an interesting story for a country-music magazine, so she looked up a bunch of magazines and typed up cards for my file on them. Now all I have to do is interview the guy and do the writing. Sounds so simple, right? Wish you were here to give me a few helping hands.

We are having a couch recovered and a table made for the darkroom. The couch should be back today, and Rog wanted me to order a couple of other small jobs while we are at it. That boy can spend my money faster than I can make it! I'll be getting about eight hundred dollars in back pay this week, and I was trying to decide if I should send it to Bradley Bilgore to invest for me. I don't want to just fritter it away, which is exactly what will happen if it is not put somewhere where "the Kid" and I can't get at it. Any suggestions??

We are slowly but surely getting our act together and finding work outside the realm of YAFI. Along with Gunilla's article ideas, the boys, Anto and Yudo, went out today and got a job for a brochure for a batik store. I sent off a package to Singapore this morning with Roger to post to the Singapore Airlines magazine. I had put together four photo essays, and hopefully, they will accept one or at least give us an assignment. Keep your eyes crossed for us!

The cameraman is finally here for YAFI. He has to do some filming for the United Nations first and will be in touch with me again about the YAFI shoot next week. They, YAFI, still don't know how many stories they need or if they need me to do the reporting. It is rather frustrating, but we will hang in there and pray they need *something*. On my Christmas card to Jerry, I said that Cinderella's feet would never fit in the glass shoes if she didn't get a chance to at least break them in. He is very understanding and encouraging, but as he said, "This isn't a bank that conducts business during regular business hours. This is Hollywood, kid, love it or leave it!" Next time I wish someone would say that to me *before* my hopes and dreams are sky-high.

One of these days, I'm not going to show up for work at all. I'll just hide out upstairs all day and soak up some sun on the porch. To look at the color of my skin, you would think I was living in Siberia instead of the tropics!

Well, madam, guess I'll go take my bath and relax for a while. The bathroom is the only room in this house where no one comes running up to me to ask: 1) Where is _____? 2) Who is _____? 3) What do I do with _____? 4.) Do you know _____? or 5) How do I _____? It's hell being the answer person to everyone I know right down to the servants. Never mind. It's nice to feel needed. Some days I feel like the mother of at least eight children.

Love you dearly. Missing you is the only thing I hate about life right now.
M.

Journal Entry,
12/17/81

Bert, the cameraman, has left without a single shot for YAFI. He said he has worked for YAFI for a year now and will not operate without the money up front. Don't we all feel that way now?? With no money and the holidays approaching, he decided to pack it up and head home. Jerry is not returning my calls. Ten weeks of hard work and hopes are down the drain. I ache inside but comfort is not forthcoming from the one who should be closest to me. A little tender support would go a long way in this situation.

Travel Indonesia magazine and UPI-Antara, two potential clients I had hoped for, did not play out as expected. Isabella from UPI-Antara was encouraging but had nothing definite to offer. *Travel Indonesia* is too small to support any more staff and seldom uses freelance work.

Gunilla is mothering six new cocker spaniel puppies. Anto and I stopped by today to have a look. They are cute as puppies always are.

Every response I have received from my queries and stories/articles has been negative. It's getting more than a bit depressing.

12/22/81

Dear Madam B.,

Three days to Christmas, but I have to keep reminding myself because there is no mass marketing, no carols playing on a radio, no decorations throughout the city. I feel so far from home in a Muslim country on the other side of the world.

This week will go down in history as "Bird Week" at the Kidder Homestead. Yesterday, I stopped off to buy a birdcage to hang from a conveniently placed hook someone left in the upstairs living room. Rog and I had been staring at it for weeks, trying to decide what to hang from it, and decided a birdcage with a nice big plant in it would just fill the spot. When Sudi and I started looking, the really nice Chinese cages were quite expensive, and for the same price, I could get a locally made one *with* a bird! Well, needless to say, I opted for the local one with the bird. It's not a particularly beautiful bird—small, black, and white, but its song is so pretty, and as if to make up for the lack of color, it sings its little heart out all day long. Kucing can't understand why I hang food up in a cage and has been leaping from all the furniture in hopes of getting a mouthful.

Today, Gunilla and I had to go to the bird market (the large central market here in the city) to meet with man who was going to arrange for a bat performance for YAFI. He had the bat all trained and now will have to wait until February or so. I had never been to the market, for good reason. I knew I couldn't be trusted to not buy a bird. Today there was no excuse, so I went with Gunilla.

It is the neatest place full of strange animals, such as mongooses (mongeese??), monkeys, bats, cockatoos, parrots, and every other imaginable kind of bird. Gunilla bought two lovely doves for her husband for Christmas. I came home with two of the cutest baby parrots. They are so tiny and fluorescent green. The female is somewhat older, tamer, and very mischievous. The male is such a timid little fellow; he just quakes when you hold him. For eight dollars, I couldn't resist.

Birds and cats are such nice, independent pets. They don't give back a whole lot of affection, but they also don't require a whole lot of attention. The parrots can't talk yet, but they are fun to hold and to have fluttering around the house. They can't fly too well yet, so I will have to clip their wings when they can.

Rog and I had thought of going to Yogyakarta to the temples in Central Java for the weekend of Christmas. Instead, we have decided to have a party on Saturday night. It's been almost a year since we had a party, and there doesn't seem to be many this year, so we figured we had better do our part and stage one. Hopefully, it won't be quite as large of an affair as last year—only fifty people.

The office is really quiet these days without any work from YAFI. I am trying to figure out ways to keep us going. Have been sending off query letters like crazy and organizing all our research files into possible story ideas. Anto has gone to Surabaya for ten days to visit his family.

Any more news on your photo submissions? Where are you sending them?

Counting the time until you will be here, and I have started a list of the places and things we can see while you are here. Don't worry, I won't play tour director too much. Just some things I think will help orient you to this part of the world.

Hope your holidays with Sue and Mac are the merriest ever. I would give anything to be there to share it all with you.

All my love to your Roger and your little zoo. Most of all to you, my dearest friend.

I love you,
M.

Journal Entry, 12/27/81 Jakarta

Christmas 1981. How quickly the years pass. Parties popped up night and day, starting on Thursday night. On Thursday afternoon, Rog and Sudi arrived, followed by a truck. In it was a genuine sate ayam maura wagon. Rog bought it for me and had it beautifully restored and painted. Around the same time, the table for the darkroom also arrived. We had a quiet Christmas morning, opening presents before breakfast. Bill arrived, bearing gifts, and we all stopped over at Nick and Jean's house for drinks. It wasn't much of a party, so we caught a cab to Steve and Sita's for lunch. I am about turkeyed out for this year. Steve's was an odd mixture of cornbread stuffing, turkey, rice, and Indonesian food.

Last night was our party. A lot of folks didn't show, and those who did were quieter and more subdued than last year. Party burnout no doubt. We went down to the club today so Rog could "swat the pill," as he calls it, with Lou. We are in the height of the rainy season, so the sun doesn't last, but everything is so green! Stark contrast to New England.

12/29/81

Dear Marthe,

Sue is in the library here at Agawam, balancing her checkbook. One of the fringe benefits— use of the premises for family. I'll have to teach her the telex machine so she can "talk" with you and Rog.

The holidays were, well, holidays. Sue and Bruce Woodbury made a super effort to be fun, and we did have a good time. It was so good to talk with you and Rog. The tree from Washington, New Hampshire, made up in fragrance for what was lacked in form. And Chocko arranged and rearranged the red satin balls on it. I expect they will be turning up in strange places from now until Memorial Day.

Your depressing letter came yesterday, and by the time you receive this, perhaps Wira Perkasa will have landed something to tide you over workwise. Don't overlook the men who handle shareholder/corporate relations for the oil companies, i.e., write the annual reports. That's a market for photos of oil-rich Indonesia. As I recall, your *Photographer's Market* book suggested a number of stock photo houses that handle such reports. You might also find some European contacts in Singapore in this area.

Did you try *Smithsonian Magazine*? They are making an impressive dent in the market of *Geo*/*National Geographic* subscribers. How about good old *Reader's Digest* and *Yankee* for human-interest stories? As you so wisely pointed out with my pictures, people are important in stories too.

Sue has been busy reestablishing old relationships. She has spent some time with the Drinkwaters and went cross-country skiing with Linda today.

Brim and Doris are distressed because some hit-and-run driver smashed the front of their car over the weekend while they were at an anniversary party at the local Holiday Inn. We're just grateful they were not in it at the time. But it's out of service, and the damage is extensive. At times like this, I realize they are aging and it's hard for them to cope with emergencies. But Doris remains strong and positive. That must be where a lot of our "Yankee lady" guts come from.

I have seen very little of Roger these days, and it really hurts. But he won't hang around the apartment/animal house. And I fully understand why. He feels he's intruding, and one more body we just don't need right now.

Sue and I are trying very hard to communicate and not let our living situation, not of either of our choosing, destroy our fine relationship. It's hard for her to be somewhere she doesn't want to be with no job and no room of her own. And it's hard for me to not resent having my life/home taken over. But time will solve the problem. Dad is being wonderfully supportive of me in spirit and sent Sue a check for $150.00 to help. She has no money, so this will buy gas to get around to job interviews.

Tomorrow, she's off to Boston to see Enid Bell and explore the modeling field. And Bruce is coming down tonight. He is not bringing his dog, King, and is renting a room at the Essex Inn. Remembering Barbara Somers and her lessons about "elastic limits," we have set the rules of no more four-legged visitors and no more overnighters when Sue and I are both in residence. A three-room apartment with two dogs, one cat, and two humans is already bursting at the seams.

Frankie is off the list forever—or at least semipermanently. Guess he is depressed and was not always up front with Sue about finances/living arrangements.

God, this really does read like an episode of a soap opera, doesn't it? Never mind. If we cry a lot, it surely beats getting ulcers.

The brightest spot is dear Mr. Mac, your beautiful old dog, and his sheer delight at being back in New England. He's almost stopped scratching, wants to be outside all the time, rolls and runs in the snow, and is as bouncy as a puppy. When are you getting one of those funny Shar-Pei dogs?

Les finally secured a $160,000 bank loan for the business against his house/wife/kids/dog. For the first time since I joined the company, we can pay a few bills. And the clients keep rolling in; small ones to be sure, but in time, it may add up to black ink on the bottom line.

I have all your letters from the last month in front of me, and it is almost like being with you!

Love you most of all,
Madame B.

Dunc and me

CHAPTER 9

A Visit from Home

Journal Entry,
1/1/82

A new year begins! We drove down here to Carita Beach on the southern coast of Java this morning. Thank God (or Allah) for Masudi because without him Rog and I would have stayed home to nurse our hangovers. He and his wife, Titi, arrived at 8:00 a.m. to drive the three-hour trip, which put us in a totally different world. Gone is the city, replaced by countryside whose beauty defies the camera lens to capture it.

So many people and karbu working the rice paddies, a real *National Geographic* special come to life. We stopped briefly, and I waded and slipped my way out into the paddy for some close shots.

When we arrived, we found Gary, Syd, and the boys sharing a three-bedroom bungalow with Chris Hammiter, her two kids, and their grandmother and aunt. Now, this is no Hyatt on the beach in Bali, although the beach is lovely. The ten thousand rupiah per night would buy five nights in Bali, but at least we are free of the city. We rented a couple of grass shacks on the beach. Literally, grass, thatched bamboo huts. Sudi and Titi are in the twin to ours next door. We have the trappings of all the modern conveniences—shower, toilet, even an overhead light with a bulb! The only problem is we have no running water or electricity. I didn't sleep too well for fear of something dropping from the roof on me all night. Roger kept saying, "Just pretend you are camping," but I have never *been* camping!!

We gave up and came home after just one night, but the trip there and back was well worth one night of inconvenience for the sights we saw and the photos I took.

1/6/82

Dear Bird Lady of Jakarta,

Please send pictures either of the birds or the smiling Kuching, whichever comes last! Chocko would go out of his little black mind. He sits in the bedroom window and drools over pigeons on the street.

What do you feed the birds? Any talking parrots? Can you let them out of their cages?

The holidays are over, and each year, some of Sue's Scrooge rubs off on me. At least this year I had a funny straggly tree, and she made a showpiece wreath out of the straw base and a plaid ribbon and some tiny dried flowers in beige and burgundy. She has a real nesting talent. But the whole performance is exhausting and expensive. Roger and I have decided it's more fun to give presents when one feels like it, not when the retailers tell us to.

There is more peace at 156 High Street these days, and it's good to have Sue and Mac there. She is most helpful with the house, keeping it neat in spite of the zoo and stacks of boxes.

Aside from all the turmoil, we have had some dialogue and are getting along very well. It's ladies only at 156, and no four-legged visitors allowed. Bruce is crushed, but so be it.

Today, Sue is in New York. She lined up a good interview in wholesale for tomorrow and had some calls to do today. We bought a beautiful basic gray flannel suit, which looks professional. Cleve's Texas jeans just don't make it in the northeast.

There's a stream of flames (old and new; hers, not mine) through the apartment, but none stay more than a few minutes. No entertaining allowed. The latest is David MacDonald of Rowley. Poor Bruce is just one of the mob!

Had a good share of religion of late. New Year's Eve, Rog and I were up in New Hampshire, and he felt the need to go to Mass, so we stopped at a fascinating Catholic bat-wing-shaped church overlooking the lake in Laconia. Lots of glass, holiday greens, red plants, lay people, and audience participation. Really so much warmer and more realistic than the last time I was in a Roman Catholic Church.

Then last Sunday, Sue and I went to the Christian Science church in Newburyport. She is really finding lots of comfort and strength in what Nana Doris holds to so firmly, and it was a lovely service. They are the most accepting people—sort of a cross between AA and a good therapist! I suppose the Lord is wondering where I'll turn up next.

Love to you. You are never out of my thoughts,
Madame B.

Journal Entry,
1/5/82

I need to sit and collect my thoughts; they are becoming suicidal! If I've been depressed about YAFI, it was at least buoyed up by the thought that when the money came in I would be able to buy a lens and perhaps work on my skills and have something to show for these last twelve weeks of pain. The money came, and all of it went to American Express. We've overextended ourselves once again. One more payment is due from YAFI, so perhaps next time I'll be able to pay myself.

We got the photo essay back from *SilverKris* magazine—a flat rejection. To round out my day, the rolls of film I shot on our way to and from the beach on New Years are all overexposed and ruined. *Nothing* is going right just now.

I'm barely restraining myself from smashing everything in the office just to satisfy the angry bile in my mouth. Do I dare to think that someday I will look back on this time and say, "Well, that all turned out for the best, didn't it?" It's hard to think that way at the moment. I want to lock myself away and pout. A good, old-fashioned cry would cleanse my soul, but I know I can't depend on a shoulder or comfort, so I'll lock it deep inside, set my jaw, and try not to be nasty to everyone in my path. I just want to be alone, but that is impossible in this house!!

1/10/82

Dear Madame B. and Sue (if she is still there),

This weekend, our bird population swelled to six, but one may not be staying. I met Gunilla and her husband, Lou, at the central bird market yesterday. They were there to replace two doves that Gunilla had bought Lou for Christmas. The doves promptly died, one after the other, in a matter of days. Both Anto and Rog had never been to this particular market, so we all went for a look. Now, I never really noticed that it was any different there than anywhere else in the city, but Rog said the smell was making him sick to his stomach, so he went back to wait in the car. There were an abundance of cockatoos for some reason; all sizes and some sulfur-crested ones as well as one with the rare apricot crest. The one that caught my eye was a lovely sulfur-crested female of medium size. She was uncommonly friendly, even to strangers, and very flashy. The price was forty-five thousand rupiah, about seventy-five US dollars, which is good for a young bird. The odd thing is that she has blue around her eyes, which somehow indicates that she is a protected species. Ordinarily, they have pinkish-red around their eyes and those with the blue are not supposed to be exported out of Indonesia.

Well, to make a long story short, she followed us home "on approval" until Monday. When I got back to the car with her, Roger said he hoped Anto had bought the bird and that it had better not have been me who did! Of course I agreed, at least until I could get her home and let her win him over. He still insists that we don't need, can't afford, and don't *want* any more birds. I'll have to work it all out with Anto and the bird market man. I have named her Bianca and hung her wooden perch out on the porch so we can see her when we are eating. She is so tame and lovable that even a confirmed scaredy-cat like myself can't help but fall in love with her. If she is around longer than a few days, I will definitely take some photos and send you a batch.

In other news, Rog is going to Singapore for a few days tomorrow. He has a new employee coming in who will be living up there. Another American, but I don't know any details.

I am rewriting some stories I started awhile back about the black magic here and the Komodo dragons. I have been having terrible luck in selling any photos or stories. So far only rejections, and I've got a drawer full of those! It's hard not to get frustrated, but since the rejections mostly come from query letters, I have to think it is how I'm trying to sell them and not the stories themselves.

By now, hopefully you have received the slides I sent. Can't wait to hear what you and the Agawam crowd thought of them. I got the photo essay back I had sent to the Singapore Airlines magazine. They rejected it, saying the quality was not up to their usual standards. I have been following their photo essays every month for a year and was really disappointed by their reply, as I felt we had sent them some very good stuff. Oh, well. Life in the creative world, right?

Hope you are keeping warm and happy.
Love, M.

1/12/82

Dearest Madam B.,

So good to talk to you this morning. The connection was as if we were right next door instead of on the other side of the world.

Yesterday, I got two letters from you, so I'll begin by answering some of the questions that I didn't get to in our phone conversation. First, about the "aviary." The other day, Anto called the office, and in the course of the conversation, he asked if I was here by myself. I thought a moment and replied that I had lots of company: Bianca the cockatoo, Ike and Mamie the small parrots, Fred, Lester, and Sport—the songbirds upstairs—Kuching, Sukarti, Sukamto, and Suparno. So, no, I can never say I'm all alone here. It seems like every room has *someone* in it if I need to find a friend!

Kuching has resigned himself to the fact that all the food in cages around here will never be a meal for him. The two parrots are both on separate wooden perches, and the cockatoo is also on a perch, although hers must be made out of metal or she eats the whole thing in one evening. They all have chains attached to one leg, leading to their perch. Ike and Mamie will probably never be tame or speak, and now Roger wants to get rid of them since his beloved Ike tried to bite him! We let Bianca loose in the office for a few hours every day to exercise. She doesn't show much interest in flying away although she will fly from wherever she is sitting to my shoulder if I call her. She is, however, very destructive and must be watched at all times if she is loose. She will eat any wood she comes in contact with and adores tearing up paper and butts from the ashtray.

The parrots and Bianca eat only corn on the cob, fresh daily from the vegetable sellers, if you please! The others all eat a prepared mix of dead ants, seeds, and nuts that I buy at the bird market. The cages have to be cleaned every day, but everyone takes a turn at it, and it's not too bad a chore. Roger shows little or no interest in them although Bianca flutters to his shoulder at every opportunity.

I have been keeping busy researching story ideas lately. Saturday, I had an interview with a lady who is a princess from Solo. She owns and operates the largest factory in Indonesia for the production of Jamu, herbal medications and traditional herbal makeup. It is not exported to the States as yet, but she has been to Washington and met with the FDA and hopes to set up some marketing there in a year or so. With all the interest in China and "back to nature" in the States now, I think she could do well if she ever gets past the red tape to export her goods.

Though I know it must be a strain on you and Susanne to be living in such tight quarters, I hope you can keep in mind the close relationships we all share. Knowing that the arrangement is only temporary, keep a good understanding of each other's needs and moods. Someday, as you say, you will look back and laugh about the winter of '82 and think, *How did we ever keep our sanity??* Be patient with each other, and enjoy the closeness I would give my eyeteeth to be sharing.

Our weather is depressing these days. The month of January is the height of the rainy season here, and it stays dark and dreary all day. Makes it tough to wake up in the mornings, and it's usually noon before I get to taking a bath and running errands. I made a vow to begin the New Year with a riding program of some kind to get back into shape. It looks like I would need a seahorse if I want to ride these days!!

Love you dearly, and you are always with me in my thoughts and mind. Hope you are keeping warm and cozy.

M.

1/13/82

Dearest Marthe,

Let me tell you how it is in the Deep Freeze of New England. Remember those big bowls we put water in for Mac? There is one beside the back door inside the kitchen. It has ice around the edges!

Chocko dropped his catnip mouse in the bowl, and it's frozen to the side! Reminds me of the mornings we would find dead mice in the horses' water buckets.

Last night, Sue put on her mittens and hat, and Mac got all excited. He thought she was going to take him for a walk. Not so. She was only going to the kitchen. Zero degrees and below, the heating system in this old building just can't cope. It runs all the time until the pipes vibrate and still never gets above sixty-five degrees. Now aren't you glad you live in the tropics??

Next item. Remember the Bali bag you left with me? Chocko was chewing on the handles, so I looked around for someplace to put it until he "grows up." Selected the top of the really tall closet next to the fireplace in the bedroom. Last night, Lydia and I were lying in bed, listening to a rustling and trying to figure out where the black devil was hiding. Up popped his head out of the Bali bag! Now tell me he's not related to Rosemary's baby??

All is well here at 156 High Street. We're healthy and getting along famously. Seemed to have coped with the underlying problems of: 1) What Sue will do for gainful employment? and 2) Where will she live? Nothing as of the moment to the first, and right where she is to the second. She has nearly completed her photo sessions with Frank Dalton for her portfolio and will be ready to hit the modeling agencies soon. She made all her contacts in New York and can only wait now for a break.

In the meantime, what's to be done? Might as well enjoy our time together, and we are doing that. The animals are spoiled but amusing. We have a diet of natural foods—sprouts, spinach and Syrian bread. We may be poor, but we are healthy.

I had a lovely twenty-four hours with my Roger at the Cape over the weekend. So nice to get away, and although we had snow on Saturday evening, a fire in the fireplace was so comforting.

When I got back to Newburyport, Sue and I went to the Grog for salads and wished so much you were with us. We are forever coming up with one-liners and stories and saying, "Marthe would appreciate this!"

Tonight, there is more snow on the way; at least that will break the bitter cold weather we have been enduring. I have a new battery for the Datsun so starting should be much more reliable. Cross your fingers that Sue can find her place in the scheme of things.

We surely do miss you so very much.
Love, Madame B.

Journal Entry,
1/29/82

Exhausted, beat up, wrung out, empty, and dry inside. The underside of my skin feels sore and raw. Depression seeps in between my clenched teeth and fists.

In a way, I'm relieved that Sue and Mac are at Mom's. It would be crazy to think there would be room for just one more depressed, unemployed person there. I would run back to that nest in a moment otherwise.

Judo has not been heard from for two weeks now. I have had to do just about all of the cataloguing, framing, and selecting of photos, all correspondence, a sales call to Bank Bumi Daya, plus tell everyone else what to do.

Rog has been busy with Ed Dillon, his boss from Houston all week. It's been a long week, and today was a total write-off, as I had to take Ed shopping all day. Thank God, at least I had exclusive use of Sudi for the day.

1/30/82

Dear Mom and Sue,

Guess I've been a bit lax about my correspondence lately. It's been a busy week around here with Roger's Houston guests. Roger's boss from Houston, Ed Dillon, here for the weekend, joined Randy, the new employee for the Singapore office. We first met Ed when we lived in Olney. He remarked that we certainly had come a long way from those days.

Randy left Monday, and Ed was here for the week, which meant we had to entertain him. Several nights, he and Rog went out looking for hookers. Now you know it was *quite* an education for the puritanical Kid Kidder!! He was aghast that Ed, or anyone for that matter, would have such an inclination. I got a good chuckle out of it and almost hoped he would carry his education a bit further and indulge himself, but he was home as soon as Ed found a girl every night. Hope Ed didn't catch any "souvenirs" on his nightly forays.

I'm getting a bit fed up with this company of mine. It's becoming more responsibility and work than I bargained for. Since I'm the only one whose native tongue is English and can also swing a passable Indonesian conversation, I end up doing both sides of the sales and marketing of our stock photos. Anto and Judo think I make a more interesting sales person to the local businesses with my fairly decent command of Bahasa Indonesia. I was on an elevator the other day in one of the downtown office buildings on my way to a sales call with a bank. Two Indonesian businessmen looked me over and proceeded to comment about me in Indonesian. As they were getting ready to exit the elevator, I piped up and said, "You really should be more careful what you say about people" in my best Indonesian! You would have loved the looks on their faces.

We received Roger's bonus check for this year and have set aside two thousand dollars for your ticket in the hopes that you can get here. We were thinking that now would be a good time if you can get away, as Sue is not too tied up and she could possibly zoo-sit for you. The rainy season is winding down, and the sun comes out every day for a few hours. Please do think about it; we both want you to come sooo badly!!

Bianca shit on my shoulder this morning, so she is in disgrace. She is relegated to her perch for the afternoon, and every time I go past, she coos funny little bird-talk I'm sorrys. Kucing was horrified that anyone would do such a thing and smugly follows at my heels. Ike is spending the day trying to thwart the chain on his foot so he can take off for vacation. Mamie is quiet for a change and probably up to no good. The songbirds are so happy that the sun is shining that they are singing themselves hoarse.

Sport, the first bird I bought, surprised us the other day by laying an egg. She then proceeded to eat it! I spoke with the man who helps me out at the bird market, and he said she would continue with this behavior until we found her an appropriate mate, a proper place to nest, or let her go completely. Since none of those alternatives were viable, Sport has enjoyed her egg for breakfast all week. This morning, she seems to have given up her tactics for freedom and, hopefully, is not too badly psychologically damaged by the whole ordeal. I thought this was supposed to be a carefree type of pet!!

Well, that's all for now from our zoo. Hope yours is doing well and that you are keeping warm.

Love to both of you,
M.

Journal Entry,
3/4/82

Most of this week has been a waste businesswise. Today, we had two meetings. In the morning, we had a second follow-up meeting with Bapak Willi from Diwi Lestari. It looks really good for at least one calendar order with possibilities for two more and some brochures.

In the afternoon, Bapak Darmawan came to the office to view some slides and talk about decorating his office. I really want to do a logo shot for him using the new filters. Sold him on the idea of using the shot in his office reception area.

Also had visits from my two regulars, Eiko and Mas Tok. Eiko and Jim are having a rough spell. I hate getting caught in the middle of things like this, especially when it involves one of Roger's largest customers. Mas Tok is so supportive of our business, and being a photographer himself, he is interested in everything we do. Of course, having the ex-president's son as a friend is not a bad thing either!

Yesterday we got a telex from Mom saying that she and Dunc want to come mid- to late April. I'm so excited I don't even dare hope that it will really come true. Dunc will really be freaked out since he's never been out of the States before. I just know that if they really do make it, it will be an experience we all will never forget.

Rog leaves tomorrow night for the States. He will be gone for about ten days.

Gunilla has started coming to work less now, as she wanted to get back into her old social circle, and with the work from YAFI dried up, there is less for her to do. I miss her terribly, but at least we still talk on the phone daily. This leaves Anto and me to make sales calls and keep plodding on through the fog.

3/11/82

Dearest Marthe,

No, Newburyport did not fall into the harbor and get washed out to sea. Les did not take the typewriter away from me. Every day, I've been looking for ten minutes to myself and have not found it until just now. For the first time since last October, we have temps in the sixties! It's not spring, but one can feel it coming. Night before last, there was one of our many mini-snowstorms. I am getting really good at scraping the windshield in record time. But winter is over!

And just to prove it, Sue and I have colds/flu, whatever the current malady is called. Everything from frontal headaches that make a lobotomy sound super, to a hack any menthol smoker would be proud to own. We've decided the only way to win is to go on a liquid diet. The menu today has been apple juice and unsweetened tea. Now don't you wish you were here???

The job situation remains the same. Sue is pounding the pavement, calling everyone we can think of, and waitressing three nights a week. She has a neat system for answering ads, follow-up dates, making appointments, and such. Says if she never gets a job, at least she can counsel on career-search methods. She has applied to everyone from the CIA to Trans National Travel to the Red Cross. Your suggestions were good, and your letter very "up" for her psyche. I feel something will break for her soon; she has so many leads out there. Meanwhile, we keep to her model's regimen—no red meat, lots of greens and fruit, brush our hair a lot, and clean our faces with special soap. She even takes Mac to the beach on good mornings for an hour workout.

The string of suitors is trailing down High Street. Bruce Brown plays big-brother lunch, dinner, and moral support. Chris Green is still about, and a new one who works as a part-time bartender. A few drop off the list and a few join.

Stay well and warm.
Madame B.

Journal Entry,
3/19/82

Came back yesterday morning from Singapore on the first flight to Jakarta. Anto was out shooting Sonia's fashion show. It seemed like I had never left.

Jakarta started erupting last night. Cars and buses were attacked on the streets, and many were burned. One guy from the Baroid office, Henry, was pulled from his car and beaten. The preelection riots have started.

Kucing hasn't been home since last night. He was vomiting at the dinner table last night, and I'm so afraid he is very sick, maybe even dead. We've found three dead rats, and I fear the worst. It's so empty without him. Doesn't do much for my already smoldering state of mind.

The quicksand is rising; my body and soul seem to be suspended in space, searching for solid bottom with half-hearted limbs outstretched.

3/31/82

Dear Madam B.,

Sorry it's been so long since you heard from me. I've been running around like crazy trying to get things ready for your visit, cleaning the house and gardens, doing all the decorating that we've put off since moving into this house. It's all starting to look quite nice, but poor Roger is confused every time he comes home, as things are moved around and he can't find anything!

Speaking of Roger, he doesn't get to Jakarta very much these days. In the last month, he has been home a total of six days. I tried to talk to him about it, but it seems I'm just one more problem on his list of things that take up his time and have to be seen to as soon as he has a free moment.

His trip to the States really took a lot out of him. When I met him in Singapore, I had hoped to persuade him to stay a day or two there so we could have time together and he could catch up on his rest. But he came right back to Jakarta for a few days and then had to go offshore. At least there he gets regular meals and lots of rest.

I realized from your last letter that you and Dunc will only be here for nine days. It will take a few days to get over the jet lag, and that doesn't leave much time to see anything but Jakarta. I had hoped we could get over to Bali for a few days also, but you won't want to see another plane for a while, so we can just hang out around here. I spoke with George and Eleanor, who work for Roger in Singapore. They said that we could bunk with them if you want to stop over there. They have a small place, but it would be fun for a night or two if you have any interest. It makes more of an impression after you have seen Jakarta, as the first time through it just seems like another big, American city. I have booked your tickets from Singapore to Jakarta and back and will confirm and telex a few days before you leave the States.

You will be most comfortable if you bring light cotton clothes and mostly skirts and t-shirts. Things are very informal, so one good dress so we can go out to dinner will see you through. Shoes should be low and comfortable, as you will really notice your height here. Everything is made for small people! I would highly recommend a good sunscreen and sunglasses, as the sun is really bright and strong these days. Be sure to pack your suit so we can hang out at the club a day or two. I'm so pale it's embarrassing but will get a weekend in on the ninth of next month when we go to a resort with Lou and Gunilla for three days.

There are a few things I'd ask you to check on before you come over if you have the time and energy. Rog mentioned he sent you a check for a new copy of the *Black Book* like the one Richelli gave me when I was there. So good for researching markets for photos, etc. If it isn't too heavy, can you bring it along? If you go to a camera store, I could always use some of those plastic pages that hold twenty slides. I think they are about forty-five to fifty cents each and are very hard (read, impossible to get here).

Two other questions. Could you please try to call Mr. Forsyth at the Design Photographers International and ask him what the hell ever happened to all the slides I sent him? The number is 212-752-3930. I received a card from him back in February saying he had received the slides that a guy sent for me from Houston, but no word since. The second is that you might receive something in the mail from *International Wildlife*. I submitted a bunch of slides and stories; they were to send any material they didn't want to me in care of you. Rog has one request, the usual *Playboy*, *Penthouse*, and any other porn that you might pick up. Not for him, of course, but for his customers. The airport customs here are very efficient and seldom open a bag. That's not to say that you should be completely honest with the custom's people, as porn is illegal here. But they won't be looking for it with a lady like you! You will not have the same intimidating situations that we faced in Trinidad. These folks are downright friendly and very helpful to foreigners.

I only wish I could kidnap you and Dunc and not let you go home until you've seen a bit of the country. Perhaps, if you like what you see this time, you'll be able to get back over for another trip. It's a lot of money for such a short stay, but I don't mean to sound whiny. Any time with you will be so wonderful!

You've no idea how much it means to me to know that each day the time grows shorter until I'll be able to wake up and say, "Today Madam B. arrives!"

M.

Journal Entry, 4/1/82

Kucing is back and seems fine. Silly little cat means the world to me.

Six days after we got back from Singapore, Rog went offshore again. He was gone six days but managed to call a couple of times. I spent my time getting ready for Mom and Dunc's visit.

When Rog did get home, we had one of our late-night discussions. He sees only two alternatives: quit his job or divorce. If it comes to that, he has said flat out that he will not quit. There is not enough time in his life for me, and if I must live my life alone, I want to really *be* alone and free to make my own decisions. I see one of two things happening. One, I leave now and the general opinion will be "Poor Martha, she got fed up waiting and left. So sad for both of them," or two, he holds on to me until I finally feel strong enough and find someone else who will love me and have time for me. In that case, the opinion will be "Poor Rog, busting his ass all those years for her and the bitch ran off and dumped him for someone else."

Where does the blame really lie? Does it matter who is to blame? Can my frozen guts ever thaw to melt and really feel again? I'm cold inside although I don't really feel much of anything but a cold hard lump where my heart used to be.

We seem to have grown so completely apart that even our memories differ radically. I brought up the violence in Trinidad, and Rog summed it up that we, at least, had escaped any real incidents. May 4 will never leave my mind; 1980 was a violent year for me. Or does he think the rape didn't happen??

4/9/82

Dearest Marthe,

Getting closer and have your letter from yesterday giving me some good suggestions about what to wear/bring. It won't really come to me that we'll be having coffee together soon until I get to Logan Airport. Right now it is still like a dream!

We are just digging out from the snowstorm of the year on Grandpa Brim's birthday, April 6. Started with dry powder snow and high winds coupled with a full moon and flood tide. There are drifts alongside Route 1A over ten feet high. Susanne and I made it to Agawam the first day, but we could not get either car out by the second. You may be sure there are a lot of confused robins wondering where spring went.

Received Rog's telex and have requested the stock Power of Attorney forms. I have your plastic sheets for slides. Also, spoke with DPI today, and Forsyth is away until Tuesday. They tell me your material has been received, but he will call me next week with further info. The *Black Book* has been ordered, and I'll surely bring it if it arrives in time. I have gathered up drawer pulls, Heath bars, porno mags, and anything else that will fit. The customs agents will surely scratch their heads at my strange cargo if they open any bags. Dunc and I plan on only carry-on bags. We have a change in Atlanta on the way to the West coast and then our connection in Hong Kong, so thought it would be better not to fight with baggage transfers. We just want to get there ASAP.

Mostly, I think it would be fun to hang out locally with you. Perhaps a day in Singapore before returning if you can come too. There must be much to do/see within the range of Jakarta that you think we might enjoy. I know the time is short. But I'm still marveling that Dunc is going overseas and that Les isn't giving me any hassle about taking the time off from work.

I will start making a list of things for us to talk about *in person*! I really never got used to your being halfway around the world. This will be the treat/trip of the century!

Thinking of you so very often and love you ever so much,
Madam B.

Journal Entry,
4/25/82

In just ten hours, a Singapore Air jet will deposit Dunc and Mom at Halima International Airport here. So much has happened, and I'm so very unprepared for their arrival. This house is in shambles in more ways than one. The workmen are everywhere, trying to fix the water systems. But worse yet is the situation with Rog and me.

I spent last night at the Sari Hotel. It all came about following a terrible fight between Rog and me. As I left the house, I took the strangest things with me. No hairbrush or comb, no clothes, no toothbrush or passport even. Instead, in my frenzied state of mind, I grabbed my jewelry, all Mom's old letters to me, last year's diary, and my camera. How am I going to put on a happy face and get through this?

Journal Entry,
4/30/82
Pelabuhan Ratu

The days have sped by since Dunc and Mom arrived. Organizing this many people and coordinating everyday life has taken every waking minute, but I wouldn't change it for anything. We came down here last night, just the three of us. Rog will be coming down with John tonight. It's so peaceful and relaxing, like another world.

The day they arrived, I was up very early to finish all the last-minute cleaning. The plane came in at 9:00 a.m., and I could barely contain myself until they walked out through customs. We hung around the house, and Dunc fell in love with my crazy bird, Bianca.

In the afternoon, we went to Heros for groceries and did a quick spin through town. Tuesday, we got up early to breakfast on the upper balcony. Everything fascinates them—all the early-morning tukans, the vegetable man, becas, and everyday activities that I no longer notice. We set out with Sudi, and our first stop was the bird market. Dunc wants to bring home a cockatoo. We looked at lots and decided to check out the legality first. It looked like rain, so we decided to go to Jalan Surabaya for shopping and antiques. We only made it about a quarter of the way down the street before we stopped for lunch at Satè Senyan. Mom loves the satè and gado gado. Dunc is like a little kid (albeit a tall one here) discovering the world all over again.

The rain had cleared during lunch, so we headed to the waterfront to Sunda Kelapa to look at the big sailing ships. The massive vessels fascinated Dunc, and although he can't speak Indonesian, it didn't stop him from chatting away with all the sailors and running up and down the gangplanks as the ships were being loaded. Mom was merrily snapping pictures. Sudi was a model tour guide and loved Dunc's excitement at his country.

We went to dinner at the Petroleum Club, a huge contrast to the down-and-dirty city tour I had taken them on during the day.

This morning, Mom and I watched the sun rise from our fifth floor balcony here at the beach resort. We got Dunc up at 6:00 a.m. for breakfast, and by 8:00, we started hiking into town. It was a pleasant walk along the road, and we got lots of great landscape and human-interest shots. We came upon a film crew working on an Indonesian movie and causing quite a stir among the villagers. After about three-quarters of the way to town, Mom was tiring, so we hailed one of the many passing minibuses that took us right to the central market. Although it was almost ten, the market was still crowded with activity and strange smells. We wandered from stall to stall, checking out the batik, tobacco sellers, dried fish, hardware, baskets, and a multitude of other items.

Across the street was the fish market. Boats were still coming in, met by dozens of sinewy men, each carrying a bamboo pole on one shoulder with two baskets suspended. The men on board off-loaded their cargo into the baskets and the basket men scurried back to a tin-roofed cement warehouse where the fish were weighed and spread out for sale. Sharks and sailfish at least six feet long, stingrays the size of a dinner table, and other assorted smaller specimens littered the slippery cement floor.

We took a dokar (donkey cart) ride up to the hotel/cottages where Rog and I had stayed over Easter vacation and had a cool drink while we rested in a shady, open-air restaurant. Another dokar ride back down to the market landed us just in time to catch the hotel bus back to Samudra Beach. We thought we had the entire minibus to ourselves until a stop in front of the local school added about forty-five small passengers. Little brown children in clean white shirts with blue skirts and shorts piled in all around us, four or more to a seat. Though they were jammed in, they behaved most politely, and the noise level was minimal. Curious eyes turned away when we tried to meet their shy stares, and I caught several comments about Mom, "the beautiful lady with the golden hair."

It was so nice to have Mom and Dunc all to myself. They are both such ardent sightseers and excellent company. I'm proud to show them the world I live in.

Rog and John arrived late in the afternoon with Anto. We all went to the buffet and cultural show for dinner. I am repeatedly amazed by Dunc's lack of self-consciousness and his bounding enthusiasm. The entertainment included various dances by Sudanese performers. At the end of the show, four lady dancers picked partners from the audience to join them. Anto and Dunc literally jumped at the opportunity, and the hotel photographer recorded the gaiety.

5/11/82

Selamat Ulang Tahun, Madam B. (Happy birthday!)

One week ago today, we were still in Singapore, enjoying the tail end of your first visit to the Far East. Needless to say, I was rather blue all day Wednesday after you left. Finished up what errands I had to do and then jumped on the 5:00 p.m. flight to Jakarta. I'm so glad that we did have that last day in Singapore, as I saw many places I had never visited and likely never would have seen had you not been there to enjoy it with me.

Reports are still coming in from people who met you and Dunc. The general consensus is that I have the neatest family anyone ever met! (That's without anyone meeting Sue. She would really bowl them over!!) Sudi talks about Dunc to the exclusion of everything else these days. He is all set to take off for Houston and get a job driving for "Mr. Duncan." Sukarti said that she was sorry she missed saying good-bye on Tuesday and keeps talking about how young and beautiful my mom is. Gunilla was enthralled with you both and made special mention that Dunc is really neat.

Now Jakarta is full of new memories for me. Every time I pass by Monas, the monument we climbed, or go to any of the places that we visited, I think of you and remember your wonderful reactions to my home. It really made me see the city again as a different sort of place instead of just the same old hustle and bustle.

I found your note in my daily diary when I got back to my room in Singapore. (I knew/hoped there'd be one somewhere!) Of course, it made me all weepy but happy to know that that morning in Pelabuhan Ratu we really did share another sunrise.

Now we've got to figure out how we can do the whole trip again and for longer next time. I'll do some traveling around Indonesia and find the best spots to visit. And, of course, you have to come back to see Bali.

Anto had to leave on Friday for his sister's wedding in Central Java. I am taking the train out in a few days to join him and photograph the whole affair. Lots to do in the office in the meantime, as we are finishing up an advertising project.

Dunc's big bird is cleaning herself up and getting quite fat for her journey to Houston. Oscar is his usual charming self, and Bianca is her usual bitchy self to everyone but me. Yesterday, I looked out of the office window to see Bianca on Oscar's perch with her perch and chain wrapped around both of them. I got them untangled, and the next time I looked, she was over on the perch of Dunc's Ladybird. Ladybird had fled to the tree, and Bianca was trying to pull her off by her chain! She is such a witch to the other two birds.

Kucing is fat and sassy. He still sleeps in "your" bed all night and seems quite content to chase the little sparrows and leave the bigger white beasts alone.

I love you dearly,
M.

The bridal party and me

CHAPTER 10

Trains Across Java

Journal Entry,
5/18/82
On the way to Surabaya

So this is to be my seat for the next sixteen-plus hours. I had rather expected something a bit more private, but at least I'm finally on the train. I had a two-day delay when I realized that I would just have to reshoot the photos of the Hotel Indonesia for the postcard job we are working on. The political slogans on the flags and banners were prolific, and there was no way to crop them out.

It's incredibly hot in here; smells something like a barnyard, and we haven't even left the station. Already an hour and a half late, and no signs of movement. My hands are sticking to the page as I write and a drop of sweat just trickled into my ear.

Later ...

It's now 7:30 p.m. We have been underway for at least a half hour but still haven't left the city limits. The air conditioning that was advertised seems to be starting up slowly or perhaps I'm just getting used to the heat.

It's now 10:30 p.m. Air conditioning is working, dinner is over, and most of the other passengers are sleeping. We are supposed to have twelve hours left to go, but I'm betting this will take longer. The lack of privacy was unexpected, as I paid for a "first class" seat. We have eighteen rows of seats in each train car, two on either side of the aisle. I have a window seat, and on my right is a young Indonesian guy who is a bit too attentive. On the other hand, it was nice to have him lead the way to the dining car. Dinner was three train cars back. The crossing between cars was a narrow platform as we chugged along in the dark. The menu was typical, traditional fare: sayur asam (Tamarind vegetable soup), rice, and fried tempeh.

The only other foreigners on the train are a Dutch couple. They are probably in their late twenties and do not represent their country well. Indonesians are sticklers for cleanliness even under the poorest conditions. These two are scruffy-looking hippies with really bad body odor.

Midnight, and we've made it to Cirebon. Our last stop was in the middle of nowhere. I went forward to check out the facilities and struck up a conversation with a steward. He figures we will make Surabaya by noon, give or take an hour. Though the Bima train from Yogyakarta back to Jakarta is more expensive, it doesn't stop at every village and town along the way, so I may opt for that on the way home.

It's now 4:00 a.m. Pekanlongan is behind us, and it is on to Semarang where they say we will change locomotives and, hopefully, pick up some time. I have discovered what it is that smells like a rotting pumpkin—the blanket/sheet/cover the stewards passed out to us when we were all dying from the heat. It's cool now, but I think I'll forgo use of said cover.

It's 7:30 a.m. The sun is up, and Semarang is behind us. We are moving slowly through the villages. Kids of every shape and size line the rails, waving, laughing, and pointing as though they've never seen a train before although this train passes every day. The houses look so frail—woven, palm-leaf walls supporting orange ceramic tile roofs. One can't help but wonder what a good, strong wind would do. I marvel at the occupants' faith in the elements.

Not much sleep last night, but I really can't complain. This is a magical journey all by myself to the heart of Java. Anto's sister is to be married in a traditional Javanese ceremony, and I have the honor of photographing it.

From Semarang they say it will be anywhere from six to eight hours. I just hope Anto can meet me at the station.

Journal Entry,
5/20/82
Surabaya

I had wanted so very much to start writing about my arrival last night, but when I finally got to bed, I was utterly exhausted. Anto met me at the station and brought me back to his parents' house. I was so tired and confused by a million introductions that I constantly felt left out and on the verge of tears. His mother had made arrangements for me to stay with family friends down the street. It is heavenly! I have a lovely, large room with a double bed, three mirrors, and a fan. Much to my delight, I even have a guling pillow, better known as a "Dutchman's wife" (body pillow). I barely had time to bathe before heading back to Anto's house for the start of the festivities.

The beginning ceremonies were for the bride, a blessing from her parents—the ritualistic bathing followed by cutting her hair into an intricate pattern around her face. It was all a bit confusing to me, and trying to photograph while staying out of everyone's way was frustrating. Just when I thought things were finishing up, the groom and his entourage appeared to meet with the parents of the bride.

Today is the actual wedding ceremony, and the reception will be held tonight.

Later ...

While I understand that Anto was needed for the ceremony and reception, it was difficult being on my own in all this. There were so many people who not only knew each other but also knew exactly what was going on. I needed a tour guide. All anyone ever said to me was "Makan, makan—sudah capai?" which loosely translates into "Eat, eat before it is all gone." It's as if they all thought I only understood three words.

In truth, the wedding was beautiful and dream-like with all the ceremonies and costumes. I was a bit taken aback by this morning's proceedings. The bride did not appear until the paperwork was signed between the families formalizing the dowry. An awful dose of chauvinism that I hadn't expected.

When all this is over, Anto and I are headed to Yogyakarta for a week of shooting temples and such. I can't get out of here fast enough.

Journal Entry,
5/22/82
En route to Yogyakarta

I'm back on a train alone. This one left Surabaya on schedule at 5:15 a.m. My "second class" seat is not as plush as the Mutiara train I took from Jakarta to Surabaya, but it's comfortable even without the air conditioning.

The strangest thing happened last night, and while I am shocked and angered, at least I feel I have a better understanding of Anto and his family dynamics and, on a wider perspective, the culture. We went out to a small restaurant for dinner. I was worried about what his mother would say about this, as she has shown an obvious dislike for me. When we got back to his house, it was in its usual chaotic state, full of guests. We asked his mother to show us the ceramic collection she wants to sell. She made a horribly disgusted face and then begrudgingly led us to a small room. As it turned out, she couldn't get into the room where the ceramics were stored, as it was jam-packed with wedding gifts.

She then turned to me and started speaking in broken English, saying she wanted to discuss a problem about her son with me. I couldn't for a moment figure out who or what she meant. Then it dawned on me that she was referring to Anto—talking about him as if he was either a half-wit kid or not standing right next to her.

She explained to me that the arts, and photography in particular, were fine for a hobby but not a life's vocation. Since Anto was still so young and irresponsible, in her opinion, he needed guidance to lead him back to school to get his degree. She went on and on about how deeply disappointed they were that Anto had not finished college and how necessary it was for someone like myself to guide him back to the "right course" so he could develop into an adult.

At first, I was dumbfounded and then thoroughly disgusted. Finally, I can only pity her. The harder she grasps at him, trying to mold his life, the further she pushes him away. But now at least I can understand why she doesn't like me. She feels I am responsible for influencing this poor, impressionable young boy away from what she thinks is the right road to follow. It's her loss, as she totally humiliated him in front of me.

Journal Entry, 5/24/82 Yogyakarta

I got into town and found a small hotel. It was noisy and dirty, so yesterday I moved to another hotel. Anto arrived last night.

Today was the true beginning of our *keliling* (adventure) as well as Anto's birthday.

We started by renting a motorcycle and going back to Taman Sari, the Water Castle. I had gone there alone yesterday but had missed a lot of it as it is being renovated. The kampong (village) has grown up around it and ancient walls have been incorporated into the houses of the villagers, so it is very hard to get a feel for how it looked when it was built.

A lovely little old man acted as our guide and took us through the entire compound. It made more sense, and I saw places I had missed, such as the masjid. This two-level, underground mosque was cool and crumbling, eerily held together and echoing ages past. Following our tour, we headed out of town to the northeast. Sixteen kilometers away, we reached Prambanan—a fantastic temple rising out of the rice paddies. Though there were tour buses and hundreds of tourists, we managed to wander around at our own pace and avoid the crowds. To look at this structure and realize that it has stood for over one thousand years gives one a sense of permanence. Ye, I couldn't help also feeling how short one's life is and how miniscule one person is in the fabric of the world.

We sat on the steps leading down from the eastern doorway to the main temple just as the sun set. I tried to collect my thoughts and realize exactly where in time and space I was. From places to temples to all the smaller experiences along the way, I have never felt emotions so profoundly, so compellingly as to actually make me sorry I was not born into this culture.

Journal Entry,
5/25/82
Yogyakarta

We spent the day at Borobudur Temple, one of the Seven Wonders of the World. This Buddhist monument was built before Cambodia's Angkor Wat and long before the great European cathedrals.

When we arrived, we were immediately swept up in a crowd of tourists. The temple is under reconstruction, and much of the lower area was cordoned off. Its massive grace is somewhat lost amidst the cranes and construction equipment until one climbs to the uppermost main terrace. Looking downward through the maze of stupas and stonework to the serene paddies and village life below or upward to the mountain of stone that forms the main stupa, life is dwarfed and man is humbled.

After the crowds with their pocket cameras followed their megaphoned tour guide back down to the buses, we were left in peace with the gentle breezes and misty mountains as a backdrop.

5/30/82

Dear Madam B.,

By now you probably think I'm lost in the heart of Central Java, wandering around, never to be heard from again. Well, that's not too far from the truth. In spirit I'm still there, though my body arrived back in Jakarta on Friday morning at 6:00 a.m.

The wedding was an amazing submersion into ancient Javanese culture but also exhausting, as I was just one of a huge crowd and the only foreigner. Anto had little time for me, and I was set adrift to try to understand the many ceremonies. Although people were very courteous, everyone knew their part in the performance as well as each other, and I felt very alone.

After three days, I headed out alone by train to Yogyakarta. Anto had a few more parties to attend, but I was spent. I arrived around noon on Saturday, found a hotel, and stashed my stuff. Yogya is in fact a city but very different from Jakarta. The lack of Western influence means it is steeped in its ancient culture. It seems to move more slowly, and the arts are everywhere. There are no wide, tree-lined boulevards and no taxis. Most of the traffic is becaks and *andongs* (four-wheeled, horse-drawn carts), as well as the usual mish-mash of antique cars and motorcycles. It felt kind of nice to be alone after the hubbub and constant chaos of the wedding.

My only complaint about the city is that it is near a volcano that has been erupting lately, and the air is filled with fine grit that gets into your eyes, ears, nose, and camera.

I lucked out and found a lovely little guesthouse that was clean and had a courtyard that was filled with songbirds in cages to wake me up with lovely tunes in the morning. My room had a traditional *permandian* bath. This consists of a small, tiled room with an open-topped, tile-sided tank in one corner. The tank has a dipper and a fresh towel nearby. The water in the tank is not heated, but remember, it is hot this close to the equator. Bathing is done by standing over the drain in the middle of the room: dip, splash, lather, dip, splash, and rinse. I brought my own soap and shampoo. Other necessities are also done over a hole in the floor with two conveniently placed footprints. If the hosts know there is a foreigner visiting, they frequently provide a small roll of rough, gray toilet paper. Again, I brought my own.

Meals were very cheap, and I found I could get fried rice with a couple of fresh fruit drinks for about $1.60. I had not brought anything to read except my Java guidebooks, and those I had pretty much memorized at this point, so I went looking for an English-language newspaper or magazine. There were none to be found, so I bought an Indonesian fashion magazine and surprised myself by being able to read all of it!

Yogya is the seat of the ancient palaces and kingdoms and is so rich in history. Java Man was found not far from there as well as his later cousin, Solo Man. It was in Central Java that the great dynasties reigned long before Europe ever got themselves out of the Dark Ages. The ruins of a palace called Taman Sari, the Water Castle, are right in the center of the city. It was an amazing feat of architectural skill that brought the ocean to the city, and the water circled around the partially underground palace, making for natural air-conditioning.

The sultan of the time who commissioned this extravaganza must have led a lovely life; this was his summer pleasure palace. He had beds in every building that leads one to think either he did a lot of resting or that his sixteen wives kept him very busy. One area, which has been restored, is an enormous sunken courtyard. In the center are three huge swimming pools for bathing. A building on one end has a sort of tower where it is said the sultan sat to watch his wives bathe. Sounds like a very horny fellow to me!

On Monday, when Anto finally arrived, we rented a motorcycle and visited the Prambanan and Borobudur Temples. One feels very small and insignificant standing beside the great stone monuments to a power that man, through the ages, has given so many varied names and faces. No matter if the builders were Hindu or Buddhist, Muslim or Christian, they all were seeking to bestow upon the earth some semblance of understanding of the greater powers that created him.

The train home on Thursday night was the absolute pits, and I was really glad Anto was there at least to share the misery. It was the dirtiest I had ridden so far, and the lights were out the whole way. We arrived early and caught a taxi to the house. Luckily, Rog had not left for work yet, as we were flat broke and couldn't even pay the taxi driver.

It was a trip, Mom, that taught me so much about the culture and people of this land, which I thought I already knew so well. To have spent ten days eating, speaking, sleeping, bathing, and living as an Indonesian was something I will cherish and never forget.

Pictures to follow.

I love you dearly,
M.

6/9/82

Dearest Marthe,

At last, a letter from you and one from Rog! I was getting frantic, worrying that you were indeed lost in Central Java. Would have sent a telex had I not heard today.

The material came back from *National Wildlife* magazine. I'm enclosing their letter. Sounds like they were pleased with what you sent.

Your letter was fantastic. Gave me a feeling for what your trip was like and how native you have become. What was Anto's family like? Is he different in his family setting? Looking forward to seeing your pictures. What a lifetime opportunity to experience the culture. I really want to come back now and see Bali and the Borobudur.

I have been reading the two books suggested in your Java guidebook—*Passage of Arms* by Ambler, the story of gunrunning during the start of World War II in Indonesia and *South of Java Head* by Alistair McLean about the last boat out of Singapore before the Japanese invasion. They are both excellent and meant something to me because I knew what the authors were talking about in those settings.

Today is moving day for Susanne, and we just loaded all the boxes and pictures she had stored here at Agawam into the company van. It will mean so much to her to have her things all together for the first time in three years.

Susanne and I have maintained a good feeling in spite of the last few weeks. I honestly believe we both relied heavily on Christian Science for our sense of harmony, and it has worked. Everyone at Agawam appreciates her devotion and professionalism. Les is beside himself with admiration, though he still gives her a hard time. Fortunately, she has her father's sense of humor and gives it right back to him.

Please send gado-gado, chicken sate, and some of Sukarti's pineapple pie. We hear that Dunc's Ladybird is on her way to America. Who will Bianca torment now? Poor Oscar?

Every day I picture something of your life—breakfast on the second floor patio, Rog coming home for lunch, your office, and Anto. It makes it all so much easier to feel close to you.

Love you most of all in the whole world,
Madame B.

Tea Plantations Puncak Pass

CHAPTER 11

Travels and Travails

6/11/82

Dear Madame B.,

Sorry to have slipped so badly in my correspondence lately. This week has been really crazy.

Anto and I received a call out of the blue last week from Pertamina, the national oil company of Indonesia. They want us to submit a proposal for their 1983 calendar. The only ideas they had were they wanted to combine culture, tourism, and the oil field in the photography. Now, culture and tourism are easily combined, but how do you also make them have anything to do with the oil field? Well, we actually did put some ideas together and submitted a proposal for about eight hundred dollars for thirteen photos and the artwork layout. When we called them on Monday, they had changed their mind and chosen the theme of "The Lifecycle: From Birth to Marriage in Indonesian Culture." It is a great idea, and I'm really anxious to do the shooting for it, though it has nothing to do with the oil field. Pertamina has sponsored many very well-done publications about Indonesia, and they are very public relations-minded. The problem is our company. We are not registered, and I have no working papers, so if anyone asks, we are going to have to do some fast talking. The second proposal calls for shots from each island with a particularly different cultural theme. It means we will have to travel to Irian Jaya, Sulawesi, Kalimantan, Sumatra, and Bali. The cost, less transport and accommodations, worked out to about sixteen hundred dollars and would afford us the opportunity to apply for company registration when we finish. KEEP YOUR FINGERS CROSSED!!

Today is the five-year mark for Rog and me. He gave me a Walkman for traveling. I replaced the backgammon board for him that we sold when we left Trinidad. Unfortunately, attitudes are not all that good after five years, and we would have been better off spending the money on a reevaluation of our marriage. The other night, we took a customer out to a very expensive place, who pointed out that we could count that dinner as our anniversary dinner and save ourselves some money. I reminded him that Baroid didn't have to pay for our anniversary dinner as we are not, contrary to popular belief, married to Baroid!!

Next Monday, June 14, Rog and I are going to Southeast Sumatra for a few days. He has to go to a Pertamina field there and invited me along to take some photos. This is the area that has been in the news lately because of the disastrous flooding.

I think of you a million times a day and relive all the wonderful times we had last month. It is so much nicer to know that you now have seen my life and can picture people and places I write about. Even if we don't get home for vacation this year, I'm trying to work out how I can get back for a few weeks sometime to refresh myself and visit with you.

Please give my love to all, but most of all to you, my best friend in this great big world.

M.

6/17/82

One day into *your* new year!

Dear Marthe,

Enclosed is the telex Susanne composed that we tried to send for your birthday. Unfortunately, due to nonpayment of the bills, our machine is down and slated to be removed. However, it is still printing tapes, so pretend this was sent. The reason we'll let our telex go is that we are not doing business with a London client anymore and can't justify the ongoing expense. Anyway, you know we were thinking of you for your birthday. We called and spoke to Anto.

Martha Kidder
Happy Birthday 2 U
Happy Birthday 2 U
We're missing you muchly
So please keep in touchly
We're anxious to hear of your jaunt to Sumatra
And trembling in fear that the natives have gotcha!
Love Susanne and Madame B.

235

6/18/82

Dear Madame B.,

Busy, busy, busy. Seems like I have to stay up all night just to get enough time to answer all my personal mail. Well, it's Friday morning, and I'm not going to do any work until I've filled you in on what has been going on. By now you must think I've broken both hands and can't type!

Monday morning at 5:00 a.m., Rog and I took off for Southeast Sumatra. He had to call on Pertamina there, and I went along for a variety of reasons: to get some shots for the calendar project, to have some time alone with Rog, and to see a part of the country I have not visited yet.

We flew into Palembang on the island of Sumatra, about forty-five minutes north of Jakarta. The city is mostly under water, and all the houses are built up on stilts. Very different from Java—everyone uses dugout canoes to get around. From there, we hired a taxi to drive us up to Prabamulih, about two hours north. Here, Pertamina has lots of old but still-producing wells and a camp that was originally built by Shell Oil. I had a strange case of déjà vu because it resembled a camp in Trinidad we had visited often that was also built by Shell many years ago. The people there, all Indonesians working for Pertamina, were very nice and really impressed by my ability to speak Indonesian. I got the feeling that Rog brought me along as a sales promotion and interpreter!!

Tuesday, I went out to some locations with Rog and a guy from the lab. While they were running tests, I searched for things to photograph. John, who you met when we all went to Pelabuhan Ratu, had given me a very expensive, new Minolta light meter for my birthday, so I practiced with that. Though it is a bit confusing, I think once I get it all worked out, it will prove to be the best tool I own. Rog has promised to do my birthday shopping in Singapore when he is there next week. I'm hoping for either studio lighting or a new slide projector. We came home on Wednesday but unfortunately not in time to receive the birthday wishes phone calls from you, Susanne, and Dunc.

I am getting fed up with dealing with some of our local customers and have made the decision to only work with private companies. The Hotel Indonesia project that Anto shot while you and Dunc were here has become an expensive lesson. We shot the whole thing on spec, and now the guy has rejected three rolls of film plus three very expensive color separations that he had previously approved. He doesn't want to pay us for any of it, and his excuse is "Well, you aren't a P.T. company (registered with the government) and you don't have a work permit, so what can you do about it?" Pertamina wanted us to produce layouts and a proposal for their calendar virtually overnight, but it has taken over a week now to decide when and *if* they want us to go ahead to shoot the photos. I explained that their time was short if they want to use Kodachrome due to the processing times and we will have to begin this month. They are still dragging their feet and haven't paid a dime (or rupiah) for our artwork and energies spent so far. At this rate, we are barely breaking even every month, and you know I am working for peanuts!

Our one bright spot is the new deal with the Yayassan Hijau, an environmental agency (private, *not* government), who is delivering about four hundred slides to me today. They have some fantastic wildlife shots and do not want to handle their own stock marketing. In addition, they regularly get requests for photos to be used in calendars and other projects. They will refer those requests to us.

Kucing is like a kitten again now that he is all recovered from his operation. This morning, he is attacking everything in sight, including the first page of this letter. He is in the desk drawer near my typewriter playing with a Ping-Pong ball that Rog placed in the drawer for some unknown reason. He is so fat and healthy now it is like having a new cat!

Bianca and Oscar are fine, though complaining regularly and LOUDLY about the lack of attention since Dunc left. He really spoiled those two. Oscar just swings and chirps his funny little call, but Bianca really screams twice a day at 7:00 a.m. and 5:00 p.m. I wonder how Dunc's Ladybird made out on the journey to Los Angeles? Has he had a confirmation of her arrival yet?

The book you sent on Nepal was here when we got back from Sumatra. I have to wait until Rog falls asleep every night to get a glance at it. Excellent information. We have been looking for an APA guide book here but have not been able to find anything about Nepal, so it will be most useful. We are gearing up for our trip in September, the first we have taken just for us in many years. Now for me to learn the language there!

Well, at twenty-seven, I look at where I am in the world and think back on where I was ten years ago. The Borobudur didn't even exist in my wildest dreams, and Jakarta was a place I couldn't have pointed to on a map. Where will I be ten years from now?

You are always with me, here in my thoughts and wherever my travels may take me.

I love you dearly,
M.

Journal Entry,
6/20/82
Cibulan

We came up to the mountains yesterday afternoon with Eiko, Jim, their kids, and another couple. The location is cool, misty, and beautiful.

This morning, Rog was up at 6:00 a.m. for a swim. The sun is warm, but the pool is icy cold. He borrowed Jim's car and driver so we could go up to Gunung Mas. It is the heart of the tea plantations, and we spent several hours taking photos and wandering among the stunted rows of tea trees.

If only we could live here and commute to Jakarta. The mountain air is so much fresher and healthier.

7/2/82

Dear Madam B.,

I'm awake early for the fifth morning in a row this week. Reminds me of working at Union Park in Trinidad! I thought I would take advantage of the peace and quiet this morning to fill you in on the latest in our household.

To give you a bit of background, I have been having trouble with Suparno and Sukamto, who you remember are my houseboy and night guard (*jaga*). Both have worked for us for well over a year, but the past few months, I've noticed things slipping badly. Before Rog and I went to Sumatra, I had spent about one hundred dollars on groceries. When we got back after only three days, the cupboards were bare. Also, things were not getting done around the house, and Sup and Suk were often missing in action. I sat them down and laid down the law, so to speak, and then started to watch even more closely. Yesterday morning, I fired both of them. Rog is away until Sunday, and Suparno's reaction was "I'll just wait until Mr. Roger comes home and speak with him." Of course this pissed me off even further that he has so little respect for me. There were a few tense moments and hard feelings all around, but that is to be expected, as this month is the Muslim Lebaran (sort of like Christmas to us), and everyone expects to receive an annual bonus.

Luckily, Anto was here, John loaned me his night guard, and Sukarti's husband is staying for a few nights. I notified our area security, you remember the light-pole-banging town crier, and was thoroughly amazed by their efficiency and cooperation in putting on an extra patrolman (for a little palm-grease, of course). Sukarti brought in a girlfriend, and the two of them are singing while they scrub everything in sight.

Rog called from Balikpapan. He is trying to catch a flight to Singapore and will hopefully be home Sunday the fourth. He says he will bring me a slide projector for my belated birthday present.

Bianca's latest trick is to unhook her perch from the tree, crash to the ground, and strut around, dragging her wooden perch while screaming cockatoo obscenities. Oscar just throws back his head and swings like a madman on his perch, trying to touch the sky.

Masudi went to a beauty salon the other night to try to have his hair straightened. He now has a wild Afro and is threatening to shave his head!

Gunilla and Lou are in the States for vacation until July 26. I miss them terribly. Their female cocker spaniel came into heat, and I had promised to take her male dog for the duration. We tried it for two days but Roger and Kuching threatened to leave, so I had to send him back.

I don't know what we will do for the Fourth of July holiday. We had talked about getting a bunch of expats together, some large trucks, and lots of flags so we could stage a good, old-fashioned, Indonesian-style rally in the streets of Jakarta.

We are planning to go to Bali for the long weekend that marks the end of Lebaran. We will go over on the last flight on Wednesday night and come home Sunday. It should be really fun, as everyone we know is going. Jakarta will be empty of expats! Nothing gets done around here anyway, and since Bali is Hindu, they are not celebrating and happy to have the business.

I got a letter from Nana saying she had received a letter from *You Asked for It*. They were acknowledging her request for a segment on Indonesia. According to the letter, the Jakarta show will air next fall. That should be very interesting, as they *never* shot any footage here to my knowledge …

Well, I really must start my day. We are still captioning and cataloguing the four-hundred-plus slides we received from the wildlife association. It is a lot of work, but they are beautiful, and I hope we can start making more money with them soon.

Love you dearly,
M.

Journal Entry, 7/11/82

I often think, *Oh, I wish I could stop and write that down.* But time and privacy are at a premium these days.

This week at least was successful. We started off with a sale of three shots to the Mandarin Hotel, finally sold the postcard shots to the Hotel Indonesia, and took an order for Lebaran cards from IndoTubine using their logo shot. Judo sent some work our way, but I don't think we'll make anything on it. It was shooting for an old customer of his, the Martha Tillar Beauty Salon. The location turned out to be a garage, the models were ten-year-old girls, and the clothing—let's just say "local disco." We arrived at 9:30 a.m. but didn't start shooting until 12:30 p.m. Total waste of time and effort in my opinion, which made me wonder what/how Judo was paid in the past.

We are pretty well organized with all the wildlife shots from Yaysan Indonesia Hijau. Friday, we made a presentation to a magazine, *Indonesia,* and though they didn't order anything right away, it went very well.

Still no word from Dunc. He promised to call when his Ladybird arrived. I hope this doesn't mean there's been a problem. It has been two weeks since I had any mail from Mom or Sue. Wonder what everyone is up to?

7/22/82

Dear Marthe,

We received your photos from south Sumatra this week. It looks a lot more like the jungle than what we saw of Java/Jakarta. Is the language the same? I have the one of the cows and village street on my desk gallery here at work.

Dunc called last night. He's very excited to have his Ladybird. I don't think he really imported it for his girlfriend, Barbara, at all! No name yet. What is Indonesian for bird, dove, pigeon, or white? He admits the prices of cockatoos in Houston these days are only a bit more than he paid in all to get her here. But there's nothing to compare with the experience of buying her in the bird market in Jakarta. It was well worth all the time and challenge to get her home, to say nothing of the endless time, expense, and aggravation you and Rog put in for her trip. She had better live to a ripe old age and be worth it!

This week, you are in Bali. Did Roger finally relax and unwind? Please send pictures.

Lebaran was featured on the local news last night. Here in Boston, as throughout large cities, there is a good-sized Muslim population, and they observe the fasting and final feasting.

There was a young boy, about twelve or thirteen years old, in the interview, and he explained the fasting and family feelings in a very mature and sensitive manner.

Tomorrow is the company outing in the parking lot. Linden offered her house on the river in Kittery, Maine, but it was just too far for some folks. Some of these people have never been south of Ipswich or north of Newbury! So we'll have our picnic on the hot-top huddled around one table and two benches. Susanne and I are doing deviled eggs and fruit bowl and then beating a quick exit if at all possible.

So many times each week, I miss your smile and presence. There are just a lot of times when no one else is close and understanding.

Thinking of you with lots and lots of love,
Madame B.

8/1/82

Dear Madam B.,

I must owe you a million letters, and you must be getting worried that I went off to Bali and never returned. Actually, I almost didn't and, upon arriving, wished I'd not bothered to come back.

I'm sitting here on this glorious Sunday, trying to piece together my thoughts and get caught up on the letters that are piled up to record heights on my desk. Don't know exactly where to begin.

Randy and Denise came down from Singapore with Rog on July 20. The servants all left that day for their annual family gatherings for Lebaran. The next night, we met up with more folks and grabbed a flight to Bali. Sonia met us at the airport. She had been there for a week and was brown as a native. There were a few bad moments when we found all our room reservations had been lost, but we managed to find a place for the night. The next day, we moved into a really neat *losmen*, traditional inn, and headed for the beach. More folks joined us, and with eleven of us for dinner on Friday night, it was mass confusion.

Sunday, Randy and Rog headed back to Jakarta with the rest of the group, but Denise and I stayed on for three more days. It's so hard to leave Bali once you get there, and the prospect of going back to the city and smog just didn't appeal. I've found my first American friend overseas in Denise. I wish we lived closer—Singapore and Jakarta are just a short flight, but still. She is another Gemini, like me, but from Texas. I do give her credit for trying to lose her accent!

Upon our return, Denise and I were met not by Masudi but rather Anto and a taxi. He said he had come back from Surabaya that morning and called Rog at his office to see where I was. Rog told him to meet me at the airport, as he was too busy to send Masudi. Denise had a flight to Singapore later that afternoon, so we went back to the house for cool drinks and to see if we could get the car later.

I found a letter waiting for me from Rog saying that he had been informed of my affair with Anto and that we were finished. It wasn't hard to see that there was something terribly wrong as I read the letter. Anto offered to take Denise back to the airport and see her off while I went to the office to find Rog.

I found him sitting in his office. We tried to make some sense of the whole thing. It turns out that my dear, devoted Sukarti decided that my Roger deserved someone better. Herself perhaps? She came to him in tears with a ridiculous story about an affair I was having with Anto. The thing that really hurt, aside from the fact that he believed her right off without asking me first, was that he didn't dismiss her for bad-mouthing his wife. It is a horrible mess, and Rog refuses to fire Sukarti or say anything else about it to her. I have to live with this sneaky witch and a doubting husband. Obviously, the effects of this incident are far-reaching and yet to be realized. It is something I would not like to ever have to go through again.

I love you and wish so much you were near.
M.

8/16/82

Dearest Marthe,

Susanne and I picked out the enclosures from the latest "Needless Markup" (Neiman Marcus) statement, so you can see how styles are going in the States. Note especially the wide variety of hemlines.

There has to be help for your help problems. You are such a generous, sensitive, and thoughtful person. Somewhere there are a couple of competent Indonesians who would appreciate you and do a good job for you and Roger. It really looks from here as though Sukarti may have had a crush on Anto and took out her rejection by trying to make trouble between him and Roger, and you were the innocent victim.

The movie of the year seems to be *E.T.* ... sort of a Disney/ *Star Wars* combination. And everyone gets to cry a little too! Did it come to the Petroleum Club yet?

Best to Sudi and his curly hair and John with his hardship-pay/Asti-Spumante lifestyle.

Most of all, best to you,
Love, Madam B.

8/24/82

Dear Madam B.,

I got a three-page letter from you yesterday, and it was, as always, the highlight of my day.

Rog has bought a TV and VCR and loves it. He is off for Balikpapan today for two or three days, and I don't think he will survive without the movies! He is up to three tapes a day, every day. In addition to the fact that it ends up costing more than a night out on the town once a week, I can't seem to get any attention. He even suggested that we could watch and eat dinner at the same time the other night. I put my foot down on that.

We are getting ready for vacation and our trip to Thailand and Nepal. We'll be leaving here on Saturday, September 4. Our plan is to play it by ear and not book definite flights since we don't know if we will want to stay longer in Thailand or move right on to Nepal. Maybe on the way back we will have time for a stopover at Lake Toba in Sumatra or make a quick trip to Bali. At any rate, we'll be back in Jakarta on September 25.

I have replaced Sukarti with two elderly ladies. They have never worked for foreigners before but are very pleasant and willing to learn. Unfortunately for Roger, neither of them can cook American food, so I am getting quite a workout in the kitchen these days, and Rog has been without a homemade pie for a week now. When I get back from vacation, I'll send them to a cooking course or teach them myself. I wouldn't mind cooking if the kitchen wasn't such a sweatbox and the counters weren't only two feet high. After an hour of bending almost double at the waist over those counters, I can barely stand upright again!

I'll try to call before we take off. Rog has been complaining that every time he leaves the city, I call you and it costs $150.00. My reply was that if he stayed home more I'd maybe have someone to talk to and it would be cheaper!

Love to my very best friend and confidant.
M.

8/29/82

Dear Madam B.,

A very strange thing happened tonight. Kucing wandered into the kitchen from outdoors at about 6:00 p.m. with his *son* in tow! His age is about right, though it's hard to tell. He's so scrawny, but the color is impossible to mistake. He has four white feet, a splotch on his chest, and a white nose, but the rest is Kucing's gray color. Even his tail is an exact miniature replica of Kucing's. Unlike most street kittens here, he is very personable and comfortable around people.

Of course, this created quite a stir. I was talking to Gunilla who was on her way to the airport. Her sister and fiancé are arriving tonight. My two "new" old ladies rushed in to oust the little beast, but he fascinated me. Kucing followed his every move but certainly was not hostile toward him. I've decided to call him Putera, which means "son of the king or leader." We'll see what Rog says, but I just can't kick him out. After all, Kucing brought him to me.

I'm trying to wind down things here and gear up for Phukett and Nepal. Anto and I are incredibly busy with eight ad agencies. We've given them all a preliminary presentation to introduce our stock photo agency. So far, we have two calendars and an ad sold. We are also cataloging new stock from the wildlife folk and shooting odd jobs. I don't want to leave just now, but hopefully Anto can hold things together.

Well, it's now Monday morning. When I got up, I found Putera sitting at the breakfast table in my seat, waiting for Kucing and me to emerge from the bedroom. Guess we have been adopted. I'll have to find time today to take him to the vet for some shots, worming, and de-flea-ing.

The mountain Gulunggung is still blowing up regularly. We really shouldn't complain because those living closer are much worse off. But the dust and ash are getting to be a real pain in the butt. The other day it was so thick you could actually see it coming down!! It was the closest thing to snow I've seen in years. I don't know if it is making the news in the States, but this particular mountain has been erupting since April. They say it is building up to a huge explosion that could have very serious effects on not only Java but also on weather conditions around the world.

Speaking of volcanoes, the other day I rented the tape *Krakatoa, East of Java*. It is your basic old Saturday afternoon kids adventure movie made years ago. First of all, Krakatoa is *west* of Java. Second, they used all Japanese actors and actresses for the parts of the Indonesians, and they even *spoke* Japanese in the movie!! Hollywood does some strange things.

So, madam, when you receive this, I'll be somewhere between Phukett Island and Nepal. I'll send lots of postcards and call you when I get home.

Love you dearly,
M.

Journal Entry,
9/6/82

Last week will probably go down as one of the worst—for this year, anyway.

Rog came back from Balikpapan and places beyond. He had Randy and Roy with him. He got on the phone immediately for an hour with George in Singapore, leaving me trapped with the other two.

We went out to dinner, but my mood didn't improve any. The next night, we were all invited to dinner at Lou and Gunilla's. As we were leaving, Putera was run over in the garage. Needless to say, it was an awful scene, and once again, my heart was wrenched up into my throat. Why does it have to hurt so much? Why do I have to feel anything at all?

Saturday, we finally got all packed for our trip. George came down from Singapore to office/house sit. Off we went to the airport, full of high hopes of escaping for a bit. I didn't have an exit permit. All is lost.

Another matter to be weighed came up last Thursday when Bert Van Muster called from Los Angeles. It seems *You Asked for It* wants to come and shoot the shows we worked on almost a year ago. I had an emergency meeting with the Department of Information and all signals are go. YAFI will decide this coming Tuesday, and I'm to call Bert and let him know if I am available. I've decided that in light of our problems, Rog could justifiably never forgive me if I cut this vacation short. I will tell Bert he most probably will have to do it alone.

God help me. I am losing my sanity. I feel only helplessness and hate for the situation my life is in right now.

Kathmandu becak driver

CHAPTER 12

A Step Toward Healing

Journal Entry,
9/8/82
Phuket Island, Thailand

Careful repairs are being made to the fabric of our life.

We spent our first true day of vacation today. It certainly was a long haul getting here. From Singapore, we flew to Penang, Malaisia, changed planes, and then on to Hat Yai, Thailand, and then took a tiny, "short" plane to Phuket.

The first hotel we got to was a disaster. Too much money for dirty grass shacks on a very rough beach with nothing for miles in any direction. We had no reservations anywhere, so we managed to grab a taxi to drive us up the island a bit to another bay. Unfortunately, Phuket is not what we expected—rather run-down; lots of young, single German guys; and a large population of Thai hookers from Bangkok. We agreed that we'd have been happier in Bali.

We have reservations for a flight to Bangkok tomorrow, so we plan to spend a couple of days there with Nick and Jean Marret. They just moved up there from Jakarta, and it will be fun to explore the city with them. From there, we will head out to Kathmandu.

I have tried to call Bert along the way to see what YAFI has planned. Perhaps I will be able to reach him when I get to the city. No matter what they decide, I can't handle any pressure just now. I'm making some serious decisions and need time out of Jakarta to do it.

Journal Entry,
9/11/82
Bangkok

Staying with Nick and Jean worked out so much better than I had ever expected. Though Jean only arrived two weeks ago, she is pleased to have company and someone to discover Bangkok with.

We moved into the Oriental Hotel today, the oldest in Bangkok and reputed to be one of the world's finest. Since we have saved so much money up to now, we decided to really splurge on one night of luxury before we head out at 4:00 a.m. tomorrow for Nepal.

Rog and I are getting along fairly well, but we both realize this may be the bitter end. One cannot live in pain and tension for eleven months of the year to enjoy one month of vacation. We have talked about things a lot since leaving home and still aren't any closer to a solution. We are two very stubborn people. I wish we could erase all the mistakes and scars and really just start over.

Journal Entry,
9/13/82
Kathmandu—Monday

Kathmandu is not for the country club set. Narrow, unpaved streets are lined with low shop fronts. The many-tiered dwellings above all boast open windows for viewing the hustling pace of life below.

Luckily, a Swiss guy who is a frequent traveler to Nepal sat next to Rog on the plane. He filled us in a bit and offered good advice on customs, airport procedures, and such. We arrived just after dark last night in the incessant rain. The airport was dreary and dank. A confusing shuffle ensued as we emerged and looked for a taxi.

Our first night here was something I will never forget. We checked into the Hotel Woodlands, which both the Swiss guy, Joe, and Lolo had recommended. It was a bit expensive (forty US dollars per night) and not very luxurious, but I suppose anything would have been a come-down after the Oriental Hotel in Bangkok.

The recommended restaurant was closed, so we picked a small café in the back of a carpet shop/hotel/antique store. The food was abominable, but what could one expect? A quick walk around, and we located another recommended hotel. We liked the neighborhood and arranged for a room for today. The rain turned the narrow streets into sloppy mud-holes, but luckily traffic of any sort other than becak, bicycle, or pedestrians was light. On our walk back to the hotel, we came upon a cow resting in the gutter contentedly chewing her cud. It appears they roam quite freely here and frequently congregate in the small squares. These crowded little plazas appear where bunches of crooked streets converge and then dart off again in every direction. The cows, however, don't "dart" anywhere, but they do seem particularly attracted to my rented yellow rain poncho.

Back to last night. We hired a becak/trishaw driver and his son to take us on a mysterious ride to Bhaktapur Durbar Square and the famous "Freak Street." Due to the monsoon downpour, it was pretty quiet, but this is the congregating spot for all the foreign tourists who have sold their passports (and no doubt their souls) for a life of hash and who knows what here in Kathmandu. We parked, and while the son of maybe ten years old and I shared a cigarette, Rog and the driver disappeared down a dark alleyway. It seemed to take forever, but after an actual fifteen to twenty minutes, I heard Rog disgustedly denouncing the driver, the rain, and everything else that came to mind. He said it was a terrifying and frustrating effort, but for twice the going price, he'd acquired a chunk of something smokeable. The smell of hash and incense snuck through your laden senses on every street corner and alley here.

We arrived back at the hotel exhausted by our emotional and physical efforts of the day and soaked.

First thing this morning, we started walking around. It would be impossible to get the true lay of the land in this city, but at least we explored our immediate area. We also moved into the Kathmandu Guest House, cheaper with a much more relaxed atmosphere. The location seems more in tune with restaurants and shopping of the younger clientele. It is populated with Europeans of our age, and the music of many languages is pervasive. The hotel is a four-story boardinghouse affair with ells, wings, jigs, jogs, and corridors running in every direction much like the city itself. I fear without Rog I would never find my way back to our room.

The rain kept up most of the day and made it tough for shooting photos. I find I can stand on a street corner and just keep slowly turning and shooting the life around me for almost 360 degrees. It is fascinating! The people are not Asian, nor are they Indian ... rather, a lovely race whose skin is smooth and warm brown. The poverty doesn't strain the dignity with which they carry themselves.

Journal Entry, 9/14/82 Kathmandu

Day #2 dawned sunny if not totally clear. We rented bikes and set out for breakfast at the Annappurna Hotel. Not bad, but my egg tasted a little funny. From there, we sought out the post office to send cards and onward to check out the Oberoi Hotel. That was not overly impressive, so we headed off on an alternate route back to town. I must say, Rog's sense of direction and map-reading skills are very impressive.

We followed winding dirt trails through the outskirts of the city that were little more than a footpath in places. These paths opened into larger spaces of tiny rice paddies and garden plots. The houses were still the tall, brick, solid construction of the city, but the air was clear, and the sun, combined with the physical exertion, soon had us sweating. Over a bridge, we started to climb into the sharp, narrow streets of the city again, dumping us in a crowded bazaar/square. After a rest and refreshment of tea, we headed back out for Dumar Square and "Freak Street." I was having a wonderful time finding abundant shots of the local color, but Rog became bored, so we pedaled back out through another section of town until we came upon the Woodlands Hotel street. An Indian restaurant looked promising for dinner but didn't open until 7:00 p.m., so we headed back to the room for a shower first. Dinner was surprisingly excellent! It's only 10:00 p.m., but I can't keep my eyes open tonight.

Journal Entry,
9/15/82
Kathmandu

Because of the tourist/hiking/climbing economy here, you can rent/buy anything you might need for the environment from tents and Sherpa guides to rainwear. We have outfitted ourselves with an odd assortment of gear, including my oh-so-necessary rain poncho. But the sun was out when we arose this morning, so we rented a motorcycle and flooded our senses with the incredible scenery on a long ride to Kakani. I said, "Oh my God! Look at that!" so many times that the words became useless to describe what my eyes told me. Tried with the camera to capture and create the awesomeness of it all, but failed to even scratch the surface, as Rog most aptly put it.

I feel my spirit slowly mending, warmed by the sun, and swirling gently upward like the hawk I saw today. He flew so close I could see his talons and yellow-spotted breast. I really think I got some great people shots today. Can't wait to develop this film.

Journal Entry,
9/16/82
Kathmandu

Started the day off sniffling and achy. Terrible cold brewing. We walked over to Dumar Mary to buy some of the colorful boxes I had so admired and to look for a yak-wool jacket for Rog. Also picked up a coffee table book and stopped off at the post office. I traded a Lacoste polo shirt and two t-shirts for an amazing ivory collar/necklace. The shopkeeper smiled broadly, showing red, betel-nut-stained teeth. We both got a bargain. She so pleased with her Western clothes, and my necklace is a beautiful wide collar of carved beads.

By the time we'd made our way back to the room, I was really dragging. Fell into bed and slept the rest of the day away.

It's raining again, and Rog has gone in search of dinner. I feel lousy.

Journal Entry,
9/17/82
Kathmandu

Oh, to have a typewriter to be able to catch the fleeting impressions my senses absorb. It's about 6:00 p.m. The bicycle bells jangle, and the pigeons are cooing and squabbling in the niches where they struggle to roost. Voices ebb and soar in so many foreign tongues that are no more intelligible than the pigeons' throaty mumblings.

Shopping and shipping filled the major part of today. We bought six netsuke figures (small ivory carvings), a pair of Nepalese mukluk-style boots, and woven slippers.

The rain has cooled the afternoon and laid the dust temporarily. The alligator fell off Roger's Lacoste shirt; it won't be worth anything in trade now.

Journal Entry,
9/18/82
Kathmandu

Another rainy day. This is becoming a bit too routine. Sold Rog's JakPak jacket to an American guy who's living in the Philippines. He'd been in Malaysia a few years also. He works for the Asian Development Bank.

Caught a minibus of sorts to Bhaktapur. This ancient town to the east was highly recommended by everyone we spoke to. Perhaps because it was raining, our senses were just getting moldy, so we were not impressed. The open countryside delights and refreshes us, but close contact with the civilization no longer charms. I'm beginning to feel like heading out, especially if the weather doesn't break soon.

Journal Entry,
9/20/82
Kathmandu

I've started getting lax about my writing and missed it completely yesterday. Guess the rain and lack of activity are to blame. Today cleared a bit. We rented a motorcycle again, a trail bike this time. It proved a bit trickier to handle, and we dumped it twice. Luckily, both times we were going very slowly. First time, we were in town trying to avoid a dog. Embarrassing. Second time, we were in the mountains attempting a U-turn and ended in the ditch. It was really cool and foggy in the foothills. Still no sight of the snow-capped peaks I'd hoped for.

Journal Entry,
9/22/82
In flight

We've just left Kathmandu and are on our way to Bangkok via Calcutta. Rog is worried that something will happen to the plane and we will be stranded in India—his worst nightmare.

The last day and a half in Kathmandu were sunny, warm, and lovely. We spent yesterday catching up on last-minute shopping and shipping a package of Christmas presents off to the States. With any luck, they will arrive before the Fourth of July!

This morning, we struggled with packing and bought another backpack to consolidate some of the smaller things. We leave Kathmandu with memories only the two of us can ever really share and hopefully lots of photos to enrich those memories. Now we begin the trek back to civilization (as we know it). It's been an interesting two weeks. We've relearned how to relax and accept ourselves again. If only the feeling of closeness we have now could last.

CHAPTER 13

Head Back, Look Ahead

9/22/82
Bangkok

Dear Madam B.,

Back again in this rainy, magical kingdom of Thailand. We caught a flight out of Kathmandu at noon. It stopped over for forty-five minutes in Calcutta, and Rog was having a fit the entire time for fear they would ask us to get off the plane for some reason and he'd be stuck in India. He even checked with the stewardess to make sure the food they served from Calcutta to Bangkok had not originated in India. His phobia goes back to our days in Trinidad and is growing worse with age.

Murphy's Law has struck again. We just called Singapore to alert Randy and Denise that we'd be coming in tomorrow for the weekend. Randy is in the Philippines, and Denise is joining him there for two weeks starting tomorrow. She said the package we sent from Bangkok has arrived but no word yet about the shipment from Kathmandu. Denise will leave us a set of keys to their apartment, car, etc. And we can only hope the Kathmandu package shows up soon. Too bad we'll miss Randy and Denise, though. They are fun people.

As we get closer to Jakarta and the end of our vacation, I find I am having mixed emotions. It feels like we have been gone longer than two and a half weeks. I'm anxious to get back and pursue Media Budaya yet also feel it is no longer of utmost importance to my life and well-being. In many ways, I'm feeling drained, having worked so hard at it and gained so little tangible evidence of success. Perhaps I'm just impatient, but I can't see any cold, hard, dollar-sign facts that all my effort has been justified. I still could not support myself with the business if I chose to, nor do I feel any less guilty about money matters than the day I married Roger. So many times on vacation, I felt reproached for spending money on clothes for myself, yet whatever he saw and liked, he felt perfectly free to buy. I never carried one baht, rupee, rupiah, or dollar in my pocket.

But here I am, bitching about petty grievances when I've just had a relaxing, fascinating vacation. No gratitude, right?

Can't wait to get back to check my mailbox and see a letter from you. It seems like so long since we had contact.

Love you dearly, as only you can possibly know.
M.

9/23/82

Dear Marthe,

Welcome back to Jakarta—home! How does it feel to be back?

Everyone has been following your progress with wonder and much interest. We call each other when we get postcards. Your card from Phuket was gray, color *and* content. Wasn't it supposed to be a resort island?

Dunc and his girlfriend, Barbara, were up for a visit. They drove up in a great big blue Lincoln with Texas plates, which, of course, confirmed everyone's ideas in Newburyport that the streets of Houston are flowing with oil money. But it did make sense to be comfortable on such a long haul. They drove all the way through to Pennsylvania, stopped for one night there, and then came straight through to Massachusetts. We had glorious fall weather, and everyone seemed to get along well. However, from Dunc's point of view, the trip was thin on the intellect department. He confided that between Barbara and Donna (Dad's lady friend from Texas), there weren't enough smarts to change a tire!

So glad you had this time with Rog. Don't feel you owe anyone a trip to the States regularly. You, Dunc, and I had our super time last spring. The future is you and Rog. Hope you both came back with new attitudes and feelings.

Wish you were here, but you are in my thoughts so many times a day.
Madam B.

9/28/82

Dearest Madam B.,

Here I am, back at the old typewriter again. Perhaps my letters will be a bit easier to read now, although it's been so long since I used this machine, there will be lots of mistakes, no doubt.

Anto has done an excellent job running the business while I was away. He sold twelve photos and has about thirty more out on spec. We are up to six calendars sold now and have had to put off two orders for custom shot advertisements since I had all our equipment with me. I'm really impressed with the way he has handled things. Also, if he hadn't been here, this house wouldn't have run as smoothly as it did. It appears that George and Roy, Roger's employees who were supposed to be holding down the fort, were busy chasing the ladies around town. Anto stayed at the house to keep things under control while they were out and away.

All in all, it was a good vacation despite all the rain we encountered. Rog and I came home so much more relaxed and ready to get back to our routines with a new feeling. The best news is that Sonny Andrews, Roger's Houston boss, has quit, so it is now only a matter of time before Rog can ease out the idiot that Sonny sent to Singapore to be Roger's boss. He is so happy it seems nothing can bum him out at the moment. Business is good, and he may rise to the seat of Baroid's Golden Boy in the Far East once again.

It really does feel good to be home, and I think Rog and I are on an even keel for the time being. We learned a lot about each other, and spending time alone made a huge difference in the way we relate to each other now. I, for one, don't want to get back into the rut and tangle of emotions that I had when I left.

Love to all, especially you!
M.

9/30/82

Dear Marthe and Rog,

Such excitement to hear from you! Your letters of September 17 and 19 came yesterday from the Kathmandu Guest House. Did the weather clear for you to see Mount Everest? There is a map in the back of my appointment book, and it's getting dog-eared from following your travels.

Loved the handmade paper and artwork on the notes. It gives me a flavor/feeling for how primitive the region must be. Hope you were able to take some pictures in spite of the monsoons.

So you see, there is life beyond Baroid, even if you have to get as far away as Nepal to find it. Of course, you are fortunate to have so many good friends, but your home in Trinidad and Jakarta seem to be the focal point for friends and business clients, and of necessity, you two are seldom alone. Those few hours at the end of a hectic day when you are both tired is not the best time to get in touch. Remember that you two are what is important.

Please don't feel guilty about not coming to the States. You are the important ones, and it is such a rat race trying to see everyone when you are here. That's not really a vacation for you two. Not even when you go to Bali with umpteen couples in tow. We here probably think of you more often and keep in touch with you and feel closer because you are not just down the street/around the corner.

Sped off to the cottage last Saturday to capture the last of the warm weather. The foliage is at about 30/40 percent and, of course, all the "leaf peepers" were out.

Marj tells me Rog is not coming to Houston this fall. If you have anyone else over there headed this way or from Houston headed your way, let me know. I would like to send a holiday package by hand-carrier. Next best is to send it to the Singapore office, right?

Lots and lots of love to you both,
Madam B.

Journal Entry,
10/4/82
Jakarta

I feel old feelings stirring; must try to remain calm and objective. The tension that creeps into and tugs at the corners of my life is self-conceived and self-imposed, yet it seems to have a force all its own that I can recognize but not check in time.

Susanne writes that she is quitting her twenty-thousand-dollar-a-year job that she began just five months ago to become an apprentice carpenter. Who knows? Maybe she will find what everyone spends his or her life looking for.

Media Budaya is humming along, but even that can't distract me from the unhappiness that is seeping back into my life.

Journal Entry,
10/17/82
Pelabuan Ratu

Rog and I came down on a semi-planned expedition late yesterday afternoon. Today was a refreshingly sunny beach day for Rog and me. Suddenly, Roy appeared. I can't believe Rog went to the extent to write him a note, telling him to join us here. He knows I don't like Roy at all, and I had thought we were having time alone.

This is such a relaxing spot, but emotions and frustrations are playing on my mind. I can't get in touch with myself, and try as I might to be loving and understanding to Rog, I can't get over the lack of sensitivity. I exist as his best buddy and pal when all I long for is the emotional bond.

Journal Entry,
10/19/82
Jakarta

I've said it, now there is no turning around. I've set my feet on the path to the unknown, alone. I've reached the end of my "elastic limits" emotionally, and I can't bounce back. My life is being propelled forward. After five years, it is scary. Not as scary as what is to come, but not the frustrating comforts I know.

For the love of God, I never set out to hurt him. It's just that I hurt so much inside and hate myself when I have to beg for his attention. He says that if I leave there will be no thought of reconciliation, nothing to hope for or even try evaluating. So be it. I must go now. If it must be under his terms, I must accept that. There will never be a better time to make this break. There will never be a change of attitude or an attempt at improving the situation. So what do I wait for? Why do I fear the unknown? Am I so weak and corrupt that I cannot believe in myself?

A sort of calm, sad, desolate emptiness has fallen over my life since I made this decision. He acts so surprised, so hurt and caught unaware. Perhaps he really is. If that is so, it sadly proves that all my tears have been unseen. All my past hopes of regaining lost footage are dashed.

It's silent, solitary, and lonely here. Sitting with the night, I watch him sleep and love him so dearly. The pain this love causes is the pain I suffer from him withholding himself from me while giving so freely to those who don't matter.

I am not wrong. I shall not fail in my journey to be happy. From within I will draw my strength.

Journal Entry,
10/21/82
Jakarta

All the talking, arguing, and agony. I look around at all I will leave behind. But leave I must for there has been far too much pain for me to believe in a new start. Like careful dancers, we tiptoe around each other's emotions. The final death dance of this marriage is being enacted, and I see only gray, empty sorrow. Why do I long to cry out, "Save me!!" when I know not from what? Or whom?

Time is growing short. We have agreed upon my leaving with the understanding that:

1. No time limit will be set, but it will be less than six months.

2. I will ease his mind by agreeing my public reason for leaving is not Roger.

3. I will be working to find a way to further my business, Media Budaya.

Now I sit in the Hotel Indonesia, waiting to give the pretest for an English language course they want me to teach. I will lie and say I must leave for "other" reasons. So many lies I live with … people trust my truths.

Journal Entry,
10/26/82

The pain in my guts is wretched. I don't know how to stop crying. Tears, like breaths of air, flow unconsciously.

Roger left for Kalimantan at 6:15 a.m. I leave tomorrow, perhaps for good. Am I doing the right thing? I am doing the only thing … surviving.

So much to do, so little time. I take so little from this space. I leave a large chunk of my heart, wounded and bleeding. A silent death.

Journal Entry,
10/27/82
Singapore

I feel so shattered and scared. What if this is all a terrible mistake that I've sentenced myself to?

Got drunk with Gunilla last night, called Mom, and cried my tears. She said, "Don't do this. You can work it out."

Please, I can't take anymore self-doubt, Mom.

Today I've played the waiting game. So much to think about and too much time to do it in. I left a love note in his sock and underwear drawer and a more serious, soul-searching letter accompanied by four packs of bubble gum on his bedside table. Why do I feel poignantly motherly in this pain of leaving?

Now I am here with Denise and am beginning to feel stronger. Not surer, but calmer.

Journal Entry,
10/29/82
Singapore

Awake before the dawn, my thoughts stray to how little time remains for me in Asia. While it will be good to see America, it is frightening to contemplate where my life will lead me. Unless Denise told Randy last night after I went to bed, he is unaware of my plans to move back to the States. It's hard to be with him now because he reminds me so of all the things I love about Roger. I wonder if Rog is home yet? Has he found my notes and letter? Later, if Denise and Randy leave today, I'll call Gunilla. She may know if Rog is still in Kalimantan. I wish I had a crystal ball to see into my future and make my questions transparent. Is all of life so full of pain and heartache?

It's midnight, and I'm alone in the apartment. It's been so long since I was totally alone. Tomorrow will be the beginning of my journey. I'm so scared. My mouth aches from all the dental work, and I couldn't eat today. I wish I had someone to talk to. Time is running out.

I called Mom. She was adamant that I not "do this." She got really mad and ended the conversation with "I won't meet you at the airport! This is stupid." I understand that she is disappointed in me and that she doesn't want to think about my life being over. I'm so tired and scared and alone.

Journal Entry,
10/30/82
Hong Kong

I'm totally alone. No one in the world knows where I am but me. I arrived this afternoon and shopped a bit as both my suitcase and trunk had to be shipped straight through. Dinner alone, drinking alone, watching TV alone. Only my thoughts to keep me company. I'm waiting for Dunc to call me back. I'm so scared of the night.

Journal Entry,
10/31/82
In Flight

Cleared customs in California, but there was a huge blowup. I guess the stamps on my passport from recent trips to Thailand and Nepal were a red flag for drug traffic. The agents brought me into a stark room, emptied my suitcase and trunk, cut open all my cigarette cartons, made me undress, and did a "further inspection." I was bleary-eyed from the flight and scared.

When they finally put me on the last flight to Boston, I could barely think. The girl sitting next to me on the flight was Indonesian. She was about five years younger than me and was on her way to meet her fiancé.

One life starting, one ending in row fifty-two.

I just hope someone meets me at the airport ...

EPILOGUE

I arrived at Boston's Logan International Airport late on the evening of Halloween, October 31. As I walked off the plane, I was confronted with people in masks and costumes. It took me a minute to realize where I was and what the date signified.

My mom did meet me. I'm sure she saw the fatigue and pain in my face. She didn't reproach me for my decision.

I never did go back to Jakarta. Rog and I were divorced in the state of New Hampshire via the US Embassy in Jakarta seven months later, on May 10, 1983. We never kept in touch. It was as if that life had belonged to someone else.

Over the next few months and years, I adapted to my "new" culture, found a job and a place to live for the millionth time, and moved on with my life.

Reverbia (working title) follows my path to reinvent myself. On May 12, 1987, I married my best friend's ex-lover. Jeff and I had two beautiful daughters, I made a career for myself, and we thrived. My thirties were a time of accomplishment as defined by our culture; an era of checking off the blanks on life's list of successful achievements. It was not without pain. I lost my dad to cancer following my brother's murder.

People persist, and this is the story of endurance.

Journal Entry,
1/5/86

Dunc's death came suddenly, violently thrusting itself first into my consciousness and then seeping into the fabric of my life.

It was the day before Christmas. Jeffrey and I were at his dad and stepmother Betty's house in Malvern, Pennsylvania. At about 8:00 a.m., the phone rang somewhere in the rambling home. Betty called out to Jeffrey that it was Susanne asking for him. He had his back to me as he listened to her. I sat up in bed and watched his fist clench, and then his hand started to shake.

He turned to me, placed the phone in my hands, and said, "Something very bad has happened, hon." As I raised the phone to my ear, he sat down behind me and began rubbing my back. I thought certainly something had happened to my dad. It was all so totally cruel and unexpected.

I found my way through an odd sort of fog, flying to Texas, not at all believing the facts. Grief is a strange state. Your mind and emotions go on overload so that you really feel nothing at all while life takes you through the hectic paces of dealing with immediate needs.

It isn't until later, much later, when supposed normality begins to set in once again, that you really begin to feel the loneliness and separation.

Made in the USA
Lexington, KY
27 August 2013

Outstanding praise for Greg Garrett
and *Free Bird*

"Best reason to read: For its cast of downright memorable characters, its fast pace and its thought-provoking message."

—*Rocky Mountain News*

"Three pages into *Free Bird* I had already fallen in love with Aunt Sister, Aunt Ellen, and Momma, and maybe with Clay Forester, too, the troubled dude who finds his way through pain to grace in this energetic, suspenseful, and touching novel. Jesus and rock-'n'-roll combine for a great read with pitch-perfect dialogue."

—Lee Smith, author of *The Last Girls*

"A story of spiritual redemption and forgiveness."

—*The Tribune-Herald* (Waco, Texas)

"Greg Garrett is a remarkable novelist who has the courage to explore in classic terms the great theme of the human soul. *Free Bird* is a splendid and deeply affecting work."

—Robert Olen Butler, Pulitzer prize-winning author of
A Good Scent from a Strange Mountain

"Entertaining . . . This wide-ranging novel makes for a very enjoyable and occasionally thought-provoking read."

—*Publishers Weekly*

"*Free Bird* chronicles the dark road trip of the soul of musician Clay Forrester, and as with any spirit journey worth a damn, Greg Garrett has made that journey by turn harrowing and hilarious, poignant and pointed, all with the final result of rendering that most rare of things these days: a book with meaning, and with heart."

—Bret Lott, *New York Times* bestselling author of *Jewel*

"Real people, real life, real engrossing, real good readin'."

—*Watonga Republican* (Watonga, Oklahoma)

"This is a first novel only in the most technical sense; *Free Bird* is a mature work from a mature writer. The book is laugh-out-loud funny and heartbreaking, sometimes on the same page, and Clay Forester's beautifully-nuanced narrative voice grows on the reader just like his character does."

—W.P. Kinsella, author of *Shoeless Joe* and
The Iowa Baseball Confederacy

(Please turn the page for more outstanding praise for Greg Garett's Free Bird)

"This book is a testament to Greg Garrett's creativity and mastery of language."

—*Texas Books in Review*

"*Free Bird* is not one story, but scores of stories that touch and influence the main story, as other lives touch our own."

—Jack Butler, author of *Jujitsu for Christ* and
Living in Little Rock with Miss Little Rock

"Although this is a first novel, the writer is adept at mixing humor, a spiritual quest, and some cuts to the chase . . ."

—*Amarillo Globe-News*

"Greg Garrett writes with intelligence, with humor, with obvious affection for his characters, with an eye for the salient detail that brings an economy to the writing that I particularly admire."

—Elinor Lipman, author of *The Dearly Departed* and
The Inn at Lake Devine

"A comical odyssey."

—*Caller-Times* (Corpus Christi, Texas)

"From lamentation to exhultation we ride cross country with a misspent soul named Clay Forester. In the late night and early morning hours one tries, without success, to turn back. When at last the story ends the passenger is at once glad to be home safely and beholden to a fine writer for a memorable journey."

—William Campbell, author of *Brother to a Dragonfly*,
National Book Award Finalist

"This is a classic odyssey story."

—*Books & Culture* (Carol Stream, Illinois)

Free Bird

GREG GARRETT

KENSINGTON BOOKS
http://www.kensingtonbooks.com

KENSINGTON BOOKS are published by

Kensington Publishing Corp.
850 Third Avenue
New York, NY 10022

All Kensington titles, imprints and distributed lines are available at special quantity discounts for bulk purchases for sales promotion, premiums, fund-raising, educational or institutional use.

Special book excerpts or customized printings can also be created to fit specific needs. For details, write or phone the office of the Kensington Special Sales Manager: Kensington Publishing Corp., 850 Third Avenue, New York, NY 10022, Attn: Special Sales Department. Phone: 1-800-221-2647.

Kensington and the K logo Reg. U.S. Pat. & TM Off.

ISBN: 0-7582-0140-0

First Hardcover Printing: March 2002
First Trade Paperback Printing: June 2003
10 9 8 7 6 5 4 3 2 1

Printed in the United States of America

TINA MARIE

Love loves what it loves.
What else can it do, being love?

Free
Bird

Prologue

"Ramblings around the River," by Sister Euless
—From *The Graham Star*, April 22, 1991

It has been a sad week along the river. Our family is so grateful to all of you for your outpouring of sympathy and support following the horrible accident that took the lives of my nephew Clay's wife, Anna Lynn, and son, Ray, in Washington, D.C. Your calls and visits have been a bright spot in this dark time. Ellen says, please, no more food. The freezers are full, and Clay isn't eating just now.

Clay has taken leave from his law practice and returned to Robbinsville to spend some time in the bosom of his family. Pray for us all, for him especially. As you can imagine, he is— we are, all of us—heartbroken. Ashes to ashes, dust to dust. But the Good Book also says that we will rise again to be with Him in glory. There will be a new heaven and a new earth and all our pain and sorrow will fade like darkness at dawn. You all know my favorite song, "I'll Fly Away," how some bright morning we'll all fly away home to God's celestial shore.

I'll return to happier news next week, God willing.

"Ramblings around the River," by Sister Euless
—From *The Graham Star*, June 7, 2000

Well, it's been a busy week down along the river. Alma Jean Shepherd came home from the hospital in Asheville Tuesday. She and Clarence say thanks for all the nice casseroles and desserts neighbors and church have brought. The freezer is full, Clarence says, but he's hard at work making more room.

Charlotte and Glennis McDowell put up sweet pickles last week. Over fifty jars between them. This hot weather has sure been good for cucumbers and okra. Brother Carl Robinson says his tomatoes are the biggest and sweetest he's ever seen. Drop by the parsonage and take a look over the back fence.

Little League baseball is taking up a lot of time for the Al Hartley family, since Tim, Tommy, and Al Jr. are all playing this year. Al says he and Nan need to hire some extra parents just to get the boys to practice.

David and Joanne Carver returned from a trip to Europe, the honeymoon trip they have been putting off for years. Good for them! I guess you'd call it a second honeymoon, since they spent a week in Myrtle Beach the first time they got married. Joanne says people in France were much nicer than she expected, and David says he saw Prince Charles outside Westminster Abbey. Drop by to see pictures, they say.

My nephew Clay Forester and Otis Miller took their act on the road last week to Greenville, South Carolina. The band played four shows and sang for a lot of our men and women in uniform. They're a regular USO, I guess you might say. Next week finds them in Charlotte. Do pray for them as they return late at night.

The azaleas are so beautiful this year. God shows his love for us in every season and in every passing day:

> *Wherever you go and whatever you do,*
> *Always remember that Jesus loves you.*

See you next week.

1

Here is how I woke on that Monday morning, the way in fact I always woke up in those days: by nine A.M., never later, someone started banging on the old upright piano downstairs in the parlor. There was no soothing prelude, none of that tuning you might get with an orchestra or two guys with guitars. Just thundering chords, then one, two, or three aging voices aimed my direction in gospel song. On that morning, it was Aunt Sister playing, and the song was "The Old Rugged Cross." I knew it was Aunt Sister by the rolling boogie-woogie left hand. She had not knowingly played boogie-woogie in fifty years, it being one of the bygone pleasures of her sinful youth, but nonetheless it got into her blood and still sneaked out where you might least expect it. Consequently, I liked her play better than the more formal chording of my mother and Aunt Ellen, although gospel piano is no humane way to wake up a man no matter who is doing it.

My name is Clay Forester, and in those days you did not have to know me very long or very well to see that I was a mess in just about every way a man could aspire to those depths. Even my stepfather, Ray Fontenot, who loved me as his own, used to drape an arm over my shoulder, draw me close, and tell me confidentially, "You know, son, you are a sorry excuse for a human being." I understand that this was his gruff way of expressing his love; I also know he was serious as a heart attack.

I used to be a lawyer like Ray, a pretty good one, in fact. But that was in the past. At the time I am telling you of, I played guitar and sang in a four-piece bar band called Briar

Patch that played all over the Carolinas. The name came from the B'rer Rabbit story, I think. None of us could remember. Briar Patch was not even a very good band, which I had to admit to myself so that I didn't get delusions, as apparently I am genetically predisposed to do. We covered other people's tunes, mostly, things we all liked and I could sing: Springsteen, Roy Orbison, John Mellencamp, Tom Petty, the usual classic rock stuff. Some Stone Temple Pilots, Semi-Sonic, Vertical Horizon, Goo Goo Dolls for the youngsters. We aspired to ska, reggae, and our own songs, but hell, we'd been known to break out Elvis and Carl Perkins in venues where the crowd threw bottles, which happened more often than I'd like to admit. It's hard to be faithful to your art when you play in the kind of places where chairs break over men's skulls and women throw beer on each other and it's a virtual lock that one or more drunken hillbillies will start screaming "Free Bird, Free Bird" until you break down and play some Skynyrd. Christ Almighty, I hate that song.

So that was my life. I once had larger aspirations, but about ten years before the time of which I speak, I suffered what I guess you'd call a personal setback, and I did not rebound from it. Or rather, I did rebound from it, but in wholly unexpected and unhealthy ways: back to my childhood home, to my old room, to a bizarre existence surrounded by old women who thought somehow that everyday life was a fitting excuse to sing praise.

Aunt Sister—Eula Mae was her given, but being she's the youngest, she grew up being called "Sister," and so there she was, sixty-some years old without a proper name to call her own—anyway, Aunt Sister switched over now to a rollicking "Onward Christian Soldiers," so I rolled out of bed, planting my feet on the floor with a reverberating thud so that the women could relax a little. They seemed to take the project of my continuing salvation seriously. Besides Aunt Sister, the women were my mother and Miss Ellen, the oldest and the scariest of the three. She was over seventy, but she still played piano at the Grace Tabernacle in Robbinsville. My mother played organ across from her most Sundays, except when she felt her life was being threatened by some new ailment, and on those occasions one of those Adams women from out Yellow Creek Road—not the ones on Talluah Road—would do their best to fill her heels. The week before, she had in fact been bedridden with colon cancer, although by Monday it was apparently far enough along into remission that she could join her sisters on the back porch to rock and shell peas and sip moisture-beaded Coca-Colas and act scandalized by my backsliding ways.

Don't misunderstand me. They were lovely Christian women, kind to children, generous to the poor and colored. But it is also true that they were capable of drawing and quartering a man with the silken strands of their words. My stepfather, Ray, in fact had moved out fourteen years before the time of which I speak, an act of sanity for which I admired him greatly, although he and my mother were still married and maintained a better relationship than most couples that I had known, my late wife and me included. He escaped; I stayed on in that household of women because I did not know where else to go, or how to live, or what to do with myself, because as I'm sure you recall, I was a sorry excuse for a human being.

I pulled on a Springsteen tour T-shirt, a pair of ratty Levi's, and my Birkenstocks, splashed some water on my face, then tramped clown-footed down the stairs so they couldn't pretend they didn't hear me and look up with badly acted surprise from some innocent conversation about my shortcomings.

"Morning," I called out as I entered the kitchen. I opened the fridge and spent a few minutes looking through it and ignoring the food already sitting at my place at the table.

"I made you some hotcakes," my mother said from the doorway to the parlor, her voice as soft as room-temperature butter. "I don't suppose they're any good now."

"Thanks, Momma," I managed to say, and I sat down to a lukewarm stack of buttermilk pancakes. She—Evvie Forester Fontenot— sat down across from me, and my eyes confirmed what my nose already knowed—that she had been to the beauty shop that morning for frost and curls. I cut and speared my first bite, poured a little more Aunt Jemima, and took another as Aunt Sister started up with "In the Garden." Miss Ellen was probably knitting: I heard her humming distractedly, then singing the end of each line before the two of them struck up the chorus in harmony, something like this:

"Hmmmmm Hmmmmm alone

Hmmmmm Hmmmmm roses."

I chewed my aging pancakes reflectively. That was what my mother's love tasted like: sweet, sticky, and stale. Hard to swallow. It clogged my chest and sometimes made me gasp for air. I took a long glug of orange juice, sour now after the syrup, and then my mother cleared her throat, her opening to edged conversation.

"What time did you get in, Clay?" Momma asked without looking up from her hands—she had gotten her nails done too, but I could see she was not crazy about the color, peach or coral or some such thing.

"Late," I said. "We played our first night at a club in Charlotte, had to drive half the night to get back."

"What'd you make? I suppose it was enough to justify playing the Devil's music on the Lord's Day?"

"Five hundred. Split five ways, less gas, less stitches for Otis."

"Sweet Jesus preserve us," she said, although it was strictly pro forma alarm, since she did not bring her hand to her chest as she would for moments of genuine distress. "Where at this time?"

"Right smack in the middle of his forehead." I drew a line over my eyebrows with my finger. "Twelve stitches. He closes his eyes, he looks like a cyclops."

She couldn't help laughing, and she hated herself for it. She did not approve of my life, but she was ever a sucker for a punch line. That must have been how my father won her; I heard that he was a funny man, even if he wasn't worth a damn in any other respect.

"You ought not to keep a drummer around that can't stay clear of those kinds of things," she said, trying to stop laughing and be solemn and motherly. "That Otis is trouble. I've been telling you for years."

"Yes, ma'am." Twenty-five years, at least. I used to go over to Otis's house in fifth grade to spin records, the beginning of her long train of rock-and-roll resentment against Otis, although after his mother died when we were in seventh grade—and to her eternal credit, since my mother is a closet racist, and Otis is the blackest of my friends, from the top of his modified 'Fro to the bottom of his Lenny Kravitz conquistador boots—my mom used to take food over and take Otis out shopping every August for school clothes.

From the time we were fifteen Otis and I put together garage bands that played pizza parlors and private parties. And when we were seventeen we put together a band that played "Stairway to Heaven" and "Layla" at a church talent show in Asheville, a band that in fact was chased off the stage and all the way to the boys' restroom by a throng of shrieking junior high girls, like something out of *Hard Day's Night* or something. What they would have done if they had caught us I will never know; all the same, I looked around daily for something that could compare to the surreal adrenaline rush of that moment.

Momma was waiting for my response, though, so I picked up in the present. "A good drummer is hard to come by. If he was just a bass player, now . . ."

She gave me an acidulous look of disapproval, but if she really knew me, she'd know that I didn't need to be lectured about alcohol and self-destruction. Since my personal setback, I hadn't so much as taken a swig of beer. When we were on stage, I sipped at a Dr. Pepper, and if I happened to see a fight brewing in front of us, I unplugged my guitar and just walked away.

There's enough pain and heartache in this life without having to go looking for it.

When I said earlier that Ray Fontenot was my daddy in all but name, I was alluding to some of that heartache, which starts early and, I suppose, doesn't let up until you die. Here it is, for what it's worth: My real father, Steve Forester, a.k.a. Steve Forrest, left us when I was still in diapers to try his luck in Hollywood. He couldn't get his car to start—it was a 1961 Triumph that Momma said he spent near as much time pushing as driving—and Momma was screaming at him and throwing things, so he abandoned it, boarded the bus to

Asheville, and then headed west from there. The car was about all he left behind, and it was about as worthless as he was: Ray and I had been trying to get that car to run for nigh on ten years and nary a peep did we hear.

He never came back, but he did write us three letters, coinciding with his three major speaking parts. In the first, he wrote about how he thought he'd be able to bring us out there shortly. In the second, he said things were harder then he ever imagined. In the third, he didn't say much beyond he wished he'd never come. There wasn't a fourth letter that I know of. No one knew what happened to him after that, and after Momma had people look for him without any luck, she had to have him declared legally dead eight years later to marry Ray. He dropped out of sight, and sometimes even out of mind, if a missing father can ever truly be called missing. And then late one night I was watching that cable show, you know the one where the guy and his little robots make fun of bad movies, and lo, there it was: *Mission to Mercury,* his starring role, in all its B-movie glory. And there he was: my dad, the so-called Steve Forrest, a dimple-jawed Rock Hudson lite done up in cheap spaceman duds. The pounding in my chest was a strange mixture of awe and embarrassment, something like Hamlet at last tracking down his daddy's ghost and finding him in a pair of Goodwill overalls.

"Momma," I called back into the house when he came on screen. "Momma, come quick."

Within seconds, she ran down the hall toward me, slippers flopping, clutching her robe about her throat. "Is the house on fire?"

"It's Daddy," I said, and I pointed to the TV. "Isn't it?"

She squinted at the screen, padded right up to the set, dropped her hands to her sides, and shook her head like she couldn't believe it. "Yes, that is your daddy." She stood for a moment more before letting out a long breath. "My God, he looks silly. And what are those things at the bottom of the screen?"

"They're robots," I said. "They're making fun of Daddy. Apparently he was one of the worst actors in the history of . . . history, I guess."

"Clay Forester," she said, and she whirled on me, "if you can't say something nice about somebody I'd thank you to keep your mouth shut." She watched my father for another moment as he piloted his cardboard spacecraft toward strange and unknown lands. Then she started bawling, which brought the rest of the house to life just as the show went to commercial.

Miss Ellen, of course, was first to arrive and take stock of the situation. "Young man," she said, exhaling frost at me, "you should be ashamed."

"I am," I told her. "Pretty near all the time."

But then the show came back on and some order was restored, explanations tendered and accepted. We settled back to watch as my father made contact with the surprisingly shapely female inhabitants of Mercury, and on one of the commercial breaks, I heated up some microwave popcorn and passed it around. It seemed to be an occasion of some sort.

"He was a handsome man," Aunt Sister offered at length.

"He always was that," Miss Ellen said. "Although it's clear now he couldn't act his way out of a paper bag. *Carousel* gave him the big head, I suppose, he was awful good in that, but whatever made him think people would love him just as much in Hollywood, I will never know."

"I do not like those robots," my mother said, and that was the last I knew about my father until Ray called while I was sitting there that Monday morning eating pancakes.

"Your mother wants me to talk to you about something," he said, his voice apologetic. "Come for lunch?"

"Gladly," I said. "But Ray, my mother is less than four feet away from me." I put my hand over the receiver and leaned forward. "Momma, what do you want Ray to tell me?"

"Oh," she said, looking her nails over again, "this and that."

I stifled the urge to blaspheme, and instead released my most piteous sigh. Two could play that game. "All right, Ray. Barbecue?"

"You bet," he said. "See you in a few, son."

I hung up and tried without success to get my mother to meet my gaze. I never realized that fingernails could be of such all-consuming interest. My aunts were singing "I'll Fly Away," the second hand on the stove clock was moving in distinct and separate clicks, and at last she got up to clear my plate.

"Well," I said. "I guess I'll get around. Go see what the old man wants. I'm sure it's important."

She paused with her hands in the dishwater, looked over her shoulder, and delivered her usual parting: "Clay, you really ought to get married again. Settle down. Take up your work. Make a real life for yourself." There was a new urgency in her voice that morning, almost a tremble for some reason I couldn't fathom; I didn't perceive that I was noticeably more distressing or distressed that morning than in weeks, months, years past. Still, I'd reached the point where I just nodded my head in agreement when she said it—nodded because it was true, all true, everything she said, and I knew it the way I knew I ought to love my country, worship my God, support my local sheriff.

"Yes ma'am," I said softly. "I surely should." And I went off to find some clothes that a man could wear without embarrassing his stepfather.

Ray and I were always the only white customers in Dolly's, which was as it ought to be. The fewer white people the better; we'd just ruin it with Elvis knickknacks and combo platters and plastic sporks, the most useless utensil on God's green earth. Bobby Blue Bland and Muddy Waters were playing on the jukebox, and barbecue here was brisket so tender it fell apart in your mouth, served on wax paper with Wonder bread, onions, and sliced dill pickles. The sauce came in plastic cups, and it was as hot and sweet and musty as love in a backseat.

I'd eaten most of my food. We'd been making small talk on North Carolina basketball and other such essential topics, and I was beginning to eye the cherry cobbler when Ray cleared his throat. Unlike my mother, Ray never cleared his throat for pleasure, so I knew that either he was choking or this was truly serious business.

"Son, your mama got a telephone call last night from Santa

Fe, New Mexico," he said, and he looked up from the table to watch how I would receive his news. "It's about your daddy."

All the meat I'd ingested became an iron lump in my stomach. "I hope to hell he doesn't think he's coming home after all this time," I said. "That train has left the station."

"No, son. He's dead. Died yesterday. The funeral's in New Mexico Friday."

Etta, our waitress, came over to see if we wanted cobbler, and I have to tell you, even with that bombshell dropped we nodded our heads at her. It was that kind of cobbler.

"So I thought since you'd need to go to the funeral—"

"Like hell, Ray," I said, then caught myself. "That man in Santa Fe was no more my father than Etta here."

"And I sho ain't no man's father," she said, slapping our bowls of cherry cobbler down in front of us. And that's for certain; her bosom weighed more than my entire body.

"You're my father, Ray, the only one I've ever had. You took me in; you raised me; you did your best to make me a good man. I don't have a father in New Mexico. Case closed."

He smiled sadly in appreciation. "Still, son, the last thing that man did was ask for you. He made a mistake, sure, and it was a big one, but—"

"He should have thought of that a long time ago." I took a bite of that crust, golden and buttery and coated with the cherry filling. "He left his family. And he never cared what happened to us after he left. No Christmas cards. No birthday cards. No hey I'm still alive cards. Good riddance, I say. Tell me that he burned to a crisp in those wildfires around Los Alamos and I'll be a happy man."

B.B. King and Lucille took up "The Thrill Is Gone," and I closed my eyes and shook my head in time to the music. I didn't want to talk about it anymore.

"Damn, son, " Ray said after a verse and a chorus. "I can't believe you're making me say this."

I opened my eyes. His face was red as his cobbler. "Well, spit it out, old-timer," I said. "I'm a busy man."

He took a good look down at the table, rubbed at a spot of

barbecue sauce there, cleared his throat. "Son, I don't believe in signs. You know that. It's a bone of contention between me and your momma, if you don't mind my saying so. Unlike some folks, God does not deign to speak to me in an audible voice and remind me to take out the trash. But yesterday, something happened."

I spooned my last bite, pushed my bowl away from me, arched an eyebrow, and waited. He looked up at me, his gaze dropped immediately, and he went on.

"I had some time on my hands last night, so I went out and put that head gasket on your daddy's car."

I nodded. "The one that came in last week. I still need to pay you for that."

"Yes, you do. But that's not what I want to tell you. I put the gasket on. I got everything tightened down. I hooked up the battery. And then I turned the key and she started."

I swallowed my last bite of cobbler and sat up straight. "You got the Triumph started?"

"I did. And she kept running. And started up again when I turned her off." He shook his head and pursed his lips, like he didn't know what to think. "We've been working on that car for ten years." He looked around, maybe to see if there was some way he didn't have to say this. "Son, don't you think it means something that last night of all nights, his car comes back to life?"

"You're scaring me now," I said. "Not with your haunted car story. But you are scaring me."

"It's got to mean something, son. Don't you think?"

I sat up straight and looked him in the eyes. "Ray, I don't care if that man's ghost walks in the door over there and starts singing 'Fever.'" Ray was a big fan of Peggy Lee. "He was not my father. You are. I'm not going to Santa Fe tonight, tomorrow, or ever. That whole damn state is on fire, anyway. Plus I've got a show tonight. And tomorrow night. And the next night. I couldn't go if I wanted to. Plus I don't want to. Can I be any more explicit?"

Ray sighed and shook his head. "No, son. I said what I came here to say. What you do with it is up to you."

"Thank you, Ray," I said, leaning across the table. "I know

you mean well. And I know the Christian thing to do would be to forgive the bastard. But I'm not interested in doing the Christian thing."

He sighed, for this was a bone of contention between us. Ray was a good Christian and devout Southern Baptist, although not so devout that he felt personally led to boycott Disney, convert the Christ-killing Jews, or shove women out of the pulpit and make sure they were at home cooking for their husbands where they belonged. I felt bad, and I hung my head a little. "Listen, I gotta go. Otis is expecting me at two."

"All right, son. When do you want to pick up that car?"

I stood there for a second and then I shrugged. "Hell, Ray, I don't know. We can talk about it later, okay? Thanks for lunch."

"Always a pleasure," he said. He got up and hugged me, and damned if there wasn't just as much love in his eyes as before we sat down to talk. I guess fatherhood suits some.

He patted me three times on the shoulders when he hugged me, like he had since I was old enough to remember being hugged; then he sat back down, and as I walked out, he waved his good-bye, one finger raised like he still had one more thing to say.

He didn't think I saw him gesture to Etta for more cobbler as I shut the door.

But I did.

2

There's a line in one of my favorite old movies where some dried-up bird of a contract actress tells Cary Grant that their life together must involve no domestic entanglements of any kind. He's a bit chagrined by the idea, even though he eventually gets rid of her and falls for Katharine Hepburn, and I think he was right to be chagrined. A man needs some domestic entanglement, and even if you tallied my mother in that category—which gets us into some spooky psychosexual territory I'd just as soon not traverse—there was otherwise so little entanglement to my life that most of the time I felt I might just slip free of the planet and disappear.

That included my current girlfriend, if you'd care to call her that. I guess it was only appropriate, seeing how I'd otherwise regressed in my life, that I took up with my high school girlfriend Tracy York when she came back on the market a couple of years ago. She had just divorced her pathetic drunk of a husband, Mark, after thirteen years of marriage. He beat her when he was drunk, and finally when he put her in the hospital, her dad, Alvin, called the cops and Ray, not in that order, and together they got her to see the light. Since wife-beating was not one of my own particular vices and drunkenness was a thing of the past for me, naturally I found his behavior loathsome, but in truth, I think my vices were just as large as Mark's, if not as lethal. Tracy just seemed to be one of those women drawn to men who are no damn good—like most women, since most men are no damn good, I feared—and maybe she just traded Mark in for a different model.

But that's a lot more analysis than we engaged in out loud.

In truth, I saw her at the Fourth of July picnic when she first came back to Robbinsville, and we got to talking, and then to holding hands while skyrockets arced over our heads, and then to some unspoken understanding that we would try to help each other in some way if we could. Ah, but that last phrase was the ticklish one, for truth to tell, neither of us really had much to offer anymore.

When two people who have lost everything come together, a strange dance ensues. If you could watch them, they might look like a couple so concerned about stepping on each other's feet—and wary of being stepped on—that they're hardly even moving to the music. Maybe only their proximity would indicate to you that they were dancing at all. And that was where we had been, and where we were.

She was not the girl I remembered. I know that I had no leg to stand on in that department, but before she married Mark she was smart, opinionated, perky, and so open that you felt like you could step into her life as through an open window. Now she resembled me in some respects—closed off, fearful, and furtive—but she was unlike me in that she was a thinker, she relived her past, she tried to figure out what went wrong. Since what Mark did wasn't her fault, maybe it was even a comfort, but since what happened to me was, and since I already knew all too well what went wrong, I tried not to think so much.

Our griefs were so different that truly it was hard to relate to each other. She lost herself, tiny pieces of self beaten loose by the fists of her brute of a husband, until there was nothing left of her and someone else had to step in to save what remained of her life. I lost everything but myself, all at once and by my own hand, and no one could step in to give back to me what I had lost, not even the God who gave Job new children, the God who told Joel that He could restore the years that the locusts had eaten.

Because I didn't want new children, and I didn't want the years.

I just wanted my wife back.

I wanted my son.

I wanted another chance, and that could never happen.

So there were, at last, only two things we had in common: both of us were damaged, maybe beyond repair; but we shared memories of an innocent time before the locusts came, a time when we cared about each other. And maybe, somehow, that could be a comfort, although I'd yet to see how we do much more for each other than help each other take another step forward toward we know not what.

Tracy used to be a dancer. I used to look down and find her spinning in front of the stage, her laughing face shining up at me, her long blond hair flung every which way by the shaking of her head. She still came to hear us play sometimes, if it was nearby, but she didn't like it the way she used to. Noisy drunks naturally didn't hold much attraction for her these days, so she didn't like most of the clubs we played, and when she did come to one of the nicer joints, she sat in a back booth and listened intently and wanted nothing more than to leave as soon as the last set was through.

Well, we'd all changed.

All of us, I guess, except for Otis. Whatever my mom might have said about him—and justly so, because sometimes his behavior was more than borderline moronic—there was something reassuring about his refusal to face the intrusion of maturity.

I went over to wake him up after my little talk with Ray about my genealogy, and found him on the floor of his living room wrapped only in a blanket. He was playing Super Mario, listening to vintage Aerosmith, and happily munching on Froot Loops straight from the box.

With a name like Otis, and the way I've described him, I know the temptation might be to expect him to be one step up the evolutionary scale from Arnold Ziffel, but truth to tell, there's more to most people than we give them credit for, even if—like Otis—they take their sartorial inspiration from Sly Stone, Jimi Hendrix, and Elton John. Otis went to Warren Wilson, a good liberal arts college in Asheville, for three years before his dad had the first of three heart attacks and he had to come back and run the Texaco station for him. He did that for nine years, until the third heart attack left him an orphan, so maybe he deserved a second childhood. At any rate, he was taking it.

He paused the game for a second to nod a greeting when I came in, and to chase his Loops with a swig of warm Budweiser.

"How you feeling?" I asked before throwing some clothes against the far wall to make a place for myself on the couch.

"Okay," he said. "My head hurts like a son of a bitch. Or it would if they hadn't given me that Percodan. Man, I love Percodan."

He was ready to drink again and I grabbed the beer out of his hand. "Do not be drinking while you're taking painkillers. We've got a show tonight. Not to mention I'd like to keep your sorry ass alive."

He looked up at me with his sad puppy eyes. "Now who ever got hurt by introducing a few innocent chemicals into their bodies?"

"Mama Cass. Jimi Hendrix. Jim Morrison. Me. I could go on."

He rolled his eyes in a "whatever" and started the next round of his game: what looked to me like Mario fighting a bunch of wild strawberries and chocolate bars, although I could have been less than lucid from my gospel-induced lack of sleep.

"Listen," I told him. "I got some news. It's kind of—I don't know—bad. Freaky bad."

"You look a little freaky," he said. How he could tell that with the attention he was giving to the game I do not know; maybe he felt something about my presence when I came in. Otis was the kind of person who talked about vibes and auras. He got in with a bad crowd of New Agers when he was in college, and once he kicked this guy's ass because his astral self shot Otis the finger. But anyway:

"Ray told me my dad was alive."

"I could have told you that," he said. "Your presence in my living room makes it an established fact."

"No," I said. "He *was* alive. Once. But now he's dead. He died yesterday. In New Mexico. Some woman called the house last night while we were in Charlotte. But maybe it's all bullshit. I mean, Aunt Sister took the message. Maybe she thinks the woman said my dad was dead in New Mexico when what she really said was, Would you like to change your long-distance provider?"

Otis put down his controller, leaving Mario to be flattened by what appeared to be a giant marshmallow. "You're shitting me," he said.

"About which part? About Aunt Sister, yes. About Ray, no. Ray said they're burying him up there on Friday."

Otis made a mournful sound and shook his head. "I'm sorry, man. Really I am. Did he burn up in those fires around Los Alamos? Did he get radiation poisoning? I have a friend at Sierra Club that says that when the Los Alamos labs burned they let loose all kinds of toxic shit. It's too bad, man. Whatever happened. But if the government killed your dad, then dude, I think you need to take up the gavel again or whatever it is lawyers have. Don't let the government get away with it. Stand up for him."

I blinked rapidly a couple of times, a pretty normal response to Otis. I'm not the only one who has it. Then I found my voice. "Otis, are you mental? I have no feelings for him. The man walked out on us thirty-five years ago. I never knew him. If they don't bury him in that space suit I won't even recognize him."

"But he was your father, man. You've got to go to his fucking funeral."

I shook my head. "The man was not a father. He was a sperm donor. And I'm a little rusty, but if I remember how that particular procedure works, he was probably happy as punch to donate."

Otis reached for the six-pack next to the couch, saw my disapproving look and interposing foot, and instead lifted a half-full glass of milk up off the table. At least I think it was milk; I did not want to investigate more closely. He chugged it down, wiped his mouth with the back of his hand, and shook his head. "Dude, you should definitely go. You should be the bigger man."

"This is not about who is the bigger man. I could be the

biggest man you ever saw. I could be so big I scare women and children and crush cars with my feet. Bigness is a moot issue here. We've got shows every night this week. I don't even have time to fly up, and Ray has this crackpot idea that since he finally got my dad's Triumph running I ought to drive it to the funeral."

Otis's eyes got big, and I could see he was getting all spacey on me. "He's right, man. It's like your dad is making amends. It makes all kinds of cosmic sense."

"Maybe so. Ray thinks it's a sign from God."

The CD player flipped to the next disk, Fleetwood Mac. Now there was a dysfunctional family for you.

"You should definitely go," he said, "as long as the radiation has died down." He looked intently at me, saw that I was in no mood to listen to more persuasion, and shrugged just like Ray. "Well, we can tell the guys about it tonight. But if you decide you want to go, don't make the band an excuse. We can put together a show that doesn't need two guitars. Or we could get one of my buddies from Asheville to sit in for you for a few gigs."

"Otis, I know I can be replaced. I don't want to go."

He shrugged. "Okay, man. Your choice. Have you talked to Tracy?"

"Not yet." I picked up something from under the heap of clothes that I thought might be a pillow. It was, and I squeezed it a few times. I liked the feel of it between my fingers. "Maybe I'll go by and see her after I leave here. I'm ready to roll."

"You sure you don't want to hang for a while? I've got more cereal. Hey, I've got Cap'n Crunch." He motioned vaguely toward the kitchen, although knowing him, it could have been in any room of the house. "You used to eat Cap'n Crunch by the boxful. Remember? It made my mom so happy. She couldn't cook for shit, but that was one thing she could give you that you liked. We'd eat cereal for dinner sometimes. She just used to stand right at that counter there and smile and smile." He stopped, bit his lip, turned his head away from me.

I sighed. Fleetwood Mac played "Never Goin' Back Again."
When it became unavoidable, I spoke into the silence.

"You miss them," I said. "I know."

"I know you do," he said without turning around.

I set the pillow back on the heap and stood. "Well, on that
upbeat note I'll take off," I said, and I raised a cautioning finger. Otis was someone who really needed a mother; maybe I
could give him mine. "One controlled dangerous substance at
a time. Do you hear me?" I picked up the six-pack and tucked
it under my arm for safekeeping.

"I hear you," he said.

"You have any more in the house?"

"Nope," he said. He wouldn't lie to me, so at least I knew
he'd just be flying on painkillers all day, not the worst thing he
could be doing.

We did our special handshake—regular shake, soul shake,
then fists top and bottom—and I stood up. "What time you
picking me up?" Otis drove the equipment van and I usually
rode with him.

He checked his watch, which apparently didn't work—he
shook his wrist, then listened to it—then looked at the clock
on the VCR, which was a line of blinking dashes.

"I'll call you when it's time," I said and opened the door.
"Later."

"Later," he said and went back to his game.

I decided I wasn't up to a serious talk with Tracy, and I certainly wasn't up to going back to the house, so what to do for
my next few hours was a quandary. As I passed the Dairy
Queen, I decided to start by wasting a half hour over a soft-
serve sundae, and as I was pulling into a space, I recognized
Tracy sitting at a window booth. She saw me, her sad face
broke into a smile, and I was caught. And I smiled back, because now that I was there, I discovered that I was genuinely
glad to see her.

"Brownie sundae," I called to the little Hendricks girl behind the counter, and I slid in next to Tracy. She was dressed
for work—since she came back to Robbinsville she did the
books for her dad's hardware store, something less than a full

time job, really—and she looked good: black slacks, a sheer black silk blouse with a black camisole beneath, sensible black flats that she had propped up on the plastic bench opposite.

"I felt a Blizzard calling me," she said, giving me a hug. "Oreo." I took a look. She was about half finished with it and it had gone all gooey, so I guess she'd been sitting there for quite a while.

I took a deep breath and scanned my hands on the table in front of me. When I realized my mother's influence, I put my hands under the table out of sight. "Can I tell you something, Trace?"

She nodded gravely. Her blue eyes, which used to sparkle, were now limpid. Still beautiful, but I could see that she had pulled back behind them, as though that were any solution.

"I just came from lunch with Ray. My real dad finally turned up after all this time. Or his corpse did. He died yesterday in New Mexico, and everybody apparently thinks I should go to the funeral. He asked for me."

"Wow," she said and reached for her cup. "What are you going to do?"

"What would you do?"

She slurped, then put the cup down, then sat quietly, thinking. I asked a good question, and now she was imagining how it might feel to be me just now. We waited until she was ready. "I don't know," she said at last. "I'll bet you can't see any reason for going. I could understand if you're too mad to go. It's quite a shock. But Clay, aren't you the least bit curious? I would be."

"Well, okay," I admitted. "I guess I am. But anyway, I can't go." I made a too-bad face. "We've got gigs all week."

She made a face too, but it was not such a pleasant one. "Don't give me that. You've chosen to live a life without real responsibilities. So don't try to act like an upstanding citizen now to get out of something you just don't want to do."

"Whoa, Betsy," I said. "I haven't chosen anything about this life," for that seemed to be true, although I guess even the act of not choosing is a choice of sorts. "And I do have responsibilities. Lots of them." At the moment, I couldn't think of one to save my life.

"You've got to sing somebody else's shitty songs for stinking drunks in dives across the great state of North Carolina." Bad sign. She only cussed when she was furious, and since that much was still true of her, I unconsciously drew my head and shoulders in like a box turtle confronted with violence. She softened when she saw my reaction, and her voice lowered. "You really should go, Clay. Find out why he asked you to. Find out who he was. Who knows? Maybe it could be important to you in some way." She moved her lips together like she was spreading lipstick; it was what she did when she wanted to choose her words carefully. "Maybe—maybe it could be a healing thing for you."

"Healing? I'm not sick," I said. She dropped her eyes to the table. "I don't need healing, really. Do I?"

She took my hand. Hers was cool and a little clammy from her drink, but I squeezed it and eventually she squeezed back. "We're survivors, Clay, you and me. That's something, I guess. But surviving isn't enough after a while. Do you know what I mean?"

I moistened my lips. "I begin to fear that I do."

"In three years, we haven't talked once about a future. Maybe that's my fault too. But both of us are halfway through our three score and ten and we're living with our parents, for Christ's sake. I want a life of my own again someday. I want to have kids. Don't you think at some point we have to pick up and move on down the road a bit?"

"I don't know," I said quietly. "I don't think I know how." I barely got it out. I couldn't believe I had said it, but she just nodded her head. It was not news to her, and she smiled sadly and took both my hands.

"Go to New Mexico. I'm asking you to. For you, first and most important. For me, maybe just a little. Maybe you'll find out that the past really is past and you won't be haunted by it any more. Maybe you'll learn something from it and move on."

"Like you've done?" I said and instantly regretted it.

"I want to move on," she said. "Maybe one day you can help me do that."

I was filled with a dangerous feeling that made me kiss her upturned lips. "Come with me," I said. "Maybe we'll make this discovery together."

She thought about it, but I could see by her pursed lips that ultimately it was going to be a no. "I'll always remember that you asked me," she said. "But you know as well as I do that Luke has to face Darth Vader alone. Yoda said so."

Well, that was true. He did.

We got up out of the booth, and I walked her to her dad's Olds, which I now saw was parked right next to my old truck. I took her in my arms and was about to kiss her when, over my shoulder, she saw Otis's six-pack of Bud in my truck bed.

"Beer?" she asked. Not in an accusing way, but a curious one.

"Huh?" I turned, followed her eyes, and explained.

It touched her for some reason, and she kissed me gently on the lips before opening her door.

"You're a good man, Clay Forester," she said. "I love you, you know."

"I know," I said.

"And you're going to New Mexico?"

I sighed and shrugged. Like Ray, I too had a problem with signs and symbols, but sometimes when they gang up on you and clang you in the head like the lid of a garbage can, only a fool can deny there's something going on. There was something out there for me to learn, or to finish. Or something. "Yeah, I guess so. I mean, if Yoda says I must. I can leave in the morning as soon as the gospel piano sounds. Hell, maybe I'll even take the old Triumph; if it breaks down before I reach Asheville I'll take it as a sign I was never really supposed to go."

"Be safe," she said. "Come back."

"Don't be ridiculous," I said. "How could I desert all my responsibilities here?"

"Uh-huh," she laughed, a ghost of the old Tracy peeking through for a moment, and she closed the door, started the car, and blew me a kiss as she drove away.

I realized, strangely, that I was going to miss her. It was an odd feeling, after all that time, to miss one of the living.

Very odd.

I got into the truck to head over to Ray's to see if that car really would start.

Because of course, as always, I had my doubts.

3

They were all waiting for me on the porch when I pulled up in the Triumph—rocking, sipping, cackling, fanning their faces with *Good Housekeeping* and *Inner Room*.

"Here he is, here he is," Aunt Sister squealed as I shut off the engine, and I swear to you, every one of those elderly ladies got to their feet and started clapping.

I felt like Engelbert Humperdinck.

But I get ahead of myself, and I've committed to putting down on paper everything you need to know, so a word or two on my so-called father Steve Forester's car. It was a Triumph TR-3, yellow, black leather interior and convertible top. The body was good, and the interior was perfect since the car had sat covered for a good twenty years before Ray strong-armed me into helping him wrestle with it, an epic struggle that I imagined then as being like Jacob and the angel, maybe, and sure to hamstring us financially if not actually pop our hips out of socket.

It was a tiny car. I could even push it up a slight incline. The backseat was slapped flush up against the front seats, and was really more of a cargo space if the truth be known. There was also a luggage rack on the back big enough to lash down a carry-on bag and not much more.

It was odd to slide into it, to fire up the engine, to listen to it idle, *putt-putt-putt* like an oversized go-cart. My father had driven this car, had washed it and waxed it, had wooed my mother in it and, for all I knew, conceived me in it. And now he was dead.

I drove off down Ray's long driveway, past towering pines

on one side and the Cheoah River on the other, and out onto Highway 129.

My father was dead.

I would never meet him, know him. Never. Of course, he would never know me, never meet my wife, see his grandson. But maybe he was better off. He had missed out on a whole lot of heartache, hadn't had to climb down in the pit with me and wallow around for the past ten years.

Son of a bitch. Who needed him? I was glad he was dead. I was so angry that I shut my eyes for a moment and had a fleeting image of myself accelerating and ramming his car into a tree, a familiar impulse, I'm afraid, but one I set aside just as quickly. Everyone would still be dead, everything would still be an unredeemable mess, and I probably wouldn't harm a hair on my unlucky head.

It was a steamy afternoon even with the top down, and I thought for a bit about driving out to the lake for a quick dip before I went home, but I had to get back and get ready for the show, which is how I found myself pulling up to the house during what I knew to be prime old-lady loitering hours.

"Otis is coming by for me at four," I said, a conversational attempt at the flying wedge I would need to get past them and inside the house.

"Plenty of time," Miss Ellen said. "Plenty of time. Sit a spell. Have a Coke Cola."

"I'd rather not," I said, as they pulled me down into an empty rocker and then settled back themselves, watching me expectantly.

I'll confess: I broke under the strain.

"What?" I asked, looking around at them. "What are you three old women staring at?"

"Ray told us," Momma said. "Told us that you're taking the Triumph out to New Mexico for your daddy's funeral. When are you leaving?"

"Tonight after the show," I said. "Which I've got to go get cleaned up for—" I rose up out of my chair.

"In a minute, Clay, in a minute," Miss Ellen said, raising a hand to magically seat me again. "We were just wondering. What made you decide to go?"

"Yes," Aunt Sister said. "Evvie said Ray said that when Ray told you about your daddy you didn't want to go."

"I don't want to go," I said. "And I didn't decide to go. I don't ever decide to do anything." Which was a lot more than I meant to say, and a lot angrier than I intended to be to these good women who were looking at me with a trace of alarm leavened by the usual superior amusement. It must be really something to be a woman and be so superior. "Everyone seems to think it's a good idea for me to go. Do I understand that right?"

"Well," Aunt Sister began, then shut her mouth, since Miss Ellen would probably want to answer and did.

"Your mother and I think it would be good for you," she said. "Close the door on the man, I say," as though it was that simple, as though, for example, recognizing that you are a wreck is all it takes to make you suddenly whole and healthy.

But what I said was, "Yes, ma'am. Maybe you're right."

"I wish you'd start while it's still daylight," Momma said. "I worry about you, driving in the middle of the night—"

"I don't think the band can do without me tonight," I said. "And I'll be fine. You know I can never go to sleep right after I play. I'll be good for a long stretch of road."

They sighed, almost in harmony. I could almost hear them thinking: Why did I have to do everything my own way?

"I've got to grab a shower," I said, rising. "Otis'll be here any minute."

"Otis will be here exactly twenty-five minutes after he's supposed to be," my mother said. "But you go on in if you've a mind to. We'll just sit out here and talk about you behind your back." And then they all gave me those gleaming beatific smiles, as if to make that truth more bearable: Yes, we're going to sit out here and talk about you. And yes, we love you dearly.

God save us from such love, I thought, but all the same I smiled back and raised a hand in a departing wave.

All my gear was already in the van, so really I just had to pick some stage clothes, which wasn't some sort of Judy Garland outfitting decision. I had on clean jeans that fit pretty well, so I pulled out a clean navy T-shirt and my red Converse high-tops. I was set. I also threw a couple of days' underwear and socks into my old road warrior carry-on bag, plus one of my dark lawyer suits, a white button-down shirt, and black shoes for the funeral, assuming I ever got that far. I'd lash that on the back of the car with some bungie cords and be ready to head out as soon as we got back from Charlotte.

After I got out of the shower, I got dressed, then noodled around a little on my acoustic guitar with some old Fleetwood Mac and Eagles, then went downstairs for a sandwich before we left.

Otis came up and rang the doorbell at 4:27. My mother let him in, kissed him on the stitches to make his head feel better, and then asked him if he felt sleepy, if he had any dizziness, and if he'd see a brain doctor about an EKG.

"Yes'm," he said, ducking his head and smiling, his standard response to my mother. "But right now I feel just fine."

"Otis, Otis, Otis," she said sadly.

"You'll have to keep an eye on him while I'm gone," I told her, to which she rolled her eyes. As though I needed to give her mothering lectures.

"What time will you boys be home?" she asked, putting her hands on her hips like we were in fact still teenagers on a curfew.

"Four," I said, looking to Otis, who nodded. "Maybe four-thirty."

"Merciful God," she said, shaking her head and turning her eyes skyward. "Send your angels to watch over them."

"Thanks, Momma," I said, bussing her on the cheek. "I'll call you from the road."

"You boys be careful," she said. "And Otis, you steer clear of trouble tonight. For me, y'hear?"

"Yes'm," he said solemnly. "I will do that."

She blinked rapidly a few times, then wiped her hands on her apron and stepped back.

"Bye, Momma," I said. "I'll call you from the road."

"Bye," Otis said.

"Bye," she said, and then we walked out to the van and headed for Charlotte. Otis had been listening to Creed, which

I liked well enough, but after two songs I asked him to change the music to something a little quieter, more contemplative.

"We can do pregame music in a bit," I said. We always liked to play upbeat stuff—Def Leppard, Aerosmith, Van Halen, UFO, Ian Hunter—to put our game faces on so we could hit the stage feeling pumped up and not a hundred years old, which was what we were becoming and what I often felt these days.

"Okay, how about some Hornsby?" he asked, flipping through his CDs.

"Pop Hornsby or jazz Hornsby?" I asked. "Because I know you like the old pop stuff better."

"Yeah, that's good stuff," he said. " 'The Way It Is,' 'Mandolin Rain' . . ." He drifted a little, then corrected his steering.

"Sure," I said. "But the new stuff kicks ass. The chord modulations, the complexity. Pat Metheny and Branford Marsalis . . ."

Otis stuck in "The Way It Is" and posed like a smiling Buddha. "There is also perfection in simplicity, my son," he said.

"Those songs are three-chord wonders," I said.

"No, man. They're simple, but the solos are lightning in a bottle."

We drove for a while, Bruce Hornsby's clear tenor flying over his piano chords.

"What the hell does that mean?" I said after we'd been driving for a while. "Lightning in a bottle?"

"It's a figure of speech," he said, looking over from his driving. "You know, like a metaphor?"

"I know what a metaphor is," I said. "Sure. Comparison of two things. You are a jackass."

He laughed, but I had to admit, the music was just right. "So," I said after a bit, "what shall we do tonight?" The crowd the night before had been mostly a rowdy rock crowd, with the usual screamed requests for Southern rock. "They didn't go for Orbison last night at all. Except for 'Pretty Woman,' which they probably thought was a Van Halen song anyway."

"Hell, let's just add some more Aerosmith and then do a twenty-minute version of 'Cocaine.' "

"Christ no," I said. "I hate that song."

"Hold the morning edition for that news flash," he said. I looked up and he was drifting over into the other lane again, so I gave a little tug of the wheel to correct it. "How about some Skynyrd or Molly Hatchet early? Kind of a preemptive strike, get it over with?"

"Hell, no. You toss in 'Flirting with Disaster' and it's not some kind of vaccination. It tells them 'Squeal for more.' "

"Point taken," he said. He was driving on the shoulder now, and I yelled at him.

"Pull over, dumbass," I said. "You can't drive for shit."

"It's just the pain pills," he whined. "I'm not doing that bad."

"Pull over," I said. "This is one disaster I can stop from happening."

He gave me a look, like he was trying to figure out if he wanted to call me on something, but what he wanted to call me on, he didn't say. He did turn on the blinker, ease onto the shoulder, and stop.

"Okay," he said. "You've got the con." He sat there, waiting. It certainly didn't look to me like I had the con.

"Well, get your ass up out of the captain's seat," I said.

"Come around," he said. "I'll climb over."

I grunted with exasperation and got out. Cars whooshed by, and a semi let out a long honk that almost startled me directly into its path.

"Jesus," I said. My heart was pounding, my hands shaking. I spread them across on the steering wheel for Otis to see. "Like I couldn't hear him already."

He looked at me again, keenly, under his brows, but I turned away from him, got my breathing under control, and shifted into drive. "Mandolin Rain" was playing, and I turned it up until I heard the words—I didn't want any songs about heartbreak just then—and then turned it clean off, and we drove in silence for a bit, if you can call the whir of out-of-balance tires and the sniveling of an overstressed Ford engine silent.

I was glad to be back behind the wheel. I'm really a good driver. I'm almost always right on top of things, alert to details, seeing the road in all directions.

Of course, it's the *almost* that always gets you.

We were low on gas—the light had actually come on shortly after we traded places—so we pulled off U.S. 74 at the Forest City exit and eased up to the pump.

"I'll pump," I said and handed him a twenty.

"You want anything?"

"Get me a Dr. Pepper. No—make it two. One for now, one for later." I came around to the pump and pulled the nozzle loose. Otis called back from halfway to the door, "Do you want some chicken? I'll buy."

"Not from this rattrap," I said. The chicken in this dive had been sitting under the infrared lamps since Hoover was president.

As I took off the gas cap and turned on the pump, a green Plymouth minivan pulled up on the other side of the island, a harried mom with several kids. The ones who got out were about three and five, boys both, and I watched them walk in, each hanging from a hand as if it were the only thing anchoring them to this world. I stood there seeing them long after the door had closed behind them.

That's when I felt the eyes on me, and I looked up and saw the boy who had stayed in the car. He was maybe nine or ten, and he had his finger stuck in one of those Harry Potter books to mark the place, but had stopped reading for a moment to watch me. He had longish hair, not a fashion statement, but simply hair creeping over his ears and eyes that needed cutting.

He saw I was looking up and blinked, but his eyes stayed on me, so I smiled a little—a tentative smile instead of a big grin, because there are some scary men in this world, and probably most of them have big smiles plastered across their faces—and then inclined my head in a nod, single, simple.

He didn't smile, just sat looking at me for a bit out of his big, serious eyes. Then he opened his book again, dropped his head, and began reading.

The mother half dragged, half carried her other two back

to the car. "We're going to be late," I heard her tell them, and after she had the three-year-old in his car seat, she came around and climbed in without even a look at me.

I was putting the nozzle back in the pump, which was how I happened to see the oldest boy one last time. He had looked up from his book again, and his face was solemn, like he was full of deep thoughts, and he just raised his fingers in a sort of good-bye.

They were long gone when Otis found me standing out there, my head down, my hand on the pump for a little extra support.

"Clay," he said, and I didn't answer him.

"Clay. If it's a heart attack, nod once."

I didn't nod, but still I couldn't answer. There was a hard lump in my chest, like my mom's pancakes had solidified: cold, heavy, cancerous, deadly.

He took my shoulder and pushed me upright, although I didn't meet his eyes. "Was it the little boys?"

I still couldn't nod. Sometimes it just hit me harder than others.

My son Ray would have been nine years old that year.

Otis took my arm, opened the passenger door, put me inside. He came around and started the van, and we got back on the highway. He looked over at me a couple of times, but I didn't say anything, and at last I could feel him getting ready to blow. The third time he looked across at me, his eyes were full of tears.

"How long, man?" He didn't expect an answer, so he forged ahead. "How long are you going to blame yourself?"

I looked out the window at the darkening woods. "How long is there?"

He pounded the steering wheel for emphasis. "You ought to give yourself a break. There was nothing you could do for them. It's a blessing that you're alive."

I looked across at him, earnest and upset, and back out into the trees. "Not for me, it isn't."

He looked away from me and took a deep breath, and it was a long time before he felt he had enough control over himself to talk. "Well, it is for me, Clay. What would I do without you? And it is for your folks. And for Tracy." I reached over and turned the Hornsby back on, loud. A root canal without anesthesia was less painful than listening to this. The music rang, rattled, and when Otis reached over to switch it off again, the silence echoed as well.

"I miss them too, Clay," he said, and there was an edge to his voice. "Ray was my godson, for Christ's sake. Do you think you're the only one who hurts?"

"I know," I croaked. "But I was the one driving."

He shook his head, and the van careened a little bit while he did it. "You had a few glasses of wine and then you went to the airport. I know you feel like you could have done something, that things could have been different, that if there's not a reason things happen, then how do we go on in this fucked-up world? But Clay"—and here he raised his right hand from the wheel and pointed at me—"if you'd been as sober then as you are at this moment, that garbage truck would still have run the red light. And they'd still be dead."

Ah, good friends. They always think the best of you. Of course, they have to, to protect their investment. "I would have seen him coming," I insisted. "I could have gotten out of the way."

He shook his head again. "I don't think so, man. But I know nothing I say makes any difference. They're still dead."

I nodded and looked back out the window. "Anybody ever tell you that you talk too much?"

"Nobody's ever gotten a word in," he said. "You know what?"

I sighed. "I'm sure you're going to tell me."

"Damn right I am. That's my job. So hear this: You think you have a handle on this. I know you, man. You see the years passing, you think you're piling so much shit on top of the trapdoor that there's no way the alligators can get out. Only it's not alligators down there, Clay. It's plutonium."

"Isn't that a mixed metaphor?"

He waved his hand dismissively and went on. "It's not alligators, it's radioactive waste, and there's no safe place in the house while it's down there."

"What's the half-life of plutonium?"

"A lot longer than your sorry ass is going to be here, believe me. Why can't you be even the tiniest little bit like me? I say anything that comes into my head, I talk about things, I try and move on. Why can't you just talk about it?"

"Thanks, man," I said.

"Which means, 'Yes, Otis, you're right,' or 'Okay, Otis, shut up and drive'?"

I just gave a narrow smile. It could mean either.

Or it could mean both.

Our gig in Charlotte was at Checker's, a hundred-seat club that had a small dance floor, a bunch of booths, and a long bar on our left that came uncomfortably close to the riser and had in fact been a contributing factor in Otis's painful evening the night before. Our equipment was already set up, but, suspicious or superstitious musicians that we were, we all took our personal gear home each night, except of course for Otis's drums—too big and bulky for casual lugging. After we got inside the club, which was cool, dark, and musty and smelled like smoke and spilled beer, I pulled out my guitars. My electric was a 1976 Gibson Les Paul, a beautiful and heavy ax with a cherry sunburst pattern. I also played an acoustic Martin on a couple of songs. I set both of them up on their stands, then started switching on amps and the sound system for a sound check, which we'd do as soon as the others arrived, and listened to Otis hitting his bass drums, *thump-thump-thump,* to check the action on his pedals.

You always knew when Rusty and Brian arrived; first you heard vague murmurings of discontent, like maybe the Children of Israel were wandering through the Wilderness somewhere nearby, murmurs that grew distinct as they approached. Anytime you walked up to them you would find them in mid-argument. I had this idea that if you went up to the living room window of their house in the middle of the night you'd find them poking each other in the chest and taking sides on Courtney Love, or mustard potato salad versus mayonnaise.

"I told you not to take that exit," Brian Gentry was saying as they cleared the back door, their guitar cases dangling from each hand. Brian, our bass player, looked like a wrestler—the actual kind, not the show-business variant. He was short, a bundle of muscles, and he bounded all over the stage like he was bouncing across the wrestling mat. He was also our second lead vocalist, a guy who was good enough to carry his own band if he wanted. "You always think I don't know where we're going. I know where we're going."

The object of this harangue, Rusty Hamilton, was tall and gangly, with red hair in a long ponytail. Sometimes he had a neatly trimmed goatee and mustache; just now, he had only a little blues mustache on his bottom lip. He had the stage presence of a totem pole, but he could throw the notes around; he was one of the best lead guitarists I'd ever worked with. When he talked, which was seldom, it was quietly, in measured tones. "You were asleep yesterday. You slept the whole way down. I woke you up when we got here."

"Hey," Brian said as they saw us. "What's on the agenda for tonight?"

"Not a damn thing," Otis said. "Let's do this damn check and go over the set at the Colonel's."

"We ate at KFC last night," Rusty said, squatting next to his case to open it. "I want pizza."

"The world does not revolve around you," Brian said, to which Rusty replied phlegmatically, "I didn't suggest that it did," to which Otis and I just looked at each other and shook our heads.

After Momma had been in their company for about five minutes, she pulled me into the kitchen to say, "Those boys. They act like they're"—and here she did her trademark lordy-lordy laugh, ha ha—"queer or something." And then she looked at me past the feigned amusement for a response.

"First, Momma," I said, "that's not a nice word. It's like saying 'nigger,' which I know you would never do." She shifted uncomfortably. "Second—and you'll pardon me, I know, for my lack of curiosity—it's none of my business what anybody does with his own penis."

"Well, I'm sure—" she began with a giggle, but couldn't think what she was sure about. The word *penis* flustered her, and so she just sort of oozed back into the living room.

What I knew about Rusty and Brian was that somehow,

despite all appearances, they were inseparable. Brian was a social studies teacher and coach in his day life; Rusty worked at a music store in Asheville giving guitar lessons. They lived in an old frame farmhouse in the foothills of the Smokies that used to be part of a pig farm, and they liked to sit around on our off nights and drink beer and watch Warner Brothers cartoons or Three Stooges. Rusty was a closeted intellectual, but he was quiet enough—and his sardonic asides funny enough—to mostly escape censure.

"There's a Pizza Hut down the street," I said. "That's what I want."

"Amen, brother," Rusty said, pulling forth his vintage Fender Stratocaster and gently setting it on its stand. Then he unpacked his Takamine acoustic and did likewise. We plugged everything in, put the microphones on the stands, made sure we were still tuned—light strings especially have a way of stretching out of whack—and then we were ready for our sound check. We yelled for Bobby Ray, the guy who owned Checker's, and he came out from the back room and slid into a booth.

Rusty and I conferred for a second about a song.

"You want to do 'Paperback Writer'?" he asked. We were still working on the backing vocals, so I shook my head. I don't like to rehearse at sound check. I like to nail a song we know backwards and forwards and leave the stage feeling like a rock god.

"Walk This Way," I suggested, and he nodded, so we shouted it back to the others. We did the old Aerosmith song straight through. I played rhythm on that one and Rusty took all the lead runs. We didn't do any of the stage business—the poses, the choreography. We just played and I sang. We all nodded our heads when we finished, and Bobby Ray gave us a thumbs-up.

"Bass is a little light," he said. "Everything else is fine. Drums sound good."

"Drums sound good," Otis said. "Give me some more of that Percodan."

"Is Brian too soft or is it the system?" Rusty called out.

"Brian."

"Damn," Brian said, adjusting the volume on his amp. "Who's trying to silence my distinctive voice?"

"If only it were that easy," Rusty muttered just loud enough to hear.

"Let's get some pizza," Otis said, balancing his sticks atop his snare and pushing back from his set. "I can hear those pepperoni calling my name."

The restaurant was crowded, but we got the circle booth back in the corner, and after we ordered two big meat-lover's pizzas, a pitcher of Bud, and a pitcher of Dr. Pepper, we looked over the set list from the night before.

"Anything y'all want to try different tonight?" Brian asked as our waitress, a little girl named Debbie, set down our pitchers. Otis was giving her his best meat-lover's smile, and I elbowed him in the ribs. "I thought things went pretty good last night except for when Otis threw his sticks at that big lumberjack-looking son of a bitch."

"Don't remind me," Otis said, smarting from the twin blows.

"I want to try a little more acoustic stuff tonight," Rusty said, looking at me. "Monday night crowd might be a little more reflective."

"Might be," I said, although I had my doubts. "Let's put it in and change it up on the fly if they're throwing beer and pretzels at us for being sensitive girlie-men." We hid a couple of softer songs in the middle of each set, pursed our lips, nodded approvingly, and hoped for the best.

As our pizza came, Brian looked over at me and said, "Hey, man, Otis told us about your phone call. I'm sorry. That's fucked up."

Rusty nodded, his mouth full. "I called Peter Bushnell this afternoon. He said he could sit in with us for a few nights. I told him if it was okay with you, we'd do it." They all looked at me.

"We can do trio stuff for a few nights if you'd rather not bring someone in," Brian said.

I waved a hand dismissively. "Peter is always great," I said. "And you can play some of that stuff I won't do."

"The penis songs," Otis chortled, almost expelling his Dr.

Pepper though his nostrils. I was infamous among my rock peers for refusing to sing songs that were too explicitly about sex or sexual prowess, which is a whole lot of songs if you think about it; I figured that a guy on the road to forty has no business pretending he's a teenager, although there are plenty of rock stars older than me doing it. Just a personal preference, that's all. Sex is a whole lot more trouble than it's worth, if you ask me.

"Yeah," I said. "The penis songs. Knock your smutty little selves out."

We ate for a bit, but I could feel them looking at me, and I knew I was going to actually have to talk about it.

"How are you feeling about this dead dad shit?" Brian asked. "This has got to be a weird thing to come up after all these years."

"It'll do till something weirder comes along," I said. I was remembering Ray sitting across from me at Dolly's, remembering his embarrassment and my hot anger. "I don't really know what to think. I'm just going to go and see what's what. Maybe there's something that'll explain . . ." Here I raised my hands vaguely. What could explain a lifetime of absence? My father left me. He went away. I never saw him again.

I shook my head. "I don't know. I just know I'm going to New Mexico."

"That'll be a nice drive," Rusty said. "It's beautiful out there."

"Beautiful?" Brian said. "You're living smack in the middle of God's country and you think desert and sagebrush—"

"One doesn't have to replace the other," Rusty said, and I breathed an inward sigh of relief. They were off again, and I was off the hook.

We sat in the booth closest to the stage as it got toward eight o'clock. We saw some faces from Sunday night—regulars or neighborhood people, I guessed. Otis was scoping out a table-full of women a few booths back, but since they were behind me I couldn't get a look at them. There were a half-dozen people sitting at the bar, probably twenty in the club when we got up to go on. Bobby Ray was going to lose some money unless they did a lot of drinking. Somehow, though, even though it was just a handful of people, there was already enough smoke in the club to choke a heifer. It smelled like the morning after at Hiroshima.

I slung the strap over my shoulder, took a pick off the mike stand (I had a dozen of them stuck up there) and tore into the seven-note introduction to AC-DC's "Sin City." I let the last note hang out in the air and attract some feedback to get their attention, and Brian yelled out over it, "Ladies and gentlemen. Children of all ages. We are Briar Patch, and we are going to rock your world."

And I know it sounds pretty ridiculous on the face of it, but then Rusty and I threw down some hard chords and the bass and drums came in and I started singing and damn, if we didn't rock the house.

4

"Man, that was a great fucking show," Otis said later when we were packed up and headed back home. It was a great show, which I guess shouldn't have surprised me, but it always did.

"It went pretty well," I said, which got Otis to hooting.

"Dude, you had them eating out of your hand. What about that pretty little thing at the front table?"

A group of UNC-Charlotte girls had come out to dance, and one of them in particular—a slender blonde in black with her hair cut like Rachel on "Friends" used to wear it a couple of years back—was dancing next to the stage and smiling and giving me the big eye.

"She must have liked the way I smelled," I said. The way I smelled right now was like barbecue ribs smoked over a bonfire of Winston Longs.

But this show had been a good one, all right. Our first set was pretty straightforward rock and roll, with some John Mellencamp and acoustic Goo Goo Dolls that let me stretch my voice a little. After we finished the set with Stone Temple Pilots' "Sour Girl," the UNC-Charlotte girl sidled over to the edge of the stage where I was kneeling to retune my guitar, and said, "You've got a great voice. Can I buy you a beer?"

I looked up at her and smiled, not my big smile, since just about nobody got my big smile in those days, just the hey, how you doing smile. Giving too big a smile is like leaving too big a tip. "So you wouldn't want to buy me a beer if I didn't have a great voice?"

She pursed her lips and turned her head slightly to one side. "That sounds like somebody sidestepping a question."

"Guilty," I said.

"And that sounds like somebody refusing to answer a question."

She was pretty sharp for a twenty-something. "Guilty again. Thanks. I don't drink."

"How about a Coke?"

I shook my head. "Thanks, though."

"Damn," she said. She raised her arm and smelled beneath it.

"It's not you, believe me," I said, and it wasn't. She was something special. "I've been standing in the pool of saliva coming from our drummer since he first saw you get up to dance."

She leaned forward so we could be all confidential. "So, then if you don't mind my asking—"

"Ask away," my outstretched palm said.

"You're a nice-looking guy, a great singer, and I'm an appreciative fan, and you're not interested in me at all." I shrugged. It was an unfortunate truth. "Are you married? Gay? Going steady?"

"Nope," I said. "Ascetic." She shrugged and gave a sad little smile, and I guess I thought that would end the conversation, but right before we started up our next set, a befuddled waitress brought me a glass of water and some crackers, "Compliments of the young lady," and I saluted her before I drank.

We talked more during the second break. Her name was Denise; she was interested in design or finance, she didn't know yet; her daddy was a Charlotte lawyer I knew by reputation as a dirty fighter on behalf of big corporations, a real bastard like I had once been, and her momma was a country club alcoholic having an affair with their maid.

"Isn't life interesting?" I said.

"That's one way to think of it," she said, and if we had both been drinking we would have shared a cynical "Cheers."

Between sets, the jukebox blared, and right now it was blaring old Police "Roxanne," which we had been getting ready to do and now would need to replace, and "Can't Stand Losing You." She toyed with the straw in her drink, which was one of those icy fruity things, margarita or daiquiri, I couldn't tell which. "So what about you, Clay? What's your interesting story?"

I was just getting ready to make up something when Otis leaned over us and said, "Pardon my barging in on your conversation. Clay, Bobby Ray wants some Skynyrd."

"God help us," I said. "I'm not playing 'Free Bird,' not unless someone holds a gun to my head. And maybe not then."

"He seems kind of ticked off. He says he asked for some Skynyrd last night. I don't remember that."

"You don't remember because he asked me last night."

Otis settled heavily into the chair next to me, trying simultaneously to smile at Denise and glower at me. It was not a pretty sight. "Dude, this is not just a fling for some of us. This is my job. Let's make him happy, okay?"

Denise leaned forward, giving Otis a good view of cleavage. I was happy for him—Otis loves cleavage—and happy for her, too. Here was some backstage intrigue. Not to disappoint, I struck my best petulant artist pose, like Norma Desmond, maybe, in *Sunset Boulevard*. Upon reflection, it was a little over the top. "I will consent to 'Saturday Night Special' or 'I Know a Little.' Maybe 'You Got That Right.' But I will not play 'Free Bird,' 'Sweet Home Alabama,' or "Tuesday's Gone" under any circumstances. That is my final word." I threw the back of my hand up to my forehead, threw my head back like an emoting silent-film actress.

"Cool," Otis said, and he rose to go consult with Brian and Rusty. "Mademoiselle," he said to Denise, tipping a imaginary hat.

"He's funny," Denise said. "And he'd be cute, but those stitches across his forehead are a disaster, design-wise."

"Finance-wise too," I said.

"What's his name?"

"That's Otis. He's my oldest friend," I said, for so he was. "From Mrs. Ferguson's first grade class on through . . . everything."

"Everything?" She arched an eyebrow and I hastened to defend my sexual preference.

"Okay. Almost everything. In fourth grade, he kicked Tommy Brando's ass because he knew Tommy scared the shit out of me. He was a big old boy. In high school we double-dated. And later . . ."

Later, other things happened.

I stood up. "Always a pleasure," I said, and I took her hand for a second. "I have to go back on."

Our last set was my favorite, but at the same time I was nervous about it. Randy had decided I was ready to play my solo version of Fleetwood Mac's "Big Love," the pluckity-pluck classical guitar version that Lindsay Buckingham plays on the Mac live album, and my fingers were not feeling up to the task. It went pretty well, though I flubbed a couple of changes here and there. My picking and plucking were not up to the standards of Rusty, who taught me to play the song in the first place, but my voice got me through it. What followed was our lone Orbison song of the night, "In Dreams," and I started playing the opening chords and singing by myself. And for whatever reason—because the people out there were drunk, or tired, or because we truly were playing well—the audience was listening. We weren't playing at them, like we had been much of the night, but for them, with them, through them.

And the recognition made me listen as I sang, and damned if I didn't start to choke up, me, of all people. I came to the point where my voice had to sail out clear and high, and I let the words float atop the notes, almost like Roy used to, singing about lost love that only comes back in dreams.

When we strummed the last chords and let them fade, it was silent. There was a long pause, and then the applause, and I was breathing again and Rusty was getting out his mandolin, and we started John Mellencamp's "Check It Out," and we were almost through for the evening.

We were in fact packing up for the evening when Denise came up to the stage again. She'd been sitting reflectively during the last songs, hadn't even gotten up to dance when we turned up the juice at the end of the set. And even as her friends were moving toward the exits, she waited for a bit, until no one was standing nearby and she could talk to me without anyone overhearing.

"You're a tremendous singer, Clay," she said, and when she got close, I could see her mascara had run. "That one song was the prettiest thing I've ever heard."

"It's by Roy Orbison," I said, because even though she hadn't identified it I thought I knew what she meant. "He was one of the great pop singers."

"What was her name?" she asked, and I suppose I could have blinked or said "Whose name?" or made a joke and avoided the question entirely, because I was an expert at all of those. But, again, I knew what she meant, and her recognition of the emotion behind the song was a forged connection between us now that I could not dishonor with dishonesty.

"Her name was Anna Lynn," I said quietly. "She was my wife."

"You must have loved her very much," she said, and then she turned away and ran for the john because she was crying and she was too old and too sophisticated to be caught with raccoon eyes.

"Dude, that's not how you're supposed to pick up girls," Otis said from behind his drum kit.

"It's how I pick up girls," I said, and of course he couldn't argue with that.

"She was sure pretty, though," he said later in the van. "You could have steered her in my direction."

We were way outside Charlotte, the highway was dark, dark, and we were the only vehicle to be seen in either direction. "Tried to, man," I said. "She said the stitches destroyed your symmetry or something like that."

"I'm symmetrical everywhere that counts," he said.

"Uh-huh." I was looking down the road; all I could see was the area right in front of the headlights. I did a lot of driving at night, and I was always amazed that no more than I could see I always ended up where I meant to be going. "Do you believe in miracles?" I asked.

"There's one right there," he said. "You asking that question right when I was thinking about it. I was just thinking that you're setting off on a great adventure. It's kind of a miracle, don't you think?"

I glanced over at him and could barely see him in the light from the dashboard. I could just see his lips move as he went on. "I mean, here I've been thinking if you don't get out of here you're never going to change. You'll die in that house. And then, out of the blue, a bolt from above, a blast from the past—"

"I get your drift, Casey Kasem. So my dad dying is a miracle? Seems pretty ordinary to me. Everybody does it these days."

He shook his head, and I could see he was preparing to get all zen on me. "You've got to learn to see the miraculous in the ordinary. Everything that happens is miraculous. That you and I are driving in this van down Highway 74 listening to Steely Dan is miraculous."

Again, even with the Steely Dan—we were listening to "Aja," which is a great song—it seemed pretty much part of the everyday to me. It's what we did just about every night, on one highway or another, with some music or other. There was a word, though, that still echoed from earlier, and first it made me laugh and then it made me wonder.

"Okay," Otis said after a bit. "I'll bite. What's eating your cereal over there?"

"Change." I shook my head and laughed again. "I'm as free as a bird now. And this bird you'll never change."

He did his Yiddish father act. " 'Free Bird'? You're drawing your philosophy from Lynyrd Skynyrd now instead of your best friend?"

"Since when do I draw my philosophy from you? Unless it's 'Hope I die before I get old.' That seems to make sense."

He laughed. Then he said, "All right, you devious bastard. You started to say something and I made the fatal mistake of letting you off the hook. Go on. Say it."

"I just felt . . . shit, Otis, I don't know. What does it mean?

I am as free as a bird. I am. I have no responsibilities, no schedules, nobody to be accountable to. Why do I need to change?"

I didn't have to turn to feel his withering glance. "Dude. That is self-evident."

And it was. I turned my attention back to the road. "Steely Dan. Man, can you believe those guys are still putting out records?"

"Nobody is putting out records any more. You're showing your age."

"Well, if I can't show you, who can I show?"

"True. Although I hope you know that there are some things I do not want you to show me."

I laughed. "And vice versa." We settled back smiling, and then the smiles faded slowly, and then we just sat, the night rushing by outside, the engine whining like an overtaxed lawnmower, before I gathered the cojones to return to what was still on my mind.

"Otis," I said.

"Here and here," he said.

"Do you think people can change?"

"Yes," he said. "Yes I do. I most surely do. But it's not easy."

"Don't I know it."

Again, the glance. "Dude, you haven't even tried to change. This trip will be the first step you've taken outside the rut you've worn for yourself in ten years."

I took a deep breath. "This is absolutely the last thing I'm going to say about this."

"Okay."

"It's a scary thing, man," I said. "I like the rut. I mean, I don't like it, but I'm content. I mean, I'm not content—"

"But you're safe. Or you think you are."

"Maybe. When I think about going back out in the world, it's like I get one of those panic attacks or something. I can feel my heart pound in my temples."

I felt his hand on my arm for a moment, and then he leaned back into his seat. "Call me anytime. Day or night. I'll take my cell phone onstage if you want me to. I'll take your call in the middle of a set. Hell, I'll take it in the middle of my solo."

"It might be an improvement," I said, glad he didn't have his sticks at hand to throw at me. But I also knew he would do it. I was that important to him. And again I was ashamed for the way I'd once treated him, the way I'd thought of myself as somehow better than he was because I was better-educated and a little higher up the social ladder. Because I wasn't better. He was stronger and gentler and sometimes even wiser than me. Always had been. "Hey," I said. "Do you remember when we used to drink a case of Budweiser of a Saturday night out at Cheoah Bend and sit on the picnic tables and watch the moon float up over the lake? How when we got toasted we'd drink a toast—"

"To eternal friendship," he said softly. "I remember it like it was yesterday."

"Was this what you imagined?"

There was a long silence then, nothing but road noise and the tape flipping to the other side, and after this uncharacteristic silence, when he spoke it was with uncharacteristic seriousness. "I couldn't have imagined that my family would be gone. That your family would be gone." He shook his head. "No, man. The only thing I got right was this. Us."

Us. This from the man I had all but written out of my life after Anna Lynn and I took up our sparkling lives as bigtime lawyers. Otis had just been an embarrassment to me when we moved to D.C. On his first visit, he had jumped into the Reflecting Pool on the Mall with all his clothes on, had attached himself one afternoon to a tour group of high schoolers because he wanted to hit on one of their teachers, and at a cocktail party at our townhouse in Georgetown, over a fine dry Merlot I had paid thirty-eight bucks a bottle for, he had engaged one of the senior partners in my new firm in an earnest discussion of the role of music in the quality of life, had in fact argued to this patron of Lincoln Center that one song by Led Zeppelin—during their seminal early blues period, of course—was worth a hundred Mozart symphonies.

It's a terrible thing to be ashamed of your past, and more terrible still to be ashamed of someone you love.

I think he knew things had changed between us. His visits dropped off in the last years we were in D.C. even though he had sold his dad's service station and had no real commitments to keep him from coming. He was up for little Ray's birth, and came back to stand godfather when we christened him in the National Cathedral—we were Episcopalians in those days. He wrote often, sending quotes and weekly wisdom for Ray to learn from when he got big enough to read, which of course, he never did.

We didn't talk about how I was feeling about the change in our relationship, and I never thought to think about how he felt. The closest we got was one time about two months before the end, when I was back from Alaska for a week and we were all walking down Wisconsin toward M Street, where there was an Ethiopian restaurant Anna Lynn really liked. Otis looked around at the shops, at the busy streets, at the clothes people were wearing, and just shook his head.

"What is it?" I asked.

He smiled a little sadly and shook his head again. "Nothing, man. I'm really proud of you. You know that?"

I nodded. I didn't get it then. I was counting the hours until he left for Carolina. But I got it later.

Otis was the first person to reach the hospital after it happened. I don't know to this day how he did it; if you want to talk about miracles, his almost instantaneous appearance at my side was nothing short of it. He was there with me, in fact, when the doctor came out the second time. Dr. Jordan, her nameplate said, and she was black, with wiry hair graying at her temples. I was sitting there with my head in my hands, and it was Otis who got up to meet her, who first saw her shake her head no. It was Otis to whom she said, her voice low and musical and tragic, "His heart stopped on the table. I tried open heart massage. His internal injuries—they were too severe." She stopped, and I could feel her eyes on me. She was measuring me to see if I had a noose around my neck and she was getting ready to pop the trapdoor beneath me. "I'm sorry. Believe me, we did everything we could."

"We know you did," Otis told her, and what I had long thought was country simpleton in him had suddenly been transmuted to a grace and gentleness I had forgotten, had never myself possessed. "Thank you for trying. Please tell your team that we appreciate them. They'll be in our prayers."

"And you'll be in ours," she said.

I looked up at her as she turned to go. She was blinking back tears, and then she walked slowly back toward the operating room. I thought doctors got used to seeing people die, but maybe you never do. Maybe sometimes you can just hide it better than others.

"Can I see them?" I called after her, and she stopped as though she had run into some barrier.

"Mr. Forester, I wouldn't," she said, turning to face me, and she bit her lip. "They're—they're not the way you want to remember them."

I nodded. I knew what she meant. And coward that I was, I didn't go to them. I didn't go, even though every atom of my body was screaming at me that there was where I needed to be, there howling like a beast over them.

But howling was never my style. I wish it were. Otis howled; when I woke in the night to find him watching over me in Anna Lynn's old rocking chair, his eyes were bloodshot from weeping.

Her parents wanted her buried in Grand Rapids, and some folks expected I'd want to bury her in D.C., but none of that felt right. I brought them back home to Robbinsville, buried them in a mountainside cemetery above Ray's place that is surrounded by azaleas, and I moved back in with my mama until I could get my shit together, a milestone I never quite achieved.

But at least Otis got me through that first night, and he and Ray and Momma got me through the next, and somehow I continued to make it through night after night without howl-

ing, without climbing inside a bottle, without driving myself
into a bridge abutment at ninety miles per.

But God help me, the joys in my life were tiny ones: a good
song and home cooking and a decent movie on cable TV in
the middle of the night.

Maybe that's how it is for lots of people. But it never feels
like enough.

It never feels like enough.

"You'll look in on Momma for me while I'm gone?" I
asked.

"Dude. Like that woman needs looking in on." But he
smiled. "But you know I'll do it."

"Thanks, man. I owe you."

"It doesn't work that way," he said. We were heading
through Asheville on I-40 now, the lifeline I'd be following all
the way to New Mexico after I picked up the car in
Robbinsville.

"Man, I wish I'd thought to leave the car in Asheville. I'd
be on the road now."

"You should go in the morning."

I shook my head. "I don't want to."

"You fit to drive?"

I did a quick internal check: fine; rolled my shoulders to
check the tension: lots; and blew into my hand to check my
breath: musty. "I feel good. I'll be awake for a while yet no
matter what. You know that. I'd like to get started before I
decide not to do it at all."

When we pulled up in front of my house and saw all the
lights blazing, my first thought was that in a twenty four-hour
span I'd lost my mother and father both. That's when Otis
pointed to the parlor window, where the sisters now gathered,
waving. "Those are some good women. They got up to see
you off."

"God help me," I said, but all the same it gave me a warm
feeling in the pit of my stomach. They were good women,
even if they drove me completely batshit. "Want to come in?"

He laughed very hard at that. "Not for a million dollars.

Hey, do call, okay? Not because you're in trouble or anything. Just to tell me what's going on."

"I'll do it," I said. Otis leaned across, and although we were not huggers, he put his arms around me and gave me a bear hug. It felt good, and I realized that although my dad had left before he could give me a brother, I'd managed to find one anyway.

It was the first time I'd ever felt glad my father left when he did. Were there other things I'd gotten out of the deal, other undisclosed and unexpected gifts? I guess I was going to find out.

"Later," he said, giving me a good slap on the back and pushing me away as though the whole hug thing had been my idea.

"Later," I said, and I climbed out and headed toward the house and inside. It smelled amazing, smelled of cooking and baking, crispy and buttery, and again I was happy I'd decided against the convenience-store chicken under the heat lamps. My mother and aunts, roused from sleep and attired in the matching monogrammed dressing robes I'd gotten them the previous Christmas, had also been thinking about miracles.

"Now," my mother said, picking nonexistent lint from my sleeve, "we couldn't let you go off without some food. You don't eat well."

"He forgets to eat," Aunt Sister said, finding lint on my other sleeve. "I worry so for him."

"Well," sniffed Miss Ellen, who liked to act as though she had no more interest in feelings than in extraterrestrials, "we've packed a picnic for you. Everything will fit in that backseat, if you can call it that."

"Everything" was three fried chickens with extra livers and gizzards, fresh baked loaves of bread, and a chocolate layer cake. Sister had made her famous cheese straws, and Miss Ellen presented me with an insulated jug of her coffee, so strong that you could walk on it. I liked to say that in another life, Ellen had either been a lumberjack or cooked for them.

"Well," I said, and it was all I could think of to say. "I'm overwhelmed." They beamed; even Miss Ellen's face cracked momentarily with something that might charitably be called a smile.

Sister and Ellen gave me quick hugs and a chorus of drive safe, don't forget to call, we'll be praying for you, and left me with my jug of coffee and my mother.

"Well," she said. Now it was her turn.

"Is this a good idea?" I asked her, not speaking of Ellen's coffee, which probably was a good idea, although no long-term health studies had been done on it.

She nodded and smiled a little, sadly. "I believe so. I didn't do right by you where your father was concerned. I hated him so for so long."

"Momma," I said in mock consternation, but she raised her hand.

"It's true, son. I know it's un-Christian. But I was so angry. So I never told you any of the good things about the man. There were a lot of them, you know."

I honestly didn't. "What do you mean?"

She sighed. "Lord, Lord. There wasn't anything he couldn't do, seemed like. He was so artistic and creative. He could act. Sing. You got your voice from him. I used to pretend other-wise—there's another sin, pride. Lord, I've piled them up over the years. You've seen the picture he drew in high school, the one on the stairway. I couldn't bring myself to take it down. And he was so funny. Even when he was leaving and he could-n't get that little car to start, he said something that had me laughing at the same time I was crying and throwing plates at him."

"I wish I'd seen it. Do you remember what he said?"

She shook her head. "No. I don't remember most of what he said, or did. I don't really even remember what he looked like when he left. That's why it was such a shock to see him on TV that time. It's been more than half a lifetime, after all." She put her hands up on my shoulders and turned me to her. "But I want you to know something. I married your father be-cause I loved him, because I believed he was a good man. And maybe he was, in his own way." She blinked and picked out a corner of the kitchen ceiling to look at. "I'm sorry I made you hate him too."

I set my coffee on the counter and pulled her close. She fit under my chin now, was in fact shrinking year by year. Someday she wouldn't be there at all. "So you did love him after all?"

I could feel her nod against my chest, felt her body-waved hair bristly against my chin stubble. "Those first years after he left, I was a wreck. Just a genuine wreck. I don't know what I'd have done without Ellen and Sister. I was sleepwalking through the days, let me tell you."

I knew all about that, the sleepwalking, but I couldn't remember anything of those days she was talking about. "Is that when they came to live with you?"

She nodded again. "They had to. I mean, Sister or Ellen had to put you to my breast when you squalled." She sniffed. "I was that far gone."

"I didn't know that."

"Well, Lord." She sniffed again. She was getting her control back. "How could you? You weren't any bigger than this." And she spread her hands apart like she was telling a fish story, and not a very satisfying one at that.

"I'm going to get going," I said, and I gave her a big hug. "Will you check on Otis while I'm gone? Make sure he doesn't overdose or have a concussion?"

"I suppose," she said.

"Make sure he's eating something besides cereal."

"We'll take him some of this leftover chicken tomorrow."

"Thank you," I said, a thanks that tried to encompass the food, the truth, and in some sense, the years she'd put me in the center of her life. "You're a good mother."

"Well, I try," she said briskly. "Are you sure you won't get some rest and get started in the morning?"

I shook my head and picked up my coffee. "It is morning, Momma."

"Well," she said, checking the clock and showing surprise, although I know perfectly well that she hadn't ever been up at 4:00 A.M. before in recorded history. "So it is."

"I'll be careful," I said. "I'll see you soon."

I walked out to the car, which started right up again, so I guess I was committed. I looked back at the house. Sister and Ellen waved and left the window, but Momma waved as long as I was in sight.

I reached the end of the driveway, looked both ways down State Highway 129, made the spur-of-the-moment decision to turn left—the roundabout way toward Tennessee, rather than right, toward Asheville and the interstate—and, wonder of wonders, I was on the road.

5

It was a beautiful night, the temperature just right with the top down, and I sped around Lake Santeetlah and farther into the Smokies on the winding highway. It had been a snap decision forsaking the interstate, and I couldn't account for it. I couldn't drive fast because of the curves and the darkness, and I had thought I wanted to get there as quickly as I could. But it also seemed right somehow, as though something or someone other than me had decided to turn the wheel and drive west.

My one regret, as I deliberated between chicken and Aunt Sister's cheese straws, was that for some reason, when I turned on the lights, the radio conked out, and while it was only AM radio, I coveted the noise. I pulled over on the way out of Robbinsville to confirm that yes, I could have one or the other, and resigned myself to a long night's silence.

But it was too quiet. Even with the purring engine—damn, Ray had done a good job with this machine!—there was too much nothing. I started to think, and I don't like to think.

So for a while, I sang. Orbison songs like "Crying" and "Only the Lonely." When I got across the Tennessee state line and was reduced to "Ooby Dooby" I knew it was time to move on. I sang Sinatra. I sang my favorites off *Songs for Swinging Lovers* and then slowed it down with some sad songs: "What's New?" and "Guess I'll Hang My Tears Out to Dry" and "One for My Baby," all the songs I used to do in the karaoke bar in Alaska. But my voice was starting to go, even with the soothing warmth of a couple of cups of coffee, and so by the time I was approaching Tellico Lake I started whistling hymns—a measure of my desperation—in between nibbling at the food so I could at least enjoy some of it while it was still warm.

I had one hand in the backseat feeling around for a leg when I began to feel the call of nature. I clamped my legs together, hoping I could ignore it for a while, but it was insistent. I'd had a big Dr. Pepper on the way back from Charlotte and a lot of coffee of late, and I was going to have to pull over, even though the road was two-lane again and narrow and with not much in the way of a shoulder. I did happen to be on the inside part of the hill instead of out on a ledge, for which I gave thanks, and I pulled over as far as I could, almost into a clump of vegetation, and climbed out carefully.

I unzipped and let loose a laser beam of a stream and felt relief almost immediately.

And then I saw the eyes in the bushes, gleaming golden in my headlights, and no more than five feet away. A mountain lion. Maybe a bear. And although I couldn't have stopped pissing in the event of a nuclear attack, I did start backing away, peeing my way back to the car.

"Oh shit, oh shit, oh shit," I said under my breath, a sort of mantra. Then I remembered that the convertible top was down even if I reached it, and realized that I was doomed.

There was a crackle as the brush parted, and the eyes moved down the slope and into the road—and when they reached the road, they were about five inches off the ground.

And although I couldn't have stopped pissing if God had commanded it, I started laughing.

What emerged from the bushes was a dog—a small, gaunt dog at that—who stepped forward onto the shoulder and sniffed tentatively at the air.

"Chicken," I explained. "My mother makes the best fried chicken in seven counties." I leaned in and took out the chicken leg I'd planned to consume before the crisis of micturition. "Here," I said, holding it out for him. "Take it."

The dog made no move to come closer. In fact, he seemed to regard me with some suspicion and actually took a giant step backward as I knelt to get closer to his level.

"Here," I said. "Doesn't it smell good? I know you must be hungry. You look like you haven't eaten in a while."

No doing. So I raised up, shrugged, took a bite of chicken, and for the second time in twenty-four hours, almost got run over by a semi—some overweight bastard sneaking around the weigh stations on the Interstate, maybe—who went whooshing by at breakneck speed.

"Jesus Christ!" I shouted, jumping out of the road, and the dog turned to flee, which was when I saw that he was missing his right rear leg. I cartwheeled my arms crazily for balance, which at least kept me from joining the foliage. When I could step back, looking and listening in both directions and hearing only the departing truck, I found the dog's eyes again, partway up the slope.

"Hey," I said as soothingly as I could with angry blood rushing through my veins. "Everything's okay here. No harm, no foul. Do you want to try this chicken thing again?"

No movement, so I got one of Aunt Sister's cheese straws and held it out. "How about trying some of this? Cheese makes it taste better."

He shuffled down the slope and the closest to me he'd been since I first saw him—about five feet away. He turned his head sideways, appraising me, and sniffed at the food. His ears flopped as he turned his head, and I saw that one of them had almost been torn off and had healed jaggedly.

"You've been taking a walk on the wild side, haven't you?" I said. "My mama would say it looks like life has just chewed you up and spit you out." I tossed him the food and he sniffed at it, then wolfed it down. Then I held out my hand, and he gave a tentative wag of what was left of his tail. His head was down, submissive, and with upraised eyes he sniffed at my hand.

"It's okay," I repeated. "I'm a pretty decent human being, as human beings go. Listen, you want to come with me a ways down the road? You stay around here, you're going to get run over or starve to death."

He turned his head again in appraisal.

"I'm not talking marriage. But there's got to be a better place for you than here. What do you think?"

He was weighing it.

"I have a whole tub of Aunt Sister's cheese straws. And it would be better if somebody else ate them. They give me gas, I'm sorry to say."

Clearly, even those on the fringes of the animal kingdom—which was obviously the place where this wretched puppy had spent most of his time recently—had heard about Aunt Sister's cheese straws, the staple of every church picnic, youth lock-in, and choir fellowship. He let me pick him up, and I put him in the passenger seat, where, after a moment's start when I put the car in gear, he began to watch the road ahead happily, his tongue lolling to one side of his mouth. He was a little unsteady as a sitter—missing such essential sitting equipment as he was, he sort of leaned a bit against the door—but all seemed to be working out.

I put the roof up until such time as I was convinced he wouldn't try to leap out, and we drove along happily for about forty-five minutes. I was starting to get tired, and my eyes were feeling tight and dry, but I thought that maybe my recent frights had added a couple of adrenaline-fueled hours to my driving capability. We crossed over the lake and finally got onto Interstate 40 about twenty miles west of Knoxville. The sky to the east was starting to gray, and I was feeling like I could make it at least as far as Nashville and maybe as far as Memphis when suddenly I took in a smell—if you can describe what I initially thought must be a truckload of festering human cadavers overturned in the road in front of us as a mere smell; I actually looked for a semi jackknifed in the ditch—that turned me into a mouth breather, for what little good it did me.

There was no such truck, of course. The road was clear of carcasses of any kind. No roadkill. No contiguous swamp exuding swamp gas.

Only then, still gasping for air, did it occur to me to look to my canine companion.

He sneaked a cross look at me then looked nonchalantly out the window.

"Was that you?" I asked, and he ducked his head and

began whimpering. It was clear that I was not the first person to ever ask this question.

"Okay," I said when I felt I was capable of rational thought again. "That was pretty bad. I've smelled less noxious things in feedlots. But you've probably been out on your own for awhile, right?" He didn't need to nod; each of his ribs was obvious. "So you've been eating roadkill and stuff for a long time, right? Of course you're going to grease the air once or twice on a diet like that."

He looked up at me hopefully, anxious to agree. I raised my hand to pronounce a papal dispensation, think no more of it, my friend, and he cringed down against the door and whimpered at the sight of it.

"Hey," I said. "Oh, hey." I lowered my hand slowly and felt around behind the seat.

"Here," I said. "Have a cheese straw." That perked him up right nice, as my aunts would say, and I was able to turn back to the road.

I love sunsets and sunrises—sunrises particularly, because there's the sense that you could be the only human being watching it. Many's the time I've lain awake for an hour or two after getting home and seen the sky go gray then red then orange and watched that ball float over the horizon and gone to sleep with a smile on my face.

This was not, apparently, my canine companion's reaction, for he took a good look at the full-blown sunset, yawned, and lowered himself onto his front paws to sleep.

It was about six o'clock when I had crossed over the Tennessee River, and the road started to feel a little bothersome when I heard the phone ring. I did not of course bring a cell phone or own such a phone, but it was unmistakably the chirping of such a phone, and since there weren't many places in my cramped environs it might hide, it took me only two rings to find it beneath my seat, and two more to figure out which one was the talk button.

"Hello?" I said into it.

"That you, Clay?" the voice of my stepfather asked.

"Is that you, Ray?"

"Hell, son, I must have left my cell phone in that car the other night while I was working on it." I could almost hear his mouth spreading with a smile as he generated this tale. "Well, since I've got you on the line, how are you doing? Where are you?"

"I'm on I-40, an hour west of Knoxville with a car full of goodies and a flatulent dog."

"Come again?"

"A dog who farts. He is in fact a three-legged farting dog, if you want the whole story, and he looks like hell. He's been out on his three-legged farting own for a long, long time."

I could hear Ray absorbing this information. "What's his name?"

"I don't have the slightest idea. Nothing much seems to suit him." I slowed down a tiny bit without thinking about it as a Tennessee trooper appeared of a sudden in my rearview, although I wasn't speeding.

"I had a three-legged bird dog once named Buster. Of course, he had to retire from bird-dogging when he lost the leg."

"Of course."

"But that was a good old dog. Does he look a'tall like a Buster?"

I appraised my canine copilot, and he looked up at me with interest. "Now you mention it," I told Ray, and so it was decided.

The trooper swooped past me doing at least ninety, and since he had no lights flashing, I wondered what the scoop was. Emergency, hunger, bladder distention?

"What does the country look like thereabouts?"

"Well," I said, taking a look around, "about like the ground around Winston-Salem. Hilly, lots of trees. Very green."

"Your mama was wondering if you'd care to call her once or twice a day to let her know you're safe. I said I believed you would not want to do that."

I flicked off the lights; it was getting light enough I didn't need them. "You believed correctly, sir. But if, for example, you and I were to talk every now and then, you could report my safety and pass on my love."

"Well, maybe I could at that," he said. "So it sounds like all is good so far. How far you going today?"

"I'm tired. I'll probably stop in Nashville for the day and sleep. Maybe I'll drive some more tonight. Maybe not."

"Well, make sure you're rested. How's the car?"

"Running okay. The generator's not charging too well. I think the belt's slipping a bit, so I guess I could try soaping it. But probably I'll just have to put on a new one."

"Don't forget to do that, son. Have fun. I'll talk to you soon."

We hung up and I smiled and smiled. Ray had never left something in a car he was working on in his entire life; I've never seen such a paragon of organization, of everything-in-its-placeness. But it was typical. That was my favorite kind of love, what I got, I realized, from Ray and Otis and Tracy even, expressive yet somehow not oppressive.

Now that the lights were off, I tried the radio, but still nothing, which was a little disconcerting; it presaged some serious further electrical problems.

"Well, Buster," I said, "I guess it'll just be some stimulating conversation today." Which was where we were when we saw that—and I admit this seems too much to believe, but I assure you it's true—leaning against the Crossville exit sign was one of those life-size crosses toted around by freaks and fanatics, and beneath it, sprawled out on the shoulder of the highway, not more than five feet from the rushing traffic, some sort of recumbent human being.

Buster started barking and I shook my head. "I don't get involved in things like this," I told him. "It's my secret of how to get through life."

Buster barked some more, which is to say he could have been protesting or arguing or just venting some steam.

"All right," I said. "We'll take a look. That's all. If he's dead, we're moving on. You may not have a taste."

I took the exit, then backed down the access road until we were just across the culvert from the cross, and there I got out.

"Stay here," I told the yapping Buster, who wanted to hop out too. "I do not have a leash for you and I didn't rescue you from a fate worse than death just to have you get bulldozed on the interstate."

Speaking of which, a car-carrying semi swooshed by just then honking its horn, and the shape on the ground didn't so much as flinch.

"Shit," I said. I approached at right angles, taking in as much as I could: a skinny white ankle seeing unaccustomed sunlight; tan coveralls like retirees might wear to putter around the house; a small plastic Safeway bag of possessions; a gray and unruly crown of hair like a tonsure. His cross had small casters underneath the long crosspiece to make the thing roll, which some people might think of as cheating, but I could see that this was one heavy mother of a cross, made from solid four-by-fours and about eight feet tall. It also had red reflectors on the back so traffic could see him better, and some foam shoulder padding to make long days of cross-carrying a tad more comfortable.

"Hey," I said, kneeling down beside him. "Hey, old-timer." I gave him a little nudge with my hand, and he stirred, rolled onto his back, and the most brilliant blue eyes I've ever seen opened and took me in with a glance.

"What is it, son?" he said, as though there were nothing out of the ordinary in lying down next to a highway, or in being awakened by somebody in that state.

"I was just checking on you," I said. "I thought you might be dead."

He sat up blinking at the morning light and chuckled, and his laugh was low and musical, like water burbling over rocks. "No, son, this isn't where that happens."

"Ah," I said, and I got to my feet so I could put some distance between us if I needed to. "Okay."

"The Lord told me I'll at least get back to Sacramento," he said, and it sounded so eminently reasonable that I just said, again, "Okay."

"My wife is in the hospital out there." He sighed. "It doesn't look good. So I'm headed that way. The Lord told me

I'll get to see her again. I just don't know what's going to happen."

"Listen," I said, before my exhausted brain could catch up to my mouth. "I can take you as far as Nashville, at least."

He smiled at the little Triumph. "In that thing?"

"Maybe we could hook your cross up like a fifth wheel trailer or something."

He got to his feet and stretched. "Ah, these wheels aren't much better than for show. I had one fall off t'other day, and believe me, I wasn't moving too fast."

"Okay," I said. "We can lash it on the back."

"All right, then. I'm obliged to you."

When he stood up I could see that he was thin and wiry, somewhere around sixty or seventy, and when he shouldered his cross and I helped him carry it across the culvert and up the slight rise to the access road, I could tell that he was a man still of immense strength. That thing must have weighed two hundred pounds.

"I see you've got a friend," he said as Buster yapped excitedly, his tail wagging.

"I met him on the road," I said. "You've certainly made a hit with him. He didn't react this way to me when I first ran into him last night."

We pushed the top of the cross up so it stuck between our seats and all the way to the dashboard, and somehow we fixed the back end high enough, propped as it was on my overnight bag and picnic basket, not to drag.

He settled in across from me, his bundle in his lap, Buster nestled down between his feet like a friendly cat.

"Again, I'm much obliged," he said, only the top part of his head visible over the cross. "My name is Matthew. Matthew Simons. I'm a sinner."

"Well, sir," I said, extending my hand under the cross, "my name is Clay Forester, and I'm sure I'd have to say the same if I were to give it much thought."

And why don't you give it much thought? It is a danger to give a Bible-believing cross-carrier that kind of opening, and if I'd been a little less tired I'd not have done it. But he didn't ask the question, didn't pull out the path-to-salvation gospel tracts. He just settled back in his seat a bit after shaking my hand with a firm grip and looked straight ahead.

"I need to warn you," I called over as we prepared to pull back on the highway. "Buster down there has a little problem with gas. I picked him up last night, and I fear he's been eating some things that aren't so good for his digestion."

"Now how bad could it possibly be," he called back, "a tiny little dog like this?" and about that time Buster again demonstrated conclusively how bad it could be and I was thankful we'd had to take the top down to accommodate the cross. Although Matthew didn't speak, I could see his eyes water, and then he began to laugh, harder and harder, and I had to join him.

"Never look a gift horse in the mouth, my daddy always used to say," he said at last. "And I suppose the same principle goes here with a free ride."

"It is pretty bad. I'm sorry."

"You can't choose your family," he said, "but you can choose your friends. Given that, there must be a reason you two found each other, although I'm hard-pressed to imagine what that might be. Lordy." And he laughed until I chimed in again, because truly it was the most god-awful thing this human nose had ever experienced, and having it come from that forlorn little package was really something. I didn't know what, but it was something.

The sun was already shining bright and warm, and I noticed that Matthew's bald crown was red and balding from days uncounted under the summer sun.

"You should use some sunscreen, sir," I said. "I believe I could pick up some at a convenience store if you'd use it."

He shook his head and brought his lips together. "The Lord'll do what the Lord'll do."

"What the Lord is going to do is give you skin cancer," I said.

He looked across at me and smiled. "Maybe so." And he settled back into his seat as best he could, which was his way of saying, so be it.

I was ever a so-be-it person too, if for different reasons, so

I didn't push. Instead I said something I'd always wanted to say: "So, old-timer, what's your story?"

"Ah," he yelled back, "just the usual. Man of God. On the road. Traveling town to town."

"On foot?"

"Mostly. If He tells me to, or if time's a-wastin' I'll catch a ride. You can mostly tell when it's His will. Not so many people stop once they see the cross."

"It's a little intimidating," I admitted. "Not to mention hard to fit."

"So there you go. I've been carrying this cross or one like it for nigh on thirty years. My wife left me some time back, took our daughters off to California."

"Where was your home?"

"Birmingham, Alabama. I used to be in the steel mills. But God spoke to me out of the fire and slag one morning and told me to get up out of there, take up my cross, and proclaim his word. I told my wife, and she said I was crazy." He smiled again, sadly this time. "Maybe I was."

"So she's your ex-wife? Is this the one in the hospital?"

"Yes. I suppose she is. My ex-wife, that is. I don't feel that way about her, but she was married two more times after me. Although she's not married a'tall just at the present time."

We passed over the Caney Fork of the Cumberland, then up a long hill. It was beautiful country, farmland and trees, and we drove for some time uninterrupted by anything other than the occasional whiff of pure phosgene from the right floorboard, and a good spell of holding the breath took care of the worst of that. I was feeling slow and sluggish and knew that I ought to be looking for a place to light and get some rest. I didn't feel right stopping just yet, especially since I'd promised Nashville when I stopped to pluck Matthew and his cross off the highway. But I kept yawning and jerking upright as I was falling asleep, and I guess I also didn't feel right about propelling Matthew and his cross off a bridge. And finally we were getting to the outskirts of town, which was as good a place to stop as any.

"Matthew," I called across to him, then said, "Sir," and put my hand on his forearm when he didn't appear to hear me.

He turned and nodded. "I've been driving all night, and I think when we get up to Nashville I'm going to have to stop and rest."

"I can catch another ride whenever you're of a mind to stop," he said. "I thought you looked a mite tired."

"Will you have some breakfast with me?" I asked, and yawned a big jaw-stretcher that threatened to break my head in half.

"If you feel up to it," he said. I saw a Cracker Barrel up ahead, thought it would do me some good to pump some additional fat into my veins, and took the exit. There was a Motel 6 just down from it, and it would do me just fine. I thought I remembered that they took pets as well, although the thought of Buster asphyxiating me in that tiny room decided me then that the car was a fine option for him. I pulled around to the back of the restaurant and parked next to a tour bus, leaving plenty of space for the cross.

Our waitress seated us and handed us menus and we commenced to browse. "Anything you want," I told Matthew. "It's my treat."

"Thank you, son. The Lord'll bless you for it."

"He's blessed me plenty for one lifetime, believe me. I'm not doing this for eternal reward. I'm doing it for you."

He closed up his menu with satisfaction and looked across the table at me. I was playing with the golf-tee puzzle on the table, trying to see if I could leave less than seven of the damn things in the holes.

"It's all the same to Him, you know. 'Verily I say unto you, inasmuch as ye have done it unto one of the least of these my brethren—' "

" 'Ye have done it unto me,' " I concluded. "25 Matthew."

Another smile creased his leathered old face. "So you had some schoolin' in the Good Book before you became a heathen."

"Had and have," I said.

"What'll you boys have this morning?" asked Carlene, our waitress.

"Boys," Matthew smiled. "Ma'am, you just made my day. I believe I can feel justified now in ordering the Old Timer's

Breakfast. Could I have hash browns and fried apples both with that?"

"Why sure, hon. Bacon or sausage?"

"Bacon."

"And how'd you like the eggs?"

"Sunny side up and soft as a woman's heart."

He was a charmer; Carlene touched at her bangs and smiled before turning to me. "All righty, then. You, sir?"

"Momma's Pancake Breakfast. I'd like the eggs scrambled, and bacon." We also ordered milk and juice, and then Carlene padded off to put in our orders.

"You haven't told me your story yet, son," Matthew said.

"I don't suppose I have," I said, piddling with the golf tees some more and actually dropping one or two on the ground so as to be able to bend over and retrieve them.

"What I'm wondering is, what brings you driving all night across the great state of Tennessee? What prompts you to stop and pick up a three-legged dog and an old man with a life-sized cross?" He fixed me with his steel blue eyes and wouldn't let me go until I spoke.

"Well, sir," I said, "it's a tale that's just as odd as anything you could want to hear." And so I told him the most recent particulars, dwelling only a little on my father's desertion and not at all on my recent life. "So off I went across the hills and hollers. And here I am now, on my way to Santa Fe, New Mexico."

He fixed me with those eyes again, measuring me, it seemed, to see what he could tell me that wouldn't overwhelm me. Then he placed both his palms flat on the table and leaned over toward me, and he spoke.

"You are on a spiritual quest, Clay," he said. "Nothing will ever be the same for you again." Then he leaned back in his chair as Carlene returned with our biscuits, and he applied butter and apple butter with practiced precision while I tilted my head and studied him for a change.

"Is that prophecy?" I asked at last, and he shrugged, his mouth full of buttermilk biscuit.

"Son, let's not talk shop over this wondrous breakfast. Although, do you mind if I stop chewing and turn thanks?"

"Be my guest," I said.

"Great Lord God," he said, "bless this place and all in it. And bless this food. Amen."

Carlene showed up with plates stacked up and down her forearms, all of which we were apparently intended to eat. And so we did, in silence for a bit, mouths too happy to speak. As our bellies began to distend, though, so did my curiosity, and so I ventured, "Did you say you've been carrying this cross for thirty years?"

He nodded. "Not this cross, of course. I go through crosses like some folks go through underwear and socks. But one cross or another. It's been a long, hard stretch. Still, I suppose the Lord knows what he's doing."

"How long since you saw your family?"

"A couple years," he said. "The girls, they backslid. Turned their backs on the Lord. I can't blame 'em really. What did He ever do for them but take away their daddy?"

"Yes sir. How old are they now?"

He reckoned for a moment. "Your age, or closeabouts. I can remember their birthdays and all, but I don't have much truck with the passage of time."

Thirty years.

"Do you miss them?" I asked.

"What I want in this life isn't important," he gruffed out, although the lump in his throat told me different.

I nodded. We all try and save our sanity somehow.

After we had finished up as much of our breakfasts as we were going to, I wrapped up some bacon for Buster, and Matthew wrapped up his for the road, biscuits and such.

"You want anything for the road?" I asked as we passed through the country store section on the way to the register.

"Some of these stick candies would be nice," he said, and he picked out a few while I paid.

"Thank you, son," he said again. We went out and extricated his cross from my cheese straws, and he shouldered it in his best cross-bearing manner. "Press on toward the prize. God'll bless you."

I believed that about as much as I believed that Haley's comet had crashed into the earth unbeknownst to us, but I just stifled a yawn with one hand and shook his strong, skinny hand with the other. "Take care of yourself, sir. I hope your trip is a good one."

"The trip home is always good," he said. "It's once I get there that was always my problem."

"Well maybe this time you'll know what to do."

He stood for a second, a sad, slow smile growing on his face, and he nodded. "I hope and pray, son. I surely do. Now you go get you some rest."

And he smiled and inclined his head, then turned laboriously and made his way up the entrance ramp and onto the highway. The last time I saw him before I turned into the motel parking lot, he had his head down, his load shouldered, and he was carrying his cross to California.

6

I dreamed of crosses spread across the landscape of what I imagined to be New Mexico: yucca plants and tumbleweeds and tufts of brown grass sprouting from white sand around me. Smoke from some unseen forest fire somewhere made me choke like a tubercular chain-smoker. I myself was carrying a cross, dragging that unwieldy wooden son of a bitch through the sand—wheels or no wheels, this was no fit terrain for such a thing—and when I reached a likely spot, I said something like "This is the place, I think," at which point I stuck my cross into the ground like a flagpole on the moon, shimmied up it, and stuck there watching the world go. I awoke groggy and confused in my cell-like room. It was late on Tuesday, near dark, to be sure. I had slept for eleven hours and I still felt tired, bone-tired as my mother would say. And why not? I was operating on a ten-year gospel-induced sleep deprivation. And so I dozed a little longer before I got up, splashed some water on my face, realized it was going to take much more than that to get me going, and took a complete shower and shave.

When I returned to the car, Buster was nowhere to be found, which was what I'd half expected. I strapped my bag onto the luggage rack and wandered around behind the motel. He was scrounging around the dumpster, licking up some kind of gray-green liquid oozing out of the bottom of it.

"Jesus, Buster, get away from that thing," I said. "Come on over here."

He walked over to me sort of sidelong, shaking his tail and ducking his head in case I wasn't the benign presence I had been up to this point. I scooped him up and rubbed his tummy, but did not accept his proffered kisses. "Thanks. I think I'll just eat my garbage firsthand."

I filled up on gas and got a newspaper to read, and then I dipped into the food packed for me. If I didn't eat it shortly, it was well on its way toward becoming dumpster material. After feeding some chicken to Buster—he needed a bowl or some such thing; no wonder he was drinking goo—I decided to toss the rest, and then had a piece of the slightly cross-squashed but still luscious sour-cream chocolate cake while I read the paper. The king of Syria dead; New Mexico wildfires mostly out but Colorado's fires raging; the Tennessee lieutenant governor's wife and young son still missing after four weeks; a committee on race in Tennessee releasing an optimistic report on future relations between blacks and whites, surprise, surprise; war in the former Yugoslavia, the former Soviet Union, and the former Congo. Why even read about it? As Molly Ivins once wrote, it was just one more thing I couldn't do anything about. I closed the paper and set it down.

Then I opened up the sports pages: Tiger Woods expected to win U.S. Open; Shaquille O'Neal expected to blow foul shots in the NBA Finals. I could at least while away a few pleasant moments reading the baseball box scores. Ray taught me how to read a box score, and I remember once he told me, "This is one thing that'll never change. My grandfather taught me how to do this; you can teach your grandchildren. Shoeless Joe Jackson or Junior Griffey, you measure them all the same way. In the box score." I was never going to have grandchildren, of course, but I did still have Ray. Thinking about it got me missing him, and so I called the house to see if he was home.

"Leave a message," was the terse reply from Ray's answering machine—he was probably out tinkering in the garage again—so I did.

"Hey, old-timer. See what you can find out about the funeral arrangements up in Santa Fe and call me back. I'm fine. Talk to you later."

Then I decided to call Otis and see where he was.

"Otis," he said after the second ring.

"Hey," I said. "You'd never guess what I'm doing."

"Clay," he said. "Damn, it's good to hear your voice, dude. Where are you?"

"On the road just outside of Nashville," I said. "So far I've picked up a three-legged farting dog and an old guy carrying a cross. I expect a fat lady and a pig-faced man at any time."

There was nothing but laughter for a second, then a whoop. "Dude, you almost made me run off the road," he said. "You must be tripping with Ken Kesey or something. Did you say a three-legged dog?"

"I said three-legged farting dog," I corrected. "Ray told me to name him Buster, which I did, although it didn't stop him from farting. Nothing could stop him from farting. He's better than a car alarm, though. Anybody had half a mind to steal this car, he'd drive them off screaming."

"I'm on the way to Charlotte," Otis said. "It's so weird to be on the road at the same time, going in different directions. The universe is really playing some changes on us."

The universe. If Otis isn't one with the universe, he at least claims to be on a first-name basis. Me, whenever he talks about the universe, I see distant stars and a whole lot of black space. I've got a perfectly good god I used to believe in, back when I still believed in things. Why get all transcendental about quarks and quasars?

"Hey," he said, remembering something. "You should call Tracy if you get the chance. She called me this afternoon to see if you got away okay. I told her I'd tell you if I talked to you."

"Okay," I said. "You've told me."

"So what're your plans, my man?"

I finished up my cake—which is to say that I ate until I knew that if I took another bite I'd be violently ill—and checked the map. "I guess I'll get around and drive for a while tonight. I want to get as far as Fort Smith, maybe Oklahoma City. I'll see how I feel. Then I'd like to get on a daytime driving schedule. I'm going to have to be on a daytime schedule in Santa Fe for this farce."

"Screw that daytime bullshit, man," Otis said. "We are creatures of the night."

"Uh-huh." I had a sudden vision of Gene Simmons of KISS, tongue extended. "Listen, say hi to the guys. And remember, you promised to stay out of trouble."

"Done and done. I've been out of trouble all day long."

"You've probably been asleep all day."

"Well, yeah, that too."

"It's a good start. Hey, I'll talk to you later."

I checked my watch. 7:30. Tracy would be at her folks'. "Let's go," I said. Buster seemed willing. I pulled onto the access road, then onto the highway, then accelerated up to a good humming seventy-five. Traffic had thinned out and I was back in the country in what felt like no time. Buster punctuated the silence with three lethal farts, spaced about twenty minutes apart. I was beginning to see that if you could get the pattern down, Buster was something like Old Faithful. You could set your watch on him.

"I think we can get to Memphis in time for dinner," I said. "I would dearly love to have some barbecue."

Buster seemed to have no opinion about it.

I picked up the cell phone and dialed, clamped it to my ear so I could hear.

"Hello," came the gruff male voice, a little put-out at having to answer the phone. It was Alvin York, who still scared the crap out of me. I'd been calling his house since I was in eighth grade. I guess some things you never grow out of. He was in his late fifties or sixties now, certainly past the prime of intimidation, but I still felt myself sit up straighter as I heard his voice.

"Yes sir," I called into the phone. "It's Clay Forester, sir. May I speak to your daughter?"

"Clay, she's already gone to bed, I think," he said, then called off to his wife Martha to confirm. "She said if you called—" and then I lost the rest to a cell glitch.

"What's that?" I shouted into the phone.

"Said to leave a number, if you could." After a moment's hesitation, I gave him Ray's cell number and hung up.

There was a lot of dark highway before we got anywhere. I smiled, then stopped smiling; it was like the universe: a sprinkling of lights, and an awful lot of dark, dark space.

It's in the dark space that dark thoughts emerge. I think it was Hemingway who wrote about how it was easy to be hard-boiled in the daytime, but at night it was a different matter, and nothing truer did he ever write. I sang for a while, but it didn't seem to work as well as the night before; I was getting farther away from my shelter and I was starting to feel the elements.

Sublimate, I told myself. Happy thoughts.

Otis and that spring break trip to Myrtle Beach, bodysurfing and drinking Busch and talking up the snooty Jewish girls from Brandeis. Otis climbing over the barriers at the Air and Space museum to climb into the ME-262 jet fighter, the docent screaming, him fleeing from security out onto the Mall.

Otis sitting beside my bed after my family was dead, watching over me to make sure that I didn't do some violence to myself.

No, you idiot. Happy thoughts.

Ray teaching me to fish. Bait fishing first: worms and stink bait at Lake Santeetlah, bass and crappie and catfish in rivers and ponds. Then, when I was older and worthy of it, fly fishing. Strict rules about how to use the wrist, about how to tie a leader, how to wade a stream. The plop of the leader and fly onto the water.

Plop. Plop.

But that brought back one of the days after Ray and Momma and Otis arrived in D.C.: Ray and I walking around the Tidal Basin.

The trees were so full of cherry blossoms that the branches couldn't hold them. As we walked, clusters of blossoms plopped into the water. The gutters and streets were full of blossoms, pink and white turning gray and black with dirt and soot.

We walked on around toward the Jefferson Memorial. I did a report on Jefferson when I was in eighth grade. For years he was one of my heroes, and the monument was one of

my favorite public spaces in D.C., so without really thinking
about it, I wandered in and stood in front of the bronze
statue, twenty feet tall on a six-foot pedestal.

"What's that in his hand?" Ray asked. "Document of some
kind. Declaration of Independence, maybe?"

I said nothing, just stood, hands in my pockets.

"A great man," Ray said.

"A dead man," I said. "Nothing left of him but words."

"Ah, but what words," he said gently. We were standing
next to the southeast wall, and Ray read:

> *I am not an advocate for frequent changes in laws and
> constitutions, but laws and institutions must go hand in
> hand with the progress of the human mind. As that be-
> comes more developed, more enlightened, as new discov-
> eries are made, new truths discovered and manners and
> opinions change, with the change of circumstances, insti-
> tutions must advance also to keep pace with the times.
> We might as well require a man to wear still the coat
> which fitted him when a boy as civilized society to re-
> main ever under the regimen of their barbarous ances-
> tors.*

"Isn't that beautiful?" Ray had asked. He was a man who
could find beauty in many places: the sun glinting on water, a
spray of azaleas, a perfectly written neoclassical sentence.

I grunted and walked back outside. Ray got us some hot
dogs and Diet Cokes from a vendor next to the Tidal Basin,
and we took a seat. Ducks paddled out on the water. I could
hear some sort of dinging, perhaps a railroad crossing, way
off in the distance. A jet soared along the Potomac on its way
to Washington National. Thomas Jefferson was still standing
behind us, tall, free, and defiant, but I could no longer see
him, could no longer even imagine him. I saw other faces.

"I can't stay here, Ray," I had said, and I was further panicked by the panic I heard in my voice. I stood up and Ray
stood with me.

"It's all right, son. We can go someplace else. Memories hit
you?"

Oh, yeah, memories. Anna Lynn and I had walked drunk around the basin late one spring night a couple of years before, celebrating her winning her first big class-action suit against a major polluter. Back in those days we thought one person could make a difference. We thought we were alive for a reason.

We thought we were going to be together forever.

"No, Ray," I said, shoving that thought out of my head as I always did. "It's not this place." I nodded at the ducks, the cherry blossoms pushed across the sidewalk and under the wheels of cars by the breeze. "It's this place." I spread my hand in a sweeping half circle: the Potomac, the Washington Monument, the Capitol, Georgetown off unseen in the distance to the northwest. "I can't stay here. I'm coming home."

He looked me in the eyes and nodded, but he asked, "What are you going to do there, son?"

I took a deep breath, let it out. "I'm going to try to stay alive," I said. But that wasn't fair. Ray was scared; I could see it in his eyes, glistening. I took another breath, let it out. "I don't know what I'm going to do, Ray, and honestly, I don't care. It doesn't feel like I'm ever going to care again. But—"

"But maybe you will, son," Ray said. "Maybe you'll grow strong and mend and learn how to go on." He put his hand on my shoulder, then moved it to the middle of my back. That hand felt strong, secure, massive—a wall to hide behind or a lifeline back to the world, whichever was needed. "I'm so sorry, son," he said, and he was weeping, and I felt a catch in my throat and thought that I might cry, too.

But I didn't, and I don't, not because I have some hang-up about men crying—I'd kick somebody's ass if they made fun of Ray's tears that day—but because it felt like an indulgence I had no right to, that I didn't deserve.

I was in fact dry-eyed as I looked over at Buster, who had brought me back to the present, to Tennessee and Interstate 40, with his singular gift.

"Happy thoughts," I said to him, and he wagged his tail, lost his balance, and fell into the front floorboard. I laughed before he gave me a withering stare and scrabbled with what dignity he could muster back onto the seat.

"I'm sorry," I said, and I was. He was now my only friend.

It was headed toward ten o'clock, and I was past the Tennessee River, through Jacksonville, but still a ways out of Memphis. "Damn it," I said. "No barbecue tonight." I stifled a yawn and Buster settled in to go to sleep. The inner man was speaking. Barbecue, he said. I must have barbecue.

"Tomorrow," I told him. I took an exit to get gas and consult the AAA map Ray had put in the dash: sixteen hours and twenty minutes of drive time to Santa Fe at fifty-five miles an hour. I had two more driving days to do that, plus I was going a lot faster than fifty-five. Barbecue, the inner man said. Stay in Memphis. Get barbecue. Drive on tomorrow.

"You keep quiet," I said. And then the universe opened up for me. I saw a billboard for Corky's Barbecue, the legendary rib place, and saw that they had a location on Germantown Parkway, not far off the interstate.

"Ribs to go," I muttered, to myself and the inner man, both of us now happy. We'd have Memphis barbecue and I'd still make Fort Smith.

Except, of course, that the universe and I weren't on a first-name basis, our mutual friendship with Otis notwithstanding.

Oh, the barbecue was wonderful. I made a mess the likes of which that little car had probably never seen before. I went through ribs like a chainsaw goes through saplings, and God saw that it was good. I got wet and dry—that is, ribs with sauce and also with the special dry seasoning—because I couldn't decide which I liked better, and even after eating them I couldn't, except to note that the wet were more of a challenge to cleanliness.

I had driven all the way through Memphis and had just crossed the Mississippi into Arkansas. The lights of the downtown skyscrapers had disappeared behind me. West Memphis, Arkansas, was an altogether seedier proposition than Memphis, Tennessee, and I was happy to be moving through it mostly in the dark. The kind folks at Corky's had given me a bunch of lemon-scented moist towelettes, and I was in the process of cleaning my face when the night began to grow darker. It wasn't an eclipse or freak atmospheric condition, I figured out pretty quickly. The Triumph's headlights were fading.

"Not a good sign," I told my canine friend. "I don't want you to go all gaseous on me, but it looks like we're going to be sidelined for a bit."

The lights went out completely, and then the engine went within seconds, the electrical system completely dead, no spark left to fire the controlled explosions of an internal combustion engine. I shifted into neutral and was near enough an exit that I could get off the highway at a pretty good clip. I was heartened to see a couple of buildings on my side of the highway, all of them lit up even this late.

Going up the off-ramp ate up a lot of our momentum, but I was able to coast into the nearest parking lot, which turned out to be Curly's Place GIRLS GIRLS GIRLS Topless if the multitude of badly lettered signs was any indication. A truck stop with an all-night diner sat the next parking lot over, but I saw a bright halogen streetlight around the back of the strip bar and thought it would be a decent place to look the car over—lots of light, and nobody around to watch. For me, having a car break down or needing help in general has always been something of an embarrassment.

So when I ran out of coast, I got out and began pushing. It wasn't much of an effort until I had to turn the wheel—no power steering—and get it around the back corner of the building. I grunted with the strain, and the steering wheel gave a bit with the effort, but we made it, me raising my hands and feeling exultant as Rocky on the steps of the Philadelphia Museum of Art, Buster with his head cocked sideways and looking at me like I was a strange new form of life.

I popped the hood and immediately saw the problem. I'd thought it was alternator-related, and it was; the smell of singed rubber coming to my nose was my first clue that the belt that had worried me some hours earlier had broken and lay tangled across the hot engine block.

"Well," I told Buster, who had his paws up on the top of the door and was balancing on his lone hind leg, "how hard can that be to fix? Get a new belt on, get the battery charged, and we're on our way again." I could check the truck stop for belts, at worst get the number of a parts store I could call in the morning. "Get ready, I'm closing the hood." Which I did, gently, so as not to startle him too much; he was a startlesome creature.

"I used to talk to my dog," came a still small voice from behind me that frankly scared the shit out of me. I jumped and whirled simultaneously—I wish I could see the replay—to find a little boy sitting on the back steps of Curly's Place GIRLS GIRLS GIRLS Topless.

He was maybe six or seven, but he was small for his age, dressed immaculately in khaki shorts and a navy Ralph Lauren polo shirt; his shoes were a little scuffed, as kids' nice shoes almost always are, but they were tiny Cole Haans, and his crew socks were an immaculate white.

"Hey," I said, trying not to use my you-scared-the-shit-out-of-me voice and failing miserably. "I didn't see you back there."

"I'm not very big," he said. "I wasn't hiding, though."

"No," I said. "I'm sure you weren't."

"You don't know my name," he said.

I nodded. "That's true. What is your name?"

His lips began to fidget back and forth and then he shook his head, his hair falling back and forth over his face, and he said "Mommy says not to tell people my name."

"Okay," I said. "Your mama is probably right."

"I like Cocoa Puffs for breakfast," he said.

"Really," I said. "I have a friend who likes Cocoa Pebbles."

"Does he like Fruity Pebbles?"

"Not as much as Froot Loops." I sat down on the steps, leaving a good distance between us so he wouldn't feel threatened. "Have you ever had Froot Loops?"

"Oh, sure," he said. "I used to eat breakfast cereal all the time when we lived with my dad. Now I have to drink barley green for breakfast." He scrunched up his face.

"Barley what?"

"It's this green stuff. Powder. You mix it with water. Mom says it's good for me. I don't like it."

"I'm big on Cap'n Crunch myself," I said. "I'll bet you didn't know that."

"I like it too."

He was a good kid. I looked into the sky and saw the

moon, almost down. "Where's your mom?" I asked, hoping maybe I didn't already know the answer. "You really shouldn't be out here by yourself."

"She's inside," he said. "I can't come in because she says it's a toxic environment."

It probably was that. "Do you sit out here all night?"

"No," he said, hanging his head. "Sometimes I sit at the restaurant. Sometimes I wait in the hotel if there's something on TV I can watch. But TV preachers were on, and they make my head hurt. And I don't want to sit in the restaurant any more. Flo smells. She makes me cough when she hugs me."

I was getting more and more angry the more he talked in his accepting way about the world as he knew it. This was a good kid, a bright kid. What kind of life was this? What kind of mother would do such a thing to her son?

Not my problem. I don't get involved in things like this, I had told Buster, just prior, admittedly, to picking up the cross guy back in Tennessee, and although all told that hadn't turned out badly, my way still seemed the best way to go through life; if you get involved you could get to caring too much, and bad things always seem to come of that.

But this was just a little boy, and it was his life we were talking about. It wouldn't hurt to call Child Protective Services or whatever they called it here in Arkansas, let them know about this little boy sitting on the back steps of a strip club in the middle of the night. And who knows? Maybe they could help his mom too, help her get a steady day job, help her get out of the life.

"I'm going in to use the phone," I said. "I wish you'd go back over to the restaurant."

"Mom is coming out soon," he said. "She gave me her watch to hold." He held it up and pointed to the eleven. "See? When the hands are on the eleven and the twelve she comes out to eat with me."

It was a cheap watch with a faux leather band, in sharp contrast to his nice clothes. On the dial face was a stick-figure drawing of a boy, and across the bottom of the face was a name: Michael.

It was the wristwatch of a proud mother.

"She'll be out in about five minutes," I said, trying to reconcile this data. "Good for you." I held myself back from tousling his hair, which clearly called out for such treatment, as I got up and stuck out my hand. "It was really nice to meet you."

He shook my hand solemnly—he had been brought up well, certainly in better society than this biker bar—and then waved at Buster, who yipped.

"Will you watch out for Buster while I'm inside?"

"Can I pick him up?"

"Sure, if he'll let you. See you later, okay?"

But he was down the steps and lifting the frantically wiggling and wagging Buster into his arms, who for a moment wasn't a battered, farting three-legged dog. He was just a puppy with a little boy, and something about the scene made me want to cry.

I haven't been in many strip clubs in my life, but this was certainly by far the seediest and the rowdiest. I heard AC-DC's "Girl's Got Rhythm" well before I opened the front door, and inside it was almost deafening. A gang of Harley riders in black leather sat against the far wall, looking up at the stage, where the feature dancer was swooping around the chrome pole clad in a scanty pair of panties and nothing else.

"What can I get you?" the bartender yelled when I asked for the phone.

"My car broke down out back—" I started to say, then held up a single finger and indicated the beer tap.

"Who's this?" I yelled when he brought the beer, which looked and smelled as good as I remembered. He knew I meant the dancer, not the beer.

"Calls herself Natalie," he said. "Been here a couple of weeks. She's good as hell."

I looked across at the stage and tried to ignore her breasts, which although they weren't big were firm and, like the rest of her, sleek and beautiful. She moved like a real dancer, not a tittie dancer, and her swings around the pole had a grace to them. She wasn't just here to shake her ass in guys' faces, although I was sure that the distinctions were lost on some of the folks here, who were the same yahooing, rebel-yelling-screaming rednecks who would have fought to get me to play "Free Bird."

I put my hand around the beer, felt the beads of moisture cool against my palm, raised it to my lips, and looked back across the room to where Natalie was dancing.

The music had changed: still AC-DC, but now it was "Walk All Over You," which fit her perfectly. She seemed to have a reserve or distance as she danced; I found it really attractive. It was like she chose to dance on her terms, whatever we might be thinking as we watched. Then she looked out across the room and met my eyes and looked away, like I was just another of these beer-swilling yahoos, and I put the beer down and scooted it out of my reach, which is what I should have done all along.

"Hey," I called to the bartender. "She belong to the kid out back?"

The bartender gave me a quick glance, then looked back down to the glasses he was washing. "What kid?"

"Nothing," I said. "Thanks." I left the beer sitting untouched on the counter—would it ever get easier?—and walked out without using the phone. Something I couldn't fathom was going on, and maybe it really was none of my business, like I'd thought all along.

The two of them were playing and laughing when I turned the corner. Michael was down on the ground giggling and Buster was licking his face. "Stop, Buster, stop," Michael was saying, although Buster and I both knew he didn't really mean it.

"Hey," I called to Michael, "I'm going over to the truck stop. Would you mind putting Buster back in the car when your mom comes out?"

"Okay," he managed to get out before Buster was on him again, yapping, tail wagging so hard he couldn't stand upright. I smiled and sighed and got my bag, and then I turned to wheel it across the dark parking lot past the slumbering, lumbering semis—running lights on, engines idling—and then back into the light.

In the store section I could have had my choice of CB radios or antennas, but nothing even remotely fan-beltish.

Sonny, who sat with slicked-back hair behind the counter sur-
reptitiously smoking Luckies, pushed me the Yellow Pages for
the Memphis area, and I wrote down the number of an import parts shop on Jackson Avenue in midtown Memphis I
could call in the morning.

Then I took a seat in the restaurant to get a cup of coffee
and—okay, I will confess—to see if I could get the scoop on
Michael's mother if she came over. Since some children's
books and crayons were piled on a table, I figured that was
probably Michael's hangout, and I grabbed a booth nearby.

"Coffee," I told the waitress, who looked like and was a
Flo: big sprayed hair, ample bosom, red lipstick, Juicy Fruit.

"You want anything to eat?" she asked me. She did smell
like cigarette smoke, although she seemed nice enough.
Maybe Michael was a little too sensitive.

"What's good?" I asked, scanning the menu.

"Best chicken-fry in three counties," she said. "Mashed
potatoes, salad, and rolls with that."

I wasn't really hungry—I could still smell the ribs on my
fingers, which brought flashing back a guilty memory of once
carrying Tracy's most intimate scent into our American government class—but I never turn down the chance to sample a
good chicken-fried steak. "Sounds good," I said. "And coffee,
black."

"All right, hon," she said, giving me a friendly wink. "You
won't be sorry."

I turned toward the window and looked out into the parking lot Michael and his mother would be coming across. It
was about ten minutes later that I saw them. She was dressed
in khakis and a blue oxford shirt, and she held his hand as
they walked. In her other hand she held a plastic grocery bag.

Flo was dropping off my food, and she was close enough
that I could see how she lit up when she saw them. "Isn't he
just the most beautiful little boy?" she asked, and I nodded.
He was certainly way up there.

They took a seat at the table catty-corner from me where
Michael's books were already piled, and Michael's mom put
her bag on the table with a rustling grunt and took out the
menu.

"Flo," she called, and Flo came over a little nervously. "What's vegetables tonight?"

"All we got left is corn, darlin'," Flo said, somehow aware that all hell was going to break loose. "Okra was gone at ten-thirty. I tried to set some back for you but someone ate it."

"Flo," she said, making a stab at calm, "corn is not a vegetable," and she pursed her lips. Then she turned to Michael and said brightly, "How about some salad and tofu?" She produced a package of tofu from her plastic bag and passed it over to Flo, who took it by one corner like she'd been handed a dead cat.

"Okay," Michael said.

Flo went off with her unaccustomed burden of soy curd, and Michael's mother was left murmuring at the menu and shaking her head. "I know better than to expect organic produce," she was saying, partly to Michael but not much. "But would it be too much to expect some things without white flour, processed sugar, or hydrogenated oils?"

"Probably so," I chimed in with what I thought was a good-natured but sympathetic shrug. "Although this is pretty good stuff." I raised a bite of my steak on my fork.

Her face rose slowly to take another look at me. She'd seen me when she came in, but had ignored me. "Would you like to know what that chicken-fried steak is going to do in your digestive system?"

"Not really, no." She looked at me, in fact, as if we'd never seen each other before, and I was doing my best to meet her there, although it's hard to pretend you haven't seen a beautiful woman naked when both of you know you have.

"He likes Cap'n Crunch," Michael said.

"It's true," I told her quizzical face. "It's my lone remaining vice."

And then, when she still sat looking at me quizzically, I said, to try and put her at ease, "Your son and I are old friends."

"Really?" It was not a friendly question. Her claws were out; this mother was poised to pounce.

"That's right," I said. "I know he likes Cocoa Pebbles—"

"Puffs," Michael said.

"Right, sorry, Cocoa Puffs for breakfast," and I ticked things off on my fingers, "that he doesn't like to watch TV preachers because they make his head hurt, that he doesn't like having barley greens for breakfast, that he has a mother who loves him very much, and that his life used to be very different."

She stood up over the table, one arm between me and Michael, and now she wasn't wary or quizzical—she was angry and scared. Very scared.

"Come on, sweetheart," she said, not taking her eyes off me. "We'll eat later. Let's get out of here."

"Hey," I said in my most calming voice. "You don't have anything to worry from me. My name is Clay Forester. I'm a musician from Robbinsville, North Carolina. My car broke down—it's the little convertible with the dog in it behind Curly's Place GIRLS GIRLS GIRLS Topless."

"Buster is his dog," Michael said.

She looked at me for a long moment before she sat again. "So he didn't send you?"

"Not that I'm aware of. He? Unless you're speaking of God, in which case I have to say, who knows? We're not on speaking terms."

With the talk of God, I had unknowingly passed from one realm to another. She lost her fear and seemed to gain some sense of surety. "Are you a Christian, Mr. Forester?"

Oh, Christ. "I never know how to answer that question," I said.

"Then you aren't," she said.

I sniffed laughter. "That's what I would have thought you'd say. Would have thought, that is, if I hadn't seen you recently in another setting."

"Whatever do you mean," she said—not a question—and she met my gaze proudly, and with her son watching the exchange avidly, I couldn't pull the trigger on her.

"My mistake," I said. "I thought maybe I'd seen you somewhere before."

"I get that a lot," she said, and then she shut down like a plant at closing time. "Honey, let's go wash your hands."

And when Michael looked back in my direction, she turned

his head forward like they were Lot and his family escaping Sodom.

"Bitch," I said under my breath. I pulled a ten from my wallet and left it on the table. Then I walked my bag across the overpass and on to the Motel 6 on the other side. I wasn't disappointed at the accommodations, at another night in a Motel 6. Actually, I was beginning to realize that I loved Motel 6. I could afford better, sure, but there was something about the monastic, cell-like nature of the place that appealed to me. It was all I deserved, I thought. Or maybe it was comforting in some sort of womblike way.

I flicked through the channels—nothing good on HBO or ESPN—wished for a good book, and turned to the window. I looked out on I-40: sparse traffic, a few stolid semis rushing commerce to the far reaches of the Empire, vacationers looking to get just a few more miles in before they crashed for the night.

And across the highway, I could see the truck stop, the lighted restaurant, and if my eyes weren't playing tricks on me, a little boy sitting alone in a window booth.

It was a long, sad night.

1

I called the import parts place at eight, got a guy named Troy Felix on the phone who got all excited when I told him what I needed and said he'd deliver the belt just to see the car, put me on hold for a bit, and then came back on with a disappointed groan.

"Mr. Forester, I don't have a belt in stock that'll fit it. And I guar-own-tee you, ain't nobody else does. But they promise to overnight it to me, and I can bring it out there to you first thing in the morning. Will that work for you?"

"Let's do it," I said, and prepared myself for a day of lounging around the Motel 6. "I can catch a few z's, maybe catch up on my correspondence." I gave Troy my number at the hotel and thanked him.

Then I climbed back into the tiny monk's bed shoved into the corner of my tiny abbey room, put the pillow over my head to drown out the road noise, and went back to sleep for a few hours.

It was restless sleep, lots of going up and down through dream states, and I must have had half a dozen garbled dreams about little boys in trouble. In some of them I was the boy; in some of them, Little Ray was in danger. But all of them had that common thread. I woke up wondering about Michael and his mother and if they were in some kind of trouble.

At eleven, I showered, shaved, and dressed to walk across to the truck stop and to check on Buster. On the way, I poked my head in at the motel office and asked Betty, the manager, to extend my stay another day.

"Sure enough," she said to me, her smile bright as a solar flare. She was somebody's grandma if there's any justice in the universe. "We're sure glad to have you another day."

Buster was underneath the dumpster again, but seemed to be there more for comfort than for comestibles. When he saw me coming he squeezed out, his tail waggling wildly.

"I'll bet you saw some interesting things out here last night," I told him. "Hang around for a bit and I'll bring you breakfast."

Flo, of course, wasn't working the morning shift, but I took the same place I'd sat last night, kind of to feel like a regular. Darla was the morning waitress. She was a scrawny girl with caved-in cheeks and a bad bleach job, but she at least didn't smell like smoke. She was probably mainlining heroin instead.

"Pancakes," I said. "Hash browns. Bacon. Two eggs, scrambled. Orange juice. And give me a couple of orders of sausage to go. Crumbled, not patties, if you can."

"I'll ask," she said, as though I was asking for escargot or béchamel sauce.

She left, and I sat looking over at the table where they had sat the night before. And had I really seen Michael over here sitting in one of these booths last night, maybe while his mom was back on stage?

I asked Darla when she came back, all bad-teethed grin be-cause the cook told her he could crumble my sausage. "I met a little boy last night when my car broke down. He was sitting back behind the strip club. Do you know anything about him? Does his mama treat him okay?"

She looked me over real good before she said anything. "Well," she said confidentially, "I'll tell you"—and here she looked around the dining room to make sure nobody was lis-tening in—"I'm not supposed to talk about them. Not so much as a syllable."

"I'm just worried about the boy," I said, trying to put on my nicest face. "It doesn't seem healthy, that's all. It's none of my business."

She cocked her head to one side and said, "No, sir, it isn't. But if it'll make you feel better and maybe put you in a tipping mood, I'll tell you this. That boy is as well loved as any little boy I know, my own two included. And I wouldn't be in that woman's shoes for all the gold in Fort Knox. And that's all I'll say." She zipped her finger across her lip.

"Okay," I said. "I had a little boy once. I just wanted to know he was okay."

"Listen," she said. "He's as okay as he's gonna get. Okay? I'll go check on your order."

I ate my breakfast slowly. I really ought to stop ordering pancakes; they're not good for you, they sit in your stomach like a lump of lead, and anyway, nobody makes them like my momma.

I dropped off some sausage with Buster and gave him the lowdown—we were stranded for the day but would get on the road first thing in the A.M.—and urged him to lay low unless he felt the need to stretch his legs, at least those he had left. Then when I got back to the room, I did something I knew was almost crazy and probably a result of sleep deprivation: I called Momma.

"Forester residence," Miss Ellen said, as she has for more years than I know, even after Momma married Ray and I was the lone remaining Forester.

"Good morning, Miss Ellen," I said. "This is your prodigal nephew speaking."

There was a moment's pause, and then a strange and unaccountable warmth as she announced to the room, "It's Clay. Clay's on the telephone." She seemed her old formal self when she returned. "I suppose you'll be wanting to talk to your mother?"

"Yes, ma'am," I said. "In a minute. How is everything there? How are you feeling?"

"I'm feeling quite well," she said, "and all of us are keeping busy. We've got church tonight, I suppose you know. Will you be able to go somewhere? Is there a good Baptist church nearby?"

"I'm stranded out on the highway west of Memphis," I told her. "I'm waiting for a part for the car. It's coming tomorrow, and then I'll have some driving to make up, but I believe I can do it without too much trouble. The only church hereabouts is one where women dance without all their clothes on. I was thinking about going there for worship tonight. Is that the kind of church that would be good for me do you think?"

I could hear her push the phone away from her and announce, "Ellie, your heathen son wishes to speak to you," and then my mother, breathless, full of questions about my well being.

"I'm fine," I said, "fine," and after the initial gust of wind, she settled down to a strong breeze.

"Are you getting enough rest?"

"Yes, ma'am."

"Are you eating well?"

"Yes, ma'am."

"Is the car running okay?"

"Yes, ma'am. Although it's got a little problem just at the moment, Ray did a bang-up job getting it going. It'll get me there just fine."

"Have you learned anything on your trip yet? Anything at all?"

I had to stop and think about that for a bit. "Yes, ma'am," I said at last. "Although I don't know just yet what it might be, I believe I have."

"Well praise the Lord," she said. "Steve Forester's death is part of a great plan for your life."

"Yes ma'am," I said. Isn't it, though? "Has anyone called Santa Fe to check on the funeral?"

"I believe Ray was going to do that this morning," she said. "The woman who called us was . . . Rosalena, wasn't that right, Sister? Rosalena Fischer. Don't know a thing about her. I suppose she's Mexican. Or Jewish. But she's probably all right nonetheless." Then she said, a little lower, "I have a suspicion that they were lovers. Him and her. Maybe living together all these years."

"Do you, now?"

"I do. I mean, why wouldn't he have found someone after all this time? I don't have any right to complain about that. And why else would she be the one who called us? Who knew your name and asked us to give you the message?"

"I don't know, Momma. Rosalena, you say."

"That's how I understand it. Mexican, like I said."

"Or Jewish."

"Right. Or maybe both."

I made sympathetic noises. Whatever dark forces had induced me to call were wearing off, and now she was just my annoying mother again. "I gotta go, Momma," I said. "Tell Ray to call me later, okay?"

"So soon?" she asked. "Why, we—"

Which was what she was saying when I hung up on her and tossed the phone away from me onto the bed. Jesus.

Take Jesus, even. If my mother understood that Jesus was a Jew, she'd probably give up her faith. I just didn't understand that, never did, and it was one of the things that really tripped me up with the whole God scene—how could you claim to follow somebody who loves everyone and then choose for yourself who you're willing to love?

Well, like the cross guy said, you can choose your friends, but you can't choose your family.

Maybe the truck stop had some reading matter besides the over-the-road magazines and travel guides I'd seen on the trucker side; surely in the convenience store one could glom a Stephen King novel to go with your Corn Nuts and Baby Ruth. A day by the pool reading trashy fiction, maybe looking over my sunglasses at the nonexistent woman who wouldn't be caught dead dipping her toe into the tepid pool of the Motel 6 in East Memphis, Arkansas, on a Wednesday afternoon—or any other afternoon, to be honest. Still, it felt like a plan, and the walk down the access road and across the highway, originally so tedious, was starting to seem common to me, like the bus ride that I used to take from Georgetown to the office in D.C., or the Blue Ridge Parkway from Robbinsville to Asheville; after a while you could do the drive without even looking up from the dash.

I fell asleep in a lounge chair next to the pool in a new pair of plenty-of-room-in-the-seat shorts I bought in the store. With a new straw hat on my head, I looked like somebody's goofy father on vacation. There was a Nordic family of four—another goofy dad, a somewhat chunky mom, and two big, chunky Aryan boys—playing loudly in and around the water, so my sleep was a testimonial to the power of hot sun and exhaustion. I had picked up what I thought was a good novel, King's *The Girl Who Loved Tom Gordon*, but I was out by mid-first chapter, and there I remained, sopping up the sun, until I woke up some hours later with a lethal sunburn on stomach, arms, legs, and feet.

I slid into the pool hoping for relief; the soles and tops of my feet felt like I'd stuck them into a toaster oven and closed the door. For a few minutes, the shock of the cool water helped me pretend I wasn't in serious trouble.

It was about six in the evening when I finally got up enough courage to make the long, slow walk back across the highway. I needed some sunburn stuff badly, and if I could just endure the pain until I got there, I thought all would be well. The blue T-shirt I had on was one of my oldest and softest, but the way it was rubbing against my chest and upper arms, it could have been lined with broken glass. Every step was misery, as my poor feet rebelled both above and below.

But then I was in the store for the third time that day, stocking up on Solarcaine and Tylenol, and five minutes later I was sitting in a truckers' shower stall slathering myself head to foot with Solarcaine and choking in a roiling gray cloud of propellant and product. I was going to be high as a kite if this stuff still had any brain-killing inhalants in it.

Once, I would have been happy about that idea, but for some reason, as I was struggling for a breath of air with even the tiniest bit of oxygen in it, it didn't seem so compelling. I would have opened the door if I hadn't suddenly had a vision of myself stepping into the corridor all oiled up like rough trade at the gay truckers' ball.

No, thanks. I figured I'd just stay in there and suffocate.

At last, the air cleared some, or at least my lungs adapted to breathing Solarcaine. I shrugged my shirt back on, pulled on my pants and lightly tied on my shoes, and limped out into the truckers' lounge.

One old boy was sitting near the showers watching *Big Trouble in Little China* on the overhead monitor. His nose wrinkled up as I approached, and he took one look at me and shook his head. "Shoo-oo-ee, boy, I've hauled pigs that didn't smell like you do. You take a bath in that shit?"

"Near enough," I said. "I haven't gotten burned like this since I was a teenager at the beach."

"Well, let's hope you never have another'n like it," he said. "You get on out of here."

"Yes, sir," I said, and I trudged on outside to air out. It was hot in the back parking lot, the heat still rolling up from the asphalt and in the air itself, so as soon as I thought I had dissipated enough toxic gases to make it less likely I'd spark a run for the exits, I went into the restaurant, eased into my booth, and waved at Flo.

"Evening," she said, coming over with a menu. "Why look at you. You're all shiny. You look like a shiny red lobster."

"Which is about what I feel like," I said. "That'll teach me to have a leisurely day by the pool."

She tsked sadly and shook her head. "Grown man like you ought to know how to take care of himself."

"It's true," I said, "it's certainly true."

"What'll you have, darlin'?"

"Start me off with iced tea, a lot of it."

"Check." She went off to pour me a glass.

I took a look outside, and there, far across the parking lot, saw Michael sitting on the steps with Buster. Michael had him sitting in his lap like a kitten and was rubbing his tummy. Buster's tongue was hanging out of his fool head. He probably hadn't had love like that in a long time, maybe not ever.

"Just breaks my heart," Flo said when she looked across the way. "Beautiful little boy like that."

"Why can't they go home?" I asked.

Flo shook her head. "Can't do it," she said. "That woman's between a rock and a hard place."

I shook my head in sympathy. Mostly I felt for the boy. I suppose that must be why after I ate my meatloaf and trudged hot-footedly home, after I lay on my back for hours trying to get comfortable, the noise from the highway bouncing around my head like a pinball, I felt compelled to get to my feet, to cross the narrow room, to pull back the curtains and look outside.

There was Michael across the way, sitting in a booth by himself. It was 1:30 in the morning by my watch, and I started cursing under my breath as I pulled my clothes on, tears of pain springing to my eyes as I dressed. "Christ almighty," I said as I pulled on my shirt. "Damn it to hell," as I pulled my pants over lobster legs. "Piss, shit, fuck, fuck, fuck," as I tied my shoes onto my even more tender feet.

What I wouldn't have given for a car that worked.

I bought a pack of cards in the truck stop store and padded into the restaurant, catching Flo's eye as I entered. It's just me, my wave said, and she relaxed and approached the booth as I sat across from Michael.

"Flo, I believe I'll have some pancakes," I told her, cutting the new deck. "Maybe you could bring some for my friend here as well. On me."

She turned her head sideways a second and made a face—pancakes were not on her instruction list from mama—but then she relented. "Okay. Two orders of hotcakes coming right up."

Michael had been coloring Scrooge McDuck in a coloring book about Donald and his known associates. He was coloring Scrooge green, like his money. I shuffled the deck, cut it, and started laying out a game of Klondike on my side of the table. I dealt out the seven foundation cards, and we worked in silence for a bit.

"You're a good colorer," I said after I felt him looking across at me. With a flourish, I laid a red seven on the one row that was going well.

"I'm okay," he said. "My mommy's really good."

I looked up at him and he dropped his head. "Did you have a good time with Buster today?"

He looked back up at me, and now a smile creased his face. He nodded, then put his head back down and returned to his coloring.

"I'm glad," I said. "Buster's a nice dog."

He looked up at me for a second, thought about what he wanted to say, and decided to say it anyway, even though it was just a whisper. "He's got really bad gas."

I laughed. There was a black eight, and I set it down. "He sure does."

He dropped his voice and leaned confidentially across the table. "Mommy says we shouldn't talk about gas. But Buster's gas is so bad she couldn't help it. He had gas while she was sitting on the steps with me." He started giggling. "Mommy was saying, 'Bad dog. Bad Buster.' And then he had gas again."

I laughed too. "He's a force of nature," I said. "Like hurricanes and earthquakes. Only with Buster, it's dog farts."

Michael was drinking milk at that moment, and he laughed so hard it spouted out his nose. He was coughing and laughing and I had to set down my cards because I was laughing and Flo was charging over to box my ears until she saw how happy he was and she started laughing too.

"Boys," she said, cleaning up the milk sprayed across the table.

"I've never seen anybody shoot milk out of their nose like that," I said when we could both breathe again. "Really. That was pretty good. That could be a marketable skill. You could join a circus and do it every night."

"Gross," he said. "My mommy wouldn't like it."

"Well, then it's a good thing she didn't see it," I said. "I won't tell."

"Promise?" His eyes were suddenly serious, and I couldn't do anything but nod and say, "I promise."

Flo brought out our pancakes and some syrup, and Michael could barely control his glee. He poured a pool of syrup an inch deep. Flo had to bring more. I helped him cut, but he could do everything else all by himself.

I had my mouth full of a too-big bite when he suddenly said something after minutes of food-induced silence.

"My dad is not being nice to my mom," he said. He didn't look up from his plate when he said it.

"I'm sorry to hear that," I said. I picked up the cards at that and slid them around on the table.

We sat there for a while in silence except for chewing and swallowing and the scrape of cards on the table.

"He hasn't been nice to her for a long time," he said.

I nodded. "My dad wasn't very nice to my mom either."

He looked up. "Did he make her cry?"

At the earliest edges of my memory, I could hear my mother weeping late at night for her husband who had gone away for good. "Lots of times," I said.

He bit his lip, looked down, looked back up again.

"Did he make you cry?"

I sighed and shook my head. "No. He wasn't around to make me cry."

"My dad made me cry," he said. "Lots of times. One time he said I was too loud, so he spanked me. He was really mad. I made him too mad. I had to go to the hospital. I cried and cried."

He looked up at me, his eyes liquid and brown. If that father had been in front of me at that moment I would have cut his throat. As it was, I could only sit and look into his eyes, sad and yearning, and distract myself from my anger by leaning my tender sunburned chest into the table and saying, "I'm sorry, Michael. I'm so sorry."

"How'd you know my name?"

"I know lots of things about you, remember?" Then I relented. "It's on your mom's watch."

"Ha. I'll bet you don't know my whole name." He crossed his arms with self-satisfaction.

"You'd be right," I said. "Do you want to tell me?"

"Michael Martin Cartwright," he said.

That name was familiar somehow, and I started to have a bad feeling in my stomach that was totally unconnected with my sunburn and the resulting nausea. I tried to keep things light: "Well, Michael Martin Cartwright, where is your daddy now?"

"In Nashville," he said. "We live at 1128 Fifth Avenue. It's a really big house. Sometimes the governor comes to eat with us."

I jotted down the address on my napkin with his red crayon and put it in my pocket. "Michael," I said, "it sounds to me like your daddy is a really important person."

His mouth fell open and he covered it with his hand. "How did you know that?"

"I'm a good guesser," I said. "A lucky guesser." I put the napkin in my pocket. "Michael," I said, "I want to tell you something. And I want you to remember it. Can you do that? You've got a really good memory for remembering things, don't you? Will you remember what I'm going to tell you?"

He nodded solemnly.

"It isn't right for people to hurt other people. Especially for daddies to hurt people. I was a daddy once, with a little boy like you. I didn't mean to, but I hurt my family too. That wasn't right. And I've never stopped being sorry for it."

He reached over and put his hand on my arm. "It's okay," he said. "Don't be sad."

"Okay," I said, blinking. "I'll try."

"Do you love your little boy even though you hurt him?"

I nodded, and when I thought I could trust my voice, I said, "Every single day."

He took his hand back and picked up his fork. "Where are they? Your family."

"They went away," I said.

"Like my mommy and me?" he asked. "Did they run away from you?"

"No," I said. "They went away in a different way."

He looked at me, and he didn't understand, and I guess maybe I wanted to tell him for some reason, wanted to tell somebody. I was a long way from home.

"They died," I said.

"Oh," he said, and he sat there silently for a bit, turning this over in his head. He took a bite, chewed, and then he asked, "Does that make you sad?"

I blinked and nodded. "Every single day." I pushed my plate away. Grief and pancakes do not mix, as I should know better than anyone. "Michael, let's keep all this our secret, okay? Your momma will worry if she thinks I know—"

"What secret?" she asked, and I jumped and banged my poor sunburned knees against the bottom of the table. I didn't hear her coming. Our conversation had been too involved and involving, I guess, or I would have seen her approach, watched her face grow red and her jaw clench, seen her ball her hands into fists. "What are you doing here? Get away from my son before I call the police. Flo!" she called.

I slid out, wincing. "I'm sorry. I didn't mean to frighten you. I couldn't sleep, and I thought—"

"What you thought is of no interest to me," she said, moving in between me and the table. "Get away from my son."

"He's nice," Michael said, but she whirled on him.

"We never talk to strangers," she said. "Never."

I took a deep breath and tried to put myself in her shoes. But it was hard, particularly hard when she was stepping on mine.

Unintentionally, I'm sure.

"I'm going," I groaned. I threw a wad of bills on the table. Maybe Flo would pass on the extra. "I'm sorry."

"You ought to be," she growled.

"Listen, lady," I growled back, "I've been here babysitting your baby while you've been—"

"It's okay," she said sharply, pulling her boy close and not coincidentally, covering his ears. "This mean man is leaving us alone now."

I opened my mouth to say something else, met Michael's frightened eyes, and decided against it. I nodded sadly to him and turned for the door. Maybe the Tylenol was kicking in, because I felt strangely calm, almost reflective as I stepped into the parking lot and again pronounced my judgement: "Bitch."

Interlude

"Ramblings around the River," by Sister Euless
—From *The Graham Star*, June 14, 2000

This is a time of much sadness as we consider the events of the past week. As many of you know, we heard Sunday that my nephew Clay Forester's father, Steve, Robbinsville High School Class of 1960, remembered for his roles in the high school musical theater productions of South Pacific *and* Carousel, *passed away Sunday night in Santa Fe, New Mexico. It was a double shock for us, as I'm sure you can imagine, since we had no idea he was still alive. Clay left for New Mexico to attend Steve's funeral in New Mexico on Friday. Please pray for him as he travels so far from home.*

Many of you have also heard the sad news that Alma Jean Shepherd came home from her doctor's appointment on Monday and found Clarence lying under the table. That nice young Dr. Modaressi made a point of telling Alma Jean to pass on to all those who brought over desserts and casseroles after her surgery that they are not responsible for the use that Clarence put them to, and truly his heart could have stopped at any time even without the extra weight he put on over the past few weeks.

Today is Flag Day! Remember as you display the Stars and Stripes to reflect on the sacrifices so many people have made over the years so that we could enjoy our freedom.

I hope to return to happier news next week. In the meantime:

Wherever you go and whatever you do,
Always remember that Jesus loves you.

8

I sat up all night, hurting and totally pissed off. I couldn't lie down; the pain was too great. It felt as though I was being pricked by hot needles. So I sat at the table in my uncomfortable chair and watched the sun come up. Two hours later, the phone rang, and I rolled over gingerly to talk to Troy, the car lover at the import parts store. I gave him directions to the truck stop: "I'm right behind Curly's Place GIRLS GIRLS GIRLS Topless. Can't miss it."

He expected to be there in half an hour or less, so I took a cool shower, sprayed myself down again with Solarcaine, packed up, and left the bag on the bed for when I checked out. Even with the sun low in the sky, I was already hurting from the heat; it was going to be a long and particularly hard day, Tylenol notwithstanding. What I wouldn't have given for Percodan.

"Buster," I called as I arrived behind Curly's. "Yo, Buster." There was a rustling in the tall grass at the back of the lot, and Buster stood up and shook the sleep off. "We'll be going shortly," I said. "I know you'll miss that little boy, but maybe we can find you another one on down the road. This is not a stable situation, I'm afraid."

I ordered breakfast to go at the counter, and nodded at Darla, who froze me out completely. Flo had apparently passed on that I was now persona non grata. I took the bag of food back and fed Buster, and then Troy pulled around back with his auto parts van and I opened the hood of the Triumph for him.

"Oh," he said, and he just stood there for a minute shaking

his head. "Oh, my. That is one bee-yoo-tee-ful car. Where'd you get it?"

"It was my father's," I said, and then I started to take it back and couldn't figure out how to do it. Too much trouble, anyway. "He left it to me."

He walked around it, feeling the curves like it was a woman. "Man. Triumph TR3A. I haven't seen one like this in years. Nineteen sixty-one?" I nodded. "All original?"

"Body and upholstery, yeah. The top too, I guess. It's been covered up for years and years."

He put on the belt for me, whistling with joy the whole time, then pulled the van around to give me a jump. When I started the car, he leaned back against his truck like a chef who had just popped a particularly savory bite in his mouth. "Mmm," he said. "Beautiful."

"I'd let you drive it," I told him as he was unhooking the cables, "except I've got to be in New Mexico tomorrow and I'm a little pressed for time."

"Hey, this was totally worth it," he said. "Oh, I brought you an extra belt, just in case. On the house."

I was gathering up Buster and putting him in the car when a big black Mercedes came squealing into Curly's parking lot. A youngish man in dark gray pinstripes—they clashed with his dark sunglasses, I thought—jumped out to check the front door, which must have been locked. He shook his head when he climbed back in; then they flung gravel in their haste to get across to the truck stop. There were three of them, all told, two in front, one in the back, and when they got to the truck stop the two younger ones hustled inside and the older gentleman in the backseat followed in a more leisurely fashion behind them.

"Damn," Troy said as he got into his van. "What do you suppose those birds want?"

"Hungry for hotcakes," I said, yawning. I was trying to keep it calm, but something was wrong about this. I waved so long to Troy. Then I gunned the Triumph across the bridge and the wrong way down the access road to the motel. I ran into my room and grabbed up my bag, flung it into the backseat, and squealed back around to the office, where Betty damn near jumped out of her shoes when I threw the door open.

"Three men, Betty," I gasped. "In a black Mercedes. Were they just in here asking about Michael and his mother?"

"It's none of my business what a mother does to keep her family together," she said. "I told them she was at the club. I didn't know what else to tell them. They were very brusque." She was babbling; Betty would make a terrific grandmother but a lousy Green Beret.

"Betty," I said. I took her gently by the arms and turned her to me. "They were in here, weren't they?"

"I sent them to the truck stop. I said they were over there getting breakfast."

"Jesus," I said. "They found her, haven't they?" Betty's eyes were big and she nodded.

"Call her. Tell her to pack up and get out of there."

"I did. She called a cab but it isn't here yet." Betty was close to tears. "And anyway, she doesn't have any place to go."

I stood up and took a deep breath. "Jesus Christ Almighty," I said. "Call her again. Tell her I'll be in front of her door in thirty seconds."

She took a good, sharp look at me. Then she picked up the phone. "This is Betty. No. No, it's not here yet. I know. I know. Listen. There's a Clay Forester here who knows something about your problem. Clay Forester."

"Michael's friend," I prompted and she repeated it into the phone. Then she hung up.

"She's ready. One fourteen."

I took another deep breath. "What can you tell me about the men who were just here?"

"The younger ones had badges. The older gentleman asked the questions. Dressed real nice, white hair. Money. The young men had a hard look to them."

"Cops?"

"Or something like. Maybe state police. Or FBI."

Jesus. Christ. Almighty. "Is there anything else I need to

know?" I looked across the way and thought I saw them climbing back into their car.

Betty took me by the elbow. "Don't let them take that little boy back. She told me his daddy broke his arm once. I know he's a bad man, and he's got a long reach. Get them a long way from here if you can."

I hadn't checked out of the motel, but she waved off my credit card. "I never saw you. You never checked in. And ten seconds from now the computer will agree with me. You get on, now."

"Thank you," I said, and she shook her head.

"You get on."

The hotel room door opened as soon as I pulled up, and Michael's mother, arms laden with paper bags, bustled out. "They're coming," I told her, and stuffed her bags in the back with mine. It was a shameful world, I thought, if this family could pack their belongings into the back of a Triumph. "Michael, climb back there. Quick, now."

Michael squealed with delight. It was like a nest for him, nestled in there among all the bags, and with Buster for comfort to boot, he'd be just fine. Mrs. Cartwright and I slid in, and we were off. I turned onto the bridge, hoping we could make it across before we met the Mercedes, but I was wrong. We were going to pass, slowly, at the exact midpoint of the bridge.

So much for my years of CIA training.

"Put your head in my lap," I said, my first best idea. Mrs. Cartwright looked at me like I'd asked her to aspirate a worm. I guess in a way, that was exactly what she thought I'd asked her to do.

"If you think for one solitary second—"

"Christ, woman, will you listen to me?" I grabbed her head, she wrestled it upright and punched me in a very sensitive spot, and the guys in the other car got a perfect view of her offended profile as they passed. The driver's mouth opened and the Mercedes stopped momentarily. Then he recovered and the car sped to the end of the bridge to turn around.

"Well, that may be the end of our little trip," I grunted, ac-

celerating off the bridge and onto the on-ramp, tires squealing. "We've got about fifteen seconds while they get turned
around."

"Sweet Jesus preserve us," she said. She turned around to
see behind us, but of course couldn't, since the back of the car
was stuffed solid. I checked the side mirror. They had dropped
one young man at the far side of the bridge and were now
doing a U in the gravel. Then they were flying across the
bridge, and that was the last I saw as we topped a rise and disappeared beyond it.

"He'll turn your hotel room upside down," I said. "Prints,
all that. They'll get a positive ID for sure."

"They got your tag," she said. "They'll know who you are
too."

"Well," I said, "they'll know who somebody is. I have no
idea who this car is registered to." For the first time, it occurred to me to check the windshield for the inspection
sticker. There wasn't one. "That's about the least of our problems right now."

I pushed the accelerator to the floor. The traffic on
Interstate 40 was sparse this far out of Memphis—nothing
like the morning rush going in—and I weaved back and forth
in traffic from the left lane to the right, checking the side mirror. I was doing about ninety-five and could probably do
more when the traffic eased up a bit. "We had half a mile on
them, and I think I can open it up some more, although they
can probably outrun us. That's a Mercedes CL-500, and it
probably has a five-liter V-8, a monster engine. Whew. That's,
like, an eighty-thousand-dollar car. You have some important
people chasing you."

"My husband's Uncle Edward," she said. "He used to be
the state attorney general. Now he's in private practice. You
can see what he's practicing."

I passed the last semi in sight and opened it up. A hundred.
A hundred and ten. Michael squealed with delight as the little
car accelerated. Roadside reflectors whished by like super-
sonic fireflies.

"They'll get a roadblock set up," she yelled over. "They've
probably already called ahead. You'll go to jail for kidnapping

or something, I'd guess. It won't stick, of course. You'll be out in twenty-four hours. But he'll have us back."

Jee. Zus. Christ. "Who are you? I'm guessing your name's not really Natalie."

"My name is Kathy. But what's more important is my husband's name: Daniel Cartwright. Lieutenant governor and soon to be the next United States senator from the Great State of Tennessee."

It just gets better and better, I thought. That's why Michael's name was familiar. I remembered the newspaper headlines back in Nashville; I guess the future senator part just slipped below my radar. All the color must have rushed out of my face, because she became momentarily kind. "If you want to pull over and let us out, I'll understand," she said. "It's an awful risk."

It was certainly worth a thought. Here I was whooshing through Arkansas at somewhere around 120 miles per hour with a fugitive woman and little boy and a farting dog, with mystery men in a big Nazi car in hot pursuit and a kidnapping rap if they caught us—if, that is, I didn't roll our car and shred us doing high-speed evasion maneuvers I'd never executed in my life.

One thing was for sure: I didn't want any more vehicular manslaughter on my hands. I slowed down. Instinctively I checked the rearview; where I'd normally see daylight, I saw Michael watching me with interest.

"I won't let them take you," I said. "But we can't outrun them. And it's too dangerous to try." The needle dipped below 100. "Where would they think we're going?"

"My only family left is a sister in Oklahoma City. But they've had her house staked out off and on for weeks."

I checked the mirror, then braked hard to avoid climbing up the back of a lumbering minivan. "So they might expect us to stay on the Interstate clear to Oklahoma City."

"They might."

"If we can take an exit unseen, I think we can mess with their minds in a big way." I nodded toward the map in the dash. "Mrs. Cartwright, you're our navigator. Michael, can you and Buster help her?"

"Sure," he said. "This is fun."

"I'm glad you think so. Now here's what we need." I checked the highway ahead. Not yet. "We're looking for an exit with a short off-ramp and an underpass. Michael, have you ever played hide and seek?"

"Sure," he said again.

"Good. You're going to help us play hide and seek with your Uncle Edward. Mrs. Cartwright—"

"If we're going to be fugitives from justice, I suppose we could be on a first-name basis."

"Okay. Kathy, I'm Clay."

"I remember. Our next exit is a mile ahead."

We were descending a long, slow grade and then ascending again. The exit would be just over the top of the hill. "Okay," I said. "We'll check it out."

I sped up a little to pass a semi, and as we went up the hill I stayed in the left lane. There was a flash of light at the top of the hill and there way back behind us was the dark Mercedes.

"Shit," I said. She shot me a look. "Sorry. Sorry. We don't talk like that, Michael." I looked over at Kathy. "They're closer than I thought."

"Do your best," she said, and she held on as I accelerated again.

As we crested the hill I threw us over into the left lane and then back right into the exit, and what I could see looked good: an underpass just ahead. "Hang on, everybody," I shouted. "Hang on tight." I downshifted and stamped on the brakes. Buster hit the dash with a yelp. I downshifted again into second, stamped the brakes, and we took the corner at thirty-five, the back end skidding until I could straighten her out. We pulled through the underpass and onto the access road on the other side, pulled up far enough that we could just see through, and there we sat.

Buster looked up at me reproachfully and started licking his shoulder.

"Sorry, dude," I said. "Emergency. Kathy, can you check your watch? We had thirty seconds on them. Can you tell me at a minute?"

"Got it," she said.

And we sat, the engine idling high, my foot raised slightly on the clutch, depressed slightly on the accelerator. Both my feet hurt like hell. It was time for more Tylenol. Maybe more Solarcaine, too. Or maybe just some morphine straight into the vein.

"Time?"

"Thirty seconds left."

"We'll backtrack," I said. "Take another highway. Something."

"Check. Twenty seconds."

I was gripping the wheel and gearshift both with white-knuckle force, and I guess I was a little keyed up. I jumped when she spoke.

"This car is too conspicuous. Any small-town cop will remember an a.p.b. on an old yellow sports car."

"I like this car," Michael said, which I was starting to think myself. But what I said was, "Your mother is a smart woman, Michael." I didn't take my eyes off the underpass. "I think she's right."

"Time," she said.

A flash of movement, and just as I eased up the clutch for a fast getaway, I recognized the big grille of a Dodge truck. He emerged from the underpass, turned right, disappeared.

"Kathy, can you find the Memphis airport?"

She nodded. "But I'm not sure—"

I raised my hand. "Silence," I said. "This plan is devious and brilliant." And I started laughing; it had been a long time since I'd been brilliant or devious, but I was once a very good lawyer. "We'll ditch the Triumph in long-term parking," I said. "And I'll rent another car."

"A bigger car," Michael suggested.

"Michael," Kathy said, shushing him. "It's a fine idea. I've saved a little money—"

"Don't worry about it," I said.

Getting help from me was for some reason making her a little testy. "I have money."

"I wouldn't take it," I said, easing back onto the road and taking the on-ramp.

"But—"

"Listen. What you did to earn that money makes it precious." I shot her a look, shifted up into third, then into fourth. "Admittedly most men—Michael Martin Cartwright excepted, of course—are not worth the dirt they're made of. But I'm helping you just because I want to. Because you deserve it. Because he deserves it. That's all. No strings. End of story."

Her face was still blank, but she nodded thanks. "God will bless you for it."

I rolled my eyes. "Oh, I don't doubt that," I said.

It was at that moment that Buster chose to release another shitbomb. "Which was just about what I was expecting," I said, and I raised my eyes to heaven. "Thank you, Lord."

"Oh dear," Kathy said, and against her will she was smiling. "Michael, you and I must pray nightly for Mr. Forester. He needs God in the worst way."

"And that's usually how I get him." We came up on the 40/55 interchange.

"Take 55 south," she said, "and we're all but there."

"All right, gang," I said. "We did it. High fives all around." Michael giggled as he slapped me five, and then his mother handed back Buster, and I would have defied the pissed-off ghost of J. Edgar Hoover for one look at the smile on that little boy's face.

"Can you drive a stick?" I asked as we approached the airport and turned onto Rental Road, and again she looked at me as if I were something on the bottom of her shoe.

"Don't treat me like my husband," she said, which I guess meant yes, she could certainly drive a stick. I stopped and she took the helm just short of the rental agencies. I told her I'd find her in long-term parking; this way the clerks couldn't have any memory of a yellow sports car.

I chose Avis, mostly for that old slogan: we're number two so we try harder. I could dig it. "I'd like to rent the biggest, blackest car you've got," I said. "Something that makes me look like a Republican for two weeks."

"Ah-ha," said the guy behind the counter, a junior-executive type with shifty eyes that betrayed he really didn't belong here. (That and the tattoo I could just perceive on the top of his left hand. He was a slacker in drag.) "Do you want to impress clients or women?"

"Either," I said. "Both."

"I've got a new Cadillac Sedan de Ville," he said, checking his screen. "They don't come bigger or blacker than this one. But it's going to run you some money." He took a good, long look at my longish hair and blue T-shirt. "Fifteen-day rental will run you $747.98, plus tax, plus surcharges, plus mileage if you go over fifteen hundred. Do you think you'd go over fifteen hundred? 'Cause then it's twenty-nine cents a mile. It adds up fast."

"I'm just driving it around town," I said, giving him a don't-worry-about-it wave. "And money I've got. What I don't have is a big black car to drive." I slid across my Diners Club, filled out the forms, and walked calmly out the door like someone who didn't have to be in New Mexico in twenty-four hours and wasn't in the meantime harboring fugitives in his other car.

I trolled long-term parking for half an hour, my pulse rising by the minute. There were open spaces here and there, but no Triumph. She was right: it was not the kind of car that would be inconspicuous. I tipped an imaginary hat at a police car easing past, then at another one the next aisle over.

This was not, I suddenly realized, a great place to hide a car, something I'm sure that would not have been lost on Mrs. Cartwright, who was irritating but extremely intelligent. The airport was a hotbed of activity.

I backtracked to Avis, and sure enough I found them, around the corner, hidden from the street. I parked a good distance away—since they wouldn't know what I was driving, another big black car creeping up suddenly might be a little scary—and then walked up.

"There were police all over the lot," she said. "I don't think they saw me, but I had to get out of there—"

I raised my hand. "I know. We'll have to dump the car and get out of town. I think you'll be pleased with our new transport, though. The contrast boggles the mind. I'll pull up behind you so we can load up quick." When I climbed into the Caddy I had a brainstorm. I called Troy at the import parts store on the cell phone while Mrs. Cartwright stuck her bags in the trunk. "Except for the vitamins and enzymes," she said. "Pack them up front because they need to stay cool."

"Hey, Troy," I said, and identified myself. "How'd you like to drive that Triumph?"

"You know I'd love to," he said. "But what are you still doing in town? You should be halfway to New Mexico."

"I need a favor," I said. "I know you've got no reason to—"

"Tell me," he said.

"I need to leave the car here for awhile. People are looking for it. I swear on my dog's life that it is my car, and that I haven't done anything wrong. In fact I'm trying to help somebody. But some bad people are going to be looking for that car on the roads and I need to stash it."

"Hey anybody with a car like that is okay with me," he said. A quick thumbs-up to my fathers, Steve the Abandoner and Ray the Fixer. "You want me to pick it up somewhere?"

"That would be great. It's around back at the Avis place at the airport. Keys are under the mat."

"Done," he said. "Call me when you get back in town. Meantime I'll stick it in the yard and put a tarp over it."

"I can't thank you enough," I said.

"Done," he repeated. "Call me when you get back."

By then we had everybody in the Cadillac without being seen, and I didn't intend to stay around for that to happen. "Let's go, gang," I said. "Ready?"

"Ready!" Michael said.

"Ready," Kathy sighed.

Buster spoke not at all, and saved his other form of communication for some time when it would be most persuasive.

We rolled out of Memphis again behind tinted windows in a car so quiet I could almost hear my watch tick. Kathy put in a Raffi tape, and within twenty minutes Michael was snoozing in back with Buster, his head at one of those perverse angles that in grown people would indicate violent death.

Raffi was singing a song about going to the zoo, zoo, zoo, which I could do without, how about you, you, you? "Can you take that out please?" I asked Kathy.

"Better not," she said. "He'll wake up without some noise." She looked tired; the early morning roust didn't agree with her, either.

"You can sleep if you like," I said. "I'll wake you if anything happens."

"Listen, I'll pay you back," she said. "Or my sister can pay you when we get to Oklahoma City."

"You really don't like to be helped by men," I said, and she looked right at me and shook her head.

"I love Michael," she said. "But sometimes I wish I could just cut that little pecker off. It'll only lead him places he shouldn't go."

"As a male myself," I said, shuddering a little, "let me strongly protest. None of us would be here without the penis."

She sniffed.

"Okay," I said. "Fine and dandy. You hate your husband. But don't cut off our penises." It was a little surreal to be conversing with a member of the Moral Majority about the male member. I hoped I could remember this conversation later to tell Otis.

"I don't hate my husband," she said. "That's un-Christian."

"Sure you don't," I said. "And these last few weeks, you've seen men at their absolute most piggish. You've had contempt for all those sad or lonely or merely horny men who wanted you to dry-hump them and stick your ass in their faces. But don't hate all men because of that."

"Well, I never," she huffed, and flashed a look at the sleeping Michael to make sure he had slept though all that. Then she crossed her arms and stared angrily out the window.

After about ten minutes of driving, she looked across at me. "I'll tell you something, Mr. Forester. When I danced, I was offering it up to God. I can't help what anyone else was thinking while they watched." And she stared at me like she dared me to find anything bizarre about the idea. She was a tough nut to crack.

Well, further talk along those lines was not worth the effort. I went another direction. "You know, you don't look old enough to be the wife of the lieutenant governor and future etcetera, etcetera. I thought there were laws about things like that, even in Tennessee."

"He's eight years older than me," she said. "But you know, he's not that old. They call him the Boy Wonder of Tennessee politics. He was elected to the state senate while he was still in law school. He was lieutenant governor when he was thirty-four. He has lots of powerful friends. And except for the Gores—who he hates, I might add—he comes from the most important political family in the state."

"Not a good man to cross," I said. We'd be coming up on Little Rock in an hour or so, and I was hoping for food and a restroom break, but even with our little penis talk I didn't feel comfortable broaching the subject. "But why won't he let you divorce him? Why'd you have to run away?"

"Another divorce would be political suicide for him."

"Another?"

She sat for a while and thought about what she wanted to tell me and how. "What I'm going to say," she said at last, "is known by a few people. But nobody would ever say this anywhere that it counts. I'm Daniel's second wife. He let the first wife divorce him, and it almost killed him in the next election. And that was supposedly amicable. I can assure you that ours wouldn't be."

"Supposedly amicable?"

"She was always the villain in our house. I believed him. Until—until things started to happen. Then I tracked her down and found out the truth. He was just as mean to her. Worse. He threw her down the stairs. She lost her baby. A lot of money changed hands to keep her quiet at the divorce."

"Kathy," I said, and I shot a look in the rearview to where Michael was still slumbering. "Your husband, if you'll forgive my saying so, is a son of a bitch. If his political future is so important to him, aren't you worried that he might—you know—throw you down the stairs too?"

She shook her head. "I've thought about that. I don't think he could have anything like that done to me. And I know he

couldn't do it to Michael. I believe—as well as he can understand the concept—that he loves him."

God save us from that kind of love. "We'll get you to a safe
place," I said. "And then we need to put some pressure on
him."

She laughed, and it was not a happy laugh. "Don't you
think I thought of that? I went to our pastor. To Uncle
Edward. To half a dozen other lawyers. I think they believed
me. I showed some of them pictures." And here she took out
half a dozen Polaroids from a larger stack in her purse and
handed them to me. They were awful: Michael, his arms covered by palm-print bruises, his poor bottom beaten raw;
Kathy with a shiner no sunglasses would cover, with bruises
up and down her rib cage. When she spoke again, her voice
was full of quiet fury. "But they said they couldn't do anything about it. Couldn't. Ha. Wouldn't, you mean." She
veered right up to the edge of tears and then skated back, and
the wall went back up to stay. "He's too powerful in the state
of Tennessee. No one will stand up to him. No one."

I gripped the steering wheel hard and clenched my teeth.
"That's not right," I said.

"No, it isn't," she said. "But this old world is full of
heartaches. That's why we have to turn our eyes to heaven."

"Please stop," I said. "I can only take so much in one
morning."

She turned puzzled eyes to me. "What are you talking
about?"

"I'd just appreciate it if you'd keep your Jesus talk to yourself," I said. "I'm on a vacation from Jesus."

The cell phone rang. It was on the seat next to me, and I
was able to pick up before it woke Michael. "Speak to me," I
said.

It was Ray. "Son," he said, "I just got a call from the
Tennessee attorney general—the man himself—and what I'm
wondering is which one of you is crazy."

"Jesus, they move fast," I said. "I thought it'd take them
longer to trace the tag."

"They ran your hotel room for prints," they said. "They
also asked me if you had an aerosol habit. Can you believe

that? I have not breathed a word of this to your mother," he said, and you could tell he was worked up almost into a lather, "but what in the name of all creation are you doing out there?"

"I'm helping someone," I said. "Since I haven't done that for a while, you'll just have to trust that I know what I'm doing. But I haven't kidnapped anyone, I haven't hurt anyone, and I don't think we're in any real danger."

That's all Ray needed to know; the word *help* was sacred to him. "You've got to dump that car, then," he said. "Damn yellow thing sticks out like a cat in a hen house."

"Already taken care of," I said. "Listen, talk to the woman riding shotgun for a second and then you get to work cleaning this mess up." I handed the phone over to Kathy. "Here, make my life easier and tell this gentleman why you're on the run."

And she did, in fifty words or less—she was a tight, tamped-down woman—and handed me the phone back.

"That's a shit-kettle you're roiling around in," Ray said.

"Thank you for that expert analysis, Brent Musberger," I said. "Any chance you can do something back there to get them to call off the dogs?"

"I'll do what I can," he said. "You have any ideas on your end?"

"Well, to start with, you can get me numbers for the Memphis and Knoxville papers," I said. "A few words from the kidnapped woman might be newsworthy."

"Okay," he said. "That's a start. But son, I have to confess. I did a bad thing before I thought about the implications of it. When they asked where I thought you might be headed, I told them you were headed off to your college reunion in Maine. I hope that won't spoil anything for you."

I went to Duke, of course, like my stepfather and his father before him. "Ray," I said, "you know I've never so much as set foot in Maine."

"Really?" he said, and I could tell he was grinning fit to swallow the telephone. "You didn't go to Bowdoin? Well, my memory isn't worth a damn anymore, is it?"

"No, sir, it isn't," I said. "But I love you just the same."

"Same here, son. Same here. You be real careful and I'll call you later."

I beeped off with a big smile on my face.

Kathy raised an eyebrow of inquiry. "Your father?"

"Yes, ma'am," I said. "My father." Fortified by the phone call, I took the Carlisle exit. A man's got a right to stop and drain his bladder, no matter what some woman might think about it.

9

And so, at last, fortified by a piss break, three bottles of Dr. Pepper, a handful of barbecue beef sandwiches, and a plastic-wrapped brownie that had been sitting on the shelf so long it was actually dusty—and a couple of bottles of Evian for the Cartwrights, the only thing in that joint that she would have let pass between her lips, although she told me, shaking her head, that plastic containers leach CFCs or some other such thing—we pressed on toward the prize. Michael was awake again, and his mother pressed a handful of capsules into his palm and one at a time, laboriously, he swallowed them with swigs of water.

"He's not getting enough antioxidants or essential oils," she said. "We've eaten such c-r-a-p—pardon my French—I worry for him."

"What's he taking?" It looked like a handful of horse pills.

"Oh, grapeseed oil, flaxseed oil, Omega-3, plus some red clover and bioflavonoids."

"All that came out of your plastic bag?" I looked over at her little grocery bag, now revealed as a magical thing.

"Oh, and there's more. She laid out on the seat one by one bottles and vials, calling off their names as she did it: barley grass powder, herbal cleansing powder, Super Ester Vitamin C, bee propolis, acidophilus, milk thistle, enzymes. I had to turn my attention back to my driving; it boggled the mind.

"Do you actually take all those?"

She looked across at me. "Do you actually ingest bleached white flour, processed sugar, and hydrogenated oils?"

I checked the label of my brownie. "Partially-hydro-genated," I said. "Is that better?"

"Cottonseed?" she asked with what I could have sworn was a smirk.

"Yes," I said.

"Does it have polysorbate or sorbic acid?"

"Well, yes," I admitted. "Both."

"You might as well get in the tub and drag a radio in on top of yourself," she said, putting her bottles back in the bag. "You'd kill yourself more efficiently."

"Well thank you for that update," I said. "Maybe I don't want to kill myself efficiently. Maybe I want to linger."

She packed away the bag and put it at her feet. Michael had forced down his last capsule, and was reading a VeggieTales book in the back seat. We drove in silence for a while, through North Little Rock and on into Little Rock proper, if indeed that can be said of Little Rock.

"Mr. Forester, where on earth are you going?" she said, after we'd been quiet for a good long while. I could see the red-rimmed blue diamond of the Arkansas flag flapping over the state house.

"I'm right in the middle of the lane," I said. Anna Lynn used to complain about my driving; turned out she was right to.

"No," she said, and if it looked like this topic had just occurred to her, it probably had. "I mean, where are you going? What are you doing out here? What's a guitar player from Robbinsville—is that right?—Robbinsville, North Carolina, doing heading west through Arkansas in the first place?"

"That question betrays some personal interest," I said.

"I'm waiting," she said.

I switched lanes to pass a slow-moving delivery van, then switched back into the right lane. "I'm going to a funeral," I said.

"Yes?"

"In New Mexico. Someone—someone I didn't really know."

"This is not satisfying my curiosity," she said.

"I'm not accustomed to satisfying people in any fashion."

"That's no kind of answer. What kind of male role model are you presenting to my son?"

I looked at Michael in the rearview. He was looking back at me and smiling with interest. I turned my eyes back to the road and prepared to be some species of role model.

"My father left home when I was a baby," I said. "I never knew him. He died in New Mexico a few days ago. I'm going to the funeral. And if you tell me I'm on a spiritual quest you'll find yourself standing beside the interstate so fast it'll make your head spin." I looked back at Michael, who was suddenly intrigued. "Not you, Buddy," I told him. "You're in like Flynn."

"A spiritual quest," she said, arching her eyebrow. "Far be it from me to suggest such a thing."

We were through downtown and the traffic was easing up. "I'm just going to New Mexico because I'm curious," I said. "That's all. Wouldn't you be?"

"Yes, I would," she said. "And it's certainly good for us that you are. God put you in the right place at the right time." She elevated her eyes heavenward and put her hands together stiffly in prayer.

"That's enough of that stuff," I growled, and then, wonder of wonders, she was grinning. "So you did that on purpose? Since when did you get a sense of humor?"

"Don't treat me like my husband does," she said, which was always the answer to my question, even if the answer itself was different.

"Far be it from me," I said. "What does that mean, anyway? You know, my whole life I always wondered what that meant."

She shrugged and yawned.

"Really," I said, "take a nap if you want to." I know I wanted to; it was cool and quiet, just a low hum of road noise, and the leather seats were smooth and soft as butter.

"I can't go to sleep around you," she said. "No offense."

"None taken," I said.

"It's just that, nice as you've been, I really don't know you from Adam. Sleep requires a lot of trust."

"Yes it does," I said. "I saw a man sleeping right next to the highway this week. He had a lot of trust."

"Hmm," she said.

"What's your sister's name?"

"Pam. Pam Standerfer."

"What kind of name is that?"

"God only knows," she said. "She certainly didn't ask us for permission before she married him. He's a backhoe contractor. Owns his own business." She sighed. "I guess I shouldn't talk," she said. "I married the lieutenant governor of Tennessee. At least he treats her well."

"I'm hungry," Michael said, although how he could still have room in that stomach after what he'd already ingested today was beyond me. "Can we get something to eat soon?"

"Sure," I said. "If your mom says okay." I turned to her and smiled. "No pressure."

"Okay," she said.

"Where would you like to eat?" she asked, just as we were passing a Cracker Barrel sign. Maybe my saliva was apparent, because Michael instantly sung out, "There!"

"It's in Conway," I said. "About half an hour. Can you wait?"

"I want to eat there," he said. "I want fried apples. And macaroni and cheese. And ice cream."

"It's okay with me," I said. "If your mom says okay." She gave me a stare that would have melted plastic.

"Okay," she said. "If you'll take some extra enzymes. Good Lord, the nutrition is all cooked out of that food. And when I think—"

"We'll be there in no time, Buddy," I said. "How's Buster doing back there? I haven't smelled him for a while."

Dangerous last words, like "Hand me that match, I don't think there's any gasoline in this can."

"Never mind," I said when it became possible to talk again. "He's doing just fine."

Kathy was still mad at me as we pulled off the interstate onto Highway 65 and then turned into the Cracker Barrel parking lot. Or at least I figured she was mad. We hadn't passed more than a dozen words, which was okay with me. I was feeling more reflective than talkative.

"I want fried apples. And macaroni and cheese. And ice cream," Michael told Wanda, our server.

Kathy rolled her eyes, sighed, and chose the lesser of evils. "I'll have the vegetable plate. Carrots, pinto beans, turnip greens, and the sweet potato casserole."

"What's the carcinogen special?" I asked Wanda.

"The what?"

Kathy kicked me under the table, a wicked jab like that old broad in the James Bond movie with the knives in her shoes. "Okay, I'll have a grilled pork chop with hash brown casserole and fried okra. Unless you have corn."

"We have corn."

"Bring me two sides of corn. It's my favorite vegetable." And I moved my foot so that I heard only the satisfying thud of Kathy's toe against the chair leg.

"That hurt," she said when Wanda walked off. She rubbed her foot underneath the table.

"I have a right to eat the way I want, especially if I'm going to pay for it. And I am."

"We can pay our part—" she began and I cut her off. Michael was playing with golf tees and didn't seem interested, although I knew he was probably used to tuning in even when he didn't seem to be. It was probably a survival trait with him now.

"Here it is: I have plenty of money. Until I get you to your sister, everything is my treat. If I get picked up on a Mann Act rap then you're going to need every penny you earned to defend yourself."

"The what?"

"The Mann Act. Passed in 1910. Interstate transportation of women for immoral purposes."

"You're an odd bird, Clay Forester," she said, a slow smile spreading across her face. "And how did you come to be rolling in dough on a musician's salary?" she asked.

"I'm independently wealthy," I said, figuring that would kill conversation; it usually did. People would laugh and move on to another topic. But Kathy just kept looking at me—that look she did where it wasn't clear that she would even breathe again until I told her the truth.

"No," she said. "Really."

"Really," I said, and I gave in. "My mother's family was well off. Then she married my stepfather, who was well off. And then I got a big insurance settlement and I was, well, well off. What I'm doing for you is not the widow's mite. I mean, I'm glad to do it. But I won't miss it. In fact, if you need more, I'd be happy to give it to you."

She shook her head, and I was heartened by the arrival of our biscuits. I opened two, spread butter on them, and opened up two strawberry jam packets to forestall further conversation.

"Let's call Pam," I said. I'd brought Ray's cell phone in for that express purpose. "Tell her we can be in OKC in about four hours. If somebody is still watching the house, it'd be best if you could pick a rendezvous. And tell her to watch out for a tail."

She just looked at me as I proffered the phone. "Where did this brilliant deviant mind come from? I thought you were a head-banger."

"People are surprising," I said. "For example, I didn't know that you knew the word 'head-banger.' "

"I was a teenager once," she said. "And although I'm ashamed to admit it, I once listened to AC-DC for pleasure." She beeped her sister's number. "Long ago, you understand. In my other life, as a sinner."

"Of course."

"Pammy," she said then. "It's me. Yes, I'm fine. We're both fine. No. They can't trace this. No. Listen, I want you to meet me. Yes, it'll be okay. You'll just have to trust me. Do you remember that place where we took the boys last summer? No, just us. The men weren't there. Right. Can you meet me in the parking lot at eight?" She smiled. "Good. Just in case, watch for company. If we see anything suspicious we'll call you on your cell phone. I know, baby. Thank you."

She beeped off and handed me the phone.

"She'll meet us outside the zoo at eight o'clock. No one's

staking out the house, but she'll be careful. And she says she has a place for us to hide. She's a good girl."

She was blinking back tears, which pissed her off. Whether it was because it was happening in front of Michael or in front of me, I don't know, but she grabbed that emotion and throttled it like she would a copperhead in a baby's cradle.

"You're ready for this to be over," I said gently. "Someday it will be."

"What do you know?" she said. Then, again, she mastered herself for Michael's sake. I could see her turn to wood; it spread up her body until she was sitting stiff and even her words came out formal. "Of course it will," she said. "By the time school starts, Michael will be making new friends."

"I've been making friends," he said, his mouth full of biscuit.

"Manners," she said.

"Sorry," he said, again with his mouth full.

I was half asleep as we drove the eastern half of the state. We crossed over into Oklahoma without incident and were headed through landscape that surprised me. I guess I thought Oklahoma looked like it did in *The Grapes of Wrath*: Dust Bowl and blowing tumbleweeds. But this was green, rolling hills, lots of trees. I couldn't tell when we passed over from Arkansas.

I could tell the growing pressure again on my bladder, though. Three Dr. Peppers and three glasses of iced tea at Cracker Barrel. Kathy was amazing, and she was having a similar effect on Michael: they could hold their urine better than any mother-son combo I'd ever heard of. "Mrs. Cartwright," I said, reverting to the formal for this request, "I need to stop and use the facilities again."

"You're a grown man, Mr. Forester," she said. "Stop whenever you need to. We could do the same." I took the Sallisaw exit and stopped at a Texaco station. "Anybody want anything from the store?"

"More water," she said. "If you wouldn't mind."

"Sure," I grunted. No more talk about water just at this precise juncture. We were relieved, gassed up, and back on the road within ten minutes. Michael was feeling tired himself

after high-fat food and the driving, and he was asleep before
we passed over Lake Eufaula twenty minutes later. The sun
was low in the sky and the world was golden, that brief
stretch when everything looks dashed with fairy dust.

I made the mistake of saying that out loud. I expected
maybe a chuckle or a nod or an isn't that so.

I did not expect her to draw herself up straight and stare
daggers at me. "Mr. Forester, if you're trying to make a pass
at me, you can just let us out here," she said. "You have not
purchased that right. Those men in the club didn't touch me
and you're not about to."

"Whoa down there, Mrs. Cartwright," I said. "Put that
horse back in the stable. I know your recent history is terrible,
but I'm not putting the moves on you. Even if I wanted to I
wouldn't know how."

"Men always know how. It's just one of the things women
hate them for."

I shook my head sadly. "It doesn't have to be this way. Men
and women do not have to be enemies."

"Only since the Garden of Eden," she said.

I shook my head again. "I don't believe that."

She snorted. "And you know so much about men and
women?"

"I was married once," I said. "We were happy for a while.
I don't know if that makes me an expert."

"And what happened to her?" she asked. "You haven't
mentioned her before now, and you're not wearing a ring, so
obviously you're not still married. What happened?" Her
voice was dripping with contempt; this kid asleep in the nest
behind me was going to ring up some serious therapy bills if
he ever really understood all his mother felt about men. "Did
you beat her? Sleep around on her?"

I felt the heat growing in my neck and my cheeks as she
was talking, could feel the iced tea sloshing around in my
stomach, and maybe I can be forgiven for what I said.

"No," I told her, biting off my words so as not to expand
upon them. "I killed her."

Well, that'll turn your conversation in a new direction, let
me tell you. She skittered next to the door, her body drawn up

against the side of the car. "Let us out," she said, and to her credit, there was only a hint of fear in her voice. "Stop the car right now or I'll scream bloody murder."

"It's not what you think, Mrs. Cartwright," I said. "But thanks for the vote of confidence."

"I'm serious," she said, and her mouth was drawn into a snarl. "Stop the car now. I have a knife and I'm not afraid to use it."

"I drank in those days," I said. "Too much, maybe. It sure seems like it now." She was rooting through her purse but her eyes didn't leave my face. "My wife and son were visiting her parents in Grand Rapids, and I went out with some colleagues to celebrate a big win. We had struck a compromise so a fat-cat corporation could avoid a big legal judgment they deserved to pay. So I was celebrating this great achievement, and I was drowning my guilt, and I was looking forward to my family coming home and maybe somehow getting back to the life we used to have."

She stopped fumbling around in the bag and she was quiet. If she had a knife, she'd found it, but her hand slid empty from her purse, and she was just watching me, because she knew that we had bumped up against my own heartbreak for the first time. Maybe it intrigued her. I can't say what goes through women's minds. "What happened?"

"I went to pick them up at the airport," I said. "Like I said, I'd had a few drinks. I didn't feel drunk. But maybe I was. Like I said, I drank a lot in those days." The sun had dipped to the horizon, and now it was in my eyes. The golden moment was over; now the light just stung. I lowered the visor for what little help it could give me.

I made my voice as neutral as I could, like I was talking about something I might have heard about on TV. "On the way home from the airport, we were sitting at an intersection. A garbage truck ran the red light. I pulled out when the light turned green. I didn't see it coming."

She waited, watching, and for some reason—maybe because I didn't know her, because I'd never see her again; maybe because she too knew something about the shape of suffering in this world—I kept talking. "I heard the horn blare. I heard Anna Lynn scream, and then she turned around and she was looking at me when the thing hit us and we went rolling over and over." And all of a sudden, there were tears in my eyes and I couldn't go on and it pissed me off.

I struggled to keep talking, to choke it down like you'd hold a hated enemy under water until he drowns. "Do you know why she looked at me instead of at the truck?"

Kathy shook her head. She was watching me, her eyes wide as if she was witnessing another truck wreck.

"She looked at me because she knew we were going to die. It was horrible. Her eyes—"

I had it under control again; I'd had plenty of practice. Nobody needed to know what was in her eyes. I cleared my throat, let out a deep breath, shook my head, cleared my throat. "Only I didn't die, you see. I didn't die."

Kathy had put her bag in the floor and she leaned forward, and there was a look of concern I had never before seen on her face. "But you did, you know. On the inside. You fooled people, because you were still walking around and so they didn't know. But you were dead from that moment on."

And of course, she knew whereof she spoke. It was so true that I lost it again, and then some. I was sobbing now, my shoulders shaking. My cheeks burned, snot was pouring from my nose, and I had to pull off the road.

There's a moment in every life that you want back. Maybe more than one, but that was my moment, when I touched the gas and pulled into the intersection. It wasn't so much to ask, was it? To have that one second over? How could one second be allowed to wreck your whole life, to kill the people you loved most?

I saw her eyes, Anna Lynn's eyes in that moment. They were full of fear, full of loss, full of blame.

If only they'd been full of forgiveness. There was so much that needed to be forgiven.

And so I sat on the side of the interstate, crying and crying and I couldn't stop. I was trying to be quiet, but still I felt as if I was shaking the whole car. It was all too much.

Then I felt a tiny hand on my shoulder, a tiny voice saying gently, "It's okay. You cry if you want to."

Michael's voice was followed by his sleepy face, and I blinked my thanks because I didn't trust my words. And there was Kathy's hand on my arm, suddenly solid, tangible. I took a series of deep breaths. I closed my eyes, held them shut, opened them again.

The moment passed.

"You should blow your nose," Michael said.

"You're right," I said, and I took Kathy's proffered tissue.

After I had honked and wiped, I put on the turn signal, *click click*, pulled onto the road, and tried to act like the whole thing had never happened. I pointed out a car with Alaska license plates. I yawned and stretched and tried to act nonchalant.

I got away with about eighteen seconds of that stuff.

"How long ago did this happen?" Kathy asked.

"Oh," I said. "That? A long time ago."

"It feels fresh. Like it just happened."

I nodded solemnly. "To me too."

"Don't you ever talk about it? About them?" She could see the answer just by looking at my face, at the sudden devastation in it. "Clay, how do you ever expect to get over it?"

"I don't expect to."

She sighed, female exasperation working past the sympathy. "You mean you don't want to." I could feel, in fact, her sympathy start to evaporate, steaming like water off a street. "You made one mistake, if it was a mistake. It was tragic. But it can be forgiven."

Nothing from me. I am a rock; I am an island.

"She wouldn't want this for you, Clay. This life you've made. It's not what she'd want. It's certainly not what you'd have wanted her to do if you'd passed, is it?"

True enough, so far as it applied, but still I showed nothing. A rock.

"God," she said, addressing the ceiling, or perhaps something beyond it, "why did you let men run the world? One crisis and they all go to pieces. No man was ever worth anything in a pinch."

"I seem to recall that Jesus had a penis."

Her lower lips contracted in her strain to keep from smiling, and at last she had to turn so I couldn't see it. "I choose not to believe that. I like to think he was like my Ken doll. Kind face, cool clothes, and completely smooth below the waist."

"You're a heretic, Mrs. Cartwright," I said. "A Marcionite, if I remember my heresies."

"A what?" She arched an eyebrow.

"I was a double major at Duke: history and religion. That was a long, long time ago. Now I don't think of either of them as particularly useful. But anyway: what made Jesus Jesus, if you believe the stories, was that he had a fully functional penis and yet he chose not to be ruled by it."

"Maybe so," she said. "You're awfully theological for a rock musician."

She was smiling again, but I was of a sudden tired unto death, and I came back testy. My very skin hurt. "Mrs. Cartwright," I said, "I have a mother and two maiden aunts who make you look like a Visigoth outside the gates. I've thrown up more of the Bible that was crammed down my throat than you will probably ever digest."

And as you might expect, she got her prim, well-I-never look, her lips drawn thin.

I should have apologized, I guess. Hell, I should never have said it in the first place. But I was tired and hurting and cranky, and I was embarrassed about my public nervous breakdown, and all I could think about was that I still had at least another ten hours of driving before I got to Santa Fe.

Maybe then, after all that, I could rest.

God, I hoped so.

I had heard this Raffi tape so many times that I knew the songs. Or maybe I had known them from a long time back. Little Ray liked Raffi, or seemed to. We heard that he was supposed to, and so we played them for him and they didn't make him scream and foam at the mouth like I did when I heard Celine Dion, so we figured it was just about okay by him.

We were listening to Raffi on the way back from the airport. I hadn't thought of that. Of course, why would I? I hadn't heard a note of Raffi for ten years.

Michael and Buster could sense the sudden tension in the car. In the rearview, they looked up at me expectantly; their experience with men was not a favorable one, and long silences or tensions could go to bad places.

"Let's sing," I said, turning up Raffi. "Want to?"

"Sure," Michael said. Kathy said nothing, just looked out the window. I'm sure she couldn't wait for this ride to end, which it would shortly. The mileage sign said we were thirty miles out of OKC, and now it was starting to look like Oklahoma. As of Shawnee the trees and green hills were a thing of the past; now it was beginning to look flat and ugly.

We sang "Willoughby Wallaby Woo," a thrilling ditty about various animals sitting on us.

"That's a funny song," Michael said after the first verse.

"But full of valuable life lessons," I said, and then we sang some more. When we finished "Willoughby Wallaby Woo," Kathy said quietly, "You have a lovely voice."

"Thank you," I said in what I hoped was a conciliatory tone. "It's my father's."

"How come you haven't gotten married again?" she asked, and the peanut-butter sandwich song started without me. "You said what happened was a long time ago."

"Married?" My head rotated without my consent, and then I forced it back to look at the road. "Are you kidding me?" As if she'd asked me how come I hadn't had a prefrontal lobotomy.

She shrugged. "You're a good-looking man. You have a nice voice. I'm sure you're not totally devoid of other good points. And you said it's been a long time. How long? Years?"

I nodded.

"So why not? Haven't there been other women?"

"Not really." I was getting my irritation back on. "I've lived a pretty monastic life. I mean, there is a woman, but it's mostly platonic. Or at least I think it is."

"Are you planning to marry her?"

"Good Christ, no." Then I remembered Michael. "Sorry."

"Why not?"

"Woman, are you so hot to get married again?"

"We're not talking about me," she said. "Of course I'm

not. My first responsibility is Michael and getting him in a good home. A safe home. I'm a long way from thinking about marriage."

"I'm a long way from thinking about marriage too," I said.

"Well, I'll bet she isn't."

"She?"

"The woman. The one you're not thinking about marrying. I'll bet she's thinking about getting married."

"Maybe she is," I said. "I don't really care to talk about it."

"You should." She sighed. Men were so predictable. It was so sad. "There are lots of things you should talk about. Holding it all inside like this really isn't healthy."

"I do a lot of talking. And I have my music. I am strong. I am invincible. I am woman."

Not even a smile. "Your music isn't going to save you," she said. "I used to sing. Singing a song is like acting. You can hide behind it, and you don't have to show yourself. It just looks like you did."

"It's not like that," I said, shaking my head. "You can live through it. Like through a story. Okay, it's not real, exactly. But it can represent your real self. It can tap into something, a stripe of love or longing like a vein of ore. You couldn't do it well if you didn't feel something somewhere."

She shook her head sadly and a little primly. "It's a shame, Clay. If I wasn't full up with what's happening to me, my heart would be breaking for you."

I tried to get her to meet my gaze. Don't people ever know when to let things lie? I clenched the steering wheel, pushed against it like it was a weight machine, like it was a four-wheeled gym, and my voice was grating even to my own ears. "I said I don't care to talk about it."

"In a few minutes I'll be getting out of this car," she said. "We'll never see each other again. I feel like I owe it to you to be honest about what I see in you."

Now I was screaming, snarling. I didn't want anybody to see anything in me. Or, at least, I didn't want them to talk about it. "I don't care to talk about it." Buster and Michael cringed away against the corner of the back seat, and Michael's eyes were big and rimmed with tears. "Anyway, woman, you should talk. I don't need personal advice from a woman who's been letting waitresses raise her son. From a woman who can somehow entertain the notion that she's been lap dancing for Jesus."

She dropped her head into her hands and I could tell she was weeping, although she was doing it quietly, so as not to let Michael know.

I was a sorry excuse for a human being.

"I'm sorry," I said. "Really."

She didn't stop, didn't look over. I looked hard at the overpass ahead; if I'd been alone in the car, that bridge abutment would have been calling my name.

"She wouldn't have wanted this for you," she said finally in a voice I could barely hear, a voice that all the same was full of strength. "She doesn't want this. Who you've become since."

"She doesn't know what it's like to be the one left," I said, and if I had been tired before, now I felt like somebody could pour me under a door. "And you don't know everything, Kathy. It's not fair to say that to me. Not until you've lived it."

"Don't you think I've lived enough? I do. I've lived all I can stand to live."

And of course, who was I to talk? What was I to say to that?

We passed Tinker Air Force Base, enormous bombers from World War Two and Korea and Vietnam somehow mounted on posts outside the gates. I pointed them out to Michael, who still said nothing, just stared out the window. I couldn't blame him for not wanting to look at me. I was just another loud and angry man.

I could see skyscrapers ahead, a patch of them rising from the plains like some strange growth or infestation.

"My God, this city is ugly," I said. "No wonder Timothy McVeigh wanted to blow it up." There was no reply; I was not so angry that I wasn't a little appalled at myself.

We were driving past oilfield supply places, scraggly trees, lots and lots of vacant lots. Downtown we passed a big public building, concrete and glass, peeling and leprous, and undergoing a facelift in the same way someone administers CPR. Still nothing, so I threw out another bon mot. "Your sister must have the aesthetic constitution of an Eskimo to survive here. Or else she's a Southern Baptist."

"We're going to take I-44 north," she said. "I'm sure there's an easier way to get there, but that's how she brought me." Her voice had all the warmth of frozen cod. She looked over at me. I didn't look back. "In fact, why don't you just take this exit. I'd like for you to drop us off here."

"No," I said. "I'll take you."

"You don't understand," she said. "I don't want you to take us anywhere. I don't want to spend another minute in your company. My son has seen enough men like you to last a thousand years."

"I'll take you," I said.

Out of the corner of her eye I could see her shake her head violently. "Let us out now, you pathetic little man."

A film of anger covered my eyes, coated my brain. Without even checking behind me I whipped across three lanes of traffic to take the exit she indicated, horns blaring behind me, a Honda Accord swerving onto the shoulder to miss us. I didn't care. My stomach was boiling and steam was coming out my ears.

She didn't give me the satisfaction of screaming or even of grabbing on tight to something. She just looked across at me and matched me rage for rage, and then she shook her head and repeated her conclusion. "You are pathetic," she said.

I bounced onto the access road and braked too hard once we got there. Things fell into the floorboard. Michael and Buster fetched up against the front seat with a thump, and Michael started crying. Buster released the master fart of his career. My eyes watered and I gagged for breath.

The car hadn't even stopped moving when she was outside it, throwing the back door open, pulling the crying Michael forth, Buster in his arms like a security blanket, pulling her plastic bags out onto the asphalt, spilling the contents of her life in her haste to get away from me.

"Put the dog back, baby," she said. She reached for Buster, but he clutched tighter still.

"No," he wailed. "No." I'm not sure he even heard her. I'm not sure he knew what he was saying no to.

"This dog isn't ours," she said, louder, and Michael was wailing still louder; derelicts were looking over from the sidewalk, and I was ready to commit hara-kiri.

"Christ Almighty, keep him," I said, and nobody heard me. So I yelled again. "Keep the damn dog. He's a worthless piece of shit. I'm sure you'll be very happy together."

They looked up at me then, and the mixture of emotions I saw there—fear, anger, sadness—was a potent brew. I sobered of a sudden like a drunk who sees flashing red lights in the rearview mirror.

"Please," I said, meaning a lot of things I couldn't possibly say. "Keep him."

Kathy nodded once, a little inclination of her head, a tiny moment of grace in a world fucked beyond recognition.

It broke me.

"I'm sorry," I said, my words fumbling over themselves in their haste to be born. "Please. Get back in. I'll take you wherever you need to go. I'll—"

She closed the doors firmly, stepped away, and raised her hands, palms toward me, washing her hands of me. Grace only extends so far.

I had never taken the car out of gear. When I saw that Michael wasn't even going to look at me to say good-bye, I put on my turn signal, the blinker clicking loud in that noxious silence.

"I'm sorry," I said, but of course there was no answer.

I watched in the mirror as Kathy took Michael's free hand and turned him around. All I could see of Buster was his tail, wagging, wagging. Life must look wonderful when you have the intellectual capacity of a three-legged garbage-eating dog.

"Okay," I said. "Fine. Good on you." I bumped back onto the access road, the stench from a cattleyard somewhere downwind on Agnew competing with the remains of Buster's parting gift. I turned the air conditioner on recirculate—as if it could help any to recycle pure phosgene—and sat beneath a dingy halogen light, waiting for the signal to change. The wind picked up, pushing yellowed sheets of newspaper past me down the street, and I saw dark, towering storm clouds far off to the west in the dying light.

My god, this was an ugly city.

And at that moment, I felt right at home in it.

10

If there is a darker place than Western Oklahoma and the Texas Panhandle at night, I hope never to see it. After I left Oklahoma City behind, I passed the occasional town: Yukon, El Reno, Weatherford, Clinton, Elk City. They were not really towns so much as momentary breaks in the darkness, the garish glow of McDonald's and Texaco and Holiday Inn at least momentarily suggesting that I wasn't driving through some primeval void.

God, I needed a drink. I ran the back of my hand across my mouth. My lips felt chapped. I couldn't have driven the Triumph; I couldn't have shifted and clutched to save my life. My feet were so badly burned I could barely rest them on the floor. In fact, my whole body radiated heat and angry pain.

And I needed to hear someone else's voice. Someone besides fucking Raffi. When "Willoughby Wallaby Woo" came on again I ejected Michael's tape violently and threw it out the window. I immediately regretted being such a son of a bitch, especially while I was fiddling with the radio and finding nothing but country western. I had just driven past Yukon, where the roadside water tower announced proudly, "A Great Place to Live: Home of the 1994 State Softball Champions and Garth Brooks." Then I found KATT FM 100.5 out of Oklahoma City, a hard rock station after my own heart, and knew that maybe I was safe from the silence for a few more minutes, at least.

But it clearly wasn't enough, even after great songs from Everclear, Creed, Van Halen, and Nirvana. It was going to take someone better adjusted than Kurt Cobain to make me feel better about myself. So I did an inventory of my few remaining friends and relations. I couldn't call Otis; he was onstage just now. I couldn't possibly talk to my mother or Ray after what I'd done; I was too ashamed. I was raised to believe that the only thing worse than cruelty to a woman, if indeed there was anything worse, was betraying your country to Mother Russia, and I had certainly been cruel, more than cruel in the time just passed.

And so I called Tracy. I thought maybe I could talk to her without having to really talk to her; I wasn't ready for that, if in fact I was ever really going to talk to her about what had happened. Still, just to hear her voice would be something, a wall to keep the creatures at bay.

The gatekeeper answered, of course, Alvin York, the sergeant major of Robbinsville. Nothing could be easy anymore. "Hello, Sir," I said. "It's Clay. May I speak with Tracy?"

"I'll get her for you," he said. "How are you, Clay? Are you safe in Santa Fe yet?"

"No, sir, I'm not," I said. "But I have hopes."

"You be careful," he said. Was that concern I heard in his voice? "That little girl's been through enough."

"She has," I said. "And I will. Thank you."

"I'll get her for you." He put the phone down and then she picked it up and said hello and my heart soared like a bird over a line of trees.

"I didn't expect to hear from you," she said.

"Why not?" I asked. "Wait, don't answer that. Is it because I'm pathetic?"

"Who says so?" she said. "If anybody but me says that I'll kick their ass."

"You cannot talk like that," I said, shushing her. "You're a good girl. And your dad will think I'm a bad influence."

"He knows that you're a bad influence. He's known it for a long time. He's been telling me so since we were fourteen."

"I blame Otis."

"Otis wasn't under the bleachers with me trying to sneak his hand under my freshman cheerleader uniform, I can assure you."

"I still blame Otis. I want to put an ad in the paper—like those things about financial responsibility?—that says I will no longer be responsible for my actions. I blame Otis. And my mother. And my missing father. I could have been a decent human being."

"What are you talking about?" she said, and her voice changed. "I can't figure out what's going on from just your voice. I wish I could see your face. Are you having some kind of therapeutic breakthrough out there on the road? Or are you just having a breakdown?"

Both. Neither. Who knew or cared? There was something else I wanted to tell her. "Tracy," I said, "You really should find someone who'll treat you better. Someone who's ready to treat you the way you need to be treated."

"Okay," she said. "Now I wish you could see my face. I'm making that face where I scrunch my eyes almost shut and turn up my nose at you. The one where I think you're talking complete bullshit?" I had to laugh. "What are you babbling about? How do you think I need to be treated?"

"You want someone who'll marry you."

"Oh," she said. "That."

I was barreling through the dark, a cone of dim light just ahead of me, lightning flashing way off to the west. Nobody said anything for a long time. I thought maybe we had lost our connection and I called her name.

"I do want to get married," she said softly. "To you. Is that so wrong? I know some guys would be pleased at that kind of news. And I want to have kids with you. You'd be a terrific father."

"I was a terrific father," I said. "Once. But that's over and done with. I couldn't go through it again. If something were to happen—"

"Oh, Clay," she said, and I could almost see her shake her head. That's what women all do to me if they're around me long enough. "You just can't live your life like that. You can't live your life forever based on the fear that someday you might lose somebody."

I took a deep breath. Sometimes you know you shouldn't say something; you know full well that it's hurtful, and damned if you don't let it fly anyhow. "Well," I said, "that's how I'm planning on doing it."

"I love you," she said. "And I hope you change your mind."

"It's not going to change," I managed to force out. "Love is the most dangerous thing I know." I shook my head. "Tracy, really. You ought to find somebody else."

"Goodnight, Clay," she said, and her voice was not icy but mournful; I could hear her love and irritation all at the same time.

The phone went dead, droned in my ear for a time, then went to beeping, then to a recorded voice that encouraged me to call an operator if I had difficulty placing a call.

I considered throwing the phone out the window, but unlike Raffi, it was blameless. I was the asshole this time. So I laid it down gently and shook my head again.

Cruel to two women in one day. A personal record, best I could recollect. Not even in my fraternity days had I ever crushed more than one woman a day.

"You are a son of a bitch and a bastard," I heard myself say out loud. No one contradicted me.

The rain in my future became the torrential downpour in my present. I lost my rock-and-roll radio station. The rain pattered down, pattered down, and the wipers sloshed back and forth—a rhythm that I thought might lull me to sleep, and would that be such a bad thing?

But I was still curious about a couple of things, so I pulled over after midnight at a truck stop in Elk City to gas up, bought a couple of cassette tapes: the Stylistics, Harold Melvin and the Blue Notes, the O'Jays' greatest hits. It was Otis that first got me to listen to all those old soul groups back in the Seventies; the Chi-Lites, Blue Magic, The Delfonics, Main Ingredient, the Four Tops, the Spinners, the Jackson Five, Bloodstone. Until then I was just your ordinary redneck white boy listening to Hank Williams Jr. or something. I thought all these black soul groups dressed like pimps, but that didn't last. Otis and I in fact learned to do a mean O'Jays before we discovered there was more of a market around Robbinsville for rock and roll. Maybe this was a wasteful purchase—I was sure I had all these tapes or something like them at home somewhere—but they were there and this was here, and I was going to need something better than right-wing talk shows if I was going to somehow get through this night.

While I was in the truck stop, I wandered. I meandered. I drifted past the coolers in back once, twice, more.

I could almost hear the foam rising off the beer in those coolers, and the cans glinted in the fluorescents like light off a hypnotist's watch.

I bought two roast beef-and-cheddar deli sandwiches, a big bag of Cheetos, a package of Oreos, some beef jerky, three artificially banana-flavored Moon Pies.

I bought a twelve-pack of Original Coors in the gold can. On sale, I noted with pleasure. I was a responsible person.

Responsible for everything.

Back on the highway, the rain pattering hard, I wolfed down a sandwich and then I cracked open a beer one-handed. It was cold in my hand, sweating, and the aroma was acrid and musty and bracing.

I used to drink Coors at Georgetown. After a long, hard morning of being law students, a bunch of us used to play softball at the big green belt down New Jersey from McDonough Hall, just north of the Capitol. Then we'd go home and open the books again in the evenings, those of us who did such things.

Someone always had a case of Coors on ice in the back of a car. In those days it was sort of romantic, this beer brewed from the icy waters of the Rocky Mountains, the beer of hunters, trappers, cowboys, and mountain men. I think Billy Rowlands, who was from Texas, was the guy who got us started drinking Coors first year, and he met some initial resistance. Most of us had been beer snobs. We drank Heineken or Moosehead. But after a hard day of moot court and a couple of hours of softball, nothing felt better in the warm afternoon than to lie sprawled in the grass and laugh and talk and drink Coors.

That's where, my last year at Georgetown, I got to know this tall blond girl, Anna Lynn Schrader, and I probably have the beer to thank at least for that, because we didn't run in the same circles and I don't know how I'd ever have had the guts to talk to her otherwise. Although we had taken one course together, Products Liability and Safety—and so at least knew each other to nod to—she was a Goody Two-shoes burning up the environmental law track, and I was a crank training for trial work. She was editor on the new *Georgetown International Environmental Law Review;* first time I ever heard her voice, she was telling Billy that she was editing articles on Mexican-American shared groundwater and marine plastic pollution. And me? I was devoting most of my energy and time during my last year to the Appellate Litigation Clinic, writing briefs for the Supreme Court and even arguing a case in front of the Fourth Circuit Court of Appeals. Anna Lynn was animated about her future; I was resigned. She had wings; I was going to be a flightless drone, if a well-paid one.

You get to know things about people by watching them play games. Anna, for example, did not play softball like the other girls. She played with abandon. She was tall and rangy, and she caught everything she could get to. She didn't care if the ball jumped up on her. She wasn't afraid to slide. She wasn't afraid to dive for the ball. She wasn't afraid to do anything. She was so beautiful and so earnest, this big blond Dutch girl from Michigan; that scared me too. When I finally insinuated myself into her company and she was directing remarks to me instead of Billy, she didn't talk about how much money she was going to make or about the rush you feel walking next to or on your way to being those in power, which was why I thought I was in law school.

No, she had this crazy idea she was going to make the world a better place.

In 1988 beer didn't taste like death and loathing; it tasted like new love. It tasted like spring afternoons and cherry blossoms and green grass and laughter, like the pealing chimes from the Taft Memorial calling off every quarter hour.

Those were good times. The best. Driving my rented Cadillac somewhere in western Oklahoma now, I took a long swig of Coors and it was like a rush of liquid gold. I felt alarm bells go off in my head and fireworks before my eyes. I saw

Anna, the way she stood at the plate, waggling the tip of the bat as the ball arced in; I saw her, her eyes red from weeping, the day she told me what I thought was the worst news that I could ever take in; I saw her in our final moment together which actually held the worst news I could take in and still survive in some fashion, when I would have given anything to have the time to tell her what I hadn't been able to tell her.

And they say Volvos are the safest cars in the world. Well, maybe they are. One of us, at least, did survive a crash with a speeding garbage truck.

My windshield wipers were going back and forth, still heavy with the rain, *thump thump thump thump*, and I took another long swig, *glug glug glug glug*.

I hadn't had a drink in ten years. They had been ten bad years, ten years of loss and remorse and anger, and I was due a little relief.

It felt good.

So did the next one.

And the next.

Before I knew it I had a growing heap of dead cans in the passenger floorboard. The hard rain and the alcohol blurred the last of Oklahoma pleasantly, blurred the yellow and white flashing lines of the roadway, even blurred the words of the song I had set on Repeat, "Betcha by Golly Wow."

The phone gurgled at my side and I fumbled for it, beeped it on. "Grand Central Fucking Station," I said, taking a drink before I went on. "What can we fuck up for you today?"

"Son," Ray said, "turn down that music and try talking to me again in a slightly different fashion."

"Sorry," I said. "Sorry, Ray. I've had a bad fucking day."

"Son," he said, and his voice took on an edge; it was late late at night where he was, and he was probably tired as hell. "An apology isn't worth a damn thing if it's immediately followed by another offense."

"No sir," I said. "It isn't. I'm sorry. Really." I turned down the Stylistics and slowed to take the Shamrock exit so we could talk.

"Damn," I said in wonder and amazement. "I'm in Shamrock, Texas." I pulled over off the access road.

"You're supposed to be in New Mexico, son," he said. "What the hell is going on with you?"

"When is the funeral?"

"Nine o'clock in the cathedral downtown. Eleven o'clock graveside at the national cemetery. It's a military burial."

"Military cemetery?"

"Your dad served his draft out in the Army National Guard. Maybe you didn't know that."

"No, sir, I didn't. There are a lot of things I don't know about the man."

I opened the door and got out. The rain was letting up a bit. It felt good, the drops splattering against my face and hands. I laughed.

"But did you hear me, son? You've got"—and here he paused to check the clock and do the math—"ten hours or so left to get there."

"I'll make it," I said. Rain dripped off my eyelids, my nose, into my nostrils. "Ray, am I a son of a bitch and a bastard?"

To his credit, he did not hesitate. On the other hand, nor did he ask me what made me bring it up. "No, son," he said.

"Am I?"

"No," he said again. "Clay, do you need me? I'll be on the next plane if you need me. I'll come to Shamrock or Lucky Charms or whatever it is. In a heartbeat."

"No sir," I said, although through the numb blur of my current feelings I felt warmth spreading across my chest. "I know you would. But this is my spiritual quest. Tracy said I had to face Darth Vader alone."

"I'm not sure exactly what that means," he said. "Although if Tracy said it, I'll bet it's good advice. She's a peach."

"You know who Darth Vader is," I said. "He fell for the dark side of the force."

"I know who Darth Vader is."

I saw Tracy hanging up on me, turning to go upstairs. But I couldn't see her face, couldn't see whether she was smiling or weeping or just shaking her head. "She is a peach, isn't she?"

"Tracy? She sure is."

"Whatever that means. I know it's a good thing. Oh, boy.

Ray, I have fucked up royally. Pardon my French. Everything. Ten years ago. Tonight. Everything in between."

"Maybe so, son. But it's not too late—"

I shook my head and clicked him off mid-platitude. It was too late. For Anna Lynn, for Ray, for Kathy and Michael Cartwright, and probably for Tracy and me.

I turned off the ringer. He would call back. And call back. I tossed the phone into the car and stood there on the access road. The horizon was a million miles in every direction, and away from the road it was so dark I imagined the coyotes needed flashlights. Hmph.

I let my head drop to the car door and closed my eyes, but the world seemed to be lurching like a ship at sea, and I opened my arms in alarm. I had forgotten how to be drunk, a useful skill I once possessed.

I raised my head again, my face completely wet, my hair matted with rain, and now I saw a familiar sign alongside the Caddy. I was standing on old Route 66, or at least a simulacrum of it; a lighted billboard farther down advertised a Route 66 museum in Shamrock proper.

And that's when I realized that this is how my father would have gone to California all those years ago. It would have taken forever, that old Greyhound stopping at every city and pissant town the old song mentioned: Amarillo; Gallup, New Mexico; Kingston, Barstow, San Bernardino. And Shamrock, Texas, too. I smiled.

"I'm getting my kicks, all right," I said. "Thanks, Dad. Thanks for everything." I got back in the car, pulled back onto the interstate, ejected the Stylistics, who were bringing me down, and tried out the O'Jays. Better.

And another beer. Better still.

The Texas high plains rushed by outside, ghostly and glistening, like something out of a painting instead of a photograph. I saw an occasional tree, so windblasted it looked like bonsai. Power or phone lines hung alongside the road from poles like crosses; the grain elevators were white and blocky and made me think of those sacred kachina dolls.

I was listening to those great songs from the Seventies— "Backstabbers" and "Love Train" and "For the Love of

Money"—when I got another signal through the blur of sensation. Urgent pee request.

There was a rest stop three miles ahead, and although this had sneaked up on me again, I had my doubts I could make it. I clamped my legs together, grabbed hold with my hand and squeezed, sped up to near ninety. I took the exit ramp with graceless haste, and all but squealed up to the back of an old Ford van plastered with bumper stickers, which was alone in front of the bathrooms.

I managed to remember the keys, and then I lurched up the pavement toward the john.

A figure materialized out of the darkness, tall, black, and female, and tried to take my elbow. "Hey baby," she said. "How about a date?" She tried to swipe her hand across the front of my pants, which would have been disastrous for both of us.

"No, thanks," I said and dodged out of the way.

I counted to 127 at the urinal, a new personal record for longest piss. Somebody back in a stall was whistling something Baroque and then paused for a moment to groan before an answering sploosh.

The hooker came up to me again on the way back. "Hey, baby," she said. "You want a date?"

"I just turned you down," I said. "Don't you remember?"

"I remember," she said. Then she smiled slyly and moved forward purposefully. "But I thought maybe you'd changed your mind."

"No thanks," I said again. "Don't ask me again."

"She has been doing that for hours," said a voice thick with Spanish sibilants. I looked down and saw what I must have missed in my earlier headlong flight to safety. A young young Hispanic woman—no more than a girl, really, eighteen at the most—sat at the curb next to the van nursing her baby.

"Poor woman," she said, looking at the hooker and shaking her head sadly.

I stopped, swayed a little to get my balance, and surveyed the scene. Across the grassy median were the half-lit slumbering semis, their engines idling up and down like giant sleeping cats. The van was the only other vehicle near, and it wasn't much of a vehicle: an old powder blue Ford Econoline with rusted-out back panels. Illinois plates. The hood was up, and I could see a guy with battered white Converse high-tops tinkering underneath. I could also smell burned oil, see the black crust caked on the tailpipe.

"Poor woman," I said, staggered back inside the Caddy, and started it up.

The O'Jays were singing "992 Arguments." I reached up to pull the car into gear.

The woman looked up at me, the baby at her breast.

"Shit," I said. "Fucking shit on toast." I let out a groan of anguish and exasperation. Then I shut off the engine, got out, reached for my wallet, pulled a couple of twenties.

"I'm sorry to bother you," I said, stepping carefully over to the woman on the curb. "Can I help in some way?"

"Help is never a bother," she said. The infant was asleep now, but still making tiny suckling noises. "Why don't you speak to the father?" She inclined her head to the front of the van.

"The father?"

"One of them," she said, shrugging. "The other is in there," and now she nodded to the bathrooms.

"The other," I said. I was well and truly drunk. "Okay," I said, and I shambled around to the front of the van.

The man turned at my approach, and I could see that he had on cutoffs and a black T-shirt. He was powerfully built, also Hispanic, handsome as Antonio Banderas. "Can I help you?" he asked, his accent thrilling, his attitude frankly belligerent.

"I know a little bit about cars," I said. I sniffed again. Yes, definitely burnt oil. Not good.

"Take a look, then," he said. "I can't make head or tails of it."

Yes, definitely a problem. I got up under the hood. "She won't turn over?"

"Not at all."

I stood tiptoe and put my head closer to the block.

"What do you think?" came a loud and hearty and distinctly un-Hispanic voice from very close at hand, and I clanged my head hard against the hood.

"Oh, that looked like it hurt," the voice said, and I struggled to focus. It hurt like hell. I put my hand to the back of my head and felt something wet, although whether it was rain or blood I did not know.

"Here, let me help you," the new voice said, and God help me, it sounded all but Irish. It was more the alcohol than the head injury, but in truth, I was a little wobbly, and I welcomed the strong hands at my elbows. They seated me at the curb near the girl, and the voice said, "Let me take a look at you. There's a bit of blood there, isn't there?" He got down on one knee in front of me, a shock of gray hair atop a large creature dressed all in black except for a stripe of white at his throat.

A priest.

"Here," he said. "Look me in the eyes, if you will."

I did. They were blue as a mountain lake, and deep-set above a bulbous nose you could have built a condo on.

"I know that nose," I said, before I could stop myself.

"And is that the truth," he said, arching an eyebrow. "And where have you seen a monstrous great honker like this before?"

And suddenly I knew. I placed the voice, the laughter, even the whistled Bach in the bathroom. I did know that nose, and the person who lugged it around. "Appellate Litigation Clinic," I said, thinking hard. "Georgetown Law, 1988."

The priest turned his head sideways in wonder, took a close look at me, and his puzzled mouth slowly sprouted a smile. "Clay," he said.

"Father Tom," I said.

"Clay Forester," he said, and his smile spread like sunlight across the broad prairie. "What in the name of all the saints are you doing in darkest Texas on such a night as this?"

"Giving you a ride," I said, and shrugged, for it was suddenly obvious that this was what I was here to do. "Your van is going to need new rings at the very least. Maybe a whole new block."

The other man shrugged. "He is probably right, Father. I can't do a thing with it."

"Of course he is, Jorge. He always was. Clay, Father Jorge Cárdenas. He just finished law school at Loyola. First in his class, unlike either of us. Jorge, my old friend from Georgetown, Clay Forester."

"It is a pleasure," he said and shook my hand. He had a strong grip. But *Father* Jorge? There were some disappointed girls in his hometown when he declared for the priesthood, I can tell you that. What did they use to call them at Georgetown? Father What-a-Waste. "And this is María and José," he continued, indicating the girl and her baby.

"Hola," she said, "again."

"And could you give us a lift then, Clay?" Father Tom asked. "We are in a bit of a hurry if the truth be know. Where are you headed?"

"New Mexico," I said. "Does that help at all?"

"Indeed it does. "We're headed toward Amarillo ourselves. Would you mind dropping us a wee bit north of town?"

"It'd be a pleasure," I said. And it would. Father Tom had been a Jesuit priest in my class at Georgetown, some years older than the rest of us; that made him close to sixty now. He was specializing in social justice issues from poverty to pollution, and so Anna Lynn loved him. If all priests were like Father Tom she would have left the Dutch Reformed Church in the blink of an eye. In fact, he'd been a guest in our home twice after we'd married, but then he got assigned back somewhere in the Midwest, and anyway, by then conditions were not so conducive around our house for entertaining guests.

I got up and went back to the car, unlocked it, and turned around, leaning against the door. The bumper stickers on their van said things like "God's Peace, not Man's Peace" and "No more Bombs for Peace." One had a peace sign inscribed over an ichthys sign.

I wondered if I had driven into some benighted alternate reality where the Sixties never ended.

Father Jorge loaded their few bags in the trunk—they were certainly traveling light, even with the baby—and I opened the back door for María. "Thank you," she said quietly. She got settled into the seat, groaning a little at the feel of the soft leather, and put the baby into her lap. Father Tom kicked the beer cans aside without a word and got in next to me.

"You wrote, I think," I said when we had pulled out onto the highway. There was no avoiding it, for he knew much of what had happened to us if not the whole horror. It was a beautiful letter, as I remembered it, full of his sense of Anna Lynn, of the shock of her loss. "After the accident. I never wrote you back."

"You had other things to deal with," Father Tom said. He turned to Father Jorge and explained, gently, "Clay lost his family in a car accident. It was some years back. But you know how these things are. Let us remember him tonight in our prayers," before turning back to me and continuing. "I just wanted you to know we were thinking of you. I said novenas for Anna Lynn and for your son. I prayed for you."

"Lots of people did," I said grimly. "But it didn't bring them back."

"No," he said. "It never does, does it?"

The baby in María's lap shifted. She looked down at it, smiled, closed her eyes.

"Where in Amarillo are you headed?"

"About fourteen miles out of town," he says. "The Pantex weapons plant."

"The what?"

Father Tom nodded to his cohort in the backseat, and Father Jorge leaned forward. "The Pantex weapons plant develops and fabricates chemical high-explosive components for nuclear weapons, assembles and disassembles nuclear weapons, modifies and repairs nuclear weapons, and performs surveillance testing and disposal of chemical high explosives."

"Oh. And why are you going there?" I asked, although I had a sneaking suspicion, what with Father Tom and the obviously even more militant Father Matinee Idol that some more Sixties tomfoolery was afoot.

Father Tom smiled and confirmed my fears. "I thought maybe you were going there for the same reason we are. That maybe you read about it on the Internet. The demonstration,

I mean. People are coming from all across the country to shut the plant down." He spread his hands. "Symbolically, of course. The business of war cannot be shut down for good."

"What is the demonstration for?"

Father Jorge spoke again. "The plant is an environmental hazard, for one thing. It's contaminated the groundwater across a four-state area."

"But that's a small thing, lad. Pantex is a site where nuclear materials are burned, where bombs are manufactured. It's a vital cog in the machinery of war. It's a prime spot to make a symbolic gesture."

"Okay," I said. "What does that mean, exactly?"

Father Tom spoke casually, as though the events he was describing had already occurred. "We'll join the other protestors. At dawn, we will commit acts of civil disobedience. María and her baby are going to join others in front of the gates. Jorge is going to join others in chaining himself to the railroad tracks so the trains carrying nuclear materials can't get in or out. And I'm going to give loud, angry Irish speeches and make people in uniforms angry and probably get the bejesus knocked out of me again. We'll all be arrested and thrown into the Potter County jail. It's a nice old jail, I'm told. You want to come with us?"

I laughed, flashing on Anna Lynn, who would have raised a fist of solidarity. There was a part of me that was tempted. But only a little. She would have done it to prove a point; I would have done it to piss people off. It was one of the differences between us—one of the stumbling blocks, it turned out. I just didn't care about anything that passionately, and she was ever a passionate woman.

I shook my head. "You know, Tom, I hate to say this after you've traveled this far and all, but I don't see the point. You'll be a momentary annoyance. It's ultimately more trouble to you than to them."

"What's the point of doing anything, then, Mr. Forester?" Father Jorge asked, clutching the headrest in front of him as if he wanted to choke it. "Don't you believe some wrongs require action, even if it is a symbol alone?"

"Now, now," Father Tom said, turning to calm him down.

"Not everyone has the activist blood in their veins. So, lad, you don't care to add this to your list of experiences, then?"

I shook my head again, a little chastened now. "I've got to be somewhere. As much as I'd enjoy getting the bejesus beaten out of me."

He laughed. "Where is it you're headed, lad?"

So I told him the story. I had it down to its component parts now and could relate it dispassionately and without feeling much of anything. I left out the people I'd met on the way, of course, and that I'd fallen off the wagon in a major way just a few hours ago. It would have been apparent to him, although I was proud at least to be driving in a straight line. Sometimes you have to pride yourself on small accomplishments.

"That's quite a story," he said when I'd finished with it. "I remembered the bit about your father. You made a joke about it first time you told me about him going off to embrace his destiny. But it's a different thing when you're saying goodbye, I suppose."

"It does put a new complexion on things," I admitted. We passed the exit for Groom, Texas, where on the north access road a huge red-and-white water tower loomed precariously over what apparently had once been a truck stop on Route 66 and was now simply an empty parking lot. I was in a suggestible state where everything seemed to have some relation to me; I was at the same time the falling tower and the ramshackle asphalt.

"I've wondered about you sometimes," Father Tom said. "You dropped completely out of sight, Clay. I asked the alumni office. You dropped your membership. The bar association couldn't find you. Where've you been, lad?"

I laughed and shook my head. "I moved home with my mother. I thought in a little while maybe I could get myself together." I raised my hands from the wheel for a moment in a sort of shrug. "That was ten years ago."

"Lord, now, has it been that long? It seems like only yesterday."

"It has. And it does."

On the south side of the interstate, a huge white monolith

came into view. THE LARGEST CROSS IN THE WESTERN HEMI-
SPHERE, a sign proclaimed, and then we saw it in its fullness,
lit like a pyre in the middle of the night, this enormous white
metal cross looming hundreds of feet above us like some
pagan idol.

"That's what it feels like to live in my mother's house," I
said. He laughed, although I was serious as hell.

"I remember you talking about your family," he said.
"Your mother and her sisters. Is your stepfather still alive?"

"He sure is," I said. "Alive and kicking."

"Retired?"

"No, he still practices. You remember him?" He nodded.
"He still does lots of pro bono work. I think his favorite thing
is representing poor black sharecroppers against landlords
and scam artists."

"Still a man after my own heart," he said. "Have you
thought of doing some work with him?"

I shook my head. "I can honestly say that I haven't given
the law any thought in ten years." And even though I hadn't,
I had been one of the most promising associates in one of
D.C.'s largest firms. I had represented General Electric as co-
lead counsel in front of the United States Supreme Court, and
that wasn't even my biggest case. It would have been a jarring
transition from that to, say, defending a black mother accused
of food stamp fraud. "I went back to playing music. That's
all."

"Still playing the devil's music?"

"Yes, sir."

"Good for you. I like a little rock and roll now and then."
He creased his forehead for a moment, trying to remember
something. "I think your stepfather went to Boston
University, didn't he?"

"Yes, he did. He never met Martin Luther King, but he was
in the law school while King was there at the Divinity School.
And Barbara Jordan was one of his classmates. I think they
were friends. He sure talks about her a lot."

"Ah, that was a fine woman."

"Ray calls her 'The Great Woman.' He'll say, 'as a Great
Woman once said.' As far as I know, he always means her. I

think he misses her." I laughed. "She was always used for object lessons around our house. Whenever I was feeling down on myself, which was pretty often—"

"Past tense, of course," Father Tom said.

"Of course. Anyway, whenever I was upset about the way the world was treating me, Ray used to remind me that Barbara Jordan didn't make law review when she was at BU. I didn't know then what he meant. Maybe not even when I was in law school. Now I think I do. Something about how people can't always know your true worth."

Father Tom nodded. "That's one to remember."

We passed another sign for the Big Texan restaurant ahead in Amarillo: 72-OUNCE STEAK DINNER FREE IF EATEN IN ONE SITTING. I tried to do the math. If it hadn't been the middle of the night, I was drunk enough to try it.

"Four and a half pounds," Father Jorge mumbled. He too seemed stunned at the idea. He was probably thinking it would feed a whole village or something, about how many pounds of grain or soybeans or whatever went to raise that cow for some glutton's table.

"That's a tremendous waste of cow," I said, catching his eyes in the rearview and getting at least a little nod in return. María was asleep, her hands cradled protectively over and under her baby. I laughed. "You know, María threw me for a loop earlier. When I asked if she needed help, she told me to talk to one of the fathers. The *fathers*. Like there was more than one."

Father Tom smiled, but his lips grew slender. "She's a good girl," he said quietly. "Jorge brought her home to stay with us in Chicago."

"María came to us from Chiapas," Father Jorge said quietly. "You know Chiapas, Mr. Forester?"

"I know it's in Mexico," I said. "The band buys organic coffee from Chiapas."

"María's father was a Zapatista there, fighting for the rights of the indigenous people. He was assassinated by a paramilitary group backed by the Mexican government." Father Jorge dropped his head, and his voice was quiet, so as not to wake her. "She was raped. Many times, by many men. Bastards." He dry-spat to his right, toward the door. "They left her for dead." He raised his head and I looked in his eyes; I would not have wanted to be one of the men who did it. "She was fifteen years old. Quince años. The good Mexican bishop don Samuel Ruiz García, of the diócesis de San Cristóbal de las Casas, he asked us to bring her to America. Father Tom arranged her adoption by members of our church. She became a citizen last year, before the child was born. So he is an American too." He nodded to himself. "An American."

I watched the mother and child, the mother herself little more than a child, the child the end product of violence and evil and lust. Her hand gently cradled his head; even in sleep she would let no harm come to him.

"How could she—" I stopped, swallowed. It was too much, opened too many doors I wanted to keep closed, locked, barricaded forever.

"Love the child of her affliction?" Father Tom asked.

"Yes," I said. "What they did to her—"

"What they did to her was terrible. Horrible. Almost beyond reckoning. But what God made of what they did . . . Well, that was beautiful. It"—and his voice softened with the deep-held conviction—"was purest grace, lad. The very essence of God."

I shook my head. "I don't believe it works that way. I'd like to. But I don't."

"Oh," he said, "but it does. Not always. Or not right away. But it does."

"Because all works for good to them that love the Lord," I said, and my sarcastic appropriation of the Apostle Paul was painful and piercing in the enclosure of the car. I snorted. "How can you drag her into what you're doing? Hasn't she been through enough?"

"She believes in what we're doing," Father Jorge said. "Anyone with eyes to see knows that the United States is the greatest weapons exporter in the world. We love our country, but we are angry about this thing. She thinks, maybe she can save some other little brown girl somewhere. Maybe she cannot. But the gesture itself is something against such a past as hers."

"So some other little brown girl will be raped by people carrying AK-47s or Uzis or spears instead of M-16s," I said. "Jesus. I can't see that it makes a bit of difference in the end. Nothing does."

Father Tom shifted in his seat, and there was the clank of empties beneath his feet. "Clay," he said, "there is a tall wooden crucifix in the church in Corte Madera, the arms blown away in some war sometime or other. Under it someone with eyes to see wrote, 'Jesus has no arms but ours to do his work and to show his love.' That is what I believe. What we believe. We must act as we think he would have us act if we are to be his arms in the world."

I laughed at him, and it was not a pretty sound.

"Clay," Father Tom said gently, "have you ever talked to a psychiatrist about your depression?"

"What depression?" I said, which I guess was a little like Captain Ahab asking, "What whale?" I laughed at him again and shook my head, but had to stop because it was making me sick to my stomach. I needed another beer, or no more. "No. I haven't seen a psychiatrist, Father, and I haven't dealt with my grief, and I haven't medicated myself so I won't feel it anymore. I don't want to lose it. I like it, in a way. The pain. It lets me know I'm alive."

"You like it because you think you deserve it," Father Tom said, and he laid his hand on my shoulder. "If you were wise enough to be a Catholic and I could get you in the confessional, I'd give you a rosary and a swift kick in the ass, and that would be the end of it. I can see that you've long ago done your penance for whatever it is that you think you did."

I certainly didn't believe it, but it was a kindness of him to say so. Although we were still some ways out from the lights of Amarillo, I took the exit Jorge indicated, and we headed off into the dark, flat plains. The road was paved but narrow, and fence posts flashed by to either side of us on the other side of deep culverts.

"I'd stick to law," I told Father Tom. "You shouldn't lecture people about their neuroses. About their suffering."

"Suffering?" Father Jorge said. I had felt him back there for a while, itching to give me the swift kick in the ass Father Tom wanted to prescribe. "What we inflict on ourselves is not suffering, Mr. Forester. This is suffering." He indicated María with his outstretched hand. "And even so, she has forgiven them. She has overcome her suffering. Transformed it into love."

And maybe she had. I admired her, for sure. "One little tragedy and men fall to pieces," I murmured.

Father Tom turned his head sideways and regarded me with an arched eyebrow.

"Just something that a wise woman told me yesterday. I think it was yesterday. I've been awake a long, long time now." I wondered where Kathy and Michael were now. Safe as this refugee, I hoped. "Maybe she was right, that woman. I couldn't have done what Maria did."

Now we saw bright lights across the plains—could see them from miles away, in fact, like the aftermath of a prison break: the tall halogen lights supplemented by spotlights playing across the fences.

Father Tom put his hand gently on my arm. "Forgiveness is easier than hatred in the long run. Something to think on, lad."

"Who do I hate? Who do I need to forgive? You've got it all wrong, Father. It won't work."

I don't think he planned to tell me any more, but in any case we were all distracted now by the flashing lights of cop cars ahead, dozens of them. Texas Highway Patrol, Amarillo police, sheriffs—maybe FBI, CIA, and NSA for all I knew. The road was blocked off well short of the gate, and we could see a milling crowd moving forward and then being pushed back by men in uniforms and riot gear.

"Well, lad," Father Tom said as we reached the outskirts of the crowd, well lit by the spotlights and TV crews, "I suppose you'd best let us out here."

It seemed so wrong, somehow. "But you're not even going

to get to the gate, Tom. You're all going to get thrown in jail for nothing."

"It's not for nothing," he said. María stirred as we pulled to a stop at the side of the road.

"Don't throw her to those wolves."

"We are doing the work of our Father, Mr. Forester. That is enough for us." Father Jorge shook his head, as though I couldn't be expected to understand.

But I understood all right, or thought I did. "Fuck you and your armless Christ, Jorge," I said, and my laughter was louder and harsher even than before. Both María and José woke up whimpering. "Christ with his arms blown off. Seems just about right to me. He belongs right up there with his blind father. God with cataracts and a white cane, tap-tapping across the earth, splattering the innocent."

The baby was crying; here was my secret identity blown again: just another loud angry man. Father Jorge looked as though he wanted to ask me to step outside, and I guess I would have gotten my ass kicked by a priest on national television—something I had never imagined might happen to me. But Father Tom waved him ahead, and he and María slid out of the car without another word to me.

Father Tom opened his door, turned to get out himself, then turned back, took my hand, and held it meditatively for a moment—strongly, although at first I tried to pull it back. His face was red with anger, but he didn't want to leave it like this. "Nothing is an accident, Clay," he said, and he squeezed my hand, hard, like you might squeeze a kid to reinforce your message, like kinetic punctuation. "I've been sent to tell you something. I don't know what it is. What's at the heart of your anguish is something no one else knows. But I think you know." He looked me right in the eyes, and his face took on a gentler cast as he saw my pain. "I'll be praying for you."

It hit me in the chest like a car door. I could barely muster a good-bye, barely register the car doors closing. I was trembling, could barely breathe.

This was exactly what it felt like when Anna first told me, like the life had been knocked almost all the way out of me and was just hanging on in my tingling fingertips and toes. This was the feeling I had been trying to avoid feeling for ten years. Somehow I fumbled the car into reverse, managed to jockey back and forth to turn around without losing my car in a culvert or sideswipe a media van, and managed to find my way back to the interstate.

Once there I checked the clock: 2:20.

I dialed the phone as I was passing into Amarillo, where construction made for some scary twisting back and forth beneath the pale halogen lights. I slowed down to keep from pinballing from one concrete wall to the other; I did not have the greatest control over my motor skills at this time.

"Otis," was the answer at the other end.

"This is the strangest trip I ever heard tell of," I began, because that was all I could say with absolute surety.

"Dude. Hey! We played nothing but penis songs tonight. 'Lick It Up,' 'Slide It In,' 'Big Balls,' 'Rock you Like A Hurricane.' First it was fun, then it got to feeling a little lame. Maybe you're right about that whole thing. And that chick—that Denise that thought you were such hot stuff?—she came in, saw you weren't here, and left like someone had tried to set her ass on fire." He stopped for a second, maybe to catch his breath. "What is that shit you're listening to?"

"Dude, this is fly. This is the O'Jays." And it was good stuff, "Put Your Hands Together," and I sang it loud for him.

There was a moment of silence on the other end. "Dude, are you drunk?"

Up ahead was a flickering flame that lit up the whole horizon. Like the burning bush, I thought. Then I figured it must be New Mexico, like maybe the whole state was on fire like Otis said, but it was too early to see that, even if it was true. Then I saw it was the burn-off for a gas well or some such thing, but it was still pretty amazing, such a big, bright flame on such a dark night in the middle of so much nothing. "Drunk? Oh-ho, Nelly. You don't know the half of it, man. First, I haven't slept in, like, three days. And let's see: today alone I've terrified two sets of already-traumatized mothers and children, pissed off two priests, had a high-speed chase with the FBI after me, delivered protesters to a top-security government weapons installation, cursed God, and made fun of Jesus. Only then may you add in that I'm drunk."

"Clay, what the fuck are you—" He stopped, got a hold of himself, then proceeded in a faux-Mr. Rogers calm. "Clay, I thought I was the one needed looking after."

"It has not been a beautiful day in the neighborhood," I said. "This trip makes *The Wizard of Oz* look like the video from somebody's grandparents' vacation to fucking Yellowstone National Park."

"Sounds like."

"Before I pissed everybody off or disappointed them, which is what I always do—" I began and then my nose wrinkled up like a brussels sprout as I passed another set of stockyards, this at the Wilderado exit. "Whew!" I said, and I was gagging. The stench made the Oklahoma City Stockyards seem like a cherry orchard; I thought for a second that maybe good old olfactory menace Buster had found his way back into the car, like one of those tabloid stories of dogs tracking their masters down a thousand miles away. I thought I was going to ralph on the Corinthian leather.

While I was buckled over, my hand brushed against something loose in the floorboard, and I brought up some of the pictures Kathy Cartwright had showed me and that got me real serious real fast.

"Otis," I said. "You still there?"

"I'm here."

"What was I saying?"

"Damned if I know. Clay, where are you, man? Pull off the road and let's talk. You're scaring the shit out of me."

"Can't do it," I said. "I've got to get to this funeral if it kills me." In the photo on top, I caught a glimpse of Michael, his shirt pulled up to show the blackened bruises across his back and arms. "But listen: I did help a little boy and his momma get away from a bad man. Ask Ray. He'll tell you."

"Good work, son," he said. "This is like *Mission: Impossible 2*. 'Difficult should be a walk in the park for you.' "

"I mean it. They were in some serious shit. They needed

help. And I helped them. That counts for something, doesn't it?"

"Who is the man who would risk his neck for his brother man?"

"Shaft," I said.

"Right on. Who's the cat who won't cop out when there's danger all about?"

"Shaft," was again the right answer.

"Can you dig it? You know, this cat Shaft, I hear he's a bad motherf—"

"Shut your mouth."

"I'm just talkin' 'bout Shaft."

"Well, we can dig him." I opened another beer. It had gone warm; I'd have to pick up some more cold ones directly. "Man, what I wouldn't give to play that scritchy-scratchy guitar. You know, that wocka-wocka sound?"

"You be the wrong color to be so righteous."

"Do not be playing homeboy with me, Otis Miller. I distinctly remember you listening to my Bee Gees album during the Saturday Nite Fever craze."

"Do not let that get out, man," he said. "I be ruined among the brothers. Hey, have you pulled over yet?"

"I have not," I said. "I'm rocketing through the black Texas night in a rented Caddy, and I'm feeling no pain. None whatsoever."

"Uh-huh."

"Oh, I forgot something. I broke Tracy's heart. I told her I didn't want to marry her, I didn't want to have kids. I told her she ought to settle down with somebody more reliable and down-to-earth. I suggested you."

"I know you were drunk when you said that."

"Flying." I ejected the tape and hit "search." "Blind." The radio rounded up a rock station crackling out of Amarillo still. Tommy Tutone. "Listen," I said, upping the volume again. "We used to do this song."

"Clay, do you need me to come after you?"

"Why does everybody keep asking me that? Shut up, man. You're making me miss the song."

"Clarence Shepherd died," he said. "I read it in your Aunt Sister's column. He was a nice old guy."

"Well," I said, "we're all going to the same place eventually." I saw the lights of a distant truck stop. "I'm at least going to have some more cold beer before I go." Some part of me recognized that I was at the place where I could go down into hard, head-banging, hungover sobriety or push on past the stupor to another buzz, and I chose buzz, hands down, pedal to the metal.

"Dude, I'm worried about you. I mean it."

I took the exit fast, with a whoop, and my head bounced off the ceiling as I said hello to part of the curb. "You should be," I said, and I hung up. Then I pulled into the lot, parked—slowly, with exaggerated drunken care—got out of the car, stretched, and turned a complete circle, my arms up high in the air. The night was dark and warm and deep, just right for swallowing me whole.

11

RIDE THE SANDIA TRAMWAY
WORLD'S LONGEST!
My eyes stung like someone had rubbed them with sand, my eyelids stuck when I tried to blink, and my throat was so dry, even with all the drinking I'd done over the past hundred hours or so, that I couldn't much more than croak along with the stereo. My back and butt and legs hurt from driving, and all of me throbbed with sunburn. Sometimes I closed my eyes, but I knew that if I did that for even a few seconds I would be asleep, and I really did want to find out what was going to happen to me.

What was left of my life was lived between highway lines and bounded by the darkness. There were flashes of light— green mile markers and exit signs, the white highway reflec- tors on the road, yellow on the shoulder—but they were simply reflecting what little light I put out. So I was grateful that, now and then, out of the night, came a sign, a light in the darkness, a carrier of meaning.

It was a long way I had come to get to where I was now.

I remembered the time Ray stood up at our Georgetown graduation party to give a toast. I knew he was going to, and I was proud to see him, this handsome and elegant man, standing in front of our professors, our new employers, our friends and family, to frame our accomplishment. He had a glass of champagne in his hand, although he did not yet raise it. I had a glass of champagne in my hand and five more in my stomach. Maybe that accounted for this strange tingling as he looked around and then began to speak.

"A friend of mine at Boston University, a Great Woman, once wrote, 'The law is supposed to be the configuration of rules and regulations which, if implemented, will lead to justice. The question is not if the law will win, but will justice be served?' " He looked down for a moment, and then out at the assembly, suddenly quiet, and repeated, "Will justice be served?" I don't know that they all—or even many—recognized the source. I did; Barbara Jordan's words always had an incredible beauty and balance. But the words themselves captured the attention, and it was now that Ray raised his glass of champagne and everyone stood and followed suit. Even my mother, even my aunts, giggling like they'd been caught browsing through dirty magazines at a 7-Eleven.

"Today we celebrate. Not, mind you, because two lawyers have been added to the roll of lawyers. If anything, that would be a matter for condolence, if still, mind you, an appropriate occasion for drinking.

"But no, instead we celebrate because of who these lawyers are, and who they will be. We celebrate because these two will be servants of the law, not lawyers who will try to make the law serve them. They will be lawyers who will seek justice. Here's to my son Clay and his future bride Anna Lynn. God bless them."

*Hear, hear*s around the room, *salud*s, and heads nodding.

That champagne didn't taste any different from the stuff that preceded, that followed. I got drunker than Peter O'Toole at a film premiere. And somehow, in the years that followed, I forgot everything he said. I became everything he despised. Everything she hated.

And driving across the high plains of the Texas Panhandle, I took another drink.

Tucumcari Tonite
Scenic Public Golf Course
1200 Hotel Rooms
Next Five Exits

The moon was full and huge; it ran in front of me like a little boy playing tag. At the beginning of the night, I had been

Charles in charge and it had been trying to catch me, but since I dropped the martyrs off at the massacre in Amarillo it had crept ahead, and now I feared it was going to get away from me entirely.

The moon was so bright that for a stretch of highway I turned off my headlights and drove dark, but then I saw headlights behind me and figured it would louse up my trip even more to have some Texas Ranger wearing mirrored sunglasses at night saunter up to my window and inform me that the Great State of Texas had some few traffic rules I had not violated but he was hard-pressed at the moment to recall what they were.

I flipped the lights back on, for all the good they did me.

Anna Lynn and I married in her home church in Grand Rapids in front of a pastor with an unpronounceable German name and a group of relatives who looked dour even in their joy. It was a plain church, almost cold, a church built by Puritans on downers. And there sat her teary-eyed parents, solid, stolid, and rich, steeped in all the Calvinistic virtues and vices, and depressing as hell to be around.

Although they were happy enough at the moment, I knew they feared Anna Lynn was making a mistake, and they were right, although they were right for the wrong reasons. They thought Anna Lynn should marry someone more like them: industrious, deeply Christian, conservative, and family-centered. They didn't know her well enough to know how miserable she would have been with someone like that. But she was also plenty miserable with me before it was all over and done.

But not at first. We honeymooned in Grenada, one of the southernmost and most unspoiled of the Caribbean islands, and a place we Americans had bombed and occupied back in 1983. It was surreal, an island paradise that had supposedly been a hotbed of Cuban Marxism before Reagan sent in the troops to protect a bunch of American medical students who couldn't get admitted into a real school.

Pardon my cynicism; I guess med school rejects have a right to feel secure too.

We landed on the one runway that made up the airport—

Anna Lynn read from her guidebook that Castro's advisers had built the runway before we booted them out—walked out of the plane onto a movable stair like something out of *Casablanca,* and then across the concrete, the world sparkling with light under a blue sky.

The airport was open-air, with huge ceiling fans instead of air conditioning. We stood in an enormous line for our bags and customs, then made our way out to the curb. Minivans booming reggae were filling up with passengers, but we got into a little Nissan Sunny, threw our bags in the trunk, and headed for our hotel on the beach.

All along the road in from the airport, goats and cows were tied so that they couldn't quite wander into the street. Bunston, our driver, said they used to roam free but cars and buses kept hitting them.

"Crunch," he said, bringing both his hands up from the wheel and clapping them together to illustrate. "Jus' like dat. I remember one t'ing—"

"Would you mind putting at least one hand on the wheel?" I said, my voice climbing into a higher register.

He laughed. "Hey, no worries, man. No worries." But he did drop a hand down to steer, and so I sat back and watched out the window.

The island was green and primitive—houses like cinderblock buildings, dazzling white laundry draped across dark green bushes, and the palm trees fifty or sixty feet tall, the tallest things on the island by official decree.

I carried Anna Lynn over the threshold of the hotel room because we couldn't remember when I was supposed to do that, and, frankly, because we thought it would be funny. She was a strapping girl every bit as tall as me, and I staggered in as far as the bed, which was where we remained until time for dinner.

"I read somewhere," Anna Lynn told me the next morning as one of those ominous minibuses careened on two wheels around a blind corner toward St. George's, the capital city, "that there were more medals awarded to American soldiers in Grenada than there were actual American soldiers in Grenada."

"Maybe it was hazardous duty," I said. "Maybe they were forced to ride this bus." Deafening reggae was booming out from under the seat, and eleven people of various ages and blacknesses were stuffed into the van with us. The seats were a zebra-skin pattern, and over the driver's head was a sticker that said "Sexy Senior Citizen."

She took my shaking hand in hers and raised it to her lips. "Nothing is going to happen to us," she said, as the beep of the horn announced our speeding approach around another corner. "We're going to lead a charmed life."

"From your lips to God's ear," I said. If another bus was coming around the corner from the other direction, we were all food for the seagulls.

But we survived that moment and plenty of others like it, and we spent an entire week doing nothing—the first time in years we'd had even a few hours of that luxury. At first, I will confess, I thought I was going to go insane without something to do, some deadline to meet, and Anna Lynn had to give me that look—you better get yourself under control, mister—and then turn her glower into a smile. And wonder of wonders, I chilled out. I kicked back.

I remembered what life was like before law school.

We strolled the tiny cobbled streets of St. George's, bought mangoes and oranges in the market place, lay for hours on the white sand beach at Grand Anse. We played volleyball with Canadians and Germans, and I cheered as Anna Lynn's team invariably won. She was, as ever, the best player out there, diving for balls no one else would aspire to, and her serve was a chilling thing to behold, like a lightning bolt from the hammer of Thor. Only I knew that she was a ringer, that she had been all-Michigan in volleyball as a girl, and I kept that info to myself—that and my joy.

We snorkled one afternoon, and since Anna Lynn had had the foresight to get her scuba certification before we left, she was able to go down scuba diving the day before we left. I stood sweating at the side of the boat and watched her, her shape recognizable but indistinct through the cool, clear water, and felt a strange chill. It seemed to be prophetic somehow, but of what?

"Oh Clay," she gushed when she came up, "I wish you could see it. It's beautiful! So much life! So much . . . everything!" She took my hand and swung it back and forth in her excitement.

"I'll bet," I said, like the wet blanket I feared I was going to become; then I feigned some excitement of my own. "I'm glad you had a good time."

At night we danced in the hotel nightclub to bad Caribbean ballads or steel bands, went for moonlight walks along the beach carrying our shoes in our hands, swam in the ocean, and made love, over and over again.

"Let's stay here," she said the night before we left, both of us about half drunk on rum punch, a Grenadan fruit punch with fresh nutmeg grated on top. "Let's practice law here. We can be barristers, you know? We can wear those funny wigs. We can eat lambi and drink rum punch and make love every night and wear our hair any way we like."

"Can't do it," I said, and the hurt look that flitted across her face told me that I could at least have said, "Wouldn't that be fun?" To my credit, I hadn't said something about how we had to get back to the real world, which was my first inclination. That would have been deadly.

But that's what I was thinking. Strange as it seemed to me then and now, I was ready to get back into that world where my life was circumscribed by others and my relationships were suspect and superficial.

It was safer, somehow, I thought, and truer to life than the idyll we shared on Grenada.

MISSION POSSIBLE: ABSTINENCE
SAY NO TO TEEN SEX

I had passed over into the state of New Mexico. I could tell by the sign, for one thing, and by the New Mexico weigh station for trucks, ablaze with light and fully staffed with highway patrol. Nothing else about the landscape looked different, but the moon was going, going, gone, and there was a strange gray fuzz across the horizon slowly becoming visible behind me.

I drove off the road once, and only running over the dark remains of a semi's blowout startled me back onto the straight and narrow. It felt like I had hit a deer or a small child. I shook my head hard, as if I could slosh around the froth passing for my brains in some meaningful way. Nothing. My eyes were so dry I moistened them with spit, thought about propping them open with toothpicks, and drove on.

My office at Welsh, Abernathy, Phelan, and Klein was on the seventh floor. It faced the Capitol, and I could just see the Washington Monument if I put my face to the glass, which I didn't do for fear of looking like someone who cared to see the Washington Monument. My desk was the size of some New England states, cherry, dark, shiny, and desolate. I had a legal pad atop the blotter, a pen holder, Anna Lynn's photo, and nothing else.

My mentor, Carroll Abernathy, told me when he checked in on my unpacking, "Clay, a cluttered desk suggests a cluttered mind. Make them think your mind is focused only on their problem and they will eat out of your hand." Carroll was the Abernathy of Welsh, Abernathy, Phelan, and Klein, and in the grand scheme of corporate law, he didn't even have to note my existence. There were dozens of partners to supervise new associates, but he'd taken a special interest in me because of my trial work. When they made the offer, in fact, he told me he thought I could be one of the best trial lawyers in the country and he wanted to work with me personally.

I took the job; maybe it proved I was desperate for praise from the rich and powerful. Maybe it just proved that I wanted to be the best at what I did.

Maybe it doesn't prove anything.

I worked long hours, not because I liked it, but because it was expected of us. New associates worked at least seventy-hour weeks. "Billable hours," Carroll said at our weekly meetings. "Bill, bill, bill." My days were marked out in increments of a quarter of an hour. Even if I made only a thirty-second phone call, we billed for fifteen minutes. It was strange, looking at my billing statements. I found five times as many hours in the day as there were supposed to be. It made me feel as though I was aging at a faster than normal rate. I had trouble sleeping, even when I got home after midnight. Sometimes I slept on the couch in my office, shaved and showered at the health club across the street, and showed up at my desk bright and early and ready to get back to work.

I told myself that Anna was working hard too, that her work was satisfying to her, that maybe she didn't miss me so much, although I missed her terribly, like rain or sunshine. I had to keep a close watch on myself, or I would catch myself mooning over her picture, losing three or four fifteen-minute billing periods to the inertia of love.

Of course, it wasn't all phone calls. I did background. I did research, looked up precedents, wrote briefs. A couple of times I took interrogatories alongside a senior litigator.

I didn't so much as walk near a courtroom.

But I would, Carroll told me during our monthly lunches. He was hearing good things about my work. I was thorough and methodical. I saw connections. I was a hard worker.

The places he took me for lunch served aged beef and martinis. He smoked cigars after, offered one to me. I puffed away at it, thinking it was like putting my head inside a smokestack. When I got home after lunching with Carroll, my scent made Anna Lynn sneeze. So I took up cigar holding, rather than smoking, which seemed to help at least a little.

Anna Lynn and I had lunch together too, sometimes as often as twice a week, and I tried to block out Friday nights to spend with her. We would go out to dinner, maybe see a movie. We made love when we got home, sometimes twice, and for a few minutes I remembered the sheer joy of love, thought it couldn't be possible to feel anything better or more meaningful. Then we fell asleep, and in a few hours, I left for the office.

She called once or twice a day. Sometimes I didn't take her calls. Sometimes I said I had to call her back. I rarely did. I didn't get to write down a .25 next to her number on my phone log.

We went to parties for clients, because Carroll wanted to show me off, and I wanted to show Anna Lynn off. We went to a reception at Kennedy Center where we met Pavarotti.

The firm rented the National Gallery of Art for an evening party, and we kissed, holding each other tightly, desperately, our bodies twined and elongated like the figures in the El Grecos.

I thought that maybe it would be enough, that she was seeing the importance of what I did, that the glitter of money was making me sparkle a little bit, too.

Then all of a sudden I knew that it wouldn't be enough and that bad things were in store for us, bad times like icebergs dead ahead.

"I feel like I'm losing myself," I told her that night after the gallery reception when we were in bed. "Like I'm losing you. Like saying one is the same thing as saying the other."

"Quit," she said. "You can be my kept man." And we both laughed and laughed. Anna Lynn's salary from her environmental nonprofit would barely cover my BMW payment.

"Can't do it," I said, although I had learned enough about marriage to say, "But wouldn't that be fun?"

"Sure you can do it," she said.

"We need the money," I said, although that was the least of my reasons for what I was doing.

"We need other things more," she said. "I just don't think you remember that. Except maybe one night a week."

"Someday I'll make partner," I said, pulling her close. "I'll be able to ruin someone else's life."

"Some consolation," she said, nipping my ear. "I hope I'm still around to see it."

She wasn't, of course. We laughed again, and then we made love, and I thought maybe I was just being paranoid. Things couldn't go on this way much longer. Someday this mad rush for partner would all be over. We'd be able to give each other more time and attention. We'd treat each other the way we had in Grenada, the way our wedding vows had said we would.

We'd actually written our vows, which made the congregation in that prim church in Grand Rapids a little nervous. Very earnest, very loving. We would always put each other first, support each other in every endeavor, love each other no matter what. They would have been impossible to follow in any case; they cancelled each other out. How can both of you always put the other first? And anyway, lawyers know how to look at vows and say, "That doesn't apply in this particular case."

Just a year after our marriage, it felt like we were complete strangers. Worse, really; complete strangers might hope to get to know each other some day.

VISIT LOS ALAMOS, BIRTHPLACE OF THE ATOMIC AGE

The Eastern sky behind me was starting to look like some kind of Georgia O'Keefe picture or something: tendrils of pink, orange, red, and purple layered up from the edge of the world. Then the sun, a big orange nuclear reactor, slipped over the horizon.

The interstate was empty. All along the highway, trucks were pulled onto the shoulders of access roads and picnic areas, their yellow running lights glowing. It was like I was the only person awake on the face of the earth.

In the summer of 1990, Carroll Abernathy took me off everything else I was doing and assigned me to the firm's highest-profile litigation: a little something having to do with a client's tanker losing eleven million gallons of crude oil in Prince William Sound the year before. Maybe you heard about it.

At first I had to shake my head. I was caught up in history, and it was too much. The previous March, Anna Lynn and I had sat in front of CNN watching the oil on the shore, two and three inches deep, the dead birds dripping with slime.

Seeing rescuers trying to help a dying bird, she squeezed my hand so hard I could feel my knuckles crack. "It's only going to get worse," she said. "There are something like seventy thousand birds migrating up there at this very moment. They don't know any better. They don't have CNN. They haven't heard that the rookeries are fouled by the biggest oil spill in history. And thousands of sea lions, too. It's a disaster of biblical proportions for the wildlife. Biblical." She squeezed again. I feared I would never be able to sign a check again. "The Federal Refuse Act and Clean Water Acts both cover this kind of thing," she said, and she spoke with the voice of an Old Testament prophet, grim as hell. "A year from now, Exxon is going to be out of business."

What was true, though, was that if Exxon had to choose between spending a tanker full of money on lawyers and staying in business, or paying plaintiffs and going out of business, it was going to do the former, and Carroll called me into his office on the one-year anniversary to say that Welsh, Abernathy, long on retainer to Exxon for other matters, was going to step up to lead-counsel status in state and federal courts out in Alaska. Already over a hundred suits had been filed, with more to follow, and he told me three things: consult with the people on the ground to find out what their strategy was; brainstorm with the defense team on ways to use the law to save our client's ass; and plan to give up my personal life for the duration.

I stood there for a moment. I had a strange pulsing sensation in my hands.

"Do we understand each other?" Carroll said. He was used to issuing orders and having people flee to carry them out. "Is there a question?"

"Wouldn't it be better from a public relations standpoint—not to mention a moral one—for our client to pay for what they did?"

He laughed, a quick hard bark that showed it had never occurred to him, and then the laugh was gone from his face and he shook his head. "Not for them. And certainly not for us. This oil spill is going to make us rich, rich men." He looked up. I considered what he said.

"The Refuse Act and Clean Water Acts are on point," I said. "I'll find a way to make them work for us."

He smiled, he turned back to his work, and I walked back to my office.

I didn't tell Anna Lynn for almost a week. I told myself it was because there wasn't an appropriate time. On the few nights I managed to come home at all, she'd been asleep for hours, and the last thing she would want was to have a conversation.

When I took off my clothes and snuggled in next to her, I ran my hand up her leg and under her nightshirt until it rested on her hip, solid and real, and I remembered that she loved me. She had married me, hadn't she? Everything was going to be all right. I was going to make partner. I was going to be home with her more often in just a little while. We only had to get through this.

The Friday morning she called me early, I was sitting looking over the motions filed by the local attorneys in Seattle and Anchorage, smart guys who had gotten off to a good start. Some of their ideas were audacious to the point of being ridiculous: for example, their contention that claims for lost earnings by fishermen or cannery workers should be offset by the money that other workers earned by participating in the spill cleanup. But other things were based on more solid ground, and could actually work: Tort reform measures passed by the state legislature could limit Exxon's payments, even for a monumentally damaging fuck-up like this. And maybe most important, if the courts bought it, they argued that a punitive damages award in one case should bar similar awards in others. Exxon would only have to pay out a big sum one time and it would be protected from having to do so again.

I was underlining something in the Clean Water Act when the phone rang. I checked my watch: 5:46. Someone who knew my direct-dial, since the switchboard wouldn't be open for hours.

"Clay Forester," I said in my best professional lawyer voice.

"Anna Lynn Forester," she said dreamily.

"Hey, baby," I said absently. I underlined something else.

"Did you come home last night?"

"No, I didn't make it," I said. "I grabbed a couple of hours on the couch."

"Well," she said, "you must have been home some time recently."

"Hmm?"

"Because you and I are going to have a baby."

I put down my pen, sat up straight in my chair, and let out a hoot. "No. Really? When did you find out?"

"About forty seconds ago."

"Did you do one of those home tests?" I slapped myself on the forehead and went on. "Of course you did. But that means you must have suspected something. Why didn't you tell me?"

"When would I have told you? Anyway, I wanted to surprise you."

"Well, you did surprise me."

"Good surprise or bad surprise?"

"Good," I said, and it sounded true; I felt good. Through my exhaustion I could feel a warmth spreading through my chest like someone had switched on an EZ-Bake Oven in there. "Very good surprise. The best."

"What are you doing?" she said. "Can we have breakfast?"

"Can't do it," I said. "I'm working on the Valdez thing."

A silence fell over the other end of the phone like she'd been sucked into space. Someone took a sledgehammer to that EZ-Bake Oven until it lay in cold plastic pieces.

"I can have dinner with you," I said brightly.

"What did you say?" she asked, and her voice was a cold breeze blowing off an ice floe.

"I can have dinner with you."

"Before that," she said. "What are you working on?"

I gulped, momentarily pondered jumping out the window, decided truth was the best strategy. "Welsh, Abernathy is representing Exxon," I said. "Carroll has me looking over some things."

You might have thought I'd told her I favored ripping newly conceived fetuses out of their mother's wombs with pruning shears. "I want you to get up from your desk and come home right now," she said, her voice level and slow, as though she was keeping control of it only by incredible effort. "And then I want us to talk about where you can send your résumé. I want you out of there."

"Can't do it," I said, and my voice too was level and slow,

although what I wanted to do was start screaming at her. "Exxon has a right to legal counsel, just like murderers and rapists and people who wear black socks with sandals. Somebody is going to represent them. It might as well be us."

"Oh, Clay," she said, and that was all she said. I put the phone back on the cradle. At eight o'clock, I had my secretary send flowers to Anna Lynn's work and arranged to pick up two dozen roses to take home. I told Carroll that I was taking Anna Lynn out to celebrate, and he slapped my back, smoked a cigar with me, and mentioned that he thought of me as his own son and he'd be proud to stand godfather for us. I felt like Michael Corleone.

So this was how you lost your soul.

DANGEROUS CROSSWINDS AHEAD

I was passed by a car with Tennessee plates, and against my will I took my mind off this strange dawn-lit lunar landscape I had wandered into for just a moment to wonder about Michael and Kathy Cartwright. I had done them wrong, I decided. What they needed was patience and quiet, and I had given them testosterone and psychosis.

And what kind of world had I driven myself into? The hills—mesas, I guess they'd be called—were layered like flavors of sherbet, red and yellow and white and dotted with dark green evergreen trees like cedars. The buildings I saw all looked like shacks. Adobe, plywood, beat-up trailers—it didn't look to me like anyone in New Mexico could raise the price of a Bomb Pop if the ice-cream man came by.

Then somewhere east of Santa Rosa, the hills disappeared. We must have been up on top of a plateau, because the land spread out flat in all directions, and there was so much sky it started to make me feel as if I was dissolving. Too much space. Too much nothing. And we all know that Nature abhors a vacuum.

The day I arrived in Anchorage, I saw a lone eagle circling over Cook Inlet. Maybe he just smelled fish, but it still felt like an omen. Alaska in the dead of winter was no place for a

Southerner to be, even if his wife wasn't great with child and so angry at him that she'd probably put a pitchfork through him if it wouldn't leave her baby fatherless.

Which my wife was.

I called every day and left messages, but it was over a week after I got to Anchorage before I got to talk to her, and even then it was no more than "I feel fine" and "Take care of yourself."

"Don't tell me about your work," she said. "I don't want to hear about it." And there wasn't much else to tell her other than what I'd been watching on HBO there in the Hotel Captain Cook, so that was that. It was cold and dark outside, and I was starting to feel that way inside as well.

As I was showing Anna Lynn's picture around to a bunch of other lawyers in Railway Brewing Co., this microbrewery in an old railroad depot on 1st Avenue, one of them—a pretty little girl from California named Becky Clausen—came over and took it from my hand. We were like a Hollywood film community out on location, and it didn't matter much if we were plaintiff lawyers or defense lawyers; when the day's work was over, it was us against Alaska.

"You must miss her," she said. She was such a tiny little thing, her hand could barely hold the picture.

"You don't know the half of it."

"How long have you been here?"

I checked my watch. "About thirty minutes." In front of me were my empty plate, the remains of a cheeseburger, and a couple of empty beer glasses.

"No, I mean in Alaska. Less than a week, right?"

I finished up another beer and nodded. "Is it that obvious?"

She shook her head and smiled. "No. It gets easier for some. I hardly think about home. I've been here for months."

"Months, huh?" I raised my finger and asked for another beer.

"Some of us were getting ready to go to a karaoke bar," she said. "Tim, Jerry, maybe a couple of other folks." Those guys nodded back. "You should come with us, Clay."

My beer arrived and I took a big swig. "I don't know." I

took another swig. "I used to sing a little bit. But I'm feeling kind of down."

"Then sing about it," she said. "Finish up and come on." She dragged me from the table, and a mob of lawyers went over to Rumrunner's, where a short, smiling, heavy-set Aleut named Karaoke Joe was serving as KJ, karaoke master of ceremonies.

"He'll get up later and do Elvis," Tom said as we took a table in the corner. "You can't tell the difference. Except for he's an Eskimo." He was a young guy going very bald, and he had passed drunk about an hour previous.

"How does this work?" I asked. "If one were disposed to do this thing."

"Write down your request and take it up to Karaoke Joe," Jerry said. He was an older guy, single, local, representing some of the fisheries. He was sober, funny, and nice as hell. "He'll find the disk if he has it, and then when he calls off your name, you go up and sing."

"I don't know," I said. Even with another drink, I was feeling about as low as the pavement. "I might just go back to the hotel—"

Becky punched me in the arm, hard; she had obviously evolved some ways to compensate for her lack of stature, unexpected violence being one of them.

"Ow," I said. I rubbed my arm. Then I took the pen she was holding and wrote down my request, and shortly before closing that night, I went up to the stage, sat on a stool, and sang Sinatra's "One for My Baby," a song about this guy who's drunk and missing his girl. There were about a dozen people left in the club besides the lawyers, who all were cheering anything that kept them from going back to their briefs, but all of them got up and gave me a standing ovation.

I mean, it wasn't junior-high girls chasing me to the bathroom or anything, but it was clear that I still had it, for whatever that was worth.

And that's how I spent most of Anna Lynn's pregnancy: in my Anchorage office writing briefs during the day, drunk and singing sad Sinatra tunes at night. Gradually Karaoke Joe started moving me up in the rotation, and finally he started jumping me to the top of the list when we came in and even letting me sing a couple of tunes, which made the tourists mad, at least until I started to sing.

"You really ought to be a singer," said Becky after the third time, when "Guess I'll Hang My Tears Out to Dry" left her in tears. She had a brassy little cheerleader's voice, and when she got up to sing—always Streisand show tunes for some reason—she switched keys a couple of times in the middle of the song.

"Coming from you," I said, tipping my imaginary fedora, "that is really career advice to savor." And then she hit me.

"You want to know why your boyfriend never calls you?" I asked.

"Why?" said gullible she.

"Because he's probably lost the use of both of his arms and can't dial the phone."

Everybody laughed, including her, although she waggled her tiny finger at me. "You're going to lose the use of something much more vital if you sass me."

"I don't have anything vital," I said, and it was the truth.

The first time I got to come home, in July, I had so much stored up to tell Anna Lynn that I tried to talk to her back as we lay in bed together on Saturday night. I didn't know if she was asleep or not, but I thought it was worth a try. We had barely spoken all day, and she had not so much as smiled at me once.

"It's not what you think," I said to her. "I'm not what you think I am. I'm still that guy you married because he sang trashy Air Supply songs to you."

She didn't laugh, and I knew she was asleep. I put a hand on her hip, on the bulge of her pregnancy, grown while I was away from her.

"I'm still in here somewhere," I said. "I haven't forgotten about justice. I'm doing my best to find it. Just wait and see."

She groaned in her sleep and then stretched like a cat. She was so beautiful I thought I was going to cry. But I was exhausted, so what I did instead was put my head back on the pillow and go to sleep myself.

The second time I came home was in August, and it wasn't

good between us then either. She was working on the environmental accords with Mexico that would have to be ironed out if there was ever to be a free trade agreement between us, and she was about to leave for a three-week fact-finding junket with some of her colleagues from the Environmental Defense Initiative, mostly to see the maquiladoras—the cheap, smoky Mexican factories along the Texas border that were replacing foundries and textile mills in the States. Her files on our dining room table were labeled "Matamoros," "Juarez," "Nuevo Laredo."

My files read "Exxon Valdez: Federal Court." And I didn't leave them out on the dining room table; they never left my locked briefcase.

Her suitcase was full of warm-weather clothes, shorts with elastic, and big T-shirts. I hovered around her while she packed, trying to be helpful, asking her about the water down there, about food, about medicines. My taxi was due to take me to Dulles in fifteen minutes, and I was looking for some place of connection, some place to anchor a bridge between us. Finally, with just five minutes left and feeling I'd already left for Alaska, I asked if I could put my head on her stomach. We thought it was a boy, and if it was, we had agreed to call him Ray. (It was not going to be Raylene or Rayann if it was a girl; we'd just have to start from scratch.)

"Hey, little Ray," I said, laying my hand gently on the bulge of her stomach and fighting the urge to cry. "How you doing in there? You take care of your momma, you hear? I'll miss you."

The taxi honked outside the town house, and I picked up my bag and stood up.

"I'll miss you," I said again.

"Safe trip," she said. "I won't wish you luck."

"Well, I will," I said. I looked at her to see if she wanted to be kissed—or was willing to be kissed. It was as if she had left the room already. "Luck," I said softly, and raised a hand in forlorn good-bye.

I tried to call her from the airport, but no one answered. Just my own voice, telling me to leave a message, which I already had.

I got so drunk on the plane that I thought they would throw me out somewhere over Montana.

Carroll came up for several days a week after that, and we had dinner at the Crow's Nest, high atop the Captain Cook. He had pheasant, I had venison, and after we'd placed our orders he just looked at the mountains and trees and then back at me and shook his head.

"We sent you a long way from home, son," he said. "What in the name of God do you find to do up here?"

"I work," I said. "At night I drink with the other stranded lawyers. We tell each other trade secrets in hopes that we can all go home sooner." I didn't tell him about karaoke. It did not seem to be a shortcut to making partner.

"So what's the news?" he asked as our salads arrived.

"All bad," I said. "Forget about your smoking gun. We have a leaking oil tanker, captured on TV. Everybody in the world knows our guy did it. There are Bushmen in the Kalahari, you walk up to them and say 'Exxon,' they say 'Valdez.'"

He laughed. "I know, I know. So what do we do to minimize our clients' exposure. Show me what you've learned."

I took a deep breath, finished chewing a bite of lettuce, and turned off my conscience. "Drag it out. Keep it out of the courts as long as possible and just drag it out."

"Why?"

"Things change. People die; people forget; plaintiffs get desperate for some, any money. You can settle for ten cents on the dollar five years from now versus going into court now."

His smile was so broad I feared for my life. "Exactly."

"I've been thinking about the settlement," I said. "It's got to be big enough to quiet people and actually make up for what they did. But there must be a way to structure it to make it palatable to Exxon too."

"Of course there is. But later, my boy. Later. For now, let's eat."

Anna Lynn called me that night after I got back to my room—the first time she had done that since we each left on our separate missions—and my heart was pounding when I heard her voice. But she sounded strange, as though she hadn't really wanted to call but for some reason she'd done it anyway. I asked how she was feeling, if the baby was moving, and her answers were short and came after a pause. "Well," I said at some point, "not much going on here if you don't want me to talk about work. Although I think I may be able—"

"Don't talk about work," she said.

"Okay," I said. "Okay. Are you all right? Is everything—"

"Well, I hope you're keeping warm," she said suddenly, her voice breaking just a bit, and then she just as quickly said, "I've gotta go," and the phone went dead.

I sat there on the hotel bed for a long time, because it was one of the strangest conversations we had ever had, and because I had the strangest feeling after it, one I'd never thought I'd connect with Anna Lynn, the most trustworthy, the most honest, truly, the best person I'd ever met.

Anna Lynn was ashamed of something.

12

The federal graveyard in Santa Fe was at the far north end of town, almost out of town, in fact, and I was there before even the funeral was set to start, so I drove around for a while. The sun was full up, and the sun beaming golden in through my side windows was penetrating me like I imagined it did Dracula at the end of all those old movies. My eyes were burning, my flesh felt like it could sizzle off my bones, and I was just grateful I'd stopped at a Love's Country Store for more beer before I'd headed north toward Santa Fe.

Dracula would not, even with the fortification of beer, have survived all those crosses on the white marble monuments arrayed perfectly in rows like those at Arlington. I passed a middle-aged woman on her knees, bent over a grave marker she had just decorated. Someone she loved was dead.

"Well, get in line, sister," I heard myself saying.

There were a lot of dead people here, so many that the cemetery had its own radio station, where, when I tuned in, I heard that my father's burial was still set for 11:00.

By then it was 10:30, so I drove up into the cemetery until I found the open gravesite where they were putting the fake green grass down—it looked positively plastic in this dusty city where turf was an anomaly—and figured it was my father. They were putting a picture up on an easel which I guess was supposed to be him, but he wasn't in a space suit so of course I couldn't be sure, and anyway, my vision wasn't so good anymore. From the car, I could see that he had short hair and his skin was dark, as if he'd spent a lot of time in the sun. I couldn't tell much else. He didn't look like a spaceman.

I drove up above it so I could look down and drink and decide if I wanted to come out at all. I was listening to 100.3, The Peak, alternative rock out of Albuquerque, and occasionally flipping over to classic rock stations 101.3 and 102.5 when something like Madonna came on. I do not find Madonna alternative, although I must always find an alternative to Madonna.

It was an effort to reach out and touch the radio buttons, an effort to screw the tops off the beer bottles. I had to do it consciously, with real concentration, and when I wasn't doing this, the world seemed to be contracting almost to a tunnel around the edges of my senses, leaving a drone of music, a bitter fizzing in my mouth, a straight line of sight to my father's grave.

I had gotten here just in time; I couldn't have driven another minute without piling into parked vehicles or taking out an acre of our nation's finest.

Cars began to pull up beneath me; people began to get out, dressed in black, slowly, reverentially. The hearse and other cars in the motorcade—a lot of them—had arrived and filled the lane beneath me.

The driver of the funeral home limo came around to give his hand to a woman in a black hat and veil, and that's when I got really interested. Although there were two chairs, she took the lone position of honor under the arcade; about a hundred more people gathered around her.

It took a while, and they had already started the service before I realized that the other chair was meant for me.

So I opened the door and fell to the ground in a clank of beer cans. It hurt; my poor sunburned knees felt like they'd been flayed open. I pulled myself up on the car door and succeeded only in slamming it against my left shin.

"Son of a bitch, Dad," I groaned. "I got here, didn't I?"

Then I made my careening way down the hill, moving from gravestone to gravestone like a one-year-old cruising from couch to coffee table to chair. I think I may have fallen; I don't remember. Neither do I know how long it took me to get down, but I remember looking up and seeing her, the veil lady, the lone family member, standing in front of me, her hand extended.

The graveside service was over; behind her, I could see that they were taking apart the sling mechanism they must have used to lower the coffin.

"You're a very beautiful woman," I told her, and although it was true, I instantly covered my mouth with my hands like I could stop the words physically. She was maybe in her forties, but her dark skin was flawless, her black hair shone under her hat, and she was perfectly made up—lips, eyes, rouge—like a Spanish movie star.

"You must be Clay," she said.

"You must be the potter," I said. I giggled. "Sorry. Sorry. Nobody ever laughs at that."

"I'm Rosalena Fischer," she said. "I was your father's friend."

I swayed and took another look at her, given this new information. "Way to go, Dad," I said.

"You're very tired," she said gently.

People never got everything right. Wasn't it obvious I was a little more than tired? "I'm exhausted to the point of death," I said. "And I'm so drunk. And I think I'm chemically depressed. I didn't think so before, but lately everyone has been telling me so." I put out a hand to steady myself on a tombstone and looked down at my feet. I had left my shoes in the car or taken them off in my odyssey down the hill; I was standing in my socks. The loss of my shoes made me want to cry. "I don't know what I'm doing here."

"You're here because I called," she said. She held her hand out to me. "Come on," she said. "My car is right over there." She indicated the funeral home limo, still waiting.

"I can drive," I said. "I have a license. I've only ever killed two people in my whole life."

"It'd be better if you rode with me," she said. "Santa Fe traffic is a little trickier than you'd find in Robbinsville, North Carolina. Your father used to complain about it."

"You knew my father?" I asked, forgetting what she'd already told me. She found my shoes a few grave markers up, came back and took my arm, and we made our leisurely way toward the limo.

"I knew your father, Clay. Better than just about anyone, I guess. As well as anyone could, anyway. He put up a high wall to keep out intruders."

"Did you love him?"

She nodded. "As well as I could. I can't claim that he returned it. He—" She blinked away some tears and I watched fascinated; someone was crying over my father. My dead father. "That's all over and done with, I guess. I loved him and I admired him, and toward the end, I took care of him as well as he'd permit. That's something, I suppose."

We had reached the car, and the driver opened the back door for us. The two of them eased me into the seat. "Why?" I asked.

"Because he was a good man," she said. "And a great artist. He made me a very wealthy woman, and even if I hadn't loved him I would have taken care of him." She held her arms out, turned her hands over so that her palms were up and out. "All of this is because of him."

"All of what?"

She buckled me into the car and they closed the door. She got in and we drove out of the cemetery. The woman was still there crying over the white gravestone.

"She's sad," I said.

"Yes she is," she said. We turned left on something called Paseo de Peralta.

"Where are we going?"

"I'm taking you to your father's house," she said. "You can rest there. And I have many things to show you."

" 'In my father's house are many mansions,' " I said. " 'If it were not so, I would have told you. I go to prepare a place for you.' John 14:2." My head nodded over with some violence as we turned a corner and whacked against the window. I jerked back erect.

"Impressive," she said. "Your father knew the Bible as well."

"But could he name the books of the Bible? I can. I can do it backwards. Revelation, Jude, Third, Second, First John,

Second Peter, First Peter, Hebrews. Oh hell. I get all the
Epistles mixed up. Corinthians, Ephesians, Colossians,
Galoshes. It doesn't matter anyway. That fat bastard Paul. So
full of himself. I wish I'd been on the road to Damascus.
While he was flailing around blind I'd have run him over with
my chariot."

We turned left at some huge hot-pink building, then right,
up a long, long hill. It was so steep I was pressed back into my
seat, and my head lolled back. "Houston, I'm pulling five
G's," I said.

"Hyde Park Drive," she said as we passed rocks, dirt, scrub
trees. "Hyde Park. Your father always thought it was funny.
A strange juxtaposition, I guess."

"Did my father love you?"

"I think he did." She smiled. "You know, Clay, my mother
was scandalized, but I asked him to marry me once."

"I asked somebody to marry me once. Did he know my
mom divorced him? That it would have been okay if he'd
wanted to?"

"Sure. He got the Robbinsville paper. Or I did, rather,
down at the gallery."

"What gallery?"

"My gallery."

"Cool," I said. "You own a shooting gallery?" I cocked my
thumb and forefinger and began shooting. "Ka-ping. Ka-pow.
What do I win?"

"It's an art gallery," she said.

"Well, that's nice too," I said. "So he said no? Why?"

"He said no. There was the religious thing. I'm Jewish.
And he said he wanted to remain celibate."

"Sex just ruins things anyway," I said. We were rising high
enough that if I looked out her window I could see out over
Santa Fe and some purple mountains majesty off to the west.

She raised a hand, brushed it aside. "I told him it didn't
matter. Sex. No sex. He wouldn't listen. He said he couldn't
marry me. I tell you, the past was still weighing on him like a
ton of bricks."

I nodded sagely. "It's like that for some people. Somebody
said that the past isn't . . . something. It's not even past. Damn,

how did that go?" I'd lost control of my brain, my mouth, and apparently my neck muscles. I just stopped myself from flopping over again as we took a turn.

"Sometimes I think he would have given up on everything if not for his painting."

From somewhere I dredged up one of my songs, rolled it around in my mouth, and took it out for a spin:

> *There's a lovely light in the sky tonight.*
> *A lovely light in the sky.*
> *Makes me wish for wings to mount up high*
> *But I don't know where I would fly.*
> *I don't know where I would fly.*

"More Saint John?" she said, smiling tenderly.

"No. Saint Clay of the Everflowing Bottle," I said.

"Your father always wanted to see you play," she said. "Are you any good?"

"I can sing the hell out of a song," I said. "As you can plainly see. Or hear. And I'm decent on guitar. That's about it. I just took it up to get girls."

"Did it work?"

"Only too well," I said.

"Your dad played some guitar too. And he had a fine voice."

"What kind of music did he like?"

"You'll laugh," she said.

"Possibly."

"Jimmy Buffet."

I shook my head. "Too much," I said. "My dad was an artist and a Parrothead."

"A what?"

"A Parrothead. A rabid follower of Jimmy Buffet."

"He was also an oblate."

"An old plate?"

"It means that as much as possible he tried to live a holy life, follow the Benedictine Rule. He was ordained through the monastery at Pecos."

I tried to get my head to stop rolling around on top of my

neck, because this was of some interest to me. "My father was a Catholic?"

"He was very serious about it. He went to Mass almost every day until the end."

"I'm not a Parrothead," I said. "I play classic rock. Do you think big-hair bands will ever come back?"

"Big hair?"

"You know. Eighties rock and roll. Crimp perms, spandex pants."

"Like Bon Jovi?"

"Yeah, sure. Bon Jovi, Ratt, Cinderella, Poison. I guess Motley Crüe never left, but is that because of the Tommy and Pamela videos or the music? And Def Leppard is still around. But I think they cut their hair." We took another turn and I hit my head on the window again. "Jesus Christ, who taught him to drive? Wonder Woman?"

"Wonder Woman." She smiled. "She was my role model. A JAP superhero."

"She's a stupid superhero," I said. "She has those stupid bracelets. Superheroes should not wear jewelry. Fighting crime is not about accessorizing." We were climbing again, a road so steep that my head rolled all the way back to the top of the seat and I was staring at the ceiling. "Okay, now I'm pulling like six G's here."

"Those bracelets are functional. They block bullets."

"They're silly."

"And she has boots."

"Boots do not make you tough," I said. "My father wears boots. It doesn't make him a cowboy."

She was laughing, and I think the limo driver was chuckling up past his little barrier. I was dimly aware that I was still talking, saying something like "You dudes stop laughing at me," and then I was aware of nothing.

The bright New Mexico sun was gone, and I was someplace dark and cool and safe.

I slept.

There were flashes of light, like those signs along the highway, or like acts revealed in the splash of lightning. I saw myself yelling at Anna Lynn, saw her face streaked with tears; I

saw myself putting a fist through the wall, heard her screaming high and unintelligible. I felt myself slide down the wall,
bump to the floor, cover my eyes with my bloody hand.

I saw the blood drip.

I saw the blood drip.

I was in the car. I had hit my head against the side window
as we rolled, and now that the window was gone I lay with
my cheek against the pavement, tangled in the webbing of my
seatbelt. I could hear little Ray breathe raggedly from his
child seat, could see a drop of blood plop onto the glass next
to my face, feel it spatter.

I looked up and saw Anna Lynn tangled in the right side of
our car, her face bloody, the white of her skull glowing in a
nakedness more obscene than nudity. Her eyes were open and
unblinking and fixed on me.

I screamed and screamed, high and unintelligible.

I covered my face with my hand.

I felt a wisp of breeze across my cheek. I lowered my hand.

I was watching the funeral, their funeral—watching myself
at their funeral. The graveside service on the hill at the cemetery at Robbinsville. I stood uphill from the grave, Ray to one
side, Momma to the other. They were weeping. I was dry-
eyed.

As they lowered Anna Lynn into the ground, I could see
myself begin to melt, turn to goo like the Wicked Witch, I'm
melting, I'm melting, could see myself ooze into the hole after
them.

Nobody seemed to notice.

Everyone walked away talking about what a nice service it
had been. A bulldozer covered us up. All that was left of me
was a pair of shoes—nice ones, black Italian leather polished
to a fine gloss.

"Sorry I'm late," my father, Steve Forester, said from behind me. He put his hand on my shoulder.

"You missed everything," I said, and I was pissed. I didn't
so much as turn to look at him.

"You better pick up your shoes."

"They're not mine," I said. "Anyway, you're not the boss
of me."

He took my arm and I let him lead me away. "My car is right over there," he said. We drove out of the cemetery, through the wrought-iron arch, and into driving snow.

"I just wanted you to know that I did make it big," he said. "I wanted to show you."

"I know," I said.

He pulled up in front of Rumrunner's, the karaoke bar in Anchorage. We walked inside and Karaoke Joe waved him on.

He got up and sang "Margaritaville."

The crowd went wild. He smiled at me from the stage.

I needed a drink, desperately.

When I woke, the room was dimly lit with sunshine coming from somewhere, and I was aware of a sharp ache in my head and a taste in my mouth like burning tires. I looked around. I was in a slender monastic room. I lay in the small bed, could see a dresser with a mirror just across the way, and one wall was nothing but bookcases full of books. The other wall was wall, with a single door, and behind me there must have been a small shuttered window, because that's where the light was coming from.

Above me on the ceiling were posts as thick as telephone poles, and the ceiling above them was wide planks of wood. The wall behind me was cool and felt of cement or sandpaper.

I got up to look at the dresser. I could just make out the raised square of a light switch next to the door, so I turned the light on. There was a picture of me from *The Graham Star*, a laminated picture of Tracy and me at the Fourth of July picnic a few years past.

But that was uninteresting. What I had thought from the bed was a mirror was something other: it was a landscape painting, about three by four, and it really stopped me in my tracks. I could tell it was New Mexico—there was the textured red and yellow and green of the desert floor, the blues and purples of distant mountains, and above it all the roiling blue and gray and white of storm clouds. A burst of sunlight crossed the canvas from the clouds in the upper left to the ground on the far lower right.

There was his name—our name—in the lower left corner,

scratched into the paint, Forester. The paint itself was thick, as if it had been laid on with a trowel instead of a brush. The landscape glowed, like it was lit from within. And I got the strangest feeling from it. The scene was foreboding, ominous, sad even, and yet there was such beauty to it that it almost gave me hope.

Almost. It would take a lot more than a painting to do that.

I opened the top drawer. Inside I found boxers, mostly blue and white. I found one pair of dress socks, dark. A lot of T-shirts. And here was a piece of newsprint, handled until it had become almost translucent. I took a look at it, too late tried to drop it.

It has been a sad week along the river. Our family is so grateful to all of you for your outpouring of sympathy and support following the horrible accident—

Sister's column from 1991.

I put it back in the drawer, closed it securely. Poking around in my father's drawers was not going to teach me anything about him. It was just going to hurt me.

I opened the door and called out into the hallway. "Hello?" It echoed. This was a long hallway or a long house. "Hello?"

"Ah," a male voice said, not too far away, and it called back, "Hello. Señor Forester, I come." And indeed he hurried toward me in something just short of a trot, a Hispanic guy in his forties, dressed in a nice pair of black slacks and a gray silk shirt. "I am Ramón Gonzales. I served your father. My wife has your breakfast ready."

"Breakfast?" I yawned, which hurt. "What time is it?"

"You have slept around the clock. It is Saturday morning."

I shook my head to get the cobwebs out. Not a good idea, the shaking. "Where is—" I didn't remember her name. "Where is the woman who brought me here?"

He nodded and smiled and revealed two gold teeth. "Rosalena," he said. "Sí. I called her when I heard you stirring. She will be here shortly. After you eat, perhaps you will want to clean up? She would like to take you for a drive."

"Great," I said. It was not great. "Ramón, I'm not feeling hungry just now." Actually, the thought of food was making my stomach contract violently. "But if perhaps there are some medicinal spirits in the house . . ."

He was already on his way, his head inclined respectfully. "This is a sad time for all of us," he said. He disappeared down the hallway, and I followed, down a set of stone stairs and into a living room with a breathtaking view over mountains, forests, valleys in three directions.

There was a clanking from the bar behind me, and I turned to Ramón. "Where are we?"

"This is your father's house. My family works for him." He sighed. "For eight years, we work for him," he corrected.

"This is my father's house?" He nodded and handed me a drink, something brandyish. I took the drink, tossed it off, handed it back, and stepped out onto one of the verandas. The house itself was enormous, of adobe construction, thick walls, lots of windows.

Below—far below, past scraggly evergreens I had never seen even in the third- and fourth-growth scrub of North Carolina, past other enormous houses built onto the sides and tops of lower mountains—was what I supposed must be Santa Fe, and then beyond it the multicolored desert, and then, on the far side of the valley, mountains looming purple.

I followed the porch on around . . . and around, and around. It went around the entire house, with stunning views in every direction. My father's enormous house was built on top of a mountain.

"Ramón," I said, upon returning to the living room, "some more medicinal spirits, please."

"Of course," he said.

I had washed my face, run my wet fingers through my tangled hair, and was sipping at my third restorative glass when the huge wooden front doors opened and Rosalena let herself in. She crossed to me, extended her hand, and smiled at me sadly. "Hello, Clay. Remember me?"

"Vaguely," I said. "I keep getting you mixed up with Wonder Woman."

"Must be the boots," she said. She was wearing them, calf-high black leather with her pants legs tucked in like riding pants.

"Where are we going?"

"I've got a full day planned for you," she said. "Your father asked me to take you to some of the places he loved and to let you talk to people who knew him. So that you'd have some sense of who he was." She shrugged, smiled sadly. "I guess maybe he hoped you wouldn't be so angry at him."

"I'm not angry," I said. "Or at least, I won't be after another glass of this very good brandy."

"Let's get going," she said. "I knew you were exhausted, but I didn't think you'd sleep for an entire day. There are a lot of things we need to do."

"Need to?" I said.

She took my hand. "Come on. Have you seen the house?"

"I think I'd need to be in orbit to see the entire thing."

"I know. It's huge. Your father wanted a lean-to. But I said, you have all these friends who will be coming to see you, these are your last days, and someday your son will come and this will be his home."

"Whoa," I said. "I don't want anything. I don't want this house. I—"

She raised her hand to shush me. "Let's talk in the car. I always think better in the car."

The car was a red Mercedes two-seat convertible, a sweet car, and she knew how to drive, downshifting expertly to run us down the mountain and down Hyde Park Drive.

"My father must have been rich," I finally said, after we'd driven a long time listening to the wind and her Joni Mitchell CD. "I mean, that house—"

"Your father was one of the great painters of the century," she said, "and he was very prolific—driven, I'd call it—and he made a lot of people rich, including yours truly."

It was a little too much to take, even on three brandies and twenty-four hours of sleep. I just lay back in the seat and watched as she drove.

We had headed out of town on 285 North, then turned off toward Nambe Pueblo. The desert landscape was strange and beautiful, like the surface of the moon. We came up over one hill and the Sangre de Cristos loomed straight ahead, green and towering, and above them jet contrails made some sort of giant ideogram miles across.

"Was he rich?"

She nodded. "But he wouldn't spend it, at least until I talked him into building the house. He lived in the back of my studio for years." She raised her hand: As God is my witness. "After he started making money, he always gave a lot to the church, to civic causes, set aside a lot of it for you. But it was important to him that he give his money away. He used to talk about what a terrible wrong it was to be rich in the poorest state in the union, in a place with so much despair and so many needs."

She took the curves fast, and when I turned to watch her driving, she just smiled and said, "I'll watch the road. You watch the country."

We sped down into a green valley, twisting and turning around blind curves as bad as in Grenada, a tiny village of adobe buildings crowding the road.

"He left you everything," she said as we climbed up out of the valley. "I'm executor, so I know. I have eighteen paintings at the gallery he said I could sell, plus there are another fifty unsold at your house, some of which he didn't want to sell. And there's the house itself. If you're not going to keep it, I could put it on the market for you tomorrow and get you two million. Maybe three."

"I don't want it. Any of it. Was he crazy? He didn't even know me."

"But he did, Clay. He knew everything that happened to you for twenty years, or at least everything in your aunt's column."

"He doesn't know me at all. And he certainly doesn't know what happened to me."

She sighed. "I guess I hoped you'd be more forgiving. You've been through a lot, I know. But lots of people have. Besides losing your father, I've lost both my parents in the last three years."

"I lost him first," I said, like a six-year-old.

"Everybody loses people they love. Have you lost so much more?" Her eyes flashed, and somewhere deep down in my cotton-candy-cushioned world I could tell I was stepping on a nerve, for all the good that awareness did.

"Did they all know they were going to die?"

"Yes. My parents both had Alzheimer's. It was a long, lingering thing. And your father was diagnosed two years ago."

"So you got to say good-bye, at least."

She nodded. "I did. And more."

I looked straight ahead. "You got to tell them that you loved them, that you forgave them, that you were sorry as hell for not making them happier when you had the chance, that you'd marry her again in a second if she'd only have you."

She looked across at me and nodded again, and the flash of fire was gone. "Something like that," she said.

"Then you've got nothing to be unhappy about," I said.

We were descending again into a valley, following a harrowing narrow road down, and all of a sudden she pulled off onto an overlook, and the view was stunning: past the village below, multicolored hills on the far side of the valley; mountains to the east with great thunderheads looming over them; and over the mesa ahead, one patch of tall clouds. Otherwise the skies ahead of us were blue and almost luminous.

"This is the painting in his room," I said, and she nodded.

"This was one of his favorite spots to paint," she said. "I brought him up here last about four months ago. After that he had to paint at the house, or he was too weak to do anything at all."

I got out of the car and stepped over to the edge of the drop-off. Tenacious sagebrush grabbed onto the slope below me.

"I need to tell you that I've got a vested interest. I want to represent the rest of the paintings he left you."

"Sure," I said. I waved my hand imperiously, like an emperor. It made me feel a little unsteady next to the edge, and she must have seen it, because she took my arm and pulled me back to the car. We drove on down into the valley through the village of Cordova, then hesitated for a moment as we pulled up onto State Highway 76.

"What's that way?" I said, indicating right and the mountains.

"Truchas," she said. "Where Robert Redford shot *The Milagro Beanfield War.*" She threw it into gear, pulled up onto the highway, and headed left, back toward Santa Fe. "He owns three of your father's paintings. Paul Newman has two."

We stopped at a little restaurant off the highway in Chimayo, a big old adobe house with lots of cars outside. We went through the restaurant and were seated in back on the patio, and I took a look over the menu, decided on the combination plate—"Combinación," the waitress repeated as I handed the menu back to her—and a beer.

"I used to eat here with your father sometimes," she said, waving flies away from her face. "But he ate here much more often alone. Every time he was out painting he would stop for the day and eat here on the way back to Santa Fe." She tapped our table. "This was his favorite spot."

My Dos Equis came, cold, the bottle beaded with sweat. I was becoming a beer connoisseur after a long layoff—that, or a drunk. Then the food followed shortly after, although it didn't look like any Mexican food I'd ever eaten. Where were the mounds of cheese? What was this strange red sauce dolloped over everything?

"It's Northern New Mexican," Rosalena said. "Not Mexican. And you should be careful. Those chunks of meat there, carne adovada? They'll be hot."

"Sure," I said. I took a bite. The chile ate a hole in the side of my mouth. I drank my entire beer and didn't make a dent in the burning. Then my water.

Rosalena was laughing. "Beer or water won't cool it off. Milk does."

I put down my glass, half empty. "Jeezus Chrish," I said.

She crossed her hands and put on a demure smile. "So," she said.

"So," I said, still trying to shoo the pepper from my mouth.

"You came."

"Against my better judgement, I have to say." I ate about twelve chips and began to feel that perhaps my mouth wouldn't be permanently disfigured.

"Why did you come?"

"Curious, I guess. Plus it began to seem preordained. And anyway, how many times in your life will your missing father die? Not more than three or four, I guess."

"Well, if you're curious, why don't you ask me some questions."

"Okay," I said. "What was my father like?"

She took a big bite of her blue-corn enchiladas—stacked instead of rolled—chewed slowly and reflectively, and swallowed. "Oh my," she said. "That is good."

I nodded my head, the cranial equivalent of impatient toe-tapping, and she smiled her acknowledgment. "I know," she said. "This was the part he tried to prepare me for, and I'm just not prepared."

"Give me something," I said, draining my beer and signaling for another. "Anything. The last time I saw him he was wearing a fucking space suit. Begging your pardon, of course."

"*Mission to Mercury?*"

I nodded.

"That was a terrible movie," she said.

"We're in agreement on that," I said.

She took another bite, chased it with some posole—what looked like hominy but was in a stew with pork and red chile. "He was a lot like you," she said. "Good heart, sad spirit."

"I am sick unto death of people talking about my spirit," I said. "Next they'll be telling me they're seeing a black aura around me. Or a black cloud, like that character in *Li'l Abner.*"

"Your father had a great gift. I suspect you did, or do. Like him, I sense that you've been broken. But like him, it comes out as self-hatred, not as viciousness." She took another bite, saw my skepticism, swallowed, and said, "Listen, kid. I'm not a Gypsy fortune-teller or something. I'm just a Jewish girl from Long Island transplanted to the desert. But I'll tell you once and for all, you have a beautiful spirit. I'll bet people in North Carolina love you. Your friends stick with you. And you make a good impression. Or I'm guessing you normally would, under different circumstances."

"Hey, I'm on my best behavior," I said. "If you don't consider the drunkenness and body odor and such." There was a rumble of what sounded like thunder and I looked up. The sky was growing dark.

She shook her head. "Don't even talk to me about behavior. Behavior is the clothes we put on everyday. I'm talking about the soul."

I snorted. The beer simply could not reach the table fast enough to suit me. "Why does everyone say things like that to me?"

She laughed. "If I were to tell you bad things about yourself, you would listen to me."

It was not a question. "Yes," I said, at last. "I would."

She nodded. "Your father," she said. "Your father all over."

"I do have a question for you," I said at length. We had been eating in silence, and I was watching dark clouds crawl over the Sangre de Cristos, where they were probably dumping rain by the bucketloads. "You said my father knew everything about me?"

"He kept up with you as well as he could through the paper. Your Aunt Sister became a very real person to me. I think I could probably recognize her by voice alone."

"I was looking through his dresser," I began, and I fidgeted a little with my napkin, moved it to my lips, back to my lap. "He knew about what happened to Anna Lynn and little Ray?"

She nodded and bit her lower lip. "Yes," she said. "He knew. He was so torn up over it I thought it was going to drive him crazy."

"A thing like that could do it to a man," I said. "But if he was so upset, why didn't he say anything? Call? Write?"

"He sent flowers to the graveside service. He wanted to come. But he thought it would be too much."

I crumpled up my napkin and threw it onto my plate. I had lost my appetite. "Too much? For who? For me? Or for him?"

She didn't say anything. I pushed my chair back and got ready to get up.

"Please don't judge him for that," she whispered. "He was afraid."

"Afraid?" I said. People from other tables looked over. I stood up. "Afraid? I needed a father. That was the most terrible moment of my life. And he wasn't there. I could have traded all the other moments he wasn't there just to have him for that."

There were tears in her eyes and she nodded. "I know. But Clay, you had a father. Ray Fontenot. And he was a good one, from everything we understood. Another father would have just . . . complicated things then."

I stood frozen; she was right, of course. "But still," I began, and then I sat down, put my head in my hands.

"He was scared," she said. "You must know what that is like. He was afraid of what you'd do or say. As sad as his life was in that respect, at least he didn't have to deal with your hatred and rejection."

"I could have forgiven him," I said, looking up.

"But would you have?" She put her napkin on the table. "He was scared. Broken. And in some ways, he never got unbroken. Some people never get over the bad things they do. The bad things that happen to them. Can you understand that?"

Those dark clouds that had been looming overhead for a while began to express themselves then, first as splatters of that long-sought rain, and then as hail, pea- and marble-sized. Before I could answer, we fled the patio—she threw down a handful of bills, which were probably swept away by the floodwaters—and ran for the car.

"Yeowtch," I said, as she raised the roof on the convertible and I stood outside doing a hail dance, arms over my head, feet flapping. Cold, hard things were bouncing off my forearms and scalp, so my dance wasn't helping in any real sense.

"Get in," she yelled, and I did, dripping, smarting, covered with welts. "My poor upholstery."

"My poor upholstery, my ass," I said. "Look at my arms. And I'm soaked to the bone. "

"And you smell all the better for it," she said. "How long were you on the road without stopping?"

"I don't know," I said. "A long time. I got sidetracked. There were . . . incidents."

We were driving back to Santa Fe in a new way, a narrow road through Chimayo, which seemed to be mostly this one road and some arroyos. Ahead of us traffic was slow because of the rain; our windshield wipers were working fast and still not doing much for visibility.

"Incidents?" she said. "That sounds . . . interesting." She got a wicked look in her eyes. "Tell me about these incidents."

"It wasn't like that," I said. "I haven't had an incident with a woman—or a man, mind you—for, I don't know, ten years, maybe. Those kinds of incidents just cause trouble. They complicate things. Not that the ones I just had didn't." I peered ahead; the rain was letting up the tiniest bit and I could see several cars ahead to a big truck holding us all back.

"Clay, you're not making the slightest bit of sense," she said. "Although I should be growing used to that. Still, you were a lawyer once, right? How did you manage that? I can only assume that at some point, stone-cold sober, you could communicate in some fashion."

"Hardee har har har," I said.

"Listen," she said, turning serious. "I'd like for you to go see your dad's best friend this evening," she said. "Take a shower first. A real one."

"I'm not up to it," I said. "Nope. No more adventures for this boy. Let alone incidents."

"Oh, I think you will be up for it, that is, when I tell you that this friend of your father's is a priest who plays on Saturday nights in a salsa band."

I inclined my head a little in response. "Okay. A priest who plays salsa. That is intriguing."

"His name is Father Nieto," she said. "I'll give you directions to Club Alegría. He plays with his band every Saturday night. If you get there before seven you can have a good talk with him before he goes on."

"Are you coming with me?"

She shook her head. "You'll talk more if I'm not there taking up so much space." She smiled. "I know I talk a lot. Plus, I don't get treated so well there. There are too many guys there trying to pick somebody up, too many fights. It's a very macho scene. Like Manhattan in the Seventies, except Hispanic. No, I'll give you directions. You can take your dad's car."

"What dad's car?" I asked, and she laughed out loud. This was going to be a nice surprise.

When we got home, she took me out to the garage and showed me. Next to a white panel van sat a cherry red 1967 Mustang convertible with a white ragtop. "It didn't look like this, exactly, when he first got here," she said. "But he fixed it up over the years. He drove a van when he went out to paint, but he drove this car for pleasure."

"He always did love convertibles," I said without thinking. "But I can't take this."

She showed me the keys. "Suit yourself. But you already know I'm a devious one. I had the rental car picked up. Your things are in the trunk."

"I don't want it," I said.

"Suit yourself," she said again, and smiled. "At least you can drive it to see Father Nieto, provided you think you can drive."

"I can drive," I said, wobbling only slightly as I grabbed the keys from her hand.

"All right, then," she said. "I'll leave the directions with Ramón. Get cleaned up, for God's sake. Then go talk to Father Nieto. Maybe I'll see you later."

She turned to go, but I threw something out after her. "Hey," I said.

"Hey," she said.

"Rosalena," I said.

"Hey," she said again.

"You're a pretty hip Jewish woman," I said.

"Thanks."

My voice softened without my realizing it. "I wish he'd married you."

She blinked wetly once or twice, surprised, before she got her smile back. "You and me both, kid," she said. "You and me both. So long."

Rosalena climbed into her Mercedes. The gravel of the driveway crackled under the tires. She backed down the mountain and out of sight. And I went in to get the hot shower and shave I'd needed for days. It felt good.

13

The car was a monument to Detroit engineering, back in the days when that phrase still signified something. The stick shift was precise and an easy throw from point to point. The clutch caught just right. The engine purr-rumbled through glass packs. "He had an eye for cars," I muttered as I downshifted to take the incline down Hyde Park Road. "I will give him that."

I drew more than my share of looks as I drove through town, more for the car than anything else, but still, everyone likes to be noticed. I checked my directions and turned onto Agua Fria headed out from town.

Way out, as it turned out. It didn't look like much of a happy place, this Club Alegría out Agua Fria Road. For that matter, I hadn't seen any cold water along the road, so I was having some serious truth-in-advertising questions before I even got in the door, although who am I kidding? I've been having truth-in-advertising issues for years and years.

"Is the Salsa Priest here?" I asked the bouncer, a big, mustachioed Hispanic guy who looked at me like I was the type of troublemaker who required some thought before admitting.

"His name is Father Nieto, hombre," he said, at last. "And he's getting set up. Are you a friend of his?"

"No, hombre. But my father was."

He straightened up and took another look at me. I tried to straighten up in response. It was futile.

He nodded. "Your father was Steve. Padre said to keep an eye for you, send you right in if you showed. Yeah, Steve was a good guy. When he and the padre got together, man, they used to make people laugh their asses off."

I swayed a little bit at this news. "Really?"

"Oh, no doubt, man. But you go in and talk to the padre. He'll tell you a lot more than I could about your dad."

And he stood aside so I could go inside. It was a multilevel place, the bar on one side, the bandstand down two tiers and against the far wall. I could see the band setting up: guitars, drums, keyboards, horns, and one priest.

I had a sudden desire to pull the cell phone out of my pocket and dial.

"Hello," Otis said.

"Uhuru, I've just beamed down to the surface of the planet."

"Clay, I am so beyond angry at you, man—"

"I'm going to approach the inhabitants. They don't seem threatening. Wish me luck."

"Listen—" he was saying as I hung up. I turned my head this way and that and listened. Nothing.

When I looked back toward the bandstand, the priest was right in front of me. He was big, balding, clothed all in black except for the white of his collar.

"Friar Tuck," I said.

He laughed, a jolly Santa Claus kind of laugh, which was the only kind of laugh he had. I could tell already that everything was large about this guy.

Including his hand, which swallowed up mine, reluctantly extended once I got a gander at his. "Clay," he said. "Rosalena told me you were on your way."

"Well," I said. "And here I am."

He pulled me over to one of the tables near the stage, seated me, took the chair across from me. "Can I get you anything?"

"Sangria would be fine," I said. I was thirsty. New Mexico was drying me out like a goddamn food dehydrator. My skin was starting to peel—partly from my hellish and still tender sunburn, I have to admit—and my poor nose was clogged with snot pralines that had gotten freeze-dried there.

"Sangria it is," he said. "Ernesto," he called in his big, hearty voice to the guy wiping down the bar. "Dos sangrías, por favor."

Ernesto nodded and went to work. There was a long uncomfortable silence. Father Nieto sat leaned across the table toward me, his elbows on the table, his face open and expectant.

When it became clear that he was going to get me to speak first, I gave him the bare minimum. "You understand that this is not the normal circumstance where boy gets together with his father's best friend for a drink?"

"Oh, I think I understand that," he said.

"Since I guess you know I didn't realize he was still alive until a week ago. Less. And then he wasn't, actually."

"I understand," he nodded, and he settled in to wait for more.

"You must be a killer in the confessional."

He laughed. "I get everything out of them," he said. "And then I help them make it right."

Now it was my turn to laugh.

He leaned forward. "Do you believe confession is a sacrament?"

I stopped laughing and leaned back, away from him. "I'm sorry, Father. But you and I don't know each other well enough to have this talk."

"Do you believe confession is a sacrament?" he repeated, and if possible, he leaned even closer. I felt like I was caught in a priestly avalanche.

"What do you mean? Do I think it's sacred or something?" Our sangria arrived, and like everything else about Father Nieto, it was big. When he ordered two sangrias, what came was two pitchers of sangria, sweating in the dry air. I poured a glassful from the pitcher set in front of me, grateful for the opportunity to pay attention to something other than Father Nieto for a moment.

He did the same, and then he took a sip, set his glass down, and continued, "No, Clay. Does it work? Not, is it sacred. It doesn't matter if it's sacred, unless it works."

"I don't understand," I said, thinking that I didn't or didn't want to, either of which was fine with me.

"Here is my question," he said, "boiled down to its essence. Does confession restore you to yourself? You confess your wrongs, you express repentance, you are reconciled with God and man. Do you believe that?"

Two pitchers began to seem just about right. I finished off that first glass and bought myself some more time pouring another. "I don't know," I said. "Maybe. Or maybe for some people. I don't know that there's anything that could reconcile me with God and man."

He laughed. "Are your sins so great? Are you, how do they say, the Guinness World Book record holder of sins? Do you carry such guilt?"

I looked him in the eye and clenched my jaw to keep from saying something I should not. What at last came out was this: "Father, I carry guilt that doesn't even belong to me."

He got to his feet. "Let's play a song," he said, leading me to the stage. "Do you know 'Margaritaville'?"

I shook my head. "Do you know any Roy Orbison?"

"Surely," he said. He introduced me to the musicians, a handful of Pacos and Rubéns. One handed me his guitar, a big acoustic that made me feel pregnant, and they looked at me expectantly.

" 'Only the Lonely,' " I said. "In A." I played the verse through, letting them see the chord progressions, then the chorus, then the bridge, and they were nodding and noodling away before I'd even finished. The horn players put their heads together and were putting some Latin flavor to the shoo-be-doos. I shrugged. "Okay." I counted off and we started.

And it wasn't half bad, me and the band playing another of the saddest songs I know to a salsa beat. Father Nieto played maracas next to me and took a harmony part. When we finished, he slapped me on the back, but it was restrained, as though through the music he had seen something about me that had not been clear to him before.

"Do you want to play that with us tonight?" he said as we walked back to our table.

"Maybe," I said. "I may be under the table before then."

"Tell me about it," he said.

"About what? Being under the table? I've just returned to alcohol in a big way. I find it very comforting. I can't believe I ever stopped."

"I know a little about alcohol. Tell me about why you are drunk."

I took another drink and acted like I didn't hear him. "Tell me about celibacy," I said. "You, me, my father. What the fuck is up with that?"

"For me, it is the state ordained by God," he said, shrugging that huge head a little to one side. "It has freed me to love more completely, because the body is no longer a part of it." He shrugged again. "For your father, it was a chosen state. He believed it was ordained to him. Perhaps it was, although I have my doubts. For you, however"—and here he shook a huge, admonishing finger at me—"it is not healthy. You are a man, out in the world. You need the love of a woman."

"I had that once," I said. "It didn't work out so well for me. Tell me something, Salsa Priest. Why was my father such a good painter? He must have been, right?"

"I am not such a judge of these things," he said. "But I will tell you what I know. He looked for more than what was there."

I didn't understand, and he saw that. "What do the paintings say to you?"

"I've only seen a couple," I said. "And I'm not much of an expert on this either. But there's . . . a light, I guess. A life. It's not just rocks and sky."

Father Nieto nodded. "Exactly. He was painting the two worlds, the seen and the unseen."

"The two worlds," I repeated, as if he'd said my dad was painting Martians.

"He was a very great artist. Anyone who can paint the face of God has to be."

"Okay," I said. "Maybe so." And although I was having a hard time holding my head straight, I poured a third glass of sangria. I only spilled a little.

He leaned forward when I set the pitcher down, and placed

his paw on my arm in a gentle yet alarming way. "Tell me, Clay," he said. "Tell me about the guilt you carry."

I looked down at his hand, then up at his face, and shook my head.

"Tell me. I am a priest, after all. Nothing of what passes between us will ever leave my lips."

I shook my head again. "I can't. I've never talked about it. Not to anyone. Everyone thinks they know the truth. But it's only the tiniest portion of it. Of the truth, I mean." I shook my head again. "I wouldn't even know where to start."

"So," he said, removing his hand from my arm and sitting back in his chair, "it has been a long time since your last confession, my son?" He smiled wryly.

"I guess you'd have to describe it that way."

He nodded, as much to himself as to me. I could see he was thinking, and he took a deep breath before he spoke again.

"There is much of your father in you."

"Isn't that from *Star Wars*?"

He smiled again and poured himself another glass of sangria. "Clay," he said, "I knew your father for twenty years. I baptized him. I sponsored his work at the monastery. I heard his confessions. I said his last rites." He took a drink, lowered the glass, looked into it. I saw a couple of orange slices floating in red liquid, but he seemed to be seeing something else. When he looked up, his face was solemn. "I loved your father. He was a good soul. More, he was my best friend, el amigo de mi corazón. I would like to help you. I would like to see the son walk a different road than the father."

I shook my head for the third and decisive time. "It's too late for that, Father. It's such a fucked-up mess—begging your pardon; I shouldn't say *fuck* in front of you." He raised a dismissive hand and I went on. "It's just that God has just screwed me over like a sailor, and nothing in the world could ever fix it. There's no point in talking about it. You see what I'm saying?"

He nodded. "So you see God's hand engineering your distress?"

I sighed and shrugged. "It doesn't matter," I said. "None of that Job shit, all right? I don't need to gather my friends and listen to them argue about it. He made it happen, He let it happen, He laughs his ass off because it happened. None of that shit matters. Just shades of gray."

He leaned forward. "Isn't it also possible to imagine God weeping at your distress? At your despair?"

I blinked away the momentary surprise and pulled my cynicism back over me like a blanket. "Maybe for someone else that would be possible. Not for me. I just can't see it."

"It can be true. If you will wish it to be."

"It doesn't matter," I said again. "There's no point in talking, even if I knew where to start."

He waved this away as well. "Look back at your life. Start at the moment when you knew that your heart was broken. That is always the best place to start confessing."

I looked at him, this huge priest who played salsa in a nightclub on Saturdays and said Mass on Sunday. There was music coming in over the speakers, some Spanish Latin thing. There was probably a name for it. Merengue. Samba. Mamba. No, that was a poisonous snake. It'd make a great dance, though, the Black Mamba.

He was watching me waiting, as he waited. He would not speak next if a black mamba slithered across his feet.

I thought of Tracy, talking about putting things behind me, of Kathy Cartwright asking, "How do you ever expect to get over it?"

I thought of Anna Lynn in the car on the way back from the airport, the silence between us so thick you could have swum it, the crash so loud after that nothingness that the noise alone could have killed.

I thought of her eyes on me.

I picked up my sangria and drained it in one long motion. I set it down on the table before us, carefully, tentatively, as though the table's apparent solidity might be an illusion.

Then I opened my mouth, and the words began to come.

His name was Ambrose. At first I didn't know if that was a first or last name. To be honest, I didn't pay much attention to him. Maybe it was his only name, like Madonna. I do know that it's a saint's name, although he didn't act like any saint I ever heard of. Well, maybe Saint Augustine in his younger, wilder days.

Oh, I knew things were bad between us. I guess you just always think that things are going to get better. I was working on the *Exxon Valdez* case, on the side of the bad guys, Father, I have to confess that as well, although I thought I could do some good. I was going to show her. I was going to show Ray. That's my stepdad. I was going to show them that I was a good person, not some corporate drone content to take it up the ass for money. Sorry, Padre.

"I have to tell you something," she told me when I got home from Alaska. She met me at the door, red-eyed from crying. That was in June of '90. That's never a good thing, is it, Padre? Always a bad sign, that look, that phrase. Especially when she follows it with, "I just want you to know that it's over now." Also always a bad sign. "It's over now."

My breath started coming fast and shallow, like I was hyperventilating, and my heart was pounding in my chest—I could actually hear it pounding—and my hands were shaking so bad that my keys fell out of my fingers and onto the kitchen floor. Then they were tingling, like I was holding onto some kind of electric wire. She had taken a seat, although she looked like she was getting ready to get up if she had to—at least, as fast as a woman that pregnant could get up.

"No," I told her. That's what I said. Just "no." I don't know if I didn't want her to say it, or if I wanted not to have heard her.

"I want you to know that I didn't do this to hurt you," she said. "Or at least, not mostly."

"Oh," I said. That's what I said next. "Oh." I sat down. I put my hands on the table so that she couldn't see them shaking. People always said I was unfeeling. What did they mean? I felt everything. I tried my voice again and heard only the slightest tremor, so I went ahead. "Oh," I said.

It started when they were on a trip to Mexico together. She told me the story like it was a history lesson, like she was telling me a story about other people, like it was just something that sort of happened, whoops, and then it just sort of kept happening, and then a couple of days ago, it had somehow stopped happening.

I kept saying "Oh," which I thought was communicating pretty well. I thought it meant "This breaks my heart," and "I'm sorry you thought you needed someone else," and "I've never been so angry in my life," and "Please tell me this is just a really bad joke." But finally she stopped pacing and reciting and crossed her arms and said, "Clay, is that all you have to say?" so maybe she was not understanding me so good after all, Padre.

I swallowed once or twice. I honestly thought that I was going to die—like that old show Sanford and Son: "Lamont, this is the big one"—that my heart was just going to explode in my chest and then finally people would know that yes, I did feel sadness and passion and rage. "He died of a broken heart," everyone would say. "Who'd a thunk it?" But it didn't happen, and I got my breath back, and finally I just asked the scariest question I could ever bring myself to ask, which was, "Do you love him?"

"No," she said. "I don't think so. I'm just so confused. I'm a pregnant raging bundle of hormones, you know."

"Apparently," I said.

She shook her head. This was no time for jokes.

"So what happens now?" I mean I know what happens in the movies. You know, either the guy goes for his gun and shoots them dead and gets the chair, or he walks away and never sees her again and she collapses in grief. Those were both appealing images, I have to say. But I didn't do either. I just sat there, my head down. I could feel the tears coming and I did not want to cry in front of her, did not want to give her that satisfaction of knowing that she had broken me, of knowing that the thought of her with another man was like a knife in my gut. So I turned away and swallowed again, and when I did, it was like I had swallowed it all, the pain and hurt, and I looked up at her, calm as could be, and just said, "It's going to be okay." Like I could just say it and make it so, like I hadn't just swallowed a bottle full of poison.

But I thought maybe it could be okay. Little Ray was born

on October fifth. I got to fly back for that, then a couple of days later, I had to be at the press conference in Alaska where the governor announced the settlement I'd brokered between Exxon and the plaintiffs. A billion dollars. Lots of money for environmental work. I didn't tell you that was Anna Lynn's field, environmental law. I thought Anna Lynn would think of me differently.

But when I got home, she was still pissed off. "It's not enough," she said, and ultimately, she was right. The settlement was rejected, Exxon went to court, and they're still ducking the five-billion-dollar award that jury gave out.

And sometime that next spring, maybe while little Ray was napping, maybe, there were more of these little accidental happenings, whoops, first one, then tearful remorse, than another, then a whole stream of them. I didn't know about it. She didn't tell me anything, not even when I came home. I guess I might not ever have found out about it except that our town house was broken into one Saturday night while we were all at dinner and they turned everything upside down: furniture, drawers pulled out and flung. I don't know what they were looking for. But in the middle of the dining room floor was a pile of letters that had been in the china hutch. I saw them. She saw them. She had Ray in her arms and I bent down first and she just said "Don't," like I was doing something wrong, or maybe like she knew the world was about to change.

Because they were from him, of course. A couple of them were just a few days old. The standard stuff. I love you. I can't live without you. I want to be with you always. I don't want to settle for hours when we can have years.

Well, Padre, I was angry. I tore them up, tore them into tiny little pieces and flung them in her face. I was screaming, Ray was screaming, Anna Lynn was screaming. None of us made a lick of sense. I put my fist through the wall, turned the china hutch over. Her grandmother's china, from Dresden. Boom. Crash. Then I sat down on the floor, with all the chips of china and shreds of paper. I said one thing: "We are the stuffed men." I know, it doesn't make sense. It's from a book

I read. Let it go. And I got up and packed my bag to fly back to Alaska.

A couple of days later I called home. I got the message that Anna Lynn and Little Ray were in Michigan at her folks', that she had a lot to think about, that if I ever came home again maybe we could sort through them.

Well, that's not the kind of thing a grieving guy alone in Alaska wants to hear, you know what I mean, Padre? I'm sure you get the gist of it.

There was this girl there, Padre. Becky Klausen. She had it all over for me. And I was lonely, but I was never that lonely, if you know what I mean. But when I got that message from my dark empty house, I called Becky and we went to this karaoke bar, and I sang "I Get Along Without You," which you probably know is this sad Sinatra song, and I thought I was doing okay, and then we went back to my room and I told her everything that had happened, and she petted me like a poor beat-up puppy, and before I knew it, we were having sex. And it wasn't even over before I rolled off her and sat on the side of the bed and told her, "This isn't what I want."

"What do you want?" she said. "Do you want to pretend I'm her?"

"I didn't realize plaintiff work warped people so completely," I told her. "I don't want you to pretend to be her. I want you to be her."

"Even after what she did to you?"

And I had to say yeah. Yeah. "It was my fault as much as hers," I told her, putting my clothes back on. "I can't blame her. I mean, look how easy it is for two unhappy people to come together looking for something."

"You must love her," she said, and then she started to cry. "Of course you do. I've heard you sing. No one's ever going to sing that way about me."

And I just shook my head and said as gently as I could manage, because Father, she really was a good girl, "Jesus, you're a mess."

She left. I sat. Somehow I got through the days. I went home for a weekend, and I was supposed to pick them up at

the airport. We were all going to try to go home and live together. You know this story? Good. I don't want to tell it.

And so that's where things were. Where they are. No one
knows that anything happened to us except for the end part.
Nobody except for Ambrose, I guess. I still see him sometimes
on Sunday morning talk shows, doing his bit for the environment. Anna Lynn said I shouldn't blame him, that he was a
symptom or something. But I did. I do. Whenever I see him on
TV I experience a momentary wavering in my support of
handgun control.

Turns out the garbage truck had bad brakes, though. Did
you know that part of the story? Ray and Carroll Abernathy
took the sanitation company to court and won a multimil-
lion-dollar settlement. Like I cared. I put it in a trust for environmental causes. I should have given it to Ambrose for his
work. Anna Lynn probably would have wanted that. But the
only way I will ever give him money is if I can put it in crates
and drop it on him from a great height.

So that's my story. Nobody knows it. They think I just
blame myself for the wreck. Like that wouldn't be enough.
But it's only the end of it. What's worst is that we left so much
unfinished. I didn't tell her that I forgave her. I don't even
know if I had forgiven her. I'm still mad at her. Do you know
how much it hurts to be angry at someone you love? I don't
know if she was going to stay or if she was going to leave me.
And I just think I deserved the chance to find out. That's all,
Father. Would that have been so much to ask?

No.

All of that is bad, but it's not the worst.

What's worst is the way she looked at me right there at the
end. Like she knew I was going to kill us all.

Like I had done it on purpose.

Maybe I did. I don't know. I don't think I did. Really,
Father, I don't think I did. But I don't know. I've never even
talked about it before. Honestly, I don't know anything.
Outside of a few songs and how to fix a car, I don't know anything at all.

* * *

The bar had begun to get busy around us while I was holding forth. Father Nieto had listened, nodded, his eyes had filled toward the end, and now his huge hand was on my head as I sat bent double with the force of my tears.

"And so," he said, his voice gentle and strong at once, "now you hold yourself apart from everyone and everything?"

I raised my head, my eyes raw and wet and burning, and indicated with one hand my self, my sad sorry sodden self. "Thou hast said."

"Your father said that you moved back home with your mother and her—how did he say it?—her horrifying sisters."

I couldn't help but laugh, even in my extremity. "They can be horrifying. But they all love me, in their own twisted ways. It's a curse and a comfort to be home." More sangria had arrived, a compelling argument for the existence of a God. I poured and drank, parched from relating my story.

"Do you know where you are at fault in what you have told me?"

"I think I do."

"Do you confess your responsibility for the distance which grew between you?"

"I do."

"Do you confess your responsibility for placing other things ahead of your family's joy, ahead of their happiness?"

I nodded. "I do."

"Do you confess that you dishonored the gifts you were given by God?"

"I do," I croaked. It felt as though a bubble had risen from my nether depths and popped open somewhere in my chest.

"And do you accept that it is your wife who bears responsibility for her decisions, for her actions, but that she has been forgiven, and that she and your innocent child are with God?"

"I'd like to believe that, Padre," I said. "It's a better story than *Mission to Mars*. And surely it would have better special effects."

"Then will you accept this penance from one who has

known you and loved you through one he loved? Who loves you through Christ who loves us all?"

"No," I whispered. "I can't,"

"Go home," he said, as though I had not spoken. "Live. Love." He raised a hand in benediction, touched it to my forehead as though he were anointing me. "You are forgiven."

"Hey," I said, pushing his hand away. "You can't do that. I'm not even Catholic. I'm not even a Christian."

He checked his watch. It was time for him to go on, to become the Salsa Priest, because he just smiled sadly and stood. "You are many things you do not know you are," he said. "And you are not many things you believe you are."

And he left me sitting there to try and digest that Zen koan. I blinked. I swilled the last of my sangria straight out of the pitcher. I called out to him, "Hey, Father Yoda. What the hell does that mean?"

He turned in the middle of the dance floor, a graceful move from such a large man. "It means what it means," he said. "It means what it means. Go with God."

Oh, I would all right. Go, that is. I drained the rest of his pitcher, then I wobbled out into the parking lot.

"Hey," the bouncer said. "You okay, man? You look like a truck ran over you."

"The priest ran over me," I said. "I'm going to get some air."

"I wouldn't do it, man," he said. "Let me get you a cab. This is not such a good neighborhood to stumble around in."

"Just want to get away," I mumbled. I weaved into the parking lot, bouncing from car to car, and then on down Agua Fria toward the bright-lighted sign of a bar that made the Club Alegría look like the Waldorf Astoria. It smelled strongly of sweat and spilled beer, a real working guy's hangout. I bought a round for the house, got drunker and drunker as the people around me chattered in español, and somewhere after midnight, I staggered out into the scraggly cedars around back to throw up. I thought my guts were going to come up. It went on for what seemed like hours: retching, my eyes rimmed with tears, thick strands of something repulsive dangling from my lips. Then I heard gravel shift and looked up from my red-tinged puddle to find four dark figures standing over me.

"Hey, pendejo," one behind me hissed. "You shouldn't wave money around like that unless you want to share it."

"You can have it," I said. "It won't make you happy. Voice of experience." I reached for my wallet, realized I'd left all but a roll of cash in the car somewhere, and then took a shot to the back of the head that brought me down hard on my side. Somebody said, "Hey, fuck you, man." Then they were kicking me in the ribs and in the back, blows were raining down on me, somebody was saying, "Bust his head open," and I welcomed the pain, deserved the pain, tried to explain that to them, and then somebody pulled the cash from my pocket and they walked off and I was lying in a puddle of my own juices.

When I woke up, the sun was coming up. It was Sunday morning, quiet as the grave. I groaned, rolled over, slowly pushed myself to my hands and knees, then with some effort, to my feet. I looked down at myself; I was caked with blood and vomit, and so I turned on a garden hose on the back wall and hosed myself down until at least I wasn't sticky and crackling when I walked.

I limped back down the street to the Club Alegría parking lot and found my father's car, still there and unharmed. The keys were in my front right pocket, jammed deep, and I guess none of my welcome wagon from the night before had thought to take them because nobody saw me drive up.

I started the car, gunned it, groaned again, and headed back toward St. Francis Drive. The Sangre de Cristos were dark blue with the sun behind them; the clouds above them floated orange and fluorescent. I turned on St. Francis, found a Texaco station open, and sloshed inside.

It hurt so much to move that I thought I had been pelted with bricks. St. Stephen if he'd lived, I thought, would have felt like this the morning after.

I got a breakfast burrito, two Dr. Peppers, and a Hostess honey bun. Kathy Cartwright, God bless her, would have done a war dance around me all the way to the checkout.

In her honor, I put the honey bun back.

When I got out to the car and managed to ease myself back in gingerly, I cracked open the first Dr. Pepper, ice cold, threw back my head, and let it glug down. It felt so good, I was so thirsty and my throat was so raw, that I drank it, the whole bottle, then started the next one. Finished it, too.

Then I just sat there for a moment, in the momentary but monumental clarity of that sugar rush, and watched the sun climb into the sky, watched the mountains turn green beneath it, watched the Sunday streets come to life.

Then I burped.

I had a full tank of gas, which struck me as significant, somehow, and so at last, I started the car, stuck it in reverse, and headed down St. Francis, south, out of Santa Fe. The mountains stayed in my rearview for some time—after I got on I-25 headed south toward Albuquerque, even—until at last I came to a long descent where I came off the black volcanic plateau and plunged down toward the Rio Grande Valley.

I was listening to 100.3, The Peak, and the music was good. The Sandia Mountains loomed to my left as I approached Albuquerque, and as I drove closer to town, at last I faced a major decision. The interchange between I-40 and I-25 could do many things: it could send me winging back east toward home; it could send me west out to California, site of my father's adventures; it could carry me south toward El Paso, maybe Mexico, maybe all the way to Chiapas if I wanted; it could whip me around and send me back to Santa Fe.

I couldn't decide. My moment of clarity had fled. Maybe I needed something stronger than Dr. Pepper, although a large part of me already doubted that.

So I decided not to decide. I would go wherever the car took me.

My lane turned into a right-hand exit onto I-40 West. "So let it be written," I said. "So let it be done."

I took the turn fast, headed west now, away from my family and friends, away from all the lives I'd lived up until then. People said my father and I were alike; maybe they were right after all.

I headed past the exits for what they called Old Town, past a Sheraton tower looming a few blocks south of the highway.

The multiple lanes became only four, two on each side, as I got outside the city and passed through the desolate plains: red sand soil, and mesas with bands of red rock around their bases like retaining walls.

That's when I saw him. Like before, I was already past him before I took him in, such a singular sight was he, but on the right shoulder, inches from the traffic on Interstate Highway 40, sat the Cross Man.

I'd already forgotten his name—Matthew something—and maybe I would have whooshed past him, since I was not the same man who stopped to pick him up before. But one other thing registered on me as I passed him: he was weeping.

The cross was lying flat, and he was sitting next to the interstate, weeping.

Common sense says keep on going; keep right on going, partner. "I stick my neck out for nobody," I said experimentally, but it didn't sound right. I sighed, pulled over, backed up on the shoulder to within about fifty feet of him. He didn't look up.

I got out, approached him obliquely—I didn't fancy him as the most stable guy under ordinary circumstances, and apparently these weren't them.

"Hey," I said, kneeling down beside him. "Hey, old-timer." I gave him a little nudge with my hand, and again the most brilliant blue eyes I've ever seen, now red-rimmed from crying and exhaustion, opened and seemed to take me in with a single glance. His face was crusted with sunburn far past the worst of my own recent experience—burns that had blistered and opened and been left untended. His lips were bloody. And although he was weeping, his cheeks were dry. His body had no moisture left for such trivial things as tears.

He looked as though he had been sitting in that one spot for a long time.

"Happy Father's Day," he said when he looked up at me, his voice shot through with bitterness as sharp as mine on my very worst days, and I recoiled like he'd bitten me.

"What?" I said. "What did you say?"

"Happy Father's Day. It is Father's Day, you know."

And it was, although I'd forgotten, being away from home

and having a dead child and all. "It's me," I said. "Clay Forester. I gave you a ride in Tennessee. I thought you were on your way to Sacramento," I said.

"This is as far as I'm going to get, son," he said. "Too tired to get up again. No reason to get up again." He turned his head up to me. "He lied to me."

"He?" I asked.

He gestured heavenward with a nod of his head. "She died before I got there. Found out three days ago. My daughter on the phone. Peggy, the youngest one. 'Don't come,' she told me. 'You got no right to come here. You left us years ago. You're not my father.' I been walking since then. Wouldn't nobody stop for me. And wouldn't matter if they had." He covered his face with his hands. "He said—He told me . . ." and he couldn't go on.

"Maybe you didn't hear right," I said gently. "Maybe he meant something else." He looked like hell—like I felt.

"You go on, son," he said, rubbing his eyes fiercely. "Go on. Leave me be."

"I'm not going to leave you here," I said. "I'm going to take you back into town. Come on, old timer." I put my arm underneath him and brought him to his feet with surprising ease. He seemed to weigh nothing at all—so little that I lifted him and carried him, bruised or broken as I was.

I buckled him into the passenger seat. "Now I'll get your cross on here somehow," I said.

"Leave it," he said. "Leave it be."

"You might feel differently later on," I said. "You might want to have it. Familiar things can be a comfort."

"I'm through with it," he said. "I'll find a new one."

I shrugged. "Okay," I said. I put the top up to protect him from the sun, got in, started the car, and headed for the next exit so I could turn around and come back into town.

"Where's that little dog you had?" he murmured, his eyes closed. "That little stinker?"

"Buster," I said. "I think he's in a good home. Or as good a home as a three-legged farting dog could expect."

"My God, but he smelled things up," he said, and I laughed.

"That was his sole gift," I said, knowing as I said it that it wasn't true.

I brought him to the Presbyterian Hospital emergency room in Albuquerque and checked him in.

"Are you his son?" they asked of course, and I shook my head. "But I'll be responsible for him." My father's money could be helpful in that much, at least. I filled out the forms as they got ready to take him into the treatment room, him so delirious with sun and dehydration and exhaustion that he barely knew me to say good-bye to.

"I'll call and check on you," I told him after they put him up on a gurney and were preparing to wheel him off. They already had IVs in him, and the young resident, one Dr. Purima, told me, "I think he's going to be just fine."

I leaned over Matthew Simons. "Everything will work out. Your girls will come around. You'll see."

He didn't seem to hear any of this, but his hand, drifting, found mine, squeezed hard. "Thank you, son. The Lord'll bless you for it." It was rote memory, maybe, or maybe, just maybe, he was finding his way back, too.

"You're welcome, Matthew," I said softly. "I hope you're right."

I turned away as they took him. The swinging doors closed behind him. It reminded me of something I had heard Ray say: "To love is to make a swinging door of your heart." Maybe he was quoting Barbara Jordan, the Great Woman. Maybe not. Anyway, I liked it.

The cell phone was lying out in the back floorboard, but I had spotted some pay phones on the way in, and I walked back through the waiting room with a real sense of purpose. Sugar or no, I seemed to be having another moment of clarity.

"Hello, Ray," I whispered when I got him on the phone. "Happy Father's Day."

"Happy Father's Day, Son," he said. "I love you."

That was as far as he could get. And then we both started to cry, and it was good.

It was good.

14

There were other calls to make, of course, but I waited until after I'd had the most incredible lunch at a place called the Route 66 Diner, a heavenly chocolate malt, a burger and onion rings to die for, until after I'd reversed my course eastward down Central Avenue—what used to be Route 66, the axis along which Albuquerque built itself—until I was back on the highway, headed toward home.

I woke up Otis—it was about one in the afternoon where he was—and started singing some Billy Paul for him, "Me and Mrs. Jones," dragging out the lyric like I was afflicted with palsy.

"Kill me now," he said. Then he woke up a little. "Clay? That you?"

"Wall to wall and treetop tall," I said.

"I am so beyond pissed at you," he said. Then he did his tight-assed George Bush voice. "You are out of the will, mister."

"I'm sorry," I said. "Really."

There was a short pause before he rejoined the conversation. "You, uh, you okay, there, pardner?"

I was hurtling around the south edge of the Sandias, and the Mustang was purring perfectly as I took a long upward grade. "I'm beginning to think that I'm gonna be," I said. "Listen, I just called to tell you I'm okay, and to apologize."

"For what," he said, and then the crunching noise of Froot Loops emanated from the phone. "Friendship means never having to say you're sorry."

"It's love," I corrected.

"Same thing," he said. "I'm going to get the whole story, right?"

"The whole story," I promised. "Small-town boy makes good. King falls from grace. The little tailor. The little engine that could."

"Are you still drinking?"

"Only the sunshine, my friend," I said. "Only the blue skies."

"I'm not awake enough for this," he said. "Call me later."

"Later," I said, and hung up. I waited until I'd finished climbing, until I was up on the high plains of Eastern New Mexico reversing my tracks, before I called Tracy. I stopped and got gas, drank more Dr. Pepper, and consumed an entire bag of Cheetos and a jumbo Butterfinger despite the remonstrating ghost of Kathy Cartwright, because, frankly, I was nervous as hell. Of course, putting all this stuff in my stomach could have accounted for the sudden feelings of nervous diarrhea that began to afflict me, the guts-in-a-coil thing that hadn't hit me much in recent years because I hadn't cared much about much of anything.

I misdialed her number twice and was getting ready to put it off for a long time, but the third time it went through, and wonder of wonders, she herself picked up the phone.

"Hello," she said, and the sound of her voice filled me with such wonder that it was all I could do not to drive into a ditch.

"Hello?" she said, and I knew from experience that she was a hair-trigger hanger-upper, so I somehow found my voice.

"Trace," I said, and then there was silence from her end of the phone. "Trace? It's me. Clay."

"Clay," she said. It was neutral, no corresponding wonder, but also no instant disconnect. I took that as a positive.

"Clay," I said. "Can you talk?"

"I have all the equipment," she said. "And don't say 'I'll say.' You're not anywhere near out of the doghouse yet, mister."

"I have so much to tell you, and maybe I can't say it all

right now," I said. "Some of it I want to say face to face. But I want you to know that I'm sorry for taking you for granted. Truly sorry."

"Are you drunk?" she asked. Maybe everyone was going to.

"No," I said. "Do you remember dancing at the prom?"

"Vaguely," she said. Nothing was going to be easy, and maybe that was okay. Maybe nothing worthwhile ever was.

"You remember we slow-danced to that song 'Always and Forever'?"

"Vaguely," she repeated, although her voice had lost its edge and I knew I had her.

"Do you remember I said that I wanted to sing that at our wedding?"

"Vaguely," she said for the third time, her voice tender as the darling buds of May.

"I still do," I said.

There was a long pause. My heart pounded, and I wiped my palms, suddenly slick with sweat.

"Talk to me," she said, and I did, all the way across New Mexico and well into Texas. I told her everything that had happened on the trip. I told her about my father, and how I thought I could finally forgive him. I told her about the ways the trip had changed me. I told her everything I had told Father Nieto, and although she was crying with me when she finished, she said something that surprised me.

"Clay, that's so sad, but it's also so good. Don't you see?"

"I don't," I admitted. "Not yet."

"I've wondered all these years how I could ever compete with Anna Lynn," she admitted. "I never told you. But you left me to think that things had been so perfect between you. Made me think of her as a martyred saint. To know that she was just like me, that you had things to work on, just like we do—oh, Clay. I can't tell you how this gives me hope."

"There's another thing," I said. "Another lie, I guess. I'm sorry. But you see, I wasn't a good father. I mean, I think I could be. Will be. But I was never there for Ray. He hardly knew me. I used to go in and see him at night, when he was asleep. I loved him. I know that. I used to sing to him, and hold my hand on his little stomach while he slept. Just to feel, you know, the life in him. His little heartbeat."

"Oh, Clay," she said.

"I miss him," I said. "I miss him a lot. I wish I had more memories."

"Oh, Clay," she said. "I'm so sorry. But we'll make new ones."

"Like Job's new children?"

"No," she said. "Like ours."

And what is a man to say to that? "Here's Amarillo," I said.

"What does that mean, exactly?"

"It means I'm going to have to hang up shortly and drive two-handed through some construction," I said.

"Is that all it means?"

"No," I said. "It means I love you very much. That I'm so grateful for you, for all you've put up with."

"Oh, that," she said, and I shushed her.

"I am," I said. "It means that even though I still think love is the most dangerous thing I know, I'm not going to be afraid. Or I'll try not to be."

"I'll help you," she said. "You know I will. We'll help each other. When will I see you?"

"Look for me Tuesday night."

"Not before then?"

"I've got some things I want to do on the way back. They'll take a little time. But I'll be there, don't you worry. Just tell your father I'm coming, and if it's after dark, let him know not to shoot me as a prowler. I know there have been times he's been tempted to."

"What kind of things?"

"Huh?"

"That you have to do?"

"Just a step in the right direction," I said. "I'll tell you all about it when I see you. Right after we make wild, passionate love."

"Well," she said, and suddenly she seemed nigh on speechless, as if someone had hit her in the face with a fish. "It sounds like I have a lot of things to look forward to."

She hung up. I had one more phone call I had to make then, part of those things I needed to do. I had to think for a second, but not much more than that, about a truck stop napkin written on with red crayon: an address. I pulled over so the road noise wouldn't obscure anything I had to say, and then I dialed.

"Operator," I said, "Nashville, Tennessee. Connect me with Daniel Cartwright, 1128 Fifth Avenue."

He answered on the third ring. "Hello," he said.

"Good morning, you son of a bitch," I said. "This is your wife's attorney speaking. I just want you to know that your days are numbered. 'And they shall know my name is the Lord when I lay my vengeance upon them.' That's Ezekiel 25:17, if you're wondering. Happy Father's Day."

Spluttering noises had started erupting from the phone after "son of a bitch," but it wasn't until I finished that he started saying "Who is this? Who the hell is this? Do you know who I am?"

I let him do that a couple of times, and then I answered him as though they weren't rhetorical questions.

"Yes, sir, I do. You, sir, are a bad man. A bad husband. A bad father. And for all I know, a bad lieutenant governor. But I'm betting you'll be a model prisoner."

And I hung up, laughing my ass off. That was enough to prime the pump.

Devious. And brilliant.

I stopped at the Potter County jail in downtown Amarillo and posted bail for a certain set of protestors still in custody. The jailer let me leave a message for Father Tom with his belongings, although it was so cryptic they asked me to repeat it twice.

"Jesus has no arms but ours," I said patiently as they wrote it down. "See that he gets that."

I drove on past the Big Texan restaurant with its free gargantuan steak, raising a middle finger on behalf of Father Jorge and tight-assed do-gooders everywhere. I stopped for the night just outside Oklahoma City, slept hard, got up, showered and shaved. Then I checked the phone book for two addresses.

The first was a men's clothing store. I didn't want just to buy off the rack, but I didn't have much choice. I walked in, gave them my stats, and went out wearing a dark-gray suit, button-down oxford shirt, Repp tie, and some great loafers. Italian leather, like the shoes in my dream.

There were already cars in front of the house when I pulled up, which was how I'd expected things to go; if you prime the pump, you get water. I walked up to the door, rang the bell, and was greeted by a flustered woman who bore some obvious family resemblance to Kathy Cartwright.

"Yes," she said, in the voice of someone who had already been put-upon to her limits.

"I'm Kathy's attorney," I said. "I had a feeling I needed to be here this morning."

She let me in, but didn't say much else beyond "She didn't say anything about an attorney. I was just telling these gentlemen that Kathy's not here. That she hasn't been here. That I don't know where she is."

They were in the living room: two OKC plainclothes cops sitting stiffly together on the couch, and in the wingback chair, rising at my approach, was the older man from the Mercedes chase.

"Gentlemen," I nodded to the cops. "Uncle Edward," I said to him.

He recognized me right away, of course; a suit is no disguise. "I don't believe I got your name," he said.

"My name, surprisingly, is immaterial. It's what I have to say that's important."

Kathy's sister—her name was Pam Standerfer, I suddenly remembered—went into her panicked spiel again. "I was just telling these gentlemen that Kathy's not here. That she hasn't been here. That I don't know where she is."

A stench like falling ker-plunk into the sewers suddenly meandered through the room; the plainclothes cops looked at each other with accusing faces, although I knew that no human being was capable of producing that odor.

"Of course you don't, Mrs. Standerfer," I said. "Although I very much doubt that these gentleman had a warrant to enter these premises, or a court order forcing Mrs. Cartwright to remand her son into the custody of Uncle Edward in the event they found her here."

"A mere formality," Uncle Edward said. "I can get one."

"Can you, now?" I said in a good Irish brogue. "You pin-striped pencil dick," I said. I stood up over him and reached for my inside pocket. One of the plainclothes guys made a surreptitious move toward his shoulder holster, so I made my movements light and clear, reaching with only two fingers while I talked. "I don't think your client wants to go to court to get his son back. In fact, I think you and he are probably so used to scaring people shitless that you've forgotten that the law is supposed to be about justice. It's easy to forget. I know. But your client doesn't deserve to get his son back." I pulled the pictures out, fanned them in front of his eyes. "He deserves justice for what he's done."

He looked up at them, his eyes opened a little wider, and he looked away. He hadn't known, or had suspected but tried not to admit it to himself. "There are lots more where these come from," I said.

Then I pivoted and showed the abuse photos to the cops, whose eyes hardened, and then they looked across at Uncle Edward with something very close to hatred. "I want it clearly understood, Uncle Edward, that these pictures, and more like them, are going to be introduced as evidence in a criminal trial that my firm and I will work toward night and day unless your client calls off his dogs and does right by his family. I mean no more harassment. I mean a divorce for my client, with no opposition from yours. And I mean a fair settlement, because you and I both know what she was driven to do to protect her child, don't we?"

He nodded, and it was with sadness. The plainclothes guys got up to leave, tipping imaginary hats to Pam as they went. "I didn't know," Uncle Edward said softly. "About the pictures. Any of that." He produced his wallet and pulled out a big roll of bills. "Please tell her I'm sorry. And to consider this an advance on that divorce settlement." I took his money, and

Uncle Edward shook his head, let out a sigh. "He's my nephew," he said at last, by way of explanation.

"I know," I said. "You can't choose your family. But you sure as hell can choose your clients."

He nodded. "Do you have a card?" he asked, opening his day planner to receive it. "I know this sounds strange under the circumstances, but I'd like to think we might do business together in the future."

"Thank you for asking," I said. "But I have a feeling that my clients from now on couldn't afford you. Oh, and sorry about the 'pin-striped pencil-dick' remark. It was just too good to pass up. Alliteration or something."

"Internal rhyme, I think," he said, closing his day planner, extending his hand, and administering a crisp shake. "But no matter. I'll convey your words to my client," he said, "and I'll see to it that things go smoothly."

"Thank you," I said.

"Thank you," he said, and inclining his head to me and to Pam, he made his way to the door.

"Tell them they can come out now," I said, handing over the wad of money. "Uncle Edward won't be back." And I too turned to go. "Tell her I'll be in touch."

"But I never got your name," she said.

"It doesn't matter," I said again. I felt like the Lone Ranger. "She'll know. Tell her it was the guy who insisted that Jesus had a penis. And that everything will be all right. For all of us. Tell her that."

"Okay," she said. "I will tell her."

And off I went. I could feel their eyes on me from the windows, so I raised a hand in a wave, or a salute—God knows Kathy Cartwright deserved both. Then I jumped in the car and off I went, into the climbing sun of Monday morning, through a city that seemed a lot less ugly today. Off I went, toward a family, friends, a woman I loved. Off I went, back toward a life that might finally be worth living.

Epilogue

"Ramblings around the River," by Sister Euless
—From *The Graham Star*, September 20, 2000

My nephew Clay Forester and his bride, the former Tracy York, were married Saturday in a service at the Grace Tabernacle. Otis Miller was best man, and Glennis McDowell was matron of honor. Brother Carl Robinson officiated at the service. The groom and my sisters Ellen and Evelyn and I played and sang. A reception followed in the fellowship hall before Clay and Tracy departed for their honeymoon, a two week drive in their Mustang convertible. The happy couple will conclude their drive and make their home in Santa Fe, New Mexico, where Clay says he intends to bone up on environmental law, take up indigents and immigrants—whatever that means—and populate a large house with children. "Oh, maybe I'll play a little salsa," he said.

We are joyful beyond expressing, although it will be awfully quiet around the house without him. Children grow up so quickly these days.

The leaves are turning in the mountains, green to golds and reds and oranges, beautiful as a painting. It's just another sign of God's love for us in every season. Think of that as you see the leaves change, and give thanks.

Author's Note

No one writes a book without help, and moreover, no one publishes a book after years and years of striving to do just that without having a list of people to acknowledge—a list of which admittedly, this accounting can only scratch the surface. While such lists are usually of no interest except to people who think they might be on them—or to curious folks who wonder if the writer knows famous people or is going to acknowledge heretofore unmentioned sexual liasions—they truly serve a vital function: to recognize the people behind the artist who helped him or her achieve something of worth. So here goes:

The *Anchorage Daily News* was an invaluable source of information on the *Exxon Valdez* disaster and the subsequent legal wrangling. Jonathan Kwitny's *Endless Enemies: The Making of an Unfriendly World* first taught me about American-sponsored terrorism, and Renny Golden and Michael McConnell's *Sanctuary: The New Underground Railroad* gave me vital background about the Sanctuary movement and the Catholic Church in Latin America. Donna Jean Garrett taught me years ago about the importance of being a committed activist, and not a little of her spirit informs some of these characters. A Spring 2000 article in the *Houston Chronicle* gave me specifics on groundwater pollution caused by the Pantex atomic weapons plant, and the *Santa Fe Reporter* covered the Los Alamos wildfires and the allegations of radioactive contamination from the Los Alamos research facilities in the summer of 2000 with its usual excellence. The work of New Mexico landscape artist Louisa

McElwain was an inspiration and a model for the art described in this book. Tennessee State Senator and good friend Roy Herron refreshed my memory on Interstate 40 as it runs through his beautiful state and also answered some useful legal and governmental questions. Kathleen Norris's *The Cloister Walk* satisfied my curiosity about the vocation of oblate. The story of the armless Christ comes from Annie Lamott's *Operating Instructions*. Thanks to all of these.

I want to thank my friends and family for supporting this dream. My parents, grandparents, brothers and sisters, Tina Marie, Jake, and Chandler all share in this accomplishment. Good friends—Tom Hanks, Trisha Lindholm, Scott Walker, Chris Seay, Bob Darden, Blake Burleson, Rachel and Andy Moore, Martha Serpas, Vicki Marsh Kabat, Frank Leavell, John Ballenger, Michael Beaty, Ray Burchette, Rick Barton, Sandy Pearce, and too many others to mention—encouraged me day in and day out. Donna Jean Garrett always believed this day would come. I hope she welcomes it now and knows my appreciation. Dozens of editors of magazines, journals, and newspapers published my work over the past twenty years as I learned my craft, for which much thanks. And my agent, Jill Grosjean, loved my words and gave me unsparingly of her time, expertise, and affection. She is a true gift. May God bless you all.

I have been fortunate enough to learn from and to be inspired by many people. These have been my teachers: Robert Olen Butler, Annie Lamott, Lee Smith, the late Andre Dubus, Richard Ford, Mary Rohrberger, the late Hansford Martin, T. R. Pearson, Leonard Leff, W. P. Kinsella, Gordon Weaver, Dennis and Vicki Covington, Bret Lott, Elinor Lipman, Jack Butler, Carol Dawson, Will Campbell, Michael Curtis, Elizabeth Cox, Marc Ellis, Gregory Wolfe, Stewart O'Nan, Rodger Kamenetz, and four others I will never have the opportunity to meet but who have taught me much nonetheless about life and art: William Faulkner, Walker Percy, Thomas Merton, and Flannery O'Connor.

The Pirate's Alley Faulkner Society of New Orleans recognized me some years ago with their prize medal, and cofounders Joe DeSalvo and Rosemary James have been my champions and friends ever since. The Society's efforts in recognizing and promoting great writing are unmatched in America, and I hope they will be able to continue their good work for years to come.

I must also thank my colleagues, my students, and the administration of Baylor University, where I have written and taught for a dozen happy years now. Dean Wallace Daniel, former dean Bill Cooper, Provost Don Schmeltekopf, and English department chairs James Barcus and Maurice Hunt have supported my work with course reductions, sabbaticals, and encouragement. I'm particularly pleased to note that *Free Bird* was written during the summer sabbatical from teaching that I was given in 2000.

Matt and Julie Chase-Daniel entrusted us with their house in Santa Fe, New Mexico, during that summer of 2000, and I believe the book could not have been written nearly as well or as quickly without their generosity. Santa Fe's spirit permeates these pages.

And the music I played in the basement of the Chase-Daniels' house while I wrote was instrumental in inspiring me to write: Bruce Hornsby's *Spirit Trail* and *Hot House*, Shawn Colvin's *A Few Small Repairs*, the Goo Goo Dolls' *Dizzy Up the Girl*, Bruce Springsteen's *Darkness on the Edge of Town*, *Lucky Town*, and *Human Touch*, Bob Schneider's *Lonelyland*, Roy Orbison's *Black and White Night*, and Stevie Ray Vaughn's entire body of work. I consider these artists to be almost cocreators of this book, although of course I will take the blame for the boring parts.

No endorsements were paid this author by Cracker Barrel restaurants, the Dr. Pepper Bottling Company, nor any of the other products, companies, institutions, places, or objects mentioned in this book. I consider myself a literary realist, and part of being a realist is creating a recognizable world. But it should go without saying that all of these real-world elements are used fictionally and should not be associated with their fictional treatments here.

Well . . . except that Exxon really was responsible for spilling millions of gallons of crude oil in a pristine Alaskan sound, but I think we all know that.

Greg Garrett plays Yamaha guitars, Fender amplifiers, and Martin strings.

And finally, I thank God, the First and Foremost, for giving me this story. I've never written so well or so quickly, and even though it almost killed me, I believe God is helping me, like Clay, to come through the darkness and into the light.

Thomas Merton closes his autobiography, *The Seven Storey Mountain,* in this fashion: *"Sit finis libri, non finis quaerendi,"* or, "Let this be the ending of the book, but by no means the end of the searching."

Amen and amen, brother.

Greg Garrett
Austin, Texas
May 2001

FREE BIRD

GREG GARRETT

ABOUT THIS GUIDE

The suggested questions are intended to enhance your group's
reading of Greg Garrett's *Free Bird*.

DISCUSSION QUESTIONS

1. *Free Bird* is a traditional journey story, where the exterior journey prompts an interior journey. How do different elements of Clay's travels prompt his inner pilgrimage?

2. How do the story's major settings (North Carolina, Washington, D.C., Santa Fe, New Mexico) influence the events of *Free Bird*? Are particular settings closely identified with particular emotions, actions, or reactions? Is the book a Southern novel, as some critics have suggested? Why or why not?

3. How would you characterize Clay's relationship to his mother? To Ray? To Tracy? To Otis? What does each party seem to get from the relationship?

4. Do you think Clay is wrong to be paralyzed with guilt over his past actions? Are some of them more defensible than others?

5. Susan Larson, book critic for the *New Orleans Times-Picayune* wrote that one of the few things that would improve *Free Bird* is if it came packaged with a soundtrack. How is music important to the novel? Does knowledge of particular songs or artists help add additional meaning to the novel? Do you find certain scenes harder to understand if you don't get the musical references?

6. Does Clay have heroes or role models he admires? Who are they, and what does he admire about them?

7. Dreams play a significant role in the book. What are some ways that dreams prompt Clay's actions? How do they reinforce themes of the book?

8. It is difficult to find a traditional marriage relationship in the novel. What do you think the novel says about love and marriage? Do you believe Clay and Tracy will be happy together?

9. Fatherhood is one of the central themes in the novel. Clay's search for his father's past, his relationship with Ray, and even his meetings with the "fathers" during his journey are

all vital elements of the book. Judging from these encounters, what does it mean to be a father? How can one differentiate between good and bad fathers?

10. Many of those who have reviewed *Free Bird* call the book's use of humor one of its best elements. What are some of the ways that the author creates humor in the story? Are there particular scenes or lines you remember with special fondness?

11. What do you consider the most important themes of *Free Bird*? What does the book seem to say about each of them? Is there a lesson or moral you take away from the novel?

12. Clay comes into contact with a number of people who seem to be—or even claim to be—fated to be in his life. At length, Clay seems to accept this. What does the book seem to say about fate and free will? Does Clay have power to choose his own course?

13. What would you say are the most important incidents in the story? Why are they important? How do they change Clay or change the course of the novel?

14. Clay mentions the song "Free Bird" by the rock band Lynerd Skynerd in the first pages of the novel, although the song is never referred to again. How else might the title be meaningful?

15. During Clay's journey, this man who claims not to care about other people aids a number of people, even if he sometimes feels forced into doing so. In the process of this story, does he become a hero? How does Clay seem to have changed by the end of the novel?

16. The relationship between law and justice is an important one in *Free Bird*. How does the author develop these ideas? Does he seem to favor one over the other?

17. *Free Bird* is a spiritual journey as well as a physical journey; Bret Lott calls it a "dark road trip of the soul." As such, it is littered with symbols and acts of faith. What are some of the ways that faith is manifested in the novel? Who are the main characters who exhibit various forms of faith?

18. In the journal *Books and Culture,* critic Betty Smartt Carter wrote that *Free Bird* is a book that assumes a shared vision of right and wrong, that the larger questions of faith, morality, and responsibility have already been settled. Do you believe the author manifests a consistent moral vision in the novel? If so, what things are right and what things are wrong?

19. Why does the book end when and as it does? In what ways do Clay's actions in the last two chapters of the book provide a fitting culmination of the plot and of the story's thematic elements?

Please turn the page for an exciting sneak peek
of Greg Garrett's next novel
CYCLING
coming in hardcover from Kensington
in September 2003!

1

It is mid-August in Waco, Texas, the Year of our Lord 1993. The mercury stands at one hundred for weeks on end, the grass goes first brown and then gray, and the parched ground cracks open. In fact, my grandfather, Jackson Bradford Cannon, Jr., called last night from his monumental home over on Austin Avenue to gleefully report the momentary loss of my grandparents' idiotic tabbycat Buster, who blundered into a chasm in their gigantic but poorly watered backyard.

"Should have seen it, Jackson," he said. (Although most people call me "Brad," my grandfather insists on calling me by our common given name; I am, of course, twice distant, JBC the Fourth. Anyway, Buster is the much-maligned cat.) "One minute he was there, the next, whoop, he was gone. I almost bust a gut laughing. Evelyn made me go and pull him out. Too bad the cracks aren't any deeper."

They are deep enough for my liking, and they are everywhere. It has been weeks since we had rain, and even some of the roads have begun to crack, mostly at the shoulders where the dry ground shrinks away from the pavement, but sometimes out in the middle of the thruway. The cracks are generally only an inch or two wide at the most, nothing noticeable for motorists, but they are potentially lethal for a cyclist, which is what I am, now and forever, even in these scorching August afternoons.

What in God's name am I doing out here? Why am I puffing up this hill in 105-degree temperatures, rivers of sweat coursing down my face, a big truck whooshing past me just inches from my left elbow? I'm not certain that I can explain it. But you are right in thinking that it's an odd time to be outdoors, let alone out riding long distances on a bicycle. Everyone else in the state of Texas sits inside in air-conditioned comfort, waiting for fall with the anticipation a snowbound Michigander must feel for spring. This afternoon, putting in thirty miles on my Specialized mountain bike, I could almost be the only living creature on the planet. The dogs, who in more temperate seasons charge out from their porches to defend their territories, now loll, panting, in the shade; the floppy-hatted retirees who normally tend their lawns and flower beds with meticulous loving care have been forced by water rationing to sacrifice their verdant St. Augustine and Bermuda for the public weal; the farmers who are in between harvest and sowing wouldn't set foot on a tractor for love or money.

I don't blame them. I shouldn't be out on a bicycle; I'm supposed to be writing, finishing a book that I have not yet even begun. Let me explain: Five years ago a New York publisher released my history of the Confederate invasion of New Mexico during the early years of the War Between the States. I didn't make this up; I first read about it in Shelby Foote's *Civil War*, and after I managed to graduate from Baylor University, a venerable Baptist institution, I spent three years rooting through the university's excellent Texas Collection, through the like-named collection at Texas Tech in Lubbock, through the Confederate Research Center up the road at Hill College. In those days I was still young enough, Southern enough, to be fascinated by military action, no matter how futile or ill-conceived—in this case, five hundred Texans rode up the Rio Grande expecting to conquer a territory almost as large as the state they'd just left—and to my amazement I filled up notebook after notebook with what I discovered in the collections. The end result was a book that has sold copies by the wagon load in Texas, sold fairly well across the South, and is apparently even bought by the occasional Yankee Civil War buff.

Following that, my publisher encouraged me to get to work on one of the two projects that I have at various times claimed to be writing—a book on the Texas Brigade and their service under Albert Sidney Johnston at Shiloh, or on the diplomatic relationship between the Confederacy and Mexico, depending on my mood. The furthest I ever got was to read a few books other people had written and decide that nothing I had to say was interesting enough for me to add, so I did not and have not. Although I know I ought to be nervous about this being discovered, I am not for two reasons: First, the whirlwind of takeovers and buyouts in New York City publishing has meant that five different editors have assumed control over my project in the last five years, and until the most recent, Eddie Todd, not a one of them has been around long enough to do more than call, introduce himself, and ask how my work is coming; second, while it seems that I must once have cared enough about something to write a book, I have no plans to write another. I have no plans, period. Consequently, as long as my slender royalties, my grandparents, and my occasional columns on Texas greasy spoons and honky-tonks for *Texas Monthly* continue to pay the bills, I am free to pretend to fill notebooks with my research, free to court in my noncommittal way the women in my life, free to pedal to my heart's content through this superheated August air.

I am reluctant to admit that there is any tense save the present, and I am not here to recount my sad stories, but since we are recalling *temps perdu* with this rolling account of my brief authorial career, I suppose that now is as good a time as any to unload the other sordid details. Everything will all come out at some point; it always does. So I guess, as Jackson might say, it's better to slap a mosquito with a bang than let her suck your blood in silence.

Here it is then, the unsavory and unalterable past: To begin with, I have been married twice and divorced twice in the past seven years. If any blame is to be attached to such a record of connubial failure, it must fall squarely on my head. I have a problem letting people get close to me. Although it's unfortunate, I can't seem to help myself; life seems easier if I just don't care too much.

Different people have attributed my fear of intimacy to different things. My first wife simply opined that I was a son of a bitch and left it at that; my second wife thought my distance was the result of my artistic temperament; if pressed, I like to say that it comes from being born and bred a male in the great state of Texas, since this seems to shut off debate at a surface level. My grandparents, however, alternatively suppose that my reluctance to connect has something to do with my past, and so it is the dark highlights of my history I must reluctantly recount for you—at least in brief—if you are to have any hope of understanding.

When I was twelve years old, my beloved mother, father, and kid brother got knocked off of Interstate 35 and into eternity by a gravel truck. While this in and of itself seems sufficient to me to justify some lamentation—I seem to recall that this kind of thing knocked Hamlet on his ass—I recognize that not everyone agrees: Fathers die, Hamlet, and mothers and brothers, too. And so they do, an ineluctable fact of life that perhaps should not—in and of itself—be paralyzing. I can say this: It is true that I loved my family dearly, that the mere thought of their fate now is like a crunching blow to the stomach. All the same, what happened to them seems like a long time ago, like another life, and not even my life, but the life of some character I read about once and then closed the book on.

This is not, unfortunately, true of everything in my past. There is something else that might account for the spare and shuttered life I lead, although many of my more recent acquaintances do not know of it except as lurid whispered gossip, the kind people in grocery stores cluck about and people in churches shake their heads over sadly.

There are gravel trucks, and then there are gravel trucks.

When I was seventeen years old, I took my girlfriend Susie Bramlett out of a Saturday night to see *Urban Cowboy* and then to the so-called Health Camp restaurant for good greasy burgers and butterscotch malts. Susie was a beautiful redheaded outdoorsy girl with a laugh as big and bright as the night sky, and she laughed at me all the time, which was one of the things that made me love her madly.

I made jokes about *Urban Cowboy* all evening, even after we had parked on a deserted country road south of town to make out. I was telling her how stupid I thought it was for even Debra Winger to ride a contraption like that mechanical bull, and Susie had thrown her head back and was laughing that laugh when a big black Lincoln or Caddy that had been creaking its way across the plank-and-trestle bridge behind us pulled up alongside and a dark-haired man with a big gap-toothed smile leaned out the passenger window and pointed a silver-plated revolver at us.

I should have done something. Should have. But I sat, stupid and stupefied, and the man behind the gun stepped from the car, ordered us to get out, and handcuffed me to the steering wheel. Then he held a knife to Susie's throat and did things I cannot recount, for your sake as much as my own. When he was finished and her body lay splayed in the creek below, he climbed back into that huge black car and drove off into the darkness, where he remains.

They never found him.

To this day I do not know why he killed Susie and let me live; he was not doing me any favor, believe me. When her body had fallen from the bridge into the creek bed with a crash that still wakes me sometimes gasping in the middle of the night, he turned to me and smiled his gap-toothed smile, and left me standing, as perhaps I have been ever since.

There is only one more thing I have to say, the saddest thing, and then I'll depart this unhappiest of subjects. It is Susie's eyes that remain with me long after I have had to resort to looking at the one picture I hid away in a drawer to recall the shape of her nose, the tilt of her head. In the one moment when I could bear to meet her gaze, her eyes were bright with the tears she had shed and wide with the horror she felt, but there was something else in them that shredded my heart so that it has ever since been strictly ornamental: I will always believe that, even in the midst of her own terror, she also understood what it had done to me to have to watch.

That's the kind of person she was.

Sometimes in the golden moment just before I wake, I am permitted a life with Susie Bramlett. In these dreams we are always holding hands and laughing, gazing into each other's eyes while children orbit us like playful moons. In these dreams I am a normal man who works and plays and mows his lawn and loves his family, and not a person who stood by watching paralyzed while hideous things were done to the person he loved most. I could happily dream those dreams forever and never again open my eyes to this waking world.

Anyway, there you have it: the whole sloppily-wrapped package that now puffs up another long hill and that answers to the name Brad Cannon. I will confess that I am an unholy mess; it doesn't take Dr. Joyce Brothers to see that. In fact, everyone around me seems to know how I could be improved, but isn't that always the way? I can spot cracks in the well-ordered facades of other people, although—unlike them—I hold myself back from offering advice. What would be the earthly good of it?

Anyway, my life is not completely out of control, not completely without shape or form. Once a semester I come back and speak to history classes at my alma mater about my tiny corner of the Civil War; once a year I do a book signing over at the Baylor Bookstore, usually for Homecoming Weekend; once every year or two I return to the building named after my grandfather to talk to beginning writers in the English Department about the craft I have mostly long since abandoned except for the occasional cranky letter to the editor composed late at night and the restaurant reviews I write when the mood strikes me and the magazine publishes when the mood strikes them.

These columns are as much a fluke as my ever having written a book; upon complaining about *Texas Monthly*'s sparse coverage of the vast expanse between Dallas/Fort Worth and Austin, the editor as much as invited me to do better if I thought I could. So I started writing about the restaurants I like—places frequented by truck drivers and farmers and janitors, barbecue places and family taco stands and meatloaf shacks on small-town main streets and soul food restaurants hidden away in back alleys. I have no assignments or deadlines, which is probably fortunate; I write when I feel like it, generally when I come home exhausted and happy from putting away a good meal at a place I hadn't known existed.

My stomach is growling now just thinking about it.

The rest of my life can be summed up thusly: I see my grandparents, a group of buddies with whom I eat lunch once or twice a week, and the women whose lives I seem to drift through, or perhaps, more properly, drift in and out of, like the tide. My grandfather, who recognizes that I am drifting even if he can't exactly put his finger on it, tells me, "Jackson, what you need is to find yourself a good woman," but I have already been married often enough to know that the problem is with me, not with the women, and that while they can entertain me for a time they cannot change my life, make me happy, or give me purpose. That I will have to do myself, if it is to be done, which I doubt.

Still, living so obviously without a purpose beyond riding a bicycle makes most rational people twitch in my presence, so when the question of my shiftless life comes up, I have taken to explaining my compulsive cycling in this way: "A few years from now," I announce, "I would like to ride in the Tour de France." I do not deceive myself; I have no more interest in or talent for that level of competition than I have current plans for the year 2020. I am too old, and—even riding thirty miles or more a day—too out of shape for such a grueling event. Still, as ridiculous as it seems, the story satisfied the first people to whom I told it, and so I now employ it at every opportunity. It is nice to be able to explain at least something about the way I live.

"How wonderful, Brad," they often say to me, their faces lit with the mere possibility of it all. "Oh, I'm sure you'll do it."

Their faith in me is touching; borne aloft on their false visions of me, I almost imagine I *could* do it, that I would *like* to do it. Then I come to this moment at around the twenty-five-mile mark when my legs decide that even thirty miles may be too much. So I shift up into the highest gears to climb an inconsequential hill, my thighs burning as though someone has injected something thick and viscous into them, and I start to laugh hysterically.

At such times, I almost believe it would be easier to try to live a normal life. Surely I could have come up with a better cover story, one without this much hard work and hardship.

When I rose at ten o'clock this morning it was already startlingly hot outside, and now my T-shirt is soaked through with my sweat and hangs from me with sodden weight. Although my ride includes several roads that offer some shade, and one wonderful half-mile stretch overgrown with towering pecan and oak and cottonwood trees that form a cool dark tunnel—all behind me now, alas—the Texas sun is lethal, and without sunscreen I would burn horribly. As it is, I am as tan as a lifeguard, and my brown hair is bleached blond. My grandmother believes I am courting skin cancer, but I tell her something else will probably kill me long before that can happen.

She does not, somehow, seem reassured by these words.

Then there's the summer wind, constant and powerful and no more cooling than the air around a blast furnace. Today I headed south initially, as I usually do, and the first eight miles of my ride went straight into the wind. The road I followed across rolling farmlands was raised and completely exposed—no trees at all except in the bottomland and only the occasional woodframe farmhouse or barn, all far back from the road and thus of no practical use to me— and the wind whistled across the pastures and past the white-faced Herefords and tail-swishing Appaloosas, rustled through the dark green fields of corn and one field overgrown with the beautiful lavender blossoms of thistles, through the towering power lines and the barbed-wire fences on its way to try and knock me off of my spinning wheels.

Despite all this, if I miss a day on the road, I find an unnamable anxiety building within me. It's impossible for me to spend a day indoors and not end up pacing like a big cat in a cage; although I'm not home yet, I'm already feeling a sense of dread at arriving there. Unlike most everyone else I know, television has never calmed me, and music or books are only a stopgap measure. When I spend too much time indoors alone it seems to me that I become too full of myself, that memories come swarming around my head like hornets, and that only by getting out here, straining, sweating, courting catastrophe, can I let the excess self squeak out of me like air escaping a balloon.

"One of these days you'll get squashed by a truck out there," Becky Sue Bradenton—the youngest of the current women—has told me, "and I'll have to spend my days nursing you back to health." She may be right, although I am strangely detached from everything her statement implies. I don't much care if I'm hit by a truck; although I can almost hear the rumble of the vehicle looming behind me, can imagine the sudden sharp impact, can even see the spot in the ditch where I'd wind up—next to that discarded pouch of Red Man—I feel indifferent to any fate up to and including death. Likewise, while some men might love to be fussed over, I have had a caretaker wife already, and I know from experience that I react badly to constant faithfulness. While I know Becky Sue will fuss wonderfully for a husband one of these days, I'm not inclined to let her practice on me.

If I should ever get hit by a truck, I hope it kills me instantly, and that my granddad sues the miscreant gravel company and wins a huge settlement.

It beats a number of alternatives, some of which I have already had the misfortune to know personally.

Greg Garrett on his new novel
CYCLING

Q: How would you compare your new book *Cycling* to *Free Bird?*

A: Well, I think readers of *Free Bird* will find lots to like in *Cycling*. My agent thinks of its narrator, Brad Cannon, as Clay's even more dysfunctional younger brother. In contemporary fiction, he reminds me most of the narrators in Nick Hornby's *High Fidelity* and Michael Chabon's *Wonder Boys*. They're all guys who are at the same time pathetic and lovable and tremendously funny. *Cycling* deals with a lot of the same issues as *Free Bird:* love, connection, commitment, forgiveness, and redemption. But I think *Cycling* is at the same time funnier and sadder than *Free Bird*. You won't find a farting dog in this book, but there is a nervous dog on tranquilizers. And you won't find a mother and maiden aunts, but I've given Brad a set of grandparents who may be my favorite characters in the book. I think Brad has even more work to do than Clay Forester. He's also overwhelmed by the past but, unlike Clay, he doesn't even consider it. For him, all there is is the present. Like Clay, his particular fixation keeps him from working toward a worthwhile future until his life has taken some twists and turns he never expected. But when that comes, it's really powerful.